ELLEN GLASGOW

ELLEN GLASGOW

A BIOGRAPHY

Susan Goodman

THE JOHNS HOPKINS UNIVERSITY PRESS   BALTIMORE AND LONDON

This book was brought to publication with the generous assistance of the University of Delaware.

The Johns Hopkins University Press
2715 North Charles Street
Baltimore, Maryland 21218-4319
The Johns Hopkins Press Ltd., London

Library of Congress Cataloging-in-Publication Data will be found at the end of this book.
A catalog record for this book is available from the British Library.

ISBN 0-8018-5728-7

Frontispiece: A self-reflective Ellen Glasgow at the turn of the century.

TO CARL

Miss Glasgow has devoted herself to the social morality of a single state, so that, in the whole history of the American novel, there is no achievement quite like hers. Some call her a novelist of manners only. But in her view manners are but the outward and visible sign (often misleading) of an inward and spiritual grace.

Howard Mumford Jones

CONTENTS

Illustrations follow page 146

ACKNOWLEDGMENTS

The writing of biography requires both a solitary journey and a silent collaboration. I am grateful to those scholars who have most enriched my own work. I must especially thank E. Stanly Godbold whose encouragement and generosity have made this project possible. With gratitude, I acknowledge my indebtedness to Edgar MacDonald, for his invaluable contributions to Glasgow research; and to Dorothy M. Scura, the editor of the contemporary reviews, who has kept Glasgow studies alive and flourishing. My book incorporates and extends the work of other Glasgow scholars besides these, including Pamela R. Matthews, Monique Parent, and Julius Rowan Raper. Linda Wagner-Martin, a pioneer in so many fields and a model for other scholars, read the manuscript, and her suggestions helped me enormously.

At times I have felt like Nancy Drew being rescued by Bess and George or Ned. With this in mind, I am forever obliged to June Hanson for her research into the intricacies of the Glasgow family genealogy and the history of Francis Glasgow's attendance at the Second Presbyterian Church; to Carrington Tutwiler for sharing his memories of his family and his mother's diary; to Welford D. Taylor for his work on Amélie Rives, his knowledge of Richmond—and just about everything else in Virginian literary history; to Patricia Pearsall for her inquiries about the Valentine family and interviews with people who knew Glasgow; to Jack Pearsall for his legal expertise; to Dede Mousseau for her help in trailing Gerald B; to Francis Foster for deciphering Ellen Glasgow's prescriptions; to Sarah Anderson Easter for memories of her father, James Anderson; to Dr. James H. Smylie and Dr. O. Benjamin Sparks III for information about the Second Presbyterian Church; to Constance J. Moore, the Army Nurse historian, for facts about Anne Virginia Bennett's military service; to Kathleen Dennehy for searching the annals of the American Academy of Arts and Letters; to Bruce Thornton for his translation of the De Graffenried family motto; and to Dottie Carroll for help preparing the manuscript. Fleda Jackson, Jerome Loving, Ellen Pifer, Mary Richards, and Charles Robinson have offered much support.

I would never have completed this book without the help of the librarians at the Alderman Library, University of Virginia, Charlottesville; the Morris

Library, University of Delaware; the University of Florida Libraries, Gainesville; the Leyburn Library, Washington and Lee University; the James Branch Cabell Library, Virginia Commonwealth University; the Harry Ransom Center, University of Texas; the Butler Library, Columbia University; Special Collections, Vassar College; Historical Collections of the Library, College of Physicians of Philadelphia; the Virginia Historical Society; the Virginia State Library; the Virginia Baptist Historical Society; the New York Public Library; the Library of Congress; the National Archives; and the Boatwright Library, University of Richmond, where James Gwyn proved to be so resourceful. I would also like to express my appreciation to the Virginia Humanities Foundation for a fellowship and to the University of Delaware for a General University Research Grant.

The Virginia Baptist Historical Society has kindly granted me permission to reproduce photographs for the frontispiece, and of Ellen Glasgow at the turn of the century and White Sulphur Springs (photographs courtesy of the University Archives/University of Richmond). Pictures of Arthur Glasgow, Henry Watkins Anderson, and Queen Marie come from the Virginia Historical Society. *The Illustrated London News* Picture Library provided the official photograph of Queen Marie, and the Special Collections Department, University of Virginia Library, provided all other photographs, with permission.

Most of all, special thanks to Carl Dawson.

ELLEN GLASGOW

INTRODUCTION

*Not for everything that the world could give would I consent to
live over my life unchanged.*

Ellen Glasgow, *The Woman Within*

ELLEN GLASGOW (1873–1945), one of the twentieth century's most acclaimed women novelists, lived her life in Richmond, Virginia, the capital of
the Confederacy. Her house at One West Main stood within walking distance of the Tredegar Iron Works, which supplied munitions to Robert E.
Lee's army. Glasgow grew up on stories of the Civil War, and the legacy she
left is itself a kind of reconstruction, a new history that contradicts and, when
necessary, flatly dishonors the old.[1] Her novels speak of a fallen South struggling to reach an accommodation with defeat, holding stubbornly to pastoral
myths as it labors to enter an industrial age. Through her fiction, Glasgow
defined many of the elements we now associate with a larger pattern of
Southern literature: a tragic sense of life, a deep-rooted pessimism, a recognition of human capacity for evil, and the decrees of history and place. Her
novels provide a chronicle perhaps second to no one's, a chronicle of Richmond and of Virginia, but also of a changing America from the Civil War to
the Second World War.

But who was Ellen Glasgow, the first Virginian woman admitted to the

American Academy of Arts and Letters and the 1942 recipient of the Pulitzer Prize for fiction?[2] To her family, she seemed moody and often self-centered. To fellow Richmonders, she figured in local lore as a gracious eccentric who had once lectured on women's suffrage in an evening dress and loved animals probably more than people. To Henry Anderson, her last fiancé, she remained an ethereal ideal who demanded more than he was willing to or could provide. And to much of the American reading public at the turn of the century, she symbolized the South itself, fighting the allure of its own broken past.

It is not surprising that Glasgow's friends and critics knew her in assorted guises, for she spent a lifetime wrestling with what she called her own "dubious identity" (WW, 130). Children, now themselves grandmothers, who accompanied their mothers to Glasgow's house might have visited Janus-like twins. One remembers how a compliment from "Miss Ellen"—"You have the most beautiful red lights in your hair"—made her feel grown up for the first time.[3] Another found the house as cold and stiff as its occupant and couldn't wait to escape.

Contemporary critics remained equally confused about Ellen Glasgow's career. If Glasgow found followers among Southern Agrarians, including Robert Penn Warren, Allen Tate, and Stark Young, who wanted to affirm the humanism they saw rooted in the rural life of their particular region, others thought she embodied the "quaint grace of the Victorian era."[4] During her lifetime, she received every major award for fiction except the Nobel Prize. After her death, younger writers ignored her contribution to Southern realism, especially her efforts to present poor whites, women, and blacks as flesh-and-blood people. Yet there have always been readers and critics who agreed with Glasgow's own contention that *Barren Ground, The Romantic Comedians, They Stooped to Folly, The Sheltered Life,* and *Vein of Iron* represented "some of the best work that has been done in American fiction" (WW, 270).

Glasgow has continued to challenge the critics. Her first biographer, E. Stanly Godbold, developed a love/hate relationship with his subject, whose "anti-maleness" tested his powers of abstraction.[5] Linda Wagner-Martin sympathized with a woman writer desperately trying until the composition of *Virginia* (1913) to pretend that she was a liberal, well-educated man. Julius Rowan Raper saw a leading proponent of psychological realism and modernism laboring to find a style. And Pamela Matthews insisted on her concern with women's issues and her commitment to female friendship in a post-Freudian world.[6]

Today most readers think of Glasgow as a regional writer or a novelist of manners. She realized that either of these categories would lead future critics to view her parenthetically, and literary history has proved her only too right. Perhaps because Glasgow wrote about a cross section of society and not the more cinematic Astor Four Hundred, she has still to receive the attention accorded Edith Wharton. Then, too, her self-styled "social history" struggles against romance and largely ignores the Gothic elements that began to define Southern literature in the 1930s. Her characters do not escape, redefine, or recreate the world. Rather, they toil within the context of a civilization she believed to be essentially uncivilized, one in which innocent souls suffer undeserved tragedies (WW, 64). Glasgow felt at a distinct disadvantage when compared to William Faulkner, who continued a tradition she pioneered, or to writers such as Sinclair Lewis coming out of the Midwest. What opportunity awaited the serious writer, she asked, who was not a literary ruffian: a stevedore, a ditch-digger, a bull-fighter, or a public enemy (CM, 53–54)? The critic Van Wyck Brooks wondered whether she appeared "too tame for Sinclair Lewis and too domesticated for Willa Cather."[7] Like many women writers of her time, she had to fight the female novelistic conventions she subverted. Unlike most, she could claim that both her skill and reputation had grown with age.

Glasgow, who manufactured an easily grasped, virtually stereotyped personality for public consumption, told two related versions of her life story: the first a tale of victimization, conflict, and isolation; the second a chronicle of will. Both were true. The early tragedies she experienced shaded all later achievements: the death of her mother, Anne Gholson Glasgow, in 1893, followed the next year by the suicide of her brother-in-law and mentor, George Walter McCormack. In the ensuing two decades, Glasgow suffered more catastrophes: the end of her relationship with a married lover, identified in her autobiography as "Gerald B"; the suicide of her brother Frank; and the death of her favorite sister, Cary McCormack, after a prolonged battle with cancer. The events she lived, the *"bios"* of biography or autobiography, always had less significance than the meaning she made of them in her fiction and her autobiography.

Writing the life of someone like Glasgow, who must in large part remain unknown, raises questions about the construction of identity and the nature of biography itself. In her autobiography, *The Woman Within*, Glasgow asks a question that haunts all writers: "How can one tell," she wonders, "where memory ends and imagination begins?" (WW, 281). This question has particular significance for a biographer. The "truth" of biography—like that of autobiography—continually evolves. It grows with the process of amendment and revision. No less than poetry, biography involves what Virginia Woolf called a "secret transaction" in which a voice answers a voice.[8]

If we accept that any writer tells, as Glasgow believed of herself, his or her own disguised story, then the biographer is also an autobiographer, whose personal narrative develops within, alongside, or in opposition to the subject's.[9] Leon Edel describes the biographer's dilemma as inherently paradoxical: "He must apprise the life of another by becoming that other person; and he must be scrupulously careful that in the process the other person is not refashioned in his image."[10] The relationship, subtle, intimate, and ambivalent, is affected by any number of personal and political factors. A biographer may choose a soulmate, an enemy, or someone in need of rescue.[11] Writing about a woman can present special problems, for the biographer must resist conventional notions about female behavior and fulfillment.[12] Perhaps the nearest approach to another's life rests on "the divination of an inexplicable presence, whether a verbal mood, or an emotional aura" of "facts" or deeds.[13] However we define the self, personality may be nothing more than a collaboration between ourselves and the world at large, a process that engaged and exasperated Glasgow from the moment she first heard words sing.

Glasgow's literary executors believed that process worth telling, and they asked Marjorie Rawlings, the author of *The Yearling,* to write her friend's biography. Long before Rawlings accepted the commission, she had a dream that eerily captures the ambiguous relationship between a biographer and a subject. "You came to live with me," she told Glasgow after visiting her in 1914:

I was away when you came, and on my return, to one of those strange mansions that are part of the substance of dreams, you were outside in the bitter cold, cutting away ice from the roadway and piling it in geometric patterns. I was alarmed, remembering your heart trouble, and led you inside the mansion and brought you a cup of hot coffee. You had on blue silk gloves, and I laid my hand over yours, and was amazed, for my own hand is small, to have yours fit inside mine, much smaller. You chose your room and suggested draperies to supplement a valance. The valance was red chintz and you showed me a sample of heavy red brocade of the same shade. I told you that from now on I should take care of you, and you must not do strenuous things, such as cutting the ice in the roadway. James Cabell came into the room and asked what the two of us were up to. (As of course he would!) (*WW,* 294)

Glasgow read the dream as an almost supernatural "transference of thought and sympathy."[14] It also reveals the complexities inherent in literary friendships and their posthumous extension in literary biography. From the biographer's point of view, the relationship encompasses burden and privilege. As Rawlings takes Glasgow's shrunken hand and leads her into the strange mansion—what Henry James called the house of fiction, or academics have come to call the canon—the generational roles reverse. Her promise to nurture Glasgow and her work disturbs Cabell because he intuits his own exclusion from female traditions that history has increasingly honored. Years later when Rawlings recalled the dream, she resented the idea of attending Glasgow: "It was my feeling . . . that her original humanity and gratitude turned suddenly to a self-assured arrogance." [15] Rawlings's recoil may be part of the biographical process itself, an assertion or reclaiming of self after the necessary suspension of judgment. Unfortunately she died before beginning the actual writing of her book, before she might have rethought the dream again.

My own "version" or vision of Glasgow's life reflects one of Glasgow's basic premises: that life and art intertwine to form a single strand. In untangling and rebraiding that strand, I have used a variety of approaches from psychological to historical, whatever has worked. While newspaper accounts, reminiscences, and correspondences have proved indispensable, any biographer of Glasgow must confront the problem of missing records. She claimed that one sister tossed out the early drafts of her novels during spring cleaning. And after Glasgow's death, with or without her prior consent, another destroyed photographs and papers. Certainly Glasgow herself had no moral compunctions about destroying documents. As a child, she and friends discovered a cache of love letters, dating from the seventeenth century, which they read aloud and then gleefully threw on the fire. [16] She may have remembered that rainy day, when despairing over the loss of mother and lover, she burned all the intimate records of her first forty years. The record Glasgow did leave was at once partial and full. According to Mark Twain, biography and autobiography inevitably consist of extinctions, shirkings, and revelations, "with hardly an instance of plain straight truth," though "the remorseless truth is there, between the lines." [17]

The structure of my book largely reflects that of Glasgow's life. Its spaces or gaps indicate the times she retreated from the world because of illness, work, or private needs. Although Glasgow traveled extensively, lived for an interlude in New York, and in later years summered in Maine, she spent most of her days in Richmond, publishing a novel every three years or so, and seeing the same circles of friends. Her days had a predictable outward rhythm that disguised her buried passions and turmoils.

Without ever writing a biography, Ellen Glasgow considered herself a "biographer of life" (*CM*, 94). Her writing notebooks contain the verses of Negro spirituals alongside detailed recipes for such favorites as batter bread and champagne punch. Like most writers she mined her life for every fictional gem, what Henry James called *le donnée*. As she aged, the balance shifted, and Glasgow lived most fully in her books. "When one is writing," she confessed, "the world of the book seems almost more real than the other."[18] There she discovered a "Reality" more profound than the selected realities that composed her daily life (*WW*, 125).

To those who might ask, as did Rawlings's aunt: "Why write the life of some obscure person?" the answer must be that these books and the person who imagined them matter. Ellen Glasgow and her work do matter. I have come to see her as a woman of great courage, someone who endured unspeakable misfortunes, including the slow disintegration of her hearing. She was also at times exasperatingly narcissistic, partly because she saw herself as a standard bearer of truth. In her novels, to which she dedicated her life and which in a sense became her life, she sought a commitment to truth beyond human frailty and pettiness, to what she called the "living pulse" of experience. This willful, self-educated, provincial Southerner, weaned on Calvinism and the science of Darwin, listened to the cries of past and present voices and found a way to make them heard.

CHAPTER I

THE DEEP PAST

1829–1887

The art of life is more like a wrestler's art than the dancer's,
in respect of this, that it should stand ready and firm to meet
onsets which are sudden and unexpected.

Marcus Aurelius Antoninus

I

To anyone other than their children, Anne Gholson (1831-93) and Francis Glasgow (1829-1916) appeared ordinary enough. The man and woman who stare from family albums look more like brother and sister than husband and wife. There is no hint, except perhaps in Anne's apathy or Francis's lurking smile, that they would provide their daughter with a daily and compelling example of one of her central themes: the thwarting of a sensitive nature by its spiritual inferior.

On their wedding day in July 1853, neither Anne Gholson nor Francis Glasgow could have suspected that they would bring ten children into the world; that two would die in infancy, a third before maturity, and a fourth by suicide; that of their six surviving children, almost all would experience debilitating bouts of depression. Instead, they looked forward to a secure future unmarred by heartbreak or the Civil War, ignorant that they would inadver-

tently repeat the patterns of their own childhoods marked by abandonment
and the withholding of love.

II

Anne Gholson grew up in western Virginia's Cumberland County, the daughter of William Yates Gholson (1807–70) and his first wife, Martha Anne Jane
Taylor (1810–31). Glasgow shared her mother's pride in their connection to
some of Virginia's oldest Tidewater families, among them the Randolphs,
the Woodsons, the Yates, the Creeds, and the De Graffenrieds, whose family
motto became a personal tenet: *Fac recte neminem time* ("Do rightly, [so that
you] fear no one"). Forebears included the Landgrave of the Carolinas and
the colonial president of William and Mary College. Ironically, for Ellen Glasgow, Virginians considered distaff ties weak enough for at least one friend to
wonder whether Glasgow's social rebellion stemmed from not being "FFV,"
that is, not belonging to the first families of Virginia.[1]

Despite Anne's background, it might be said that she had been born into
tragedy. Her mother's death ten days after her birth left the as-yet-unnamed
baby and an older brother, Samuel Creed, practically orphaned. In what
would become a familial pattern, Anne's care fell to Rhoda Kibble, a black
woman who would die in her adopted daughter's service. Family legend,
echoing the formulaic plots of plantation novels, has Anne's mother hand-
ing the newborn to Kibble with the request, "Mammy, bring her up for me"
(*WW*, 299). Glasgow mythologized the scene in "Whispering Leaves," the
story of a nurse whose loyalty and protection extend beyond the grave.

To some extent life and fiction did coincide. Anne promised always to
care for Kibble, and Kibble's children and grandchildren formed part of Ellen
Glasgow's extended family. Kibble's daughter, for example, acted as Glasgow's wet nurse. In turn, Glasgow paid the school tuition for Kibble's great-
granddaughter, sent members of the family copies of her novels, and contributed to the upkeep of cemetery plots. Anne Gholson's inauspicious start in
life ultimately had a bearing on several generations of Virginians, white and
black. It also had an impact on Southern literature, for her daughter would
make interracial kinship bonds a major strand of her revisionary history of
Virginia.

Within three years of Glasgow's birth, her mother experienced another
major loss. Her father, William Yates Gholson, moved to Mississippi, where

THE DEEP PAST 9

in 1839 he married Elvira Wright and began a second family. Later he freed his slaves and moved north to Cincinnati. The reasons he did not send for the children of his first family remain obscure. To all appearances he deserted them.[2] Anne did not correspond with her father directly but kept in touch through her half-brother, William Yates Gholson Jr. Communication stopped for many years following William's death in the Civil War. It did not begin again until 1866, when, with a guile none of her children would have credited, Anne approached her father through an intermediary, her 11-year-old daughter, Emily. Emily wanted to know how she could have a grandfather and never see or hear from him. William replied to his granddaughter's letter. Now that the "ice was broken" (to paraphrase Anne), father and daughter resumed an intermittent correspondence.[3]

After Anne's father left Virginia, she was adopted by her great-uncle Chancellor Creed Taylor (1766–1836). In better days, Taylor had founded the Needham Law School (1821), acclaimed for an apprenticeship system that spawned practitioners, old-time Southern orators, rather than scholars.[4] Some of Virginia's most celebrated lawyers, including Anne's father, had trained at the school's "moot" or simulated court. Taylor and his wife, the eccentric Sally Woodson Taylor (c. 1774–1861), were kind, elderly, and ill—hardly the ideal guardians for a young girl. With her sharp, wizened face, Aunt Taylor reminded her niece of a good witch, one who preferred a red Morocco coach to a broomstick. Predictably, much of the child's daily care fell to servants, already feeling torn between chores and family responsibilities of their own. Taylor's deteriorating health and his depression over financial reverses lent Needham a somber air.

Before Anne reached her sixth birthday, Creed Taylor died. He had hoped to live long enough to discharge his debts, but at last even the long avenue of cedars had to be sold. Ellen Glasgow wove that bit of family history into her novel The Ancient Law (1909). After Taylor's death, Anne and her brother remained with their aunt at Needham, fighting the despair of genteel poverty. All that would remain from this time, except shreds of anecdote, were two lone goblets and family portraits by C.B.J. Fevret de St. Mémin, an aristocrat who fled the French Revolution. The portraits, which Glasgow hung in her drawing room, proclaimed their owner's social standing, while capturing some distilled essence of the past.

As with Anne, his own experiences had ill-prepared Francis Glasgow for the intimacy of marriage or family life. He grew up in Rockbridge, a county neighboring Anne's Cumberland, on the plantation that had been in his family for three generations. His grandfather, Arthur Glasgow, had been a pioneer, who came to the United States about 1766 with his brothers Joseph and Robert. Settling on the James River in the wilderness of Rockbridge County, they named their plantation, which covered between four and five thousand acres, Green Forest (the meaning of the Gaelic *Glasgow*). The large plantation included what would become the small towns of Buena Vista and Glasgow. The Glasgows took their family motto—"Lord, Let Glasgow Flourish"—to heart. About 1800, their prosperity allowed them to tear down their log home and build a brick house that featured a two-story porch and white columns. Francis Glasgow was born in this house, the fifth of nine children from the union of Katherine T. Anderson and her cousin Robert, one of Arthur's three surviving sons. Glasgow thought her father's homestead "simple and very modest" in comparison to the Tidewater places of her mother's relatives.[5] The Glasgows were, in fact, the largest landholding family in Rockbridge County. The 1860 census lists the personal property and real estate holdings of Francis's father, Robert, as totaling $35,000—almost $1,000 more than the combined assets of forty of his neighbors. Despite their wealth, the Glasgow men led spartan lives. From his father, Francis learned to value austerity, a trait Ellen thought as "Roman" as it was Calvinistic.

Glasgow associated Needham with her mother's Episcopal faith and Green Forest with her father's Presbyterianism. Her own soul seemed a battleground where opposing and hostile armies of each parent contended. If Needham approximated a cultured English aristocracy, she held Green Forest responsible for three generations of iron-willed church elders. Glasgow's own father served as an elder for thirty-three years, and with his death in 1916 the family line of succession ended. Because Glasgow could never dissociate her vision of her father's religion from the man himself, she saw Calvinism as a punitive, authoritarian, and irrationally sentimental system. Among her grievances against her father, she listed his singing over and over again on Sundays his favorite hymn: "There Is a Fountain Filled with Blood." But however much she saw her father as a Southern Bismarck calling for blood and iron, she reluctantly linked his Scotch-Irish heritage with the fortitude or "vein of iron" (later the title of her 1935 novel) she thought necessary for survival.

In a strict Calvinist household where every earthly affliction seemed divinely appointed by God, Francis Glasgow learned to consider emotion an indulgence, sensuality a sin. He became an increasingly taciturn man, who appeared like his Calvinist forebears to need neither comfort nor pleasure.

According to his daughter, "a God of terror, savoring the strong smoke of blood sacrifice, was the only deity awful enough to command his respect" (*WW,* 85). Patriarchal rather than paternal (86–87), he had never in her memory changed his mind or admitted a mistake. Glasgow felt that her father's despotic personality made him the last man on earth her mother should have married. "He gave his wife and children everything," she decided, save love, "the one thing they needed most" (15).

How can we reconcile Ellen Glasgow's memories of her father with the earnest, even passionate young man who appealed to her mother? The couple met at the home of his uncle, Joseph Reid Anderson, during a visit Anne made to her Grandfather Taylor in Richmond. Their families occupied identical Greek Revival mansions at 110 and 113 West Franklin, a wealthy Richmond neighborhood not far from the Capitol. The young people could not have had a more romantic setting for quiet talks than the Anderson garden, which covered more than half a city square. Francis saw a young woman with skin so fair and fine that friends had nicknamed her "the lily." Anne saw an imposing young man with a brilliant future. Francis had studied law and then gone into business with his uncle, the president of the Tredegar Iron Works and one of the South's leading industrialists. Marriage promised Anne independence and financial security. To someone who grew up in her circumstances, Francis's reputation for steadiness and kindness proved irresistible.

Anne could not have known that she was marrying a man who in his single-mindedness resembled her father. When William Gholson served on the Ohio Supreme Court, he "knew nothing of the parties but their names on the docket; nothing of the cause but from the evidence; nothing of the result and its consequences but the judgment which the law pronounces." Francis Glasgow believed as strongly in the doctrines of religion as his father-in-law believed in the letter of the law.[6] Each man could be ruthlessly inflexible. Ellen Glasgow would not admit to herself that a man as devoid of compassion as her father could have understood his wife for a single minute.

III

From the outset of their marriage, Glasgow's parents needed emotional resources that neither had. Within a year, Anne gave birth to their first child, premature and stillborn. On January 31, 1855, Francis recorded in the family Bible the birth of Ellen Glasgow's eldest sister, Emily Taylor. Every two or three years he entered another name: Annie Gholson on July 9, 1857; Joseph Reid on March 26, 1860;[7] Sally Cary on January 4, 1863; and Arthur on May 30, 1865, a month following Robert E. Lee's surrender at Appomattox.

The welfare of the Glasgow family had always been tied to the fortune of Tredegar Iron Works. Occupying five acres between the James River and the Kanawha Canal, the Works consisted of an armory rolling mill, with nine puddling and four heating furnaces, a spike factory, a cooper shop, a pattern storage attic, and three tenement buildings that housed the slave labor force. Sick or injured slaves unable to work their usual ten-hour day as skilled or unskilled laborers received treatment at a segregated hospital.[8] In its own "peculiar" version of slave labor, the Tredegar functioned like a self-contained, nineteenth-century model village, fostering social ideals to reach economic goals. Food was said to be good at the Works and clothing adequate, but more important the management respected slave family groupings.[9] In 1861 slaves constituted half of the firm's 900 workers;[10] on the eve of the war, that figure had nearly doubled.

The fate of the Tredegar and its agents depended on the fortunes of the South. Richmonders predicted—falsely, as it happened—that a Northern victory would mean the confiscation or the destruction of the Works. Management, hedging bets until December 31, 1861, accepted a federal government order for cannon. On the floor of the foundries, munitions for the North and the South lay like corpses in parallel rows,[11] a macabre projection of the scene soon to be enacted at Bull Run.

Although Francis Glasgow had freed his own slaves before the war, he never wavered in his allegiance to the Confederacy or to the company whose employees and conscripts formed the Tredegar Battalion, a unit that served in Richmond and on the front lines. From 1862 to 1864, he managed blast furnaces for the Tredegar in the counties of Botetourt, Allegheny, and his own native Rockbridge. He drilled his subordinates as if they were going on active duty, and all the time never stopped worrying about the defection of his enforced workers, who included convicts as well as slaves. When the enemy appeared, his men would bank the fires and retreat into the woods. Oddly enough, federal forces threatened the operation less than hungry Confederate soldiers, who swarmed through the countryside like locusts looking for grain. News of the Emancipation Proclamation stirred the Tredegar slaves to rebellion before Francis punished the leaders, effectively stopping the revolt. In various manifestations, economic and sexual, the thing not named but imagined—the "real" relationship between her family and their black employees—would become for Glasgow a moral debt and the subject of fiction.

The war separated the Glasgows as it did so many families. While Francis protected the interests of the Tredegar, Anne lived in Botetourt County on a farm named Far Enough. Needless to say, it was not. Contending with hungry babies and stragglers from both armies, Anne found herself deserted once again. Like Francis, she deemed Union troops less dangerous than her compatriots. After one terrifying day of fending off scavengers, she dispatched a servant with a request to General David Hunter of the federal army: could he place a guard on her front porch? Tearing the note in two, Hunter snapped, "Tell her to make her damned Rebel husband come home and protect her" (*WW*, 38). That night a colonel from Massachusetts who had witnessed Hunter's outburst knocked on Anne's door and offered to guard her family. Glasgow claimed that for years she heard his name repeated in her mother's morning and evening prayers.[12]

At the end of the war, Francis wondered how the Union could be reconstructed over the graves of the Confederate dead. Nevertheless, he swore allegiance to the federal government, received a federal pardon, and dreamed of beginning again far from the ruins of Richmond. Ever since ill health had forced him to live a planter's life for a year in the middle 1850s, he had thought about returning to Green Forest. Now he hoped to restore the ravaged homestead to its former splendor. As Arthur's first birthday approached, Anne Gholson Glasgow surveyed her bustling family. "We have employed a female teacher in our family," she wrote her long-absent father, "& Emily & Annie are at their lessons every day. Our eldest boy is five years old, is reading now & very much interested in his book. Little Cary is three years old & the pet of the household. Our baby boy . . . is Gholson from head to foot."[13] The teacher, a large, genial woman named Virginia Rawlings, became one of the family and an indispensable companion for Anne.[14] Glasgow remembered her as having a Roman profile and the first short curly bob she had ever seen on a woman. (In the 1930s, Glasgow adopted a similar hairstyle.) Most of all, she remembered Miss Virginia as a storyteller who "knew only the drama that was reality" (*WW*, 38).

In 1865, Francis resumed his management of the Tredegar Iron Works, one of the few businesses to escape the flames when Richmond fell. During the war, the company had run cotton to England and realized enough capital to get the plant back into full production, despite the need for extensive renovation and rebuilding. Their first contract came from the federal government. Richmond itself hovered on the verge of lawlessness. Confederate soldiers released from Northern prisons daily staggered into town. Racial tensions escalated as the citizenry disputed the rights of the black populace.

And just blocks from the Glasgows' narrow three-story house at the corner of First and Cary, the Gamble Hill Cats, Shockoe Hill Cats, and Church Hill Cats, gangs of young boys who had witnessed the battles of the Confederate Army, armed themselves with rocks and waged their adolescent version of war with pistols, shotguns, and slingshots that could hurl half a brick.[15]

The Glasgows fared better than many of their neighbors, some of whom depended upon former slaves for greenbacks and food from the U.S. Commissary. While the maintenance of their large family threatened to consume the assets that had survived the war and the Reconstruction acts, they still held Tredegar stock, the value of which increased with the company's new contract. Their four-bedroom house on Cary Street afforded little privacy for a growing family, but, shaded by large tulip trees, it still seemed an oasis among the turmoil. There Kate Anderson was born on January 14, 1868. Living only ten months,[16] she was followed by Francis Thomas on September 2, 1870, the year that Virginia came back into the Union. Three years later Ellen Anderson Glasgow arrived, so small and frail that she had to be carried on a pillow.

The financial panic in late September of 1873—five months after Glasgow's birth—heralded the beginning of a long depression. The bankruptcy of several Northern railroads heavily indebted to the Tredegar threw the Works into a receivership that lasted nine years. Richmond's industrial district experienced plant shutdowns and massive layoffs of both black and white workers. The city wore a general air of mourning, most apparent on Memorial Day when thousands of ladies dressed in black wandered "silently and tearfully among the graves" in Hollywood Cemetery.[17] The same economic necessity that had doomed the South to defeat determined, as Ellen Glasgow understood, her father's actions. Francis began to hold fast to property for the sake of his family. He spent nothing on himself except for books. Never a cheerful or a generous giver, he began to see his children almost as antagonists, their immediate needs to be weighed against those of the future. Ellen always remembered that she could not have a doll with real hair because her family had "lost everything in the War" (CM, 12).

For most of her life, Glasgow believed that she had entered the world on April 22, 1874, but in examining the family Bible she discovered that her father had recorded her birth as April 21, 1873. Glasgow attributed the difference in year to an inadvertent copying mistake, the difference in day to temperament:

As I came into the world precisely at four o'clock in the morning, by the testimony of all concerned, I suppose Father had considered it was still night, while Mother, a more sanguine spirit, who welcomed ten children with joy, had dreamed of the more confident morning. (*WW,* 5)

After Glasgow's precarious beginning, Anne became increasingly protective of her children. The death of her next baby, Samuel Creed (October 1875), naturally magnified her fears for their safety. Before the family could begin to grieve for the newborn taken by diphtheria, the eldest son, Joseph, died from the same disease. Anne felt devastated. Her sorrow seemed to run like a "nerve of grief" (*WW,* 16) through Glasgow's childhood. Nothing could comfort her, not even the birth on January 31, 1877, of Rebe Gordon, who displaced Ellen as the youngest child. When she saw the new baby in her mother's arms, Ellen Glasgow wept bitterly.

IV

Glasgow's first memories concern her mother and her nurse, Lizzie Jones. If Anne Gholson had three mothers—the mother who gave her birth, the aunt who sheltered her, and the servant who raised her—Glasgow had two. Jones joined the family three years after Rhoda Kibble's death in 1870. Jones, who had "belonged" to a Cumberland family (*WW,* 19), assumed care of the one-month-old Ellen. The childhood Glasgow did have she owed to Jones. The "dark, lean, eager colored woman" and the "small, pale, eager little girl" (*WW,* 21) roamed the back alleys and hills of old Richmond, from the governor's house in Capital Square to the City Almshouse, beyond Shockoe Cemetery. With equal affection Glasgow remembered the owner of the apothecary shop, the policeman on his rounds, Mrs. Staples's green parrot, and the local rag-picker, who appears in *The Sheltered Life* carrying a hempen bag and a hickory pole to poke out scraps from the trash-heaps (*SL,* 36). Glasgow exhibited none of the fears or shyness that would later plague her, and at least two childless couples she met on these excursions approached her parents about adoption. Like Eugenia Battle in *The Voice of the People* (1900), Glasgow may have adopted some mannerisms of black dialect. She certainly remembered many of Jones's sayings, such as "the Lord made us all, and He must bear with us," to the end of her life.[18] These years, which seemed in retrospect an endless spring, could only belong to childhood, a time before most children become aware of class or race.

Glasgow found her first muse in Jones. Each night, as Glasgow prepared for bed, the two would continue the story of the evening before. Whether the character of Little Willie appeared first to her or to Jones, Glasgow did not remember. With him she could be pursued by bears, lost in trackless forests, or shipwrecked with the Swiss Family Robinson. The very room seemed to glow not just with light from the candles and fire, but with the intensity of words. Glasgow served a kind of aesthetic apprenticeship with Jones, in which she awakened to the importance of place, the appeal of nature, and the joys of language. She never forgot the milk-white waxen blossoms of the pipsissewa she and Jones found hiding under leaves in the woods and the sensation that had rushed over her three-year-old self with the recognition of its beauty.

Of all places, Glasgow best loved Jerdone Castle, the family's 485-acre farm in Louisa County, about thirty miles northeast of Richmond. Originally built in 1752, Jerdone Castle's secret closets and cupola afforded wonderful hiding places for the youngest children and their new friends, Lizzie Patterson and Carrie Coleman, whose family had inherited and then sold the farm to the Glasgows. Glasgow's friendships with Patterson and Coleman lasted her lifetime. In colonial times, Jerdone Castle (like almost every other house in Virginia) had welcomed George Washington for a night—but only after its mistress had attended to her chores and chickens.[19] When the Glasgows took possession, the fields of the castle, once known for their rich harvests of wheat, corn, and tobacco, had long been left to run wild. They provided an example of what Glasgow would come to see as nature's "evolution," and more than forty years after her first summer there she divided her favorite novel, *Barren Ground* (1925), into sections called "Broomsedge," "Pine," and "Life-Everlasting." When Glasgow's mother developed a dislike of Jerdone Castle, and her father sold it for a substantial profit in 1887, it nearly broke her heart.[20] She and Jones had baptized its every tree and knew each one by name.

Glasgow thought of places as she did of writing. They seemed an extension of her personality, living both in themselves and through herself. She never lost her fascination for the almshouse, where Jones's friends petted her, or the cemeteries, where the Glasgow women planted flowers for remembrance.

From her earliest years, Glasgow lived in separate but overlapping worlds.

Jones gave her a glimpse of another world, which her presence in part disrupted. Glasgow failed to realize that she, a protected visitor, entered Jones's world solely by permission. Her sense that she knew and could write about blacks came from her relationships with Jones and various members of the Kibble family.

Jones mediated between Glasgow and the mother whose duties, along with childbearing, kept her mysteriously distant. Jones's presence and Anne's absence affect Glasgow's presentation of her two mothers. Lizzie Jones emerges as an individual and Anne always appears the perfect lady of rose-and-lavender scented pages, later satirized in *The Romantic Comedians* (1926) and *They Stooped to Folly* (1929). Glasgow defines her mother either as a figure in a Victorian postcard—her face framed in "the doorway, beyond the tall red and white oleanders" (*WW*, 23)—or almost exclusively in terms of Anne's imagined longings.

Glasgow, who associated her creative self with a dispossessed woman like Jones and her social self with a martyr like Anne, had a difficult choice. One mother was "owned" in the sense that she worked for the family, and the other was "owed." Glasgow's earliest memory, in which the identities of these women merge, highlights the difference: "My mother and my colored mammy bend over me. . . . I remember passing from arms to arms" (*WW*, 4). The possessive "my" suggests a different relationship when applied to Glasgow's mother as opposed to her "colored mammy." While Mammy's presence seems to acknowledge the limitations of Anne's ability to nurture her children, Anne's gentility highlights Mammy's servitude.[21] To reject Jones, Glasgow would have had to shed the self she had constructed in her image. Instead, Glasgow internalized the other or the opposing self whom Jones represented, becoming a rebel and a writer. Her two lives reflected her two mothers. She continued her adventures with Little Willie by night, and she studied to be a lady by day.

From her mother, Glasgow learned debilitating lessons about womanhood. Anne raised her daughters according to the precepts of her grandfather, Judge Thomas S. Gholson, who in his 1859 address "Woman and Her Mission" preached that woman should be "the helpmate to man, the confiding sharer of his joys, the sweet counsellor, and always the fond, firm, and abiding friend."[22] A woman's charm (and power) lay in her innocence (or ignorance), her ability to suffer in silence, her piety, and her devotion to family, servants, and the poor.

A young girl's education, as Glasgow herself satirized in her novel *Virginia*

(1913), emphasized the "superiority of man and the aristocratic supremacy of the Episcopal Church" (9). Although Richmond had instituted a public school system after the war, girls of Glasgow's class usually attended private schools run by indigent spinsters. Their days began with prayers and ended—for an additional fee—with music lessons or calisthenics. It mattered to no one that teachers, such as Lizzie Munford—the model for Glasgow's Miss Batte ("batty")—had neither aptitude "nor any special strain of intelligence." They represented a certain class and set of antebellum ideals, never, in Glasgow's words, having "lived beyond the battles around Richmond." [23] People respected Miss Munford because they remembered how she thanked the soldiers who carried her brother's body back from the war.

Because of health problems, Glasgow had very little formal schooling, probably less than a year. She remembered a month here and there and one final humiliation. Glasgow felt disgraced by her ignorance of math and science, which earned her the last bench in class. During recess a girl bullied her into surrendering her lunch of buttered biscuits, a slice of chicken, a sponge muffin, and an apple. Between classes, Glasgow bolted. "Mother alone understood," she thought. "Mother alone could protect me from this despair of being different, of being outside the world." "Look at the white rabbit," an older girl taunted (WW, 48). Once home, her mother tucked her into bed, darkened the room, ordered cocoa, rubbed her brow with eau de cologne, and sent for the doctor. He gave the girl and her mother the advice they wanted: Glasgow should not return to school this year. The headaches must stop or she might not live to womanhood, a state which, given her mother's example, would bring chronic pain. Herself a partial invalid, Anne supported, maybe encouraged, her daughter's delicacy.

The configuration of Glasgow's family and the larger culture it mirrored made her separation from Jones inevitable. In Glasgow's seventh year, Jones went to live with the Pattersons at Reveille. Her loss tore Glasgow's world apart. The circle of her friends, "in every shade of white, black, or yellow . . . melted away. The stories in the evenings were over. Little Willie had vanished. It may be he was dead. Whatever had happened, he never came back after they let Mammy leave" (30). No one could be trusted. Always a delicate child, Glasgow became more so after Jones left, her "sick headaches" or migraines continuing through adulthood. The French would have called her "une sensitive." Lizzie Jones declared—with irony or exasperation—that Glasgow had been "born without a skin" (5).

V

Sometime after Ellen Glasgow's tenth birthday, her mother changed in the space of a single night—or so it seemed to her daughter—from an engaging, inquisitive woman into a chronic invalid. Night after night, she paced in anguish, driven back and forth by a thought or a vision from which she tried in vain to escape. Her youngest daughters, awake in the adjoining room, listened, powerless to help. They partly blamed themselves for their mother's illness. Glasgow felt that her brother Frank, just three years older than herself, alone of Anne's children had never failed her. "In the environment in which we lived," Rebe wrote on the anniversary of their mother's birthday, "it was hard to physically show love and affection—but if I only had!" [24]

Friends and neighbors thought the Glasgows a morbid family, and the children may have inherited more than guilt from their mother. The oldest daughter, Emily, allegedly suffered from bouts of mania, and the four youngest children, Cary, Frank, Ellen, and Rebe, from depression. Possibly homosexual, Frank was a loner who would later commit suicide. Rebe considered herself cursed with sentiment and commonly woke up in the middle of the night thinking about every unpleasant and tragic thing she had ever known. Her worrying had an obsessive quality. She couldn't, for example, eat food prepared by someone she thought "immoral." Glasgow wrote openly to friends about her periods of despondency and lassitude. Contrary to rumor and to the memories of people who knew Glasgow when they were children, no available records show her having been a patient for recurrent nervous disorders at the nearby Tucker Sanitorium. She certainly did not have a suite reserved for her sole use and furnished with Oriental rugs and Chippendale furniture. When Glasgow did check into the Tucker Sanitorium during her last illness, she needed specific medical treatment. If, at other times, she had removed herself to the sanitorium, she would have done nothing more than many Richmonders who periodically used the facilities for a retreat. Glasgow had a fascination with psychology and was the first to recognize that not only her mind and character were affected by her mother's illness; it also shaped her future life (WW, 61). She knew that the past, its regrets and scars, failed sympathies and missed love, could not be laid aside or forgotten.

The exact nature of Anne's illness remains unknown, though Glasgow told friends that her mother had found her father "sleeping with one of the colored maids." "That's why she couldn't keep a maid," one explained, "he

did it all the time."²⁵ Rebe's son, Carrington Tutwiler, remembers that his
mother's hatred of her father also stems from this time; however, his memory differs in an important detail: she and Ellen never forgave their father for
keeping a black mistress during their mother's illness. This variation of the
story suggests that Francis's behavior may have been a response to Anne's
spells of irrationality and depression rather than the cause of it. In other
words, the source of the family problems could have been more biological than environmental—a topic that Glasgow made the subject of her first
novel, *The Descendant* (1897). All we do know is that whatever Anne Glasgow
surmised, discovered, heard, or imagined about her husband's affairs, she did
not suffer like a "true woman" in silence.²⁶ At 52, her emotional life may have
been further complicated by severe symptoms of menopause. Glasgow believed that the years of war and childbearing had left her mother bereft of the
physical and emotional resources needed to cope.

Glasgow blamed her father for her mother's illness. To her, he seemed a
consummate hypocrite. Where the community saw a model citizen, deeply
religious and committed to public service, she saw an archetypal villain
whom she compared to the murderous Duke in Robert Browning's "My
Last Duchess." In her fiction, Glasgow characterized men like her father as
sophisticated Simon Legrees. She dismissed his work as a city alderman from
1880 to 1890, during which time Richmond's black population received much
needed and long overdue benefits: a new school, an armory, fuel provided for
the poor, and improved neighborhood streets and lighting.²⁷ Neither did she
acknowledge that the Second Presbyterian Church—which in its first hundred years of existence (1845–1945) had only three African American members—chose him to head an 1885 fundraising effort to build a black sister
church.²⁸

Glasgow mocked as "sentimental" her father's devotion to his church and
its charismatic minister, Moses Drury Hoge, sometimes called the Patrick
Henry of the Southern pulpit. Remembering that he beat Arthur for refusing
to change Sunday schools,²⁹ she failed to understand that her father used religion as she used her writing, to control experience. His daily routine began
with family prayers, and the week revolved around church services, once
midweek and twice on Sunday, where for years (from the nation's centennial
year, 1876, to 1899) he could be found in the second pew of the church's north
transept. When the congregation shifted after Hoge's death, he inherited the
first pew. Its hymnbook rack, a cast-iron copy of da Vinci's *The Last Supper*,

symbolically joined the major aspects of Francis Glasgow's life: his devotion to his church and his place of employment, the Tredegar Iron Works.

In his daughter's imagination, Francis Glasgow never shrank to human size. His almost epic presence dominated her childhood and cast a shadow over her life. Her first memory associates him with pain and isolation:

> I open my eyes and . . . beyond the top windowpanes, in the midst of a red glow, I see a face without a body staring in at me, a vacant face, round, pallid, grotesque, malevolent. Terror—or was it merely sensation?—stabbed me into consciousness. . . . One minute, I was not; the next minute, I was. I felt. I was separate. I could be hurt. I had discovered myself. And I had discovered, too, the universe apart from myself. (WW, 3-4)

Glasgow metaphorically links her father and the setting sun, whose intrusion seems to thrust her from the seamless, preconscious world she had shared with her mother and Lizzie Jones. Conveniently overlooking the source of her own "irrepressible Scottish sense of humor" and obdurate will, Glasgow acknowledged no paternal legacy except the tawny-brown color of her eyes and a share in a trust fund (WW, 3-4, 16). At times her hatred blazed as "jealous and as strong as love" (D, 156).

Glasgow's antipathy toward her father has never been—and perhaps can never be—fully explained.[30] Multiple secrets like the Glasgow family ghosts remain entombed, at times even enshrined, in the deep past. Whatever the truth of Francis Glasgow's character and activities, his daughter believed him a contemptible philanderer. By confiding his sexual proclivities to close friends, she helped to feed the rumors that circulated Richmond for decades. This "secret" may have seemed less shameful, more socially acceptable, than those imagined. In Glasgow's fiction, for example, Virginia (1913) and The Sheltered Life (1932), the sexual exploitation of mulatto women produces a second, unrecognized family. The South's most obvious and collective secret may also have been one of Glasgow's own. Irita Van Doren, one of Glasgow's literary executors, supposedly told another friend that Glasgow had a black half-sister.[31] Available records neither support nor disprove this report.

Glasgow thought her father a fraud, and there exists some evidence to support her view. Known to boast that he came from a long line of elders, he attended only one out of thirty-seven elders' meetings between February 1868 and April 1870 at the First Presbyterian Church, and only twenty-eight of the seventy-nine "governing meetings" at the Second Presbyterian Church from 1908 to his death in 1916.[32] These meetings, where the elders discussed membership and finances and ruled on irregularities in behavior, including drunkenness and adultery, were crucial for the day-to-day running of the church.

Greater sins aside, Francis Glasgow indulged in at least one secret pleasure forbidden to members of the Second Presbyterian Church. His granddaughter Josephine (the daughter of Annie Glasgow Clark) remembers: "I always associated my grandfather Glasgow when a little girl with a strange and not unpleasant aromatic odor. Later in life I realized what it was. It was from the angostura bitters that he used in his whiskey."[33] By the time Josephine received her goodnight kiss, her grandfather had drunk his evening toddy. Josephine's use of the word "whiskey" may be a generic term, for Irita Van Doren recalls that she almost never served gin, a drink frequently flavored with bitters and perhaps reminiscent of her father. Of course, Glasgow, who served mint juleps and her own favorite old-fashioneds, could have had an aversion to gin because of its Hogarthian affiliation with the "lower classes."

With the exception of Frank, the children tended to sympathize with one parent or the other, the two older sisters and Arthur supporting their father; Ellen, Cary, and Rebe their mother. Yet Glasgow's relationship to both parents was more complicated and ambivalent. Her illnesses, including the severe headaches triggered by proximity to her father, aligned her with her mother while excusing her from the things she did not want to do. Overtly Glasgow blamed her father for her mother's unhappiness. Covertly she criticized her mother's behavior in tyrannical, neurasthenic characters, such as Angelica Gay (*The Miller of Old Church* [1911]) or Lavinia Timberlake (*In This Our Life's* [1941]).

Glasgow's earliest efforts at writing highlight the conflicts in her family. In one poem, she wishes to

> Drift to the land where I long to go,
> Leaving behind me the world's sad choices. (*WW,* 36)

This poem foreshadows her later pessimism, while the earliest surviving story, "Only a Daisy," anticipates her fictional concern with women's issues. Even as a child, her conventionally feminine exterior masked a fiercely rebellious and unorthodox heart.

"Only a Daisy," written at age 7, may have been inspired by one of her friends, who went to a dance clothed as a daisy. By the end of the evening, the daisies sewn onto her costume had begun to compost, and she "smelt awful." [34] In Glasgow's Cinderella story, the daisy wishes she were a rose:

> It was the evening before he should go away and the earl was walking in the garden with a young girl. "Let me give you a flower before you go," she said, "for it is the last time I will see you before you go," and she stooped to pluck a tall white lily that grew near, but the young man stopped her. "No," he said, "I will have this little daisy. I will keep it and it will remind me of you." She plucked the daisy and handed it to him. They stood together and talked for a little while and then the girl turned and went into the house. The young [man] stood still a moment, pressed the daisy to his lips, then hurried away and was soon lost to sight in the darkness. And the little daisy was content at last to be "only a daisy." [35]

This story contains the major themes of Glasgow's life: alienation, accommodation, and acceptance. It already presents a sense of isolation as desirable, a sign of election.

VI

Between the ages of 10 and 15, Glasgow never felt "free from the pressure of anxiety, from the sense of foreboding, and of something else, strange and terrible" (WW, 65) hanging over her. She could no longer hide under her bed and derive comfort from sucking a cube of flavored gelatin. People may have believed that "the less a woman knew about life, the better prepared she would be to contend with it" (CM, 90), yet the young girls of Glasgow's class were less protected than might be supposed. Afternoons could find them at the slaughterhouse with their brothers, evenings at a fancy dress ball for grownups. Their world, at once genteel and violent, teemed with contradiction. No one seems to have complained, for example, that during recess at Miss Lizzie's school in 1885 the girls witnessed a public hanging.[36] For Glasgow, the world outside her house became increasingly nightmarish. Her memories of Richmond are threaded with acts of senseless cruelty: the cries of boys stoning a dog, the sight of black convicts laboring in Hollywood Cemetery, the fate of a crippled girl abused by her family.

Little as the world of adults made sense, girls like Ellen Glasgow still had to be trained for their "proper sphere." By 1880, the Glasgows could afford to vacation at the expensive resort of White Sulphur Springs in the mountains of western Virginia. Life at "the White" had a ritualistic quality. Days melted into one another as guests swam or rode in the mornings, strolled or napped during the afternoons, and drifted into the ballroom after tea.[37] With other guests who escaped Richmond's oppressive heat, the Glasgows observed the comings and goings—duly noted in local society columns—of "belles." Richmond, too, had its "society." On Saturdays, young girls donned party dresses and attended a dancing school held above a Richmond barber shop that exuded the fragrance of exotic perfumes and strange spices. While Glasgow's health may have barred her from dance classes, she did hear stories about real-life beauties, such as May Handy or Mary Triplett, over whose reputation two men fought a duel. These stories taught girls to view themselves as objects of art. Noticing the vividly complexioned May Handy enter church, for example, one man supposedly gasped, "By God, that woman is painted!" May Handy, the subject of portraiture, responded with a pun: "By God she *was* painted." Such stories carried with them the implied cost of being, like Ellen's mother, a "flower" of the Tidewater.

Glasgow's fears about impending womanhood can be read in another early story, "A Modern Joan of Arc," set two years into the Civil War.[38] The heroine's family, which has an absent father, a beautiful mother, and a loving mammy, resembles the Glasgow household. Determined to find her father, Sally marches off, trailing a sword behind her. She wonders whether the Yankees will burn her at the stake like the lady in Mother's story, but instead they return the exhausted child to her mother. Recovering her manners, Sally thanks her rescuer for not setting her afire. The story illustrates the narrow parameters of a little girl's—and by extension a woman's—life. Sally's non-adventure has initiated her into the ranks of all those silent martyrs waiting for their men to return from glory. The female heroic represented by Joan of Arc exists now in minor social rebellions, such as Sally's insistence on thanking the enemy. She learns (and perhaps reflects her author's dawning belief) that women's adventures must be mannered and internal, lived in an imagined and private region.

The most accomplished story from this time, "Prairie Flower," shows Glasgow's awareness of the complicated relationships between black and white Southerners. It touches on themes of female sexuality and racial divisions, both of which she would develop over the course of her career.[39] In this story, a man named "Brown Bill" threatens a woman named Rose. The men in Rose's life—a young cowboy, her brother "Gentleman Jamie," and her fiancé—save her honor by ostracizing Brown Bill. Later Glasgow would examine in novels like *Virginia*, *The Sheltered Life*, and *In This Our Life* the relationship between Southern women and racial oppression.

From the first, writing proved both empowering and disabling. Glasgow asserted her dominance over her younger sister, Rebe, by calling her "Shadow" and demanding that Rebe stop whatever she was doing to hear her newest poem. Rebe, not without a will of her own, retaliated by refusing to listen. In its broadest strokes, Glasgow's life can be seen as a struggle to control the words that determined her immediate reality. The strength of that need found expression in an idiosyncratic version of "house" the sisters played. One of the girls would point and say, "That's *my* chair." Then she would leave the room. During her absence, the chair had to remain empty.

Glasgow may not have known her multiplication tables, but she knew the names of all the characters of Scott's novels and Shakespeare's tragedies. Her memory for poetry ranged from Gray's "Elegy Written in a Country Churchyard" to "Sigh no more, ladies, sigh no more." She especially loved the "tremendous rhythms" of Dryden and would sing aloud:

> Fallen, fallen, fallen, fallen,
> Fallen from his high estate . . . (WW, 53)

The sounds and rhythms of words gave her an acute, physical pleasure. After Glasgow overheard her older sisters read some of her verses to amused friends, she wrote in secret. This initial silencing, which made her want to champion those who could not speak for themselves, further reinforced her sense of difference.

In one instance, storytelling transformed Glasgow into the heroine of her own drama. When teenagers, she and Lizzie Patterson dressed as gypsies by coloring their faces with burnt cork, hitched a pony to a cart rigged with red curtains, and drove down Franklin Street in search of customers. The novelist William Dean Howells happened to be visiting his brother in Richmond that day and playfully shooed the girls away: "I want no gypsies on this place," he told the future recipient of the medal named in his honor. "Get out!" [40] After Lizzie's father heard of the escapade, he ordered them first to wash and change and then to return every penny of their ill-gotten seven dollars with an apology.

Remembering her childhood, Glasgow never understood how she came to be a novelist. The answer probably lies in her own family, whose story during and after the Civil War seemed as compelling as any fiction. In the beginning of her career, Glasgow defined the past in terms of historical necessity rather than individual psychology. Every adult seemed to have a story about how the war or Reconstruction reshaped his or her life. The stories that Glasgow heard at home came mainly from a "chanting chorus" (CM,

12) of female relatives. Besides Virginia Rawlings, who could make the most ordinary event seem extraordinary, her father's Aunt Bec could summon the Bible and *The Waverley Novels* "from the grave" (*WW*, 38). Their voices resound in the biblical cadences of Glasgow's fiction and its emphatic realism, for her "social history" continues the classical form of the historical novel that the Hungarian philosopher Georg Lukács admired in novelists such as Scott.[41] The tradition flows from novels of social realism in the eighteenth century, to the human comedy of Honoré de Balzac and the Wessex sagas of Thomas Hardy. Glasgow read all these authors and acknowledged their influence. When conceptualizing her history of Virginia, for instance, she consciously or unconsciously drew on Scott's understanding of the evolution of Great Britain. Like him, she sought to balance warring extremes.

Glasgow analyzed the friction between the aristocracy and the rising middle class by embedding it in what she called the "tragic conflict of types" (*CM*, 12). Usually her protagonists embody the social trends and historical forces of their period. Reading Scott, Balzac, and Hardy, she realized that the portrayal of history must be immediate, connected in some felt way to the lives of real people. The theories of evolution taught her that the present exists as a consequence of past events. From her Aunt Bec and other female relatives who tended the graves in Richmond's Hollywood Cemetery, she learned to remain faithful to an imagined past. And from Lizzie Jones, the friend of her youth, she learned the magic of words.

VII

Unlike Glasgow's own fiction, the story of Ellen Glasgow and Lizzie Jones had a happy ending. When Glasgow visited Lizzie Patterson at Reveille, she found her old nurse unchanged. After the girls got into bed, Jones would follow them to her own. From her bed in the far corner of the big attic nursery at Reveille, they could see Jones's "Star of Bethlehem" quilt rise and fall with the sound of her voice. Slowly the room would fill with happiness as "the fairies and ghosts and talking animals that Mammy would evoke from her secret magic" (*WW*, 33) came to tell their tales. People believed Reveille to be haunted, and Ellen Glasgow thought its spirits friendly.

Despite her affection, Glasgow came to patronize Jones, whom she described as

> an extraordinary character, endowed with an unusual intelligence, a high temper, and a sprightly sense of humor. If fate had yielded her even the slight-

est advantages of education and opportunity, she might have made a place for herself in the world. But Jones could neither read nor write, and since she had not attracted her own race in her youth, her emotional life was confined to the love she lavished upon the children she nursed. (*WW,* 18)

This characterization grows out of the popular mythology that portrayed the mammy as loving "her white children more than her own." Recalling nostalgic poems like "Me and Mammy" or novels such as John Pendleton Kennedy's *Swallow Barn* (1832), it continues traditions, sometimes actual but usually fictional. The role of "mammy" obscured the individuality of Lizzie Jones. How much, for example, could Glasgow have known about Jones's life apart from her family? Like other black female citizens of Richmond, Jones probably had extensive kinship networks, whether or not she married; and she may have belonged to one of the local Baptist churches as well as several secret societies that promoted black education, political involvement, and economic advancement.

Glasgow's relationship with Jones highlights her ambivalent relationship to much of the past. In the preface to her Civil War novel, *The Battle-Ground* (1902), she argued that the culture of the old South had been "shallow-rooted at best" because it depended upon the "enforced servitude of an alien race" and not on "its own creative strength" (*CM,* 13). She saw no irony in the fact that One West Main could not run without a company of servants, most notably James Anderson, who returned in the middle of each night to load the furnace as other men had fed the Tredegar fires. Nor did she, by her own account "the most unsentimental woman in the South,"[42] realize how she projected the domestic ideals of an antebellum age. The limitation of Glasgow's self-knowledge is highlighted by a remark of Anderson, her cook for forty years. Once asked if he had any dependents, Anderson answered, "Seven children and Miss Ellen."[43]

In 1925, more than thirty years after her world "tore in two," Glasgow made a pilgrimage to Evergreen Cemetery looking for Jones's grave. She discovered it neglected and unmarked. "I always felt badly that I had never seen how it was attended to," she wrote Rebe:

I found it entirely obliterated. No one would know that any one was buried there, and I remembered the way that old woman used to walk that long distance to the end of her life and the years when she went to Hollywood every spring and planted flowers while I was in New York, and the other years when she worked there with Mother and Cary. I engaged a man to make a mound over it and I am going to have a marker put over it.[44]

With the placing of that marker, Glasgow paid the kind of tribute to Jones that Alice Walker would pay to her literary foremother, Zora Neale Hurston. Of all the legacies of Glasgow's past, perhaps none had more power than the memory of Jones's voice.

As Glasgow approached adolescence, however, she had little sympathy for the "lingering poetry of time and place" (*WW,* 104) she would later associate with Jones and Southern literature itself. Family histories, no less than historical romances, seemed to falsify experience as she knew it. She wanted to explore whatever was real and vital in her own heart.

CHAPTER 2

SHARP REALITIES

1887–1895

*We see only what our own natures allow us to see: to know
others rightly, we must not view them from our own
standpoint—our rules and ideas, but from theirs.*
        Cary Glasgow, *A Successful Failure: An Outline*

I

WHEN ELLEN GLASGOW was 14, her family moved to One West Main, the
house she would occupy for the remainder of her life. A stroll through the
neighborhood took one by the former home of Jefferson Davis's secretary
of state, Judah P. Benjamin, and the Grace Episcopal Church, whose rector, Dr. Landon Mason (a descendant of the Revolutionary War hero George
Mason), had been one of Mosby's Rangers.

Originally built by a wealthy tobacconist, the Greek Revival mansion,
"overgrown with ivy and wisteria and half-concealed behind box and magnolia trees,"[1] always seemed a place unto itself. Even after the First World
War, when a garage stood on the site of the Benjamin house and the smell
of smoldering dumps tainted the summer's air,[2] an antebellum charm of
leisured elegance prevailed inside. Rooms lined with books and family portraits opened into the airy front hall where one might divine the smells of

spiced rose leaves, cape jasmine, or burning cedar logs. Guests slept on pink monogrammed linen sheets and were served mint juleps or old-fashioneds in eighteenth-century glass goblets. A prelude to lunch, the cocktails were, as one friend learned, strong enough "to lay anyone out."[3] On special occasions, such as Hugh Walpole's visit in 1920, friends listened to the Negro Sabbath Glee Club sing spirituals on "Miss Ellen's" back porch. By 1929, the gray stucco walls of One West Main could no longer shut out the noise made by heavy traffic rumbling over the uneven bricks. Down the hill, the Tredegar, sadly reduced by the supremacy of steel, endured, an atavistic symbol of the old and new Souths.

Glasgow would write all but one of her novels, for the most part, in One West Main. To her chagrin, she found that she could write in few other places. When she was 14, however, she wanted nothing more than to leave the house behind.

For Glasgow, adolescence resembled her own civil war. The twisted lives she led stood always on the verge of unraveling. The first crisis concerned her brother Frank. Growing up, Glasgow adored Frank. He seemed to understand everything she felt and could not express and, like those who most attracted her, he had a romantic air of resigned defeat. With Frank, she had continued the wanderings begun with Lizzie Jones. She remembered their visiting the cabins of former slaves where they heard poor whites criticized for being shiftless and unintelligent. Glasgow incorporated these experiences into *The Voice of the People* (1900) and *Barren Ground* (1925).

Francis Glasgow put an end to childhood adventures by sending Frank to the Virginia Military Institute. The boy—"shy and delicate . . . with immense brown eyes, and handsome, reserved features"—needed, in his father's opinion, "hardening" (*WW*, 65). Although Frank did not appear a likely candidate for a military school, he endured his training to the end and graduated in 1891.

The institute was no place for a 17-year-old boy who still liked to play with his younger sisters, especially one unsure about his sexual orientation. Established in 1839 so that the arsenal at Lexington might be protected, and considered the West Point of the South, VMI trained the sons of "Virginia's first families." Francis Glasgow, for example, enclosed in his son's application a family genealogy. When the public thought of the school, they remembered that Stonewall Jackson had taught there in 1851, and that Lee had praised its graduates. No one publicized the brutal hazing that also formed part of its history. More than one boy had to be carried to the hospital with injuries deliberately inflicted upon him by upperclassmates. In 1852, the year before Frank's admittance, a young cadet complained that he had "been through so much ducking, and twisting" that he would not have gone there had he known the extent of the hazing.[4] While cadets could be dismissed for hazing, students and faculty alike considered it part of the tradition.

Frank never spoke about his school experiences. He may have been one of those shunned for fighting back. Whatever happened, the boy who returned home for the holidays bore little resemblance to the brother Glasgow loved. He began to live alone among, rather than with, his family. Ever obedient and respectful of authority, he nonetheless burrowed deeper and deeper into himself. His retreat, which might have been the "safest defense against life" (WW, 67), went unnoticed by his father, who wrote the headmaster that "it is very gratifying to us to have a good account from Frank."[5] Thinking of Frank, Glasgow later encouraged Julian Meade, an aspiring writer who had attended VMI and hated it, to write a story about a sensitive boy whose well-meaning parents condemn him to a similar torture.[6]

The year of Frank's transformation also marked the beginning of Glasgow's long and open war against her father. Not again would she believe that older people knew better. The incident that triggered her rebellion happened in Anne's absence. Glasgow's mother and younger sister, Rebe, went to visit Anne's brother Samuel in Holly Springs, Mississippi, where he now practiced medicine. During this time, Glasgow's father and older sisters decided to "give away" Anne's ailing dog. When Glasgow discovered that two men from the Tredegar had carted off the dog in a bag, her long and brooding resentment against her father erupted. She hardly distinguished between injury to the animal and injury to her mother. Her anger masquerading as righteous indignation, she picked up a vase and hurled it against the wall. It was an exhilarating experience. She felt like Andromeda, who, having waited long enough for Perseus, tore her own chains free. This first act of defiance unleashed greater ones. Following Frank's lead, she withdrew from her family, despising their "sanctimonious piety," their hypocrisy and pretense (WW, 71–72). She refused to attend divine service, an act that other members of her father's congregation would construe to his embarrassment. Like her heroine in Barren Ground (1925), she vowed, "I will not be broken" (BG, 460). And, if she won her liberty, she also lost whatever remained of childhood.

II

Like most adolescents, Glasgow felt herself a composite of multiple selves: one gossiped with girlfriends about beaux; another hungered for meaning. How could there exist together this much mystery and pain? Sometimes she felt changed beyond recognition; and at others, like any pretty and popular young woman. At 16, Glasgow attended her first ball in Charleston, South Carolina. It was a St. Cecilia Ball, given once in January and twice in February. The dance itself had no set presentation of debutantes, and girls who went for the first time could wear colored dresses. These informalities made the ball no less exclusive. Legend has it that more than one young man became an upstanding citizen after the board threatened to revoke his invitation. The evening she went, Glasgow wore a white organdy dress with flounces that would swirl when she waltzed. In her hair, she pinned a red rose. The secret success of the balls to this day resides in the unwritten rule that no guest be overlooked, no lady neglected, no stranger unwelcomed.[7] The young men pledged to make every girl a belle. Two years before, when visiting Frank at VMI, Glasgow had attended a dance and been neglected. This night the world seemed hers. Little did she suspect that her chaperon saw her as "a hopeless difficult lump, dumb as a dolphin . . . never in all her much experience [had she] ever chaperoned a more unattractive and impossible debutante."[8] The truth of the evening matters little, for Glasgow felt herself admired; she knew—to echo another woman writer—what happy women felt.[9] She saw herself at the center of a brilliant and unforgettable affair.

The following June, Glasgow went to Commencement at the University of Virginia where she flirted and felt all "the glorified sensations of a Southern belle in the Victorian Age" (WW, 78). Freed from her cage of self-consciousness, she looked forward to a normal life complete with husband and children. The future held many difficult choices, but they did not have to be by default. The realities of childhood—the unnamed fears, ever-present anxieties, and unconquerable desolation—seemed finally blunted.

III

Although Glasgow anticipated a "normal" life, she already thought of herself as a writer. In retrospect, she wondered whether "any other obstinate author could ever have received so little understanding encouragement" (*CM*, 10–11). When she thought about Edith Wharton's fortuitous start in letters, she felt jealous. She herself had found no friendly critic to teach her how to write. Crediting her success to a "natural distrust of the easiest way," she claimed, "my only critic was within" (52). In truth, Ellen Glasgow may not have become a writer—or not the writer we know today—without the support of two friendly "critics": her sister Cary and her brother-in-law George Walter McCormack. Glasgow idealized them both. They composed her chosen family, separately and together filling the voids from childhood. They helped to determine the course of her emotional life and her artistic development.

A decade separated Glasgow from Cary, the youngest of her older sisters, making intimacy difficult. Glasgow avoided Emily who gave sanctimonious advice, and Annie and Cary seemed like distant goddesses exhaling a rarefied air. In the family, each of the elder girls had a special distinguishing attribute. People thought Emily pious, Annie pretty enough to make her Sunday school pupils read the Koran, and Cary brilliant. Glasgow timorously watched the spectacle of her sisters' lives, which seemed to center mostly around courting: a bland admirer casting sheep's eyes at Emily; another listening in amorous abstraction to Annie's thin, sweet voice pipe, "Douglas, Douglas, tender and true" (*WW*, 58). As Glasgow's own shyness wore off in adolescence, she stopped calling them "Sister Emily" or "Sister Annie" and assumed a more equal, less deferential, stance. Cary responded to the change and invited her friendship. For the first time, Glasgow realized that in her own right she might be an interesting person.

Glasgow's portrait of Cary's life in *The Woman Within* shows how closely she identified with her older sister. The short biography recalls "Only a Daisy," her early story about the misunderstood young girl:

> [Cary's] intellectual integrity must have prepared for her a tragic fate, in a period when truth walked alone, and the second best was exalted. She had singularly winning charm, an iridescent personality. Even when she turned away to the strange gods of heterodoxy, her older friends were still ardently faithful, and remained devoted until the end of her life. Wherever she went, she invariably drew the best and brightest about her. But a girl who read Darwin and Henry George in the last decades of the nineteenth century was known as "the eccentric Miss Glasgow" to the orthodox youth who walked home from church with her sisters. (*WW*, 57–58)

Cary's life reads much like Glasgow's version of her own. The "real" Cary, the idiosyncratic twists of her mind, the things that outraged or absorbed her, remain a cipher. Other than Glasgow's testimony, there exists scant record of Cary's heretical or even liberal views. There is, however, a record of her being received into communion at the First Presbyterian Church on November 13, 1868, and the Second Presbyterian Church on June 2, 1882— six years after her father and mother became members.[10] As we might expect, Glasgow both followed and rejected her sister's example. Forgetting that her eldest brother, Arthur, also rejected Presbyterianism, she wanted to align herself with her mother and then her sister whom she surpassed.[11] In later years, she characterized herself as the family's foremost "rebel against the Calvinist conscience" (WW, 59).

While Glasgow admired Cary for her skepticism, she admired her daring more. At 20, Cary had wanted to write novels. Her first and only book served as a primer for the young Ellen Glasgow. Inspired presumably by William Dean Howells's A Modern Instance (1881), A Successful Failure: An Outline (1883) recounts the aborted love affair between a young doctor, Joel Harden, and a divorced woman, Frances Howard.[12] Its rebellious and passionate heroine marries a man who schools her sensibilities and breaks her heart. Attracted by her aura of suffering, Harden regrets but honors her history: "It appeared to him that he had no right to take advantage of the circumstance [the divorce] which had wrought the very being of the woman he loved."[13] He can neither deny Frances's past nor imagine a future they can share. She resolves their dilemma by removing herself to New York. In the tradition of her male Glasgow namesakes (Francis Senior and Junior), Frances Howard dedicates the rest of her life to upholding the status quo. Foreshadowing the span of Ellen Glasgow's heroines, from Rachel Gavin in The Descendant (1897) to Roy Timberlake in In This Our Life (1941), she assumes that hard work can stifle thought. Is her life a failure? Cary, obliquely endorsing Presbyterian precepts, would have her readers answer no.

Although her book received little attention, Cary herself presented living proof that women could and did write. Her experience fed, rather than inhibited, her sister's competitive spirit. Ellen Glasgow saw her mother turn into a semi-invalid as menopause approached, yet she also saw her sister scribbling. Resembling those ordinary women who paved the way—as Virginia Woolf argues—for extraordinary women, Cary made it possible for her sister to envision a different future. Beautiful and literary, she epitomized everything that Glasgow wanted to be.

Cary was herself a transitional figure, a link between the "true" and the "new" woman. Her profound, unbreakable sympathy (WW, 84) made her seem of all the daughters the most like their mother. Her contemporaries thought her "unorthodox" because she supported a woman's right to work and vote. She did not, however, question refined notions of female sensibility or sexuality. The protagonist of an extant short story, "The Renunciation," for example, cannot fully dedicate himself to the Virgin Mary until he recognizes the ravaged features of his sweetheart in the face of an aging prostitute.[14] Cary's sympathies do not extend to the prostitute Ellen Glasgow would have championed.

Following the pattern of many women writers, Glasgow preferred to see herself as an anomaly, defining her life—like Cather and Wharton's—in opposition. She drew no comparisons between *The Descendant* and *A Successful Failure,* despite their anonymous debuts, "unladylike" subjects, and strong heroines. On the contrary, she either denied or minimized her sister's influence on her early work: "I had never met a novelist, or indeed any sort of writer in the flesh," she says of herself at the turn of the century, "and the whole profession existed for me as a tribe slightly fabulous" (*CM,* 18). Forgetting that Cary had struck at least a small blow for realism nearly two decades before *The Descendant* (1897), she imagined that all the brave young men wrote Henry James novels. Her compatriots knew more about the art of living, she declared, than they did of the fine arts. And, to a large extent, she was right. At the end of the nineteenth century, Southern writers felt hampered by their environment and its aura of self-satisfaction. After the Civil War, the South had no major publishing firms, and Southern writers had difficulty publishing their work with Northern presses. In the 1860s and 1870s, sentimental or humorous stories set in antebellum days found the largest audience. Their popularity continued into the 1880s, when local colorists led the way for more realistic depictions of daily life.[15]

Richmond, which could boast of four daily newspapers at the turn of the century, had always had a long and respected tradition of memorists, diarists, historians, and novelists. Among its early writers, the city could claim William Byrd, Thomas Jefferson, Patrick Henry, John Marshall, and Edgar Allan Poe, the dejected cousin (as Allen Tate called him) of all Southern writers. Poe had worked for the *Southern Literary Messenger* from 1834 to 1837, but Richmond honored him posthumously. Charles Dickens, Matthew Arnold, William Makepeace Thackeray, and Oscar Wilde all visited and received warm receptions, though Richmonders thought Wilde—with his knee britches, ruffled shirt, shoulder-length hair, and a fat sunflower stuck in his coat—"a queer Englishman."[16] Notwithstanding her sense of artistic isolation, Ellen Glasgow lived in a city rich with literary allusion. Just blocks away from One West Main, she could have encountered James Branch Cabell dreaming his own dreams. By the first two decades of the new century, Glasgow would be able to list many writers among her Richmond friends, including the novelists Mary Johnston and Henry Sydnor Harrison, critics such as Emily Clark and Hunter Stagg, and the historian Douglas Southall Freeman.

Instead of entering into Richmond's artistic or intellectual life, Ellen and Cary Glasgow created their own version of the Brontës' secret childhood world. The sisters began writing for one another, posing and answering aesthetic questions about the nature of art and the purpose of life. Their literary dialogue—or apprenticeship for Glasgow—may also have been a kind of contest that highlights the sisters' temperaments. In *A Successful Failure,* Cary had asked what is the "greatest good," which her heroine had defined as "unselfishness of action." [17] Cary believed that art needed to be grounded in human suffering, comprehension, and empathy, or the artist risks becoming an isolate or a parasite.[18] Glasgow took a different position in her poem "The Greatest Good," which argues that art—even the transitory song of a nightingale—has more permanence than death and provides more comfort than love.[19] This paradigm, at odds with yet realized through her sister, became the guiding principle of her life.

IV

George Walter McCormack (1868–94) held a certain appeal for women with intellectual or artistic inclinations, and he met two of them in the Glasgow household. Five years younger than Cary and five years older than Ellen, he had the "face of a poet and the mind of a scholar" (*WW,* 58)—a dangerous combination for both sisters. His Scotch-Irish father and Santo Domingan mother also made him the product of diverse heritages. In Charleston, his family seemed exotic because they spoke French.[20] McCormack, who had attended the University of Virginia School of Law (1885–87) and passed the South Carolina bar in 1889, enjoyed mentoring the Glasgow sisters. He guided their reading toward his own beloved area of political economy. "Until I met Walter," Glasgow avowed, "I had never known a man with an intellect of the highest order" (*WW,* 88).

Encouraged by McCormack, Glasgow began to study wages and conditions of labor, a field that had similarly captured her distinguished relative,

Mary Clare De Graffenried (1849–1921). De Graffenried lived in Washington, D.C., where she hosted a salon catering to well-known scientific and political figures. She worked for the Department of the Interior and published articles in such leading magazines as *Harper's, Century,* and *Forum.* In 1891, she received the first prize offered by the American Economic Association for an essay on women wage earners. Two years earlier, she had shared the prize for an article on child labor. De Graffenried corresponded with Cary and provided Glasgow with another example of a woman writer—in her case one who chose to remain single.

Glasgow's studies offered an escape from an unsatisfactory reality. Why didn't people rebel when they had nothing to lose? What kept them in their place? They also brought her into closer, though largely imagined, contact with McCormack. Reading his books, she participated in an intimate dialogue that made her feel she knew him better than anyone else, Cary not excepted. His notes and underlinings in William Graham's *Socialism New and Old* or Francis A. Walker's *Political Economy* seemed to provide a window into his mind, even his soul.

Glasgow, who remained a good but conventional student, believed that books could change lives. Like *The Descendant*'s Michael Akershem, she spent long plodding hours memorizing the vocabulary, definitions, and systems that Walker outlined in *Political Economy* (*TD,* 20). Finishing the book, she exulted, "Tant pis!"[21] Next she turned to philosophy. Over her father's objections, she devoured Kant, Schopenhauer, Lecky, and Gibbon's infamous chapter deriding the early Christians.[22] She had already acquired from her father's library the rudiments of a liberal education. Now she read contemporary works on evolution, spiritualism, socialism, philosophy, history, and psychology. Herbert Spencer's *Principles of Sociology* (1896), Friedrich Nietzsche's *Zarathustra* (1902), and V. C. Desertis's *Psychic Philosophy* (1901) all testify to an ardent search for meaning.

Glasgow began to begrudge any time away from reading, as though her life depended upon it. Friends and family warned her about turning into a bluestocking: "Didn't intellectual women end as either temperance workers or women's right's advocates?" She was, the now-familiar refrain went, too attractive to be strong-minded (*WW,* 90). Their warnings fell on deaf ears. When Walter recommended *The Origin of Species,* she studied it until "she could have passed successfully an examination on every page" (88–89).

For Ellen Glasgow, Charles Darwin's beliefs were to the body what Francis Glasgow's were to the soul. *The Origin of Species* freed the doctrine of competition from the last restraint of moral law and showed how warfare between individuals, species, or social communities, at least in the plant and animal worlds, could lead to evolutionary progress.[23] Although Glasgow refused to see evolution as either benign or beneficial, Darwin's book became a substitute bible, its theories influencing most of her early books and her interpretation of her own experience. The "religious persecution" (WW, 91) that Glasgow suffered at home for reading Darwin seemed minor when compared to the temporary sense of identity and authority his ideas afforded. He became a kind of intellectual father, whose views on heredity vaguely echoed those of her own father on predestination.

Glasgow's confidence in her newfound knowledge led her to take an examination in political economy from George Frederick Holmes, a renowned economist at the University of Virginia. In her need for external approval, she resembled myriad women writers who resented their exclusion from universities and sought to educate themselves in the sciences or classics. Elizabeth Stuart Phelps's relationship with her father, Austin Phelps, or, for that matter, George Eliot's relationship with George Henry Lewes parallels that of Glasgow and McCormack. These women, not least of all Glasgow, needed male validation of their intellect. Professor Holmes awarded Glasgow a "pass with distinction" in a subject that women at "Mr. Jefferson's University" could not formally study until years after Glasgow's death.[24] In her eyes, this achievement made her the intellectual equivalent of a man. Holmes's recognition of her ability gave her the courage (the "certification") to study any other prohibited subjects she desired, even prose fiction.

Initially Cary endeavored to dissuade her sister from attempting what "she herself had tried and failed as a girl" (WW, 83), but Glasgow's first draft of The Descendant, originally entitled Sharp Realities, began to take shape. Glasgow borrowed the title, which spurns the moonlight-and-magnolia tradition popularized by Thomas Nelson Page, from the seventeenth-century playwrights Francis Beaumont and John Fletcher. The idea came during a visit to the University of Virginia. An older woman, supposedly deploring her "dangerous ignorance," felt duty-bound to apprise the flirtatious 17-year-old "delicately and painfully" of the facts of life (WW, 78). It defies common sense to believe that Glasgow—given her version of her parents' history or her place in the family—would still have known nothing about reproduction. More likely, the conversation prompted her first thinking about the social repression of female sexuality, a topic she would later address in her Queenborough trilogy: *The Romantic Comedians* (1926), *They Stooped to Folly* (1929), and *The Sheltered Life* (1932).

Through the winter of 1890 and the next, Glasgow threw herself into causes and activities Walter McCormack could approve, while remaining aloof from the entertainments that would have brought her into contact with eligible young men. She volunteered at the City Mission and the Sheltering Arms, the only free general hospital in Virginia. Although the squalor repulsed her, she supported the institution for decades to come. Glasgow found it especially troubling that the patients — like so much "inanimate matter" (*WW*, 81) — had resigned themselves to circumstances. The inability to understand others left her feeling both humble and no less impatient at 60 than 17. For the rest of her life, she retained a distaste for the drudgery of charity work. While she enjoyed giving to individuals, she preferred others to wrap packages and serve meals. She wanted the intellectual stimulation of good talk rather than good works. Glasgow's desire to find people of like minds led her on to politics. Her brief stint as a Fabian Socialist did little to alter her already pessimistic view of human nature. She remained, in her own mind, less in search of "abstract truth, than of a very private and personal destiny" (*WW*, 83). During this period, no one suspected that what Glasgow really sought was "God": "In my own rebellious way," she wrote, "I was trying to find Him" (93). The discovery might yield what she truly sought: that elusive creature she called herself.

Glasgow's experimentation with different identities shows her trying to fix this person who passed as Ellen Glasgow. Signing her name Ellen Glasgow, Ellen Anderson Glasgow, Ellen Gholson Glasgow, and Eleanor A. Glasgow, she alternately aligned herself with either her mother's or her father's sides of the family. These seemingly incompatible combinations underscored her confusion. How could she meld her different and evolving selves into one?

V

On the evening of March 24, 1892, George Walter McCormack and Cary Glasgow married. The local paper reported on its front page that the "luxuriant" Glasgow home had been decorated with palms and plants, "while smilax and occasionally a few sprigs of yellow jasmine . . . entwined *bric-a-brac* and balustrades." Tastefully attired in white corded silk with pearl trimmings,

Cary held a huge bouquet of roses and lilies of the valley. The candelabras in the front parlor "shed forth glistening rays of light," which accented the texture of her grandmother's pearls and "real" lace veil. Virginia Rawlings, the children's teacher who had become an adopted aunt, came for the ceremony, performed by Moses Drury Hoge. To readers of the Richmond Times Dispatch, the couple's future seemed secure. He was a "prominent young lawyer" from "one of the oldest and best-known families in South Carolina"; she "a lady of rare accomplishments and qualifications," having achieved "more than one literary success." [25]

The first year of his marriage, McCormack ran for the House of Representatives on the Reform ticket. The Reformers had adopted the Ocala Platform (named after Ocala, Florida, their 1890 convention site). They were to be the party "of the people, for the people." Supported by the Populists and the Southern Alliancemen, their platform denounced unfair taxation, the lien system, railroad overcapitalization, and, not least, racial discrimination. During the winter of 1892 the Populists stood for the yearning middle and lower classes. They presented themselves the sworn foes of any monopoly.[26] The Southern Populists defended the black population's political rights and condemned the convict lease and lynch law. They based their strategy on cross-racial alliances between regions and between disparate groups of workers, such as farmers and factory hands. In Georgia, where the Alliance had elected the governor, the farmers extended the powers of the railroad commission, placed restrictions upon banking corporations and railroads, strengthened state inspection of fertilizers, and established a Negro college.[27] The Ocala Platform aligned McCormack against his own class interests since his family's income (from the Chicora Fertilizer Company) depended on the state's policy toward phosphate. It also assured his defeat. After the election, he continued to practice law with a succession of partners in smaller and smaller offices.

Glasgow admired McCormack's integrity and saw his failure as a comment on the epoch, not the man. "Even today, after forty years," she wrote in The Woman Within, "I burn with moral indignation, because so much brilliance, so much pure intellectual fire and radiance, was wasted, in an age and a place that valued tepid sentimentality" (100). Glasgow saw McCormack as Scarlett O'Hara saw Ashley Wilkes, a man out of time with the present. McCormack remained as near a soulmate as Glasgow ever found.

Cary and Walter's move to Charleston did not lessen their involvement with Glasgow's education. From Charleston, they sent books and eventually a subscription to the Mercantile Library in New York City. Writing in secret, with the collusion of her mother, Glasgow produced a 400-page manuscript. Cary advised her sister not to repeat her own disappointing experience with the local firm of West and Johnson. Somewhere in the advertising pages of a magazine, they found the name and address of a "distinguished" literary critic in New York City. For fifty dollars, he could be induced "to give advice to young authors, and to assist them in selecting the right publisher" (*WW*, 95).

The sisters devised a plan that would get Glasgow to New York. For some months now, she had been having trouble with her ears. The Richmond doctors thought it a temporary condition; however, Glasgow's almost clairvoyant terror of deafness helped Cary convince their father that she needed to consult a specialist. They knew of a "handsome, and very strict, Southern lady, in depressed spirits and reduced circumstances" (*WW*, 95) who received girls from "good" families. Conveniently, a group of Richmond parents decided that their daughters needed some exposure to the opera to finish their educations, and Glasgow accompanied them to New York. During one of their window-shopping excursions to Fifth Avenue, she slipped away. Cary had saved fifty dollars from her wedding money, and this as well as the manuscript entitled *Sharp Realities* already lay in the hands of the unknown literary adviser.

Arriving at the appointed hour, Glasgow met a stock character out of melodrama, an elderly, gray-haired man wearing a soiled velvet coat. After much rummaging around, he finally unearthed her manuscript from beneath a mountain of papers. Its wrapper appeared to be still intact. Without reading a word, he began to ask her a series of personal questions that ended with a proposition: "Is your figure as lovely in the altogether as it is in your clothes?" The man then demanded a kiss and tried to force himself on her. She looked, he insisted, too pretty to be a novelist. Like many victims of sexual assault, Glasgow partly blamed herself. "I was too startled," she explained, "or too stupid to understand." This particular assault recalled others. As a child, she had "hated to be pawed over—especially pawed over by elderly uncles." Glasgow finally escaped without having to consent to the kiss he demanded for her release. Bruised, disgusted, and angry at herself, she had a messenger retrieve the manuscript the next morning. Safely home, she threw the manuscript on an open fire with the resolve that she would "never write again." She acted as though the fire could purge her body and memory itself. Writing had made her more vulnerable, not less. In retrospect, Glasgow tried to make light of the incident, which left an indelible mark. Afterwards she loathed "red and juicy lips" and attributed them in novels to older predatory males (*WW,* 96–97).

Glasgow's depression lasted less than six months. Out of the ashes of *Sharp Realities* walked the protagonist of *The Descendant,* Michael Akershem, a person as angry and rebellious as Glasgow herself.

VI

In late October 1893, Glasgow received staggering news that again led her to destroy her work-in-progress. Anne had gone with Cary to a summer resort in the Virginia mountains where she contracted typhoid fever. Within a week she died. When Glasgow left the house at all, she sat in the small garden at the back or under the shadows of the tulip poplars on the front pavement. She found some comfort with her sister Annie's family in Norfolk, Virginia. With her niece Josephine, she could both revisit and recast the past. Josephine—born at One West Main and named after Joseph Reid Anderson —linked three generations. Anne Glasgow had given this first grandchild the silver baby cup that had belonged to Kate, the daughter she lost in infancy.

Glasgow, who wanted her niece to have everything she had not, tried to shape her development. She sent her a handmade album of well-known works of art as well as books, such as Hans Christian Andersen's fairy tales.[28] In the book's cover, Aunt "Lellie"—Josephine's pronunciation of "Ellen"— wrote:

> From the cares of our dull earth,
> Turn to things of better worth
> Here within thy very door
> Lies a world of fairy lore.
>
> Fairy skies are always blue,
> Fairy hearts are always true,
> Through the pages night and day
> Princesses and princes play.
>
> In this magic fairy-land,
> Palaces eternal stand.
> Here the rose is always red,
> Here the flower is never shed.

Here no lover sues in vain,
Here the dragon's always slain,
Here 'neath skies of daffodil
Good's triumphant over ill.[29]

In the days following Anne's death, Glasgow's version of her family's romance became permanently fixed. Pain seemed a family legacy, the predestined result of her parents' marriage. There remained no intermediary, whether real or imagined, between the children and their father. Frank could not bring himself to mention Anne's name. Glasgow readily accepted hereditary arguments for the development of personality, which her subsequent reading of Sigmund Freud and Carl Jung modified without radically altering, and liked to think that her mother had bequeathed her "some generous prenatal influence."[30] She did not have the luxury of looking at her mother over time and with adult eyes. Such scrutiny may have necessitated a reevaluation of her father's character or at least her mother's participation in an unsatisfactory marriage.

Glasgow felt that she could bear what she had to bear by adopting a philosophy of "humane stoicism," but she would not pretend pain away (WW, 138–39). Her identity depended on a loyalty to her experience. She retired more and more into her own increasingly bitter world. Without realizing it, she imitated Anne's neurasthenic behavior. The house revolved around her illness, and Emily spent hours trying to tempt her invalid's appetite with special foods. In retrospect, nothing separated the sensibilities of mother and daughter. Glasgow's interpretation of her mother and brother's relationship offers an example. Anne had been, she wrote in her autobiography, "the only human being who ever saw Frank as he really was, incurably faithful in his affections, and yet completely disillusioned with life, wanting nothing from experience, because all experience seemed to him to be inadequate" (84). The analysis is, of course, Glasgow's own attributed to Anne, and it underscores the narcissism at the heart of their relationship. When Anne died, Glasgow lost a mirror, both benign and terrifying. At the same time she gained an as-yet-unrealized freedom.

The period after Anne's death had the added terror of Frank's retreat—not unlike Glasgow's own—into a deep "invulnerable reserve" (84). Ellen and Rebe clung together, afraid to speak of their brother's behavior or to comfort him. Frank never spoke his mother's name again and began to devote himself to his father, almost as if he was seeking punishment or martyrdom. On Sundays, his one day away from his office at the Tredegar, he went horseback-riding. That single pleasure ended when his father objected to his riding on the Sabbath. From then on, Frank spent the afternoon reading the Bible to his father or taking him to church for the second service.

Glasgow wondered why her brother never rebelled: "It may be that he felt nothing, not life itself, was worth making a fuss about" (85). The nature of his ennui may have been biochemical, since depression ran in the family; it may also have resulted from a violation that destroyed his trust in the world. Glasgow did not speculate that he might have been afraid of something, people, his longing for male friendship, even life itself. Frank's almost exclusive duty to his father further alienated him from the sister whom it saved. His sacrifice spared her from the usual exactions demanded of unmarried daughters.

Glasgow's mourning, like Frank's, had a kind of aggressive magnificence, an extravagance to it that rebuked those who could return to life's routines. Whatever sympathy she felt for her father evaporated when she learned that he had sold Anne's pet mare to be used for light hauling at the Tredegar. Glasgow saw the act as a desecration of her mother's memory. Father and daughter could not make themselves understood to one another. She wondered why he failed to realize that it would be better to shoot the mare than sell her into servitude. He wanted her to know that the animal had fallen with a kind of fit in the street. Glasgow wanted to purchase the animal, but she had no money of her own. The incident taught her that economic independence provided the only real power.

Feeling persecuted by life generally and her father immediately, Glasgow struggled to find a way to free herself from hate. Repeatedly she cautioned herself that malice and envy could not hurt her unless she let it. The real enemy lay within. At 20, she still underestimated the blows that come from those we love.

VII

In the early summer after Anne's death, Glasgow looked forward to a visit from Cary and Walter despite a feeling of foreboding. The couple dispelled her fears. Although Walter looked drawn and pallid (a state she ascribed to acute spinal pain and financial woes), the two acted like young lovers (WW, 99). Before he left for New York on business, brother- and sister-in-law took a stroll and talked about "life." Still grieving, she confessed her attraction to suicide. He protested: "I want to go on until I see what folly the world will commit next. Sheer curiosity, if nothing else, would keep me clinging to life" (100). A day later he was dead—apparently by his own hand.

The Richmond papers hushed up the questions arising from McCormack's death. On June 18, 1894, he had registered for two days at Smith and McNell's, a Washington Street hotel. He called himself S. J. Otey and listed his home as Atlanta, Georgia. That night he ate dinner in his room. At about 9:40 P.M., a porter heard a revolver go off and roused the night clerk. They found McCormack lying on the bed, clad only in his underwear, a .38-caliber revolver beside him. He had left the room in otherwise perfect order, as though he did not want to cause unnecessary trouble. In addition to a suit, a complete change of underwear, and twenty-three cents, he had with him a half-emptied bottle of prescription medicine, a guide to the city, and a novel entitled A Ruling Passion. The flyleaf contained his pseudonym (probably taken from the secondhand book) and an address: corner Washington and Fourteenth Streets, Augusta, Georgia.

When the Southern papers reported that the man's underwear bore the initials "G. W. McC." and that he had possessed legal documents for a case before the courts in Charleston, South Carolina, McCormack's law partner realized the victim's identity. He telegraphed George Battle, a friend of McCormack in the New York district attorney's office, asking him to make certain. Meanwhile, a young, stylishly dressed woman had already identified the dead man as her scorned suitor, Jasper I. Beall. According to her, Beall had also called himself S. J. Otey and had migrated from the South three years ago, settling in Perth Amboy, New Jersey, where he edited a newspaper.[31] She told the police that he had threatened to kill himself after she refused to marry him. Battle had to convince the woman that the man was McCormack and not Beall before the body could be returned to Richmond. "Well," she responded, "he looked just like that, anyway."[32]

If Ellen and Cary read or heard about the young woman, they seem to have dismissed her as a sensation seeker. The sisters contended, as did the local newspapers, that McCormack's death "undoubtedly" resulted from "mental depression caused by bad health . . . [and] too close application to business matters."[33] Glasgow thought herself "the only person who could feel and know why he had chosen the one way of escape" (WW, 101). To turn-of-the century Richmonders, suicide or "self-murder" seemed an act of weakness or insanity, something more appropriate to the lower classes or those driven to it by pain or financial losses. To Glasgow, suicide made the thought of continuing in loneliness and pain bearable. No one seems to have considered the possibility that McCormack had been murdered. If the unsubstantiated rumors about his homosexuality and excessive drinking were true, he could have gone back to his room with a stranger and been robbed. The adoption of an alias hints at a secret life, one that may have ended in unforeseen tragedy.

Cary never recovered from her husband's death. She spent her days in Hollywood Cemetery and her nights brooding as her mother had. "It was agony to watch her," "to listen to her, year after year" (101), Glasgow recalled. Cary used the entire insurance of her inheritance to erect a large tombstone on her husband's grave, a gesture that beggared her. Rebe later complained that the marker dominated the Glasgow lot and asked a stonemason to see if it was possible to remove the urn and lay it flat beside Cary's.[34] Rebe resented McCormack because he had killed both Cary's future and Ellen's faith in love. "To think of the unceasing wheel that grinds out birth and life and death," she later admitted, "fills me with an acute nausea."[35]

Glasgow explored the idea of suicide in a short story she published five years after McCormack's death. The plot of "A Point in Morals" (1899) centers on an "alienist" (psychiatrist) who decides to help a rogue take his own life because it will spare his family further pain. Glasgow argues that the most developed civilizations do not necessarily place the highest value on either human life or happiness,[36] a theme that framed her own life story and became the focus of Barren Ground and Vein of Iron.

Glasgow felt that her family resembled the characters of a Greek tragedy because a sense of doom touched them all, from the eldest to the youngest (WW, 101). At the end of the first year of mourning, salvation came, as it had in past tragedies, through intellectual endeavor: Cary moved back home and "persuaded herself that the more widely she read, the more companionable she might be with Walter, when they met in eternity" (101). The sisters began reading classical philosophy and recent theories of biology and ethnology.

For all that Glasgow claimed not to derive the slightest benefit from these studies, the margins of the books tell a different story. Shortly after McCormack's death in 1894, she quoted Sophocles: "It is best never to have been born, and next best to escape as soon as possible." (The year of the McCormacks' marriage, she had written the same line in her copy of The Teachings of Epictetus.) In Alexander Bain's book on mental science, Glasgow modified a quotation from Descartes—"God's perfection requires pre-determination" —by drawing a line through the prefix "pre."[37] Over the next three years, she returned again and again to *The Thoughts of the Emperor Marcus Aurelius Antoninus*. Between its pages, she pressed flowers, a poppy, a pansy, a sprig of green, and every year from 1894 to 1896, she copied (and dated) lines that held special meaning.[38] They served as a personalized record of her reading and moods. The year 1895 brought some resignation: "Things are as they are," she recorded, "and will be brought to their destined issue." By 1896, she found comfort in the ideas that "things must all return whence they came according to Destiny,"[39] though suicide remained an option: "I will depart whither no man shall hinder me to dwell," she copied at the new year. "For remember this always, and hold fast to it, the door is open."

As Glasgow struggled to come to terms with grief, she also struggled to find a code for living. The passages she marked or underlined in Aurelius give a sense of how she defined herself and her growing ambition. Aurelius echoed what she had learned from experience: to expect nothing, fear nothing, and be satisfied with present activity.[40] Glasgow particularly noted passages that emphasized self-reliance, the transitory nature of fame, the naturalness of death, and the world's indifference or cruelty.[41] "This man chose not to live," she wrote of herself and perhaps McCormack, "but to know." For Glasgow the choice appeared both either/or and paradoxical. At 21 she also felt that she knew too much of living, too little of happiness. Already feeling life overrated, she more determinedly turned to her writing, which allowed her some control. Writing alone could help her break the "clankless chain" that bound her. "No more a slave to hope I cringe or cry," she wrote in "The Freeman," a poem from the 1890s:

> Captives to Fate, men rear their prison walls,
> But free I am.[42]

VIII

With McCormack as her muse, Glasgow secretly began work on *The Descendant*. She surprised Cary and Rebe with a complete manuscript, which she read to them aloud. They immediately recognized her talent. The project revitalized Cary, who threw her whole being into puzzling out the "whys" of each character's thoughts and feelings, motives, and actions. "Without her help and sympathy," Glasgow acknowledged, "I doubt if I should ever have had the spirit to take up again the old discouraging struggle" (*WW*, 103).

The Descendant intellectualizes Glasgow's personal concerns by embedding them in scientific and psychological theories of the day. With Rebecca Harding Davis, the author of *Life in the Iron Mills* (1861), she led the way for American "naturalists" such as Theodore Dreiser and Frank Norris, whose *McTeague* (1899), the story of a lower-class hero's rise and fall, has some parallels with *The Descendant,* its predecessor by two years.[43]

The epigraph of *The Descendant* comes from the nineteenth-century German philosopher Ernst Haeckel: "Man is not above Nature, but in Nature." Again, like many nineteenth-century intellectuals, Glasgow struggled to understand what part heredity and environment played in determining character. The history of her family seemed to demonstrate fin-de-siècle anxieties about the evolutionary degeneration of the human race into madness and chaos. Glasgow had a special interest in theories, such as those of Max Nordau, that equated genius with neurosis or illness. Forever the pessimist, Nordau insisted that cultural evolution followed the birth of geniuses, whose ability to reason compensated for their amorality. He divided "degenerate" artists into two categories, "mystics" and "egomaniacs," and feared that artists like Richard Wagner, a notorious anti-Semite, and Paul Verlaine, an equally notorious sensualist, could bring civilization to the brink of entropy.[44]

In *The Descendant,* Glasgow explored Nordau's faces of degenerate genius.[45] Her novel follows the careers of Michael Akershem, the editor of a radical newspaper *The Iconoclast,* and Rachel Gavin, a painter of brilliant promise. Michael, the illegitimate son of a poor field worker, wants to deny nature: "With two hands and a brain to guide them he would create a new Michael Akershem, as God had created a new Adam" (*TD,* 28). Instead he creates, like the Doctors Frankenstein and Jekyll, a monster with a "genius for destroying" (39). Rachel, on the other hand, shows nature to be the enemy. Not wishing to compromise Michael's principles, she agrees to live with him without the benefits or the protection of marriage. The decision, which makes her a social pariah, also reduces her to an artist manqué. Love supplants every concern, and her masterwork, "Mary of Magdala," remains half-finished.

The McCormacks' marriage had taught Glasgow the woman no less than Glasgow the novelist that domestic experiments predictably result in tragedy. Michael yearns for middle-class respectability and gradually comes to view Rachel as an impediment. After they separate, he figuratively kills himself, shooting the protegé who questions his commitment to social change. His resulting imprisonment grants Rachel a modest freedom. Between copying dressmaker's models, she returns to her painting of Mary Magdalene, transforming "the rough peasant . . . with traces of sinful passion and suffering upon her face" (82) into a self-portrait:

> In the whole strong-limbed figure, of which the mud-stained drapery seemed to accentuate the sensuous curves, a living woman moved and breathed. . . . Above her head a full moon was rising, casting a pale-lemon light upon her garments, falling like a halo about the head of one scapegoat for the sins of men. (264)

The novel ends with Michael's release and Rachel's "reward" (276): the dubious privilege of nursing her former lover, now dying from tuberculosis.

Glasgow used writing, as The Descendant highlights, to come to terms with those warring elements in her own nature. Michael cannot escape the inheritances of blood or Rachel those of sex. From whom Michael acquired his name we never know, but the surname implies a foreign, even a semitic, origin.[46] Michael foreshadows Glasgow's realistic treatment of other outsiders, most notably African Americans. If, like Aurelius, Glasgow believed that "a name is but sound and echo" (TD, 185), The Descendant demonstrates that those echoes reverberate from generation to generation, shaping individual and cultural identity. How much, and how consciously, we might wonder, did Glasgow herself fear the old adage that "blood would tell"? Her sense of futility can be read in the epigraph to Book IV, which comes from Ibsen: "It is not only what we have inherited from our fathers and mothers that walks in us. It is all sorts of dead ideals and lifeless old beliefs. They have no vitality, but they cling to us all the same, and we can't get rid of them."

Glasgow presents two equally fatal models for the artist: theory, which constrains Michael, and emotion, which paralyzes Rachel. Together they represent the parallel and competing traditions commonly characterized in American letters as male and female. Because Michael does not recognize the personal in the political, his art is devoid of humanity, while the more mystical Rachel tears her painting from her very being, transforming personal trials into collective grace. The portrait's title emphasizes the historical, the actual woman (Mary of Magdala), rather than the mythical one (the Magdalene), herself a composite of three women: Mary Magdalen, the first witness to the resurrection; Mary of Bethany, the sister of Martha and Lazarus; and Mary, the repentant sinner of St. Luke's Gospel.[47] The novel traces the descent of woman, rather than man (to twist Darwin's title), by emphasizing Rachel's connection to both the reformed prostitute and the woman who handled the body of Christ.

In *The Descendant*, Glasgow poses a question that woman writers, such as Elizabeth Stuart Phelps in *The Story of Avis* (1877), have asked for centuries: when the greatest enemy is neither God, man, nor devil, but a woman's own heart (*TD*, 83), how can she reconcile the conflicting demands of sex and vocation? New women like Rachel, who believe themselves liberated, soon find themselves making concessions to old traditions. Granting that Rachel's steadfastness tames Michael's aggressiveness by subordinating it to maternal love, Glasgow shows how much she loses or jeopardizes in the process.[48]

For Glasgow, *The Descendant* served as a personal manifesto. Proclaiming her rejection of the South's "insidious sentimental tradition" (*WW*, 104), she intended to follow in the footsteps of Zola, Ibsen, and Tolstoi. To Glasgow there would have been no irony that these, and indeed all her favorite authors, were men. It mattered only that these writers looked ruthlessly at human manners and refused to falsify life as they saw it. Life could be, and for the most part was, a struggle between the sexes, whereas art for Ellen Glasgow surpassed the men and women who gave it birth.

CHAPTER 3

NO PLACE OR TIME

1896–1900

Of encouragement that was misunderstanding, I had, I think,
a little more than my share.

Ellen Glasgow, *A Certain Measure*

I

HOW DID A SHELTERED young woman like Ellen Glasgow come to write a book like *The Descendant?* What fed the emotions or passions she needed to write? The answer lies partly in fin-de-siècle culture with its emphasis on distinguishing difference—whether among races and civilizations or between the sexes—and partly in Ellen Glasgow herself. Each of the novels in her evolving "history," for example, has a protagonist who, by deviating from "type," highlights analogous social and political transformations in American society. The same might be said of Glasgow. When she thought of herself as a beginning writer, she declared, "I did not belong in any place or period I had so far discovered" (*CM*, 10).

Glasgow both resented and nursed her sense of difference, measuring her genius to the exact degree she deviated from types such as the Southern belle or the romantic novelist. One admirer paid her a supreme compliment when he remarked that the woman and the artist in her were equally wonderful.[1]

Glasgow hid her cynicism from most people. With Henry Adams, she shared a decidedly pessimistic view of the future and of human nature mitigated by a Calvinistic belief in the merits of labor and suffering. She worked for everything she had ever had, from health or knowledge to the "very elements" of her own identity. "But I was willing to struggle," she wrote in her autobiography. "I had never asked of life anything more than the fair rewards of endeavor" (WW, 113). She repeatedly learned to her chagrin, however, that life could not be trusted. It meant to "defraud" her of everything she held precious (113), and with only a pen for a rapier she struck back at real and imagined injustices. It would take her sixty years to discover that she could do little to change herself, let alone the world in which she lived.[2]

II

In her early twenties, Glasgow faced her greatest affliction. No matter how much she wanted to believe heartbreak and illness requisites of genius,[3] she could not bear the idea of what she now faced: a world slowly growing silent. She conjured painful moments from the past to act as talismans against the future certainty of deafness. She remembered watching Dr. Patterson's buggy recede into the twilight, the sight of other children healthy enough to play outside, her parting from Lizzie Jones, and her mother's "slow martyrdom" (WW, 112–13).

Glasgow's first trouble with her ears had begun after her mother's death. Bouts of violent crying had exacerbated a hereditary condition affecting the Eustachian tubes, previously damaged from influenza. Like many hearing-impaired people, Glasgow suspected that she might be losing her mind. Fear slowly began to govern all social situations: fear of chance encounters with people, fear caused by sudden noises and imagined sounds, fear of failure and ridicule. Glasgow developed what she called a "morbid sensitiveness" that stalked her "in a panic of terror" (152) for the greater part of the years to come. Over the next decades, episodic panic attacks circumscribed her movement and increased her dependency. These attacks could have had, as many physicians currently believe, a biological origin. They could also have been triggered by the strain of trying to function "normally." Glasgow had no tolerance for "difference" when it made her powerless or conspicuous. The stereotype of the "stupid old deafie," for example, still prevailed at the turn of the century. The sight or the very sound of the word "deafness" made

Glasgow feel anxious. The fear of betraying an ailment had become itself a malady.

Although society tends to minimize the effects of hearing loss, it looms as one of life's greatest traumas.[4] Glasgow's reactions to what Samuel Johnson called "the most desperate of human calamities" reveal the depth of her "vein of iron."[5] The same infirmity drove Beethoven to the brink of suicide. This response might seem more understandable for a composer, but Beethoven dreaded being an "outcast" as much as living without sound. "There can be no relaxation," he confessed, "no refined conversations, no mutual confidences. I must live quite alone and may creep into society only as often as sheer necessity demands."[6] When Glasgow read the autobiography of the writer and political economist Harriet Martineau (1802–76), she recognized not only another person who loved truth for truth's sake—"not for any earthly reward or any spiritual gratification or luxury"—but also someone who continued a productive career in the face of deafness.[7] How many similarities Glasgow saw between herself and Martineau, of whom deafness made "far too much of a talker," she never admitted. Both women protected themselves by dominating or, as Martineau explained, by not allowing "a fair share of time and opportunity to slower and more modest and considerate speakers."[8]

Glasgow never fully accepted her situation. Deafness remained, in her own words, "a wound in the soul" from which there was "no escape until death." Because she felt the need to keep her problem secret, it made her feel almost schizophrenic, as if she were split "in half from center to surface" (WW, 113). Whatever charm she had once possessed seemed to have evaporated. Believing that the threat of inherited deafness presented an obstacle to marriage, she refused to confide her problem when pressed by a potential suitor. In a society that worshipped female perfection and routinely published the photographs of young girls with any promise of beauty, a physical infirmity could make a woman feel less desirable, even unfeminine. Not only a source of humiliation, deafness proved a source of shame, a sign—as in Ibsen's *Ghosts* (1881) and *Hedda Gabler* (1890)—of degeneracy. While Glasgow and her sisters hoped for a cure, they covered her impairment so effectively that their brother Arthur did not realize her condition until it could not be ignored.

The effect that Glasgow's impairment had on her writing is difficult to determine.[9] From the beginning of her career, she relied on long passages of description and epigrammatic summations of character as substitutions for dialogue. This choice or accommodation gradually hardened into an aesthetic judgment. It disturbed her, for instance, that critics praised Ernest Hemingway's extensive use of dialogue. While knowing that her own talents lay elsewhere, she still pushed herself in her comedies of manners to advance the plot through dialogue. There she successfully replicated the slangy speech of the postwar young—"all the little things," as one friend phrased it, that "you don't say to a deaf person." [10]

Glasgow took especial pleasure in the musical nature of her prose without caring for music itself. Words sang to her in ways that music couldn't. When writing, she would often find herself "bound and enslaved by *words*, just as Gulliver . . . awoke to find himself bound and enslaved by the Lilliputians" (*WW*, 127). Words allowed her to restructure the world to match her experience. In a Glasgow novel, characters reveal themselves through their responses to music, not directly as in a Cather novel, but through the melodic representation of individual consciousness. James Branch Cabell, one of the few people to recognize the musical nature of Glasgow's prose, actually scanned a passage from *Vein of Iron* (1935), in which Grandmother Fincastle drifts in and out of sleep. [11] Glasgow included the scanned passage in *A Certain Measure* without giving Cabell credit for his insight. Instead she used it to illustrate a style that springs naturally from the characters themselves and the situation:

> Wéaving ín and oút of her bódy and sóul, and
> knítting her ínto the pást as she knítted lífe íntŏ
> stóckings, móved the famíliar rhýthms and páuses—
> nów—of the hóuse; and móved as a cásual wáve, as
> bárely a mínute's ébbing and flów, in the tímeless
> súrge of predéstinátion. (*CM*, 182)

Glasgow never found a cure for deafness, but she learned to compensate. Eventually she carried a hearing device that indiscriminately amplified every sound. Her voice lost much of its range and inflection and struck listeners as "metallic" or "strident." [12] The less attractive aspects of her personality— hypersensitivity, pessimism, and emotional detachment—form part of Glasgow lore but are themselves a common and terrible legacy of deafness. [13] She certainly sympathized with the misanthropic poet whose verse she clipped from a newspaper:

> I wish I loved the human race;
> I wish I loved its smiling face;

I wish I liked the way it walks;
I wish I liked the way it talks;
I wish when introduced to one
That I could feel "what jolly fun."

Glasgow's difficulties with conversation made intimacy wearisome, yet they never made her unneighborly. One West Main opened its doors to visitors each afternoon and to dinner guests on Sunday.

The complications of social intercourse did, however, reinforce Glasgow's affinity for solitude. Like most deaf people, she turned to animals for the emotional comfort once found with friends and family.[14] Never a believer in what she called the "anthropomorphic fallacy," Glasgow identified with dogs as other tormented and exiled souls. Their sympathy seemed almost palpable. To borrow a phrase from her 1905 poem "Spirit-Loneliness," she dwelt apart among her kind:

My soul has never found its speech,
And to the self within myself
No human voice can ever reach;
The world is deaf, the world is blind,
I dwell apart among my kind.[15]

Glasgow's sense of difference became with time a mark of her superiority. "A sensitive mind," she concluded, "would always remain an exile on earth" (WW, 271). But if she learned to laugh at her own tragedies, she still felt the vast, impersonal anguish of life itself. Work, and work alone, made the struggle worthwhile.

III

In 1896, no one beyond her immediate circle had heard of Ellen Glasgow, and getting The Descendant published seemed even more difficult than writing it. Cary finally suggested that Glasgow contact Dr. Holmes, the man who had tested her on political economy. Cary seemed to remember that he had a friend—or maybe the friend of a friend—who published textbooks. Meanwhile, Glasgow met Louise Collier Willcox, whose brother Price Collier worked as a senior editor at Macmillan. Collier interceded on her behalf, and Glasgow forwarded the manuscript to the president of the company, George P. Brett. A month later, she arrived in New York for a six-week stay.

During that time, she hoped to meet writers and editors who could further her career. More than anything else, she wanted the right to be heard (*WW*, 110), as though "hearing" guaranteed "being."

For his sister's sake, Collier reluctantly invited Glasgow to lunch at Delmonico's, and between the first and the last course made it clear that he wanted "no more writing from women, especially women young enough to have babies" (107). Afterwards he wrote to Brett asking his opinion of the manuscript. Brett replied that "the new woman sort of thing" had been worked to death. Scribner's had just published Frances Hodgson Burnett's *A Lady of Quality* and Houghton Mifflin, Elizabeth Stuart Phelps's *A Singular Life*. He thought that Glasgow's book showed promise and with training and "not a little" advice the author might develop. He didn't know. She might improve and then a rival firm, like Harper's (*The Descendant*'s eventual publisher), would reap the profits from subsequent books. What did Collier think?

Collier read the book and pronounced it riddled with "hobble-de-hoy vulgarity," pseudo-sophistication, bad grammar, and childish rhetoric. Miss Glasgow, he assured Brett, apart from being uneducated, unintelligent, and sheltered, showed absolutely no promise. Already ambivalent, Brett decided to reject the manuscript. Because Collier did not want Glasgow (or his sister) to know that he had had a hand in refusing *The Descendant*, Brett wrote Glasgow to explain that his firm could not publish the book in its present form. There must be, he assured her, at least a dozen houses interested in her type of work.[16] He later admitted that he had never ceased to regret his decision. Glasgow's account differs slightly: Brett told her that it ranked as "one of the two gravest mistakes he had ever made as a publisher." He should have read the manuscript himself and not left the decision to others (*WW*, 109).

Once home, Glasgow decided to follow Cary's original plan. She brought the manuscript to the University Publishing Company of Virginia, where another skeptical editor, a Mr. Patton, read it. One reading made him a believer, and he vowed to get the book published if he had to build a firm himself (112). Instead he recommended *The Descendant* to Century, which conditionally accepted it, insisting that the first chapters be revised. Glasgow would never again have difficulties getting her work accepted.

Because she began publishing early, Glasgow differs in some ways from her chief rivals, Edith Wharton (1862–1937) and Willa Cather (1873–1947). Wharton's first novel appeared around her fortieth birthday, and Cather could not afford to quit her editing job until she had published her third novel, *O Pioneers!* If the design of her career makes Glasgow odd woman out, the structure of her personal life brings her back into the fold. None of these women writers had the distractions (or the pleasures) of motherhood, and all had the support of people who loved them, whether it was Wharton's "inner circle" of male friends, Cather's female companions,[17] or Glasgow's sister Cary, and later her secretary-companion, Anne Virginia Bennett.

While still ignorant of the fate of her first novel, Glasgow began a second, *Phases of an Inferior Planet* (1898). The old headaches had returned and with them a profound despondency. Both these patterns—of composition and depression—would continue throughout Glasgow's life. She exhibited many of the symptoms ascribed to neurasthenics at the end of the century: exhaustion, reduced appetite, fears, dyspepsia, cold hands and feet. (Her circulation was so poor that she slept in colored stockings that had to be carefully laundered and pressed the next morning. Later she wore gloves when typing.) While these symptoms can be indicative of specific undiagnosed illnesses, Glasgow took at various times small doses of strychnine and marijuana, an accepted treatment for nervous disorders. Neurasthenia had become a fashionable disease of the upper classes, thought to afflict overly ambitious souls—those who worked with their brains rather than their muscles.[18] No wonder doctors saw Glasgow as an almost textbook case of a female "neurasthenic."

Thinking that Glasgow teetered on the verge of nervous collapse, Cary persuaded their brother Arthur, who lived in London near St. James Park, to invite her to London for a kind of rest cure. Arthur, a bachelor in his early thirties, could afford the gesture. Eleven years earlier (1885), he had graduated from the Stevens Institute of Technology in Hoboken, New Jersey. After working for utility companies in Maine and Missouri, he had become the general manager and chief engineer of the Standard Gas and Light Company of the City of New York. With another graduate of Stevens Institute, Alexander Crombie Humphreys, he formed Humphreys and Glasgow of London (1892), which designed and constructed the first productive large-capacity "water-gas" fuel plant in England. In 1894, Humphreys and Glasgow opened a firm in New York City. Humphreys directed the New York enterprise and Arthur remained in London.[19] Their firm flourished.

On April 18, 1896, Ellen Glasgow, accompanied by the Humphreys family, boarded the Cunard liner *Etruria*, a record-breaker at 20 knots. Her first sea voyage proved exciting. The captain gave her a tour of the chart room, and a young man made his preference for her company unmistakable. On shore,

Arthur immediately handed her £30 to buy clothes and make a good impression. Glasgow regretted that her brother Frank could not have escorted her, but she found Mr. Humphreys kind and congenial. Like a typical tourist, she took long walks through streets familiar from books. With guidebook in hand, she haunted the British Museum and the National Gallery, usually sitting for long stretches before one or two paintings—Turner's "Building of Carthage" or Sebastian's "The Raising of Lazarus." Images of the Holy Family and of strong, tender madonnas reminded her of what she had lost or never had.

Glasgow felt at home in England because she had, in her own mind, come to the land of her adopted fathers, Charles Darwin and Thomas Hardy. She saw herself as part of a long tradition of English prose masters. Despite her protestations about being a "modern," the early books of her social history read like Victorian novels. With their clear beginnings, middles, and ends—not to mention the obligatory double climaxes—they could have been published as the standard three-deckers. Hardy's ties to place, his love of nature, and his sympathy for women made him one of Glasgow's favorite writers. When she visited Oxford, Hardy's Jude seemed to walk "like a shadow along her right hand." Glasgow felt no less impassioned about Darwin. At Westminster Abbey, she wept at the foot of his grave. "To think," she told Cary, "what that stone with the words Charles Robert Darwin Died Nov. 12, 1882 covers." How could people walk over the spot chatting? "One should just stand silent and think."[20] At Darwin's tomb, she placed a rose and wrote a poem, which no doubt failed to express the depth of her feelings:

> England's greatness: this abides unchanging,
>   Won by arms that sound no loud refrains;
>   When all wars and warriors shall have perished
> Truth remains. (*Poems*, 52)

Glasgow's visit to London signaled her reluctant return to the world: "One may travel from the North Sea to Jericho," she wrote Cary, "and one cannot alter one jot or tittle of one's nature or destiny." She believed that happiness lay "not in getting what you want, but in learning to want what you get." As most devotees of travel believe, the change of scene worked its magic. Glasgow began to notice the charming colors of the latest London fashions and envied Englishwomen "such heads of hair."[21] Ostensibly for Arthur's sake, she agreed to be stylish and exchanged the full mourning she had worn the last three years for somber shades of green and red.

Glasgow did not confide in Arthur about her deafness. Their daily round of engagements, from afternoon calls to evening theater, predictably made her feel anxious and self-conscious. "I wonder what Arthur would have done had I been quite stupid," she complained, "he watches me so closely." She felt that she must act the part of an American girl and that to others she appeared "a wild and strange vision."[22] Despite her nascent interest in how men responded to her, she found the chimpanzees in the zoo more interesting than Arthur's friends. At least they didn't expect to be entertained.

Glasgow never had an easy relationship with Arthur—or he with her. They got along best with the Atlantic Ocean between them. He thought her difficult and ungrateful, and she patronized him. "Poor fellow," she told Cary, "he has so much sentiment about his relations. . . . Arthur is one of the most romantic persons in theory I ever met. He is still troubled by the fact that we haven't taken the positions in the world our father took."[23]

That summer Glasgow visited the Highlands of Scotland, imagining that she had come to her "home in the past" because of her heritage and her adoration of Scott (WW, 120). September found her in Paris at the tomb of Napoleon.[24] Paris meant nothing to her in and of itself, except for its association with one moment of joy. There she received a cable from Cary: Harper's had accepted the manuscript of an anonymous author they believed to be Harold Frederic, the author of the bestseller *The Damnation of Theron Ware*. For reasons of his own, Patton had decided to bypass Century. Glasgow did not care. With the blue acceptance slip in her hand, she walked in a stupor down windswept streets littered with yellowing leaves. At last, she felt that she had found the secret to happiness. The past no longer mattered. The "continuous adjustment of character to calamity" had brought its own reward.[25] She swore to be a great novelist or none at all.

I V

Imagine for a minute Glasgow arriving back in New York at the end of September, 1896. It was one of those sweltering fall days that catch you by surprise. And picture her standing outside Harper's in Franklin Square: a petite woman in white gloves, a summer fur draped like a scarf around her neck, and a hat perched at a jaunty angle. On that morning, she tells us, "the firm of Harper seemed . . . to be a haven for wandering souls, and for lost aspirations." She had to remind herself, as she entered the building, that one novel does not make a novelist. "Wasn't the American literary scene dotted with such tombstones to promising authors, who had died when they were born?" For herself she wanted more than "a memorial of what might have been" (WW, 123).

If Colonel James Thorne Harper still hoped to greet Harold Frederic, he did not have cause for regret. *The Descendant* proved something of a sensation. The literary world buzzed with speculations about the identity of its anonymous author (*Reviews*, 1–14). A few readers objected to the novel's pessimism or oppressive fascination with the doctrine of heredity, but the reviews were overwhelmingly positive. It took three months for Glasgow to be identified or to allow Harper's to release her name. In June, when her photo began to circulate, it excited nearly as much comment as the book itself.[26] An author whom critics thought "distinctly, almost audaciously, virile and vigorous" (*Reviews*, 7) appeared to the public swathed in white ruffles and feathers that cascaded from her bare shoulders to her exposed ankles. Readers saw what they had been culturally conditioned to see: the image of a little girl perched on a chair in her father's library or a debutante sitting out a dance.

Once reviewers knew Glasgow's gender, those who had previously emphasized her uncompromisingly masculine vision began to stress her feminine intuition and sympathy. Glasgow emerged as the heir to George Eliot and Emily Brontë, the only other female "geniuses" reviewers seemed able to name. "Never did appearance so belie a person's occupation," Clarence Wellford wrote in *Harper's Bazaar* (*Reviews*, 8). What first intrigued people about the young writer, however, eventually disturbed them. With her ladylike demeanor and penetrating mind, she seemed a Southern version of the new woman, whose demands for political, economic, and in some cases sexual equality threatened the status quo.[27]

Unlike Wharton, Glasgow would not have traded "all her brains and her art and the success they brought her to have been one of those women whom men find irresistible."[28] She considered her femininity a personal and marketable asset. People noted her almost childlike hands and feet, small enough to fit into size-3 shoes, or her eyes, which were the same color but a shade darker than her mass of bronze hair. The more fanciful compared her features to those of a finely carved cameo.[29] Having evaded the confines of gender, Glasgow now demurely acceded to their symbolic trappings. The contrast between her "feminine" facade and "masculine" mind apparently caused this woman with a penchant for scent, lace-trimmed negligees, and high-heeled shoes more amusement than anguish. "It is incredible," an elderly relative declared (and Glasgow liked to repeat), "that a well-brought-up Southern girl should even know what a bastard is" (*CM*, 9).

The contrast between the content of the book and its author's "old and prominent" Virginia heritage (*Reviews*, 6) intrigued readers. Glasgow may have rejected the lingering fragrance of magnolias in Southern letters, but she and her publisher used those tropes, as movie stars do today, for monetary advantage. Sales of *The Descendant* rose, and Glasgow, becoming a minor celebrity, had her first lessons in marketing and advertising. The third edition, with Glasgow's portrait as frontispiece, sacrificed notions of feminine modesty to merchandising hoopla. From the very beginning of her career, Glasgow seems to have realized that the public wanted its writers to be as glamorous or at least as distinctive as their characters. Having grown up on tales of the Civil War and Reconstruction, she knew that history endures by its appeal as myth.[30]

Glasgow's public story, in its broadest strokes, remained unchanged. *The Woman Within*, begun in the late 1930s, echoes the earliest interviews she gave in the 1890s. After one winter of dancing, she eagerly studied science and philosophy, writing in secret. "I had to stop a dozen times in Michael's most exciting predicaments," she told reporters about *The Descendant*, "to see whether a certain flower looked better on the left or the right side of a hat" (*Reviews*, 9). To her friend and rival James Branch Cabell, she became nothing short of a skilled actress gracing a carefully devised stage. Her ample Victorian house, filled with "Glasgovian treasures" hinting at former aristocratic opulence, charmed interviewer after interviewer.[31] They repeated her story until it became legend: "This bright-looking young girl, with keen brown eyes and chestnut hair and the very daintiest of feet," had renounced society for "her own chosen pursuits" (*Reviews*, 8). The public loved the performance.

Professional exigencies and psychological needs fixed Glasgow's self-narrative. She declined, for example, to speak of her deafness or Walter McCormack's suicide. Over time her public narrative became *the* narrative: a kind of psychological snare that kept her the victim of an unimaginative father and an undiscerning public. Glasgow characterized herself as a rebel and an exile partly because she understood that literary historians wanted their geniuses indebted to no one. Although she seems more akin to an artist like Henry James, who lived largely for his work,[32] the choices that she had to make about self-representation align her with other women writers, including Gertrude Stein, whom she personally liked against everyone's expectations.

Glasgow never realized the paradox inherent in being both the daughter of gentility and the spokeswoman of the people. "Where at the end of the nineteenth century," she asked in her autobiography, "could one find the Revolution?" Remembering Lizzie Jones, the poet and fellow Southerner, Adrienne Rich supplies the obvious answer: in your own backyard.[33] As Rich understood, Glasgow's "radicalism" had its limits, for she championed the rights of women like Jones in her fiction, while benefiting from their service and loyalty.

At the turn of the century, Glasgow did not have to defend her "difference" as a woman. The literary world paid court to the one woman writing "like a man in a nation of men writing like a woman" (Reviews, 24). Hamlin Garland, known for his realistic stories of midwestern farm life, declared The Descendant "one of the most remarkable first books produced within the last ten years." He had read the book in a single sitting, its characters seeming so real that he allegedly forgot their author's gender. Nonetheless, the areas he singled out for special praise might be considered female terrain: Glasgow's depiction of women and of spiritual struggles. Recognizing her as a writer who would never "dodge, or pander to weak readers," he echoed Emerson's welcome to Whitman and extended her a "cordial greeting" (Reviews, 12).

Garland generously offered himself as a mentor to the younger writer by calling at One West Main. The visit hardly satisfied his curiosity. He found Glasgow shy and slightly alarming. He could not reconcile her sanguine manner with the confession that happy people irritated her. The discrepancy between Glasgow's youth and tone, which had all the bitterness and anger of old age, disturbed him: "Her work will not be pleasant," he decided, "but it will be original and powerful."[34] He could not know that his presence caused Glasgow, who could barely decipher his speech, "agonizing tension" (WW, 137). As he sipped iced tea and pondered the "marked personality" that lay behind his hostess's seemingly gentle facade, he struggled to make conversation.[35] Glasgow seemed powerless to help him.

Age or background aside, these two self-taught writers had much in common. Garland's interest in Glasgow had been piqued by his study of John Fiske's books on evolution and Virginia's colonial history. Like Glasgow, he had grappled with the works of scientists and philosophers. Garland sensed in Glasgow a kindred soul, someone who had sworn to write only what was "sound, solid, and true-to-life" (AA, 189). She too felt strongly drawn to a synthesis of democracy and spirituality, to a realm beyond realism, what Garland called "veritism." Years after his visit to One West Main, Glasgow disingenuously claimed that she would have called herself "a verist had such a term come her way" (CM, 28). Alternately indignant and nostalgic about the past, each of these writers tested the borders of "regionalism." Garland aggressively assumed and revitalized the term; Glasgow stridently avoided it. In her mind, the public coupled women regionalists with sentimentalists, those second-rate writers who wore rose-colored spectacles.

It is not surprising that Garland thought Glasgow "disturbing." No matter how irrational, she had somehow hoped that the success of her novel would cure everything that ailed her, including deafness. Depressed and ill, she preferred to avoid people rather than ask them to raise their voices. Because Glasgow found it increasingly hard to mask her infirmity, Richmond seemed suffocating and insular. New York, where she visited twice a year seeking treatment from one aurist or another, offered an alternative. There she could live as anonymously as she wished or visit friends met through her publisher. For probably both psychological and physical reasons (such as the lack of enclosing greenery, fewer allergies, and the hum of background noise), she heard better there. Nor with her doctors did she have to pretend to be a fully hearing person.

In New York, Glasgow met other members of the literary old guard, many as ready as Garland to embrace her. At the Authors Club, the winter of 1898, in a suite of rooms provided by Andrew Carnegie and decorated with portraits, busts, and framed manuscripts of its members, she conversed with future members of the American Academy of Arts and Letters. Their sunny natures did not harmonize with her mood or her view of herself as a writer. The club's ranks included editors, such as Henry Mills Alden of *Harper's* and Richard Watson Gilder of *Scribner's Monthly* and *Century Magazine*, a woman, Harriet Beecher Stowe, and Glasgow's childhood nemesis, that shooer of gypsies, William Dean Howells.[36] "For more than one full generation all the well-thought fiction in America was infected," Glasgow unfairly said of Howells, "by the dull gentility of his realism" (WW, 141). While many of Glasgow's generation shared this view, the inheritances of region, gender, and temperament made Howells an easy scapegoat, perhaps the natural enemy.

To Glasgow, men like Howells seemed mannered, elderly, and oddly immature. She considered them emissaries of literary capitalism and what she liked to call "evasive idealism" or a maudlinly optimistic attitude toward life.[37]

In Glasgow's mind, willful optimism amounted to lying. She saw the Southern tendency to want to make the story better—or women prettier and families more distinguished—as pernicious, perhaps the greatest single factor keeping her region from joining the twentieth century.

At the time of Glasgow's visit, business at the Authors Club centered on protecting copyright. In 1898, they tabled a motion supporting Zola's efforts to free Alfred Dreyfus, the French Jew falsely accused of treason. The official record reads that too many members objected to the frank nature of Zola's work, not that anti-Semitism may well have prevailed as it did in so many institutions at the turn of the century.[38] Glasgow believed that the Dreyfus trial offered proof of Europe's organized corruption.[39] She resented—at least in retrospect—a fraternity that "had created both the literature of America and the literary renown that embalmed it" (WW, 139).

After the publication of her first novel, Glasgow began studying the craft of fiction—to use Percy Lubbock's phrase—as thoroughly as political economy. She turned, with a few exceptions, to European masters. Her own eclectic reading taste encompassed Lafcadio Hearn's books on Japan, Victor Hugo's Les Misérables, and Leo Tolstoy's Anna Karenina. She read the novels of Henry James from cover to cover, next turning to Flaubert and Maupassant, whose Une Vie seemed to her nearly flawless. She wanted to get beyond form, no matter how perfect, to "reality" itself, to forge a prose style that could embrace every breath of being, one "so pure and flexible . . . it could bend without breaking" (WW, 123). Discovering War and Peace, she experienced a "revelation from heaven." Tolstoy's "simple fidelity" (125) to an inner vision seemed at once the end and the truth of art. From Tolstoy or from Balzac, rather than Cabell,[40] she most likely got the idea for her "social history," a term that Cabell used to describe her work in a 1925 review of Barren Ground.[41] Like Balzac, Ellen Glasgow imagined writing a history of manners. She wanted to be the first American to write the history so many historians had neglected.[42]

V

Glasgow's achievement gave her new status at home. Even her father agreed that she needed a private place to work, and a little second-floor room with a window facing Main Street soon housed the familiar texts on philosophy, political economy, and science. Glasgow liked to entertain close friends in her study, sometimes staying up long after midnight reciting original poems like the one entitled "In a Buddhist Temple" (*Reviews*, 9). From that room, she sent — to use Emily Dickinson's phrase — letters to the world, corresponding with her newly acquired literary agent, Paul Revere Reynolds, and the associate editor of the *Atlantic Monthly*, Walter Hines Page (1855–1918).

Glasgow's relationship with Page had developed during the fall of 1897, when she entered the last stages of writing *Phases of an Inferior Planet*. At first the friendship promised to fill the gap left by the death of McCormack. Eighteen years her senior and firmly established in the vanguard of American letters, Page proved an invaluable ally and adviser.

Page and Glasgow came from similar backgrounds and shared opinions about Southern character and politics. No less a proponent of Jeffersonian Democracy, Page blamed the feudal backwardness of the "modern" South on Confederate hero-worship by people he called "Mummies." Born in Cary, North Carolina, Page came of pioneer stock, and despite his disapproval of sectionalism and the institution of slavery, his family had owned — like the Glasgows — a few slaves. He supported equal education for black and white Southerners of both sexes and more opportunities for the common man, a subject of Glasgow's third novel, *The Voice of the People* (1900). A social critic, if not a cultural force, Page promoted his native region whenever possible. He corresponded with other progressive Southerners, such as William P. Trent, Edwin Alderman, C. Alphonso Smith, and Edwin Mims.

With Page, Glasgow could be funny, charming, and unashamedly self-promoting. "I am working upon my book and I have absolute confidence in its dramatic development," she wrote him. "It is going to be worth my while and worth your while and if I send it to you and you do not want it for the *Atlantic* you will be very blind and I shall be very wrathful." [43]

Page periodically offered Glasgow practical advice. Perhaps thinking of the sexist responses to Glasgow's first novel, he observed that "the everlasting clatter about the colour of an author's hair . . . makes a good reputation commonplace." [44] Too many authors of promise had scattered the influences that ought to have gone toward the steady building of a great reputation. The public, he warned her, eventually regards these "professional" writers as "literary operatives" — a fate Glasgow also reckoned worse than death. When he cautioned against publishing anything but her most "important and significant" work, she wished that she could recall the few short pieces already sent to magazines (AA, 182). She recognized him for what he was, a broker of literary reputations.

The shape and tone of their correspondence became the model for Glasgow's dealings with other influential men of letters, notably Alfred Knopf and Frank Doubleday. From them she wanted what every author wants: the widest audience for her work, the best quality of production, and the largest return. She revised, for example, her contract with Harper's, demanding that 10 percent royalties be paid on all copies of *The Descendant*. For her second book, she insisted on 15 percent royalties for the first 5,000 copies sold and 20 percent thereafter.[45] When it seemed as though Harper's might delay the publication of her second novel, she wrote Paul Revere Reynolds that it "would mean sacrificing the best selling season of the year" (AA, 184). She also instructed him to place one of her poems in an English journal to create a market for a projected volume of verse. Because she believed that English writers had a greater chance of fame than their American cousins, she called English publication a "*must*."[46] As early as November 1897, she told Reynolds to begin negotiations for an English edition of *Phases of an Inferior Planet*. Hoping to capitalize on the success of *The Descendant*, she would nevertheless be willing to accept the "lowest terms" (a nominal royalty) to secure the proper firm: Heinemann's first and Sampson, Low & Co. second; then maybe John Lane or Dent. Should Heinemann's not want it, she preferred a "young enterprising" company that would take a "special interest in pushing" her books (AA, 181). She need not have worried. Heinemann's agreed to her terms. Possessing a natural aptitude for business, Glasgow had more in common with her brother Arthur than she might have liked to admit.

Publishers found her difficult because she had no abiding loyalty to them. Her work was her life. She desired to do justly and fairly by it, she told Page in 1897, adding as an afterthought, "and by my publisher."[47] Page complained that women writers, including Ellen Glasgow, required extra attention: "Their imaginations are more easily excited by the hope of success, and few of them have had business experience," he reasoned. "They want to be fair and appreciate frank dealing. Yet they like to have everything explained in great detail."[48]

Frank Doubleday, Page's future partner, shared his friend's opinion of women writers generally and of Glasgow particularly. She exasperated, even intimidated, him. She was, he contended in a chapter entitled "The Lady or the Tiger," "rather a pretty woman, and [as the world's most cantankerous letter writer] she needed to be": "In the first place, she writes in a hand that can be read only with the greatest difficulty; in the second place, her pen is dipped in blue vitriol; in the third place, it leaves a sting that is apt to last for a long time."[49]

Managing her own career, Glasgow could not win. Her business acumen made her at best a "tiger," at worst a "bitch." Men such as Page and Doubleday patronized her as a neurotic because they resented her independence. Her femininity stymied them. Doubleday expected that when he chastised a recalcitrant author she would listen meekly, not smile and call him a "cave man." In defense, he took her irony as flirtation and countered by asking her to sign an agreement promising to be "good." He knew, of course, that such a document wasn't worth the expense of the paper.[50]

No matter how much Glasgow wanted to rely on the advice of her agent or publisher, she counted only on herself. She had few models of happy marriage, few examples of women writing, and scarcely any instances of women directing their own careers. In her first published story, "A Woman of To-Morrow" (1895), she addressed this dilemma. The heroine, Patricia Yorke, must choose between love and career. On one side, she feels all the "womanhood" within her quivering with desire; on the other, a "man's" ambitions struggling to survive (RD, 9). Ambition wins out:

> There were many scores to be settled between Patricia and that public, and she had little doubt as to which would be the victor. . . . Resistance only stimulated her. She was not afraid. The public might resist, but she, Patricia Yorke, she, the embodiment of freedom and the twentieth century, would carve her name, and indelible mark, upon its constitutional history.[51]

Ten years later, when Patricia learns of her nomination to the Supreme Court, she feels nothing but the need to return home to see what her life might have been. There she finds the landscape barren, her former lover's house weatherbeaten, his wife worn from childbearing. The sight reconciles her to her original choice, "its strong, bold lines unaltered" (RD, 13). As the story suggests, Glasgow saw her own options at the turn of the century in either/or terms: love or ambition, children or books, others or self. In the end, she had, as she informed Page, little choice. She wrote not to amuse or to sell, but to live.[52]

VI

Glasgow had high hopes for her second novel, *Phases of an Inferior Planet*. The dedication to Cary suggests that she may have seen it as a companion to *The Descendant*, whose title page read: "To G[eorge]. W[alter]. McC[ormack]." And in key ways it seems to echo the earlier book by tracing the parallel and intersecting careers of an artist, Mariana Musin, and an intellectual, Anthony Algarcife. They meet and fall in love at the Gotham, a New York rooming-house, where Anthony toils on a scientific treatise and Mariana dreams of singing opera. Poverty and the death of their infant daughter, Isolde, erode their marriage. They divorce and eight years later meet again. Mariana is now Mrs. Gore, and Anthony the agnostic leader of the High Church movement. Their plans for remarriage end with Mariana's death from pneumonia. If Glasgow aimed "to impress the miserable doctrine that life is not worth living" (Reviews, 28), one critic declared, she had succeeded.

Although Glasgow sets the lovers' story in a larger constellation, the material has the characteristics of veiled autobiography. Mariana possesses Glasgow's hair and eyes; she suffers from nervous exhaustion and craves "complete submergence of soul in idea."[53] The product of opposites, an Irish Catholic mother and a French Protestant father, she teeters between the father who christened her "Marie" and the mother who called her "Mary Ann." "I will be both," she announces, "I will be Mariana" (Phases, 19). The solution brings to mind Glasgow's own combinations of family names: Ellen Anderson Glasgow, Ellen Gholson Glasgow, and Ellen Anderson Gholson Glasgow. Perhaps more self-critically, Mariana's ambitions exceed her talent: she has "a clear and brilliant voice, but . . . a voice in miniature," and already lacking its first freshness (14). The woman, who would give half her life to play Lucia di Lammermoor, descends to the music hall.

The protagonists of Glasgow's second novel again highlight the dilemma of the woman artist split between the feeling Mariana exudes and the intellect Anthony venerates. He can't distinguish one note of music from another. She can't distinguish political economy from home economics: "There was something in the first page about a 'web of muslin,'" she tells Anthony of her encounter with John Stuart Mill, "and, somehow, it suggested to me the idea of making a bonnet" (108). Mariana's extravagance of feeling and Anthony's misuse of language represent potential hazards to any artist. On Sundays he delivers sermons that he refutes in anonymously published scientific essays on Monday.

Living in an era obsessed with scientific ordering,[54] Glasgow wrote a novel that breaks down the very categories she employed when characterizing her life.[55] On one hand, it debunks the superiority of man over woman, motherhood over career, and intellect over intuition. On the other, it questions whether anything can grow from the divorce of feeling and intellect, maleness and femaleness. The death of Anthony and Mariana's daughter underscores Glasgow's ambivalence about the future.

Glasgow thought that *Phases of an Inferior Planet* extended her mastery of her craft. The writing had involved three complete revisions, taxing her to exhaustion. Any substantial changes in content and organization Glasgow typically made in the second version and substitutions of words or condensing of phrases in the third. The surviving manuscript contains few major changes from the printed text apart from the cutting of clauses and the addition or removal of adjectives. Nevertheless these changes reshape the tone of the text. They show Glasgow struggling to correct some of her early writing problems, including her tendency to pontificate or explain too much—a practice for which critics have continuously faulted her.[56] They also show her trying to remove herself from the text by moderating value judgments: for example, "repellent humanity" becomes merely "humanity" (*Phases*, 8). Glasgow obviously worried about the complexity of her heroine. She did not want her to appear too much of a new woman or a femme fatale; therefore, a "decisive shrug" becomes an "exquisite" one (5), and when Mariana inclines her head for posterity she does it without the "gracious lifting of her lashes" (9).[57] The changes made Mariana the type of feminine and independent woman whom Glasgow herself admired.

The public's response must have deeply disappointed Glasgow. Many reviewers commented on the novel's excessive length and strange title. *Literature* cautioned that the book—"emotional, unconventional, and uncomfortable"—would hardly appeal to the ordinary healthy English reader" (*Reviews*, 29). More sympathetic local papers such as the *Richmond Times* verified the Glasgow family's genealogy as well as Ellen Glasgow's literary genealogy by comparing her to Hardy (24). With the anonymous publication of her first book Glasgow had largely escaped the prejudice shown to woman writers. Now she found herself accused of inexperience, sentimentalism, melodramatic plotting, unoriginality, and unwholesomeness:

> The wife who deserts her husband solely because of the poverty for which he is not to blame cannot be accepted as the adorable creature the author believes her to be without blunting the moral sense. The husband . . . who poses as a saint, because it pays, cannot be admired . . . without profanation of holy things. (*Reviews*, 30)

Glasgow had divined some inkling of the novel's problems from Walter Hines Page. Thinking it ill-conceived, he bluntly stated: "It was a book that she ought not to have written"—an opinion she echoed in her autobiography.[58] Neither the Old Dominion nor the Scribner's editions of her work include *Phases of an Inferior Planet*. Sensing that both her New York novels had been "experimental failures" (*WW*, 129), she sought a subject closer to home. This proved to be the most significant artistic decision of her life. She would set all but one of her future novels in Virginia.

VII

In the spring prior to the publication of *Phases of an Inferior Planet*, Glasgow had begun work on *The Voice of the People*, her first social history. She would work out—or superimpose—a design for this cycle over the next two decades. Now she planned "to write a series of books that would deal with the Virginian background, from the Civil War, down to the present" (*WW*, 129). Hawthorne, she decided, would not be read today if he had not come from New England, and she applied the same theory to herself and the South. In this new novel and the ones to follow, Glasgow wanted to ground her imagination in the exact knowledge of place. Predicting that the first book in the series would take two years to complete, she hoped to be "repaid" emotionally and financially (AA, 187).

Research took Glasgow and Cary to Williamsburg in May 1898, where they met another Richmonder who would become important to Glasgow: James Branch Cabell (1877–1958). Only four years younger than Glasgow, he possessed the same cultivated air, aristocratic manners, and "a face tempered with melancholy" she had found endearing in Walter McCormack.[59] And like McCormack, he seemed victimized by his time. Glasgow heard about Cabell before she saw him. The month before she arrived in Williamsburg and just months before his graduation, Cabell and three of his classmates had resigned from the college, emphatically denying rumors of their homosexuality.[60] At home in Richmond, Cabell quickly realized that his withdrawal might seem like a confession. After consulting a lawyer, he asked for reinstatement. The College of William and Mary found no evidence of what it considered misconduct, and Cabell graduated with his class in June.

To Glasgow, Cabell appeared "grave, inscrutable and disdainful." "I was young enough," she writes in her autobiography,

> to feel that he was a romantic figure, innocent but persecuted, and I admired his aristocratic detachment, the fine, thin modeling of his features, and the enigmatic quality of his expression. There was, too, even a flash of envy in my heart as I watched him. What was an unjust passing scandal compared to the permanent burden of deafness? Silly people might avoid him, but at least

he did not have to wear out his nerves pretending that he heard all they were saying. (*WW,* 133)

No matter how much Glasgow romanticized Cabell—or sought McCormack in every man she encountered—nothing came of their meeting. Their affinity existed mostly in her imagination. Could she have dreamed that some day she would lobby for his membership in the American Academy of Arts and Letters? Or that late in her life he would write a cruel review of one of her books?

VIII

When, in 1898, Arthur visited One West Main, he found the house inhospitable and his sisters alarmingly low-spirited. He decided that they needed a more dramatic change of scene than their fall excursion to the mountains of Shawville, Virginia. Arthur intended that his sisters should travel in grand style, and on February 4, 1899—with the negotiations for the publication of Glasgow's third novel still incomplete—she, Cary, and Rebe sailed for Egypt.[61] They left two days before a great blizzard buffeted Richmond for fifty-five hours. Snow fell to a depth of seventeen inches, forming drifts from three to eight feet, and bringing trains, streetcars, mail delivery, and public schooling to a halt. At the beginning of the Glasgows' Atlantic voyage, passengers crawled on all fours along the flooded decks in sixty-five-mile-an-hour winds.

On board the *Allen,* Glasgow literally found herself "between two shores," the title of a short story that *McClure's* published that month in an issue also featuring Stephen Crane's "Marines Signaling Under Fire at Guantanamo" and Rudyard Kipling's "The White Man's Burden." [62] Sailing from the United States to England, the heroine, confined to her cabin from seasickness, meets a man who lets the other passengers assume they are married. He is one step ahead of the law, and the relationship provides him with a disguise. By the end of the voyage, he has recovered morally and she physically. Together they look forward to a new life in the old world. For Glasgow, the passage also signaled a fresh start, a chance to regain health and emotional energy.

The sisters disembarked at Gibraltar on the third of March. Several days later they stayed up all night to watch the ship's approach to Genoa. "Genoa is intensely picturesque," Rebe recorded in her journal. "And yet, for me, it will always have a shadow connected with it, for I wept many, many bitter tears the day I was there."[63] On the voyage, Rebe and Ellen had grown fond of Max, one of the ship's cabin boys. Small for his twelve years, Max had become a kind of mascot to the passengers, who built up his strength with fruit and cookies. When he fell ill from pneumonia not far from Genoa, they collected enough money to admit him to a hospital. Rebe and Ellen visited Max and took some comfort in seeing him lying between spotless sheets, his head resting on an eiderdown pillow. Rebe assumed that he would die and twice kissed him goodbye. The story had a double coda: not only did Max live to return to sea, his parents, unable to earn a living in Germany, later "begged" Glasgow to find a janitor's place for them in the United States. She declined. "After all," she rationalized, "what can one do with one's world?" (WW, 149). Glasgow's sympathy had its limit, as her 1922 novel, One Man in His Time, illustrates. The heroine tries to help people like Max's parents by gentrifying tenement housing. They want none of it and rent the new housing to young professionals. The experiment proves to have been more selfish than altruistic.

The Glasgows traveled like tourists in the sense that they observed people and things from a safe distance. From Genoa, the sisters went to Naples, then to Alexandria, and on to Luxor, where they boarded a boat called Rameses the Great. At each stop, they inspected the local bazaars, and Rebe noted scenes that would make "exquisite" watercolor studies, including one of women washing clothes in a cavernous stone fountain. They rode donkeys to Karnak and crept on their hands and knees through crannies and crypts to read inscriptions made visible by magnesium lights. After the Rameses tour ended the third week in March, they traveled on to Smyrna, Constantinople, and Rome.

Glasgow spent a good part of the trip alone. At Cooks in Rome, Rebe had met two Cambridge students, one from Switzerland nicknamed "Swissy" or "Cousin Hans," and the other from Bedford, England, nicknamed "Trinity." Rebe soon paired off with Trinity to visit the Acropolis and other romantic places preferably at sunset. "Heavens knows I appreciate being loved," Rebe confided to her diary. "I hope I may always be a true friend to him as long as he needs me." Life called, and she yearned "to live one pulsing, red-blooded moment." Anything was better than "to exist through years of drowsy indolence."[64]

As Rebe courted and Cary enjoyed the company of a Mr. McClintock, Ellen recuperated: "She is simply indefatigable about sightseeing," Rebe wrote, "and I am so glad that she has improved that much" (38–39). The trip

that took Rebe away from what she considered her dull and colorless existence in Richmond passed for Glasgow in an aching whirl from one sight
to another. Like a miser, she hoarded moments both "sublime" and uncom-
municable. Struggling to be satisfied with her portion in life, she related
whatever she saw — whether the Hall of Columns at Karnak on the Nile or
Hadrian's Villa — to her reading. In Rome, where she put red poppies on
Shelley's grave (and Rebe did on Keats's), she thought of the Italian philosopher Giordano Bruno (c. 1548–1600). The Inquisition had burned Bruno at
the stake for repudiating the doctrines of transubstantiation and the immacu-
late conception. Glasgow also favored a pantheistic view of life, and she may
have equated her gradual loss of hearing with his slow torture. Yet no matter
how much she sought or desired an absolute truth, she believed it an illusion.
At Thebes, she contemplated the paradox of enduring monuments marking
a transitory existence and underlined Marcus Aurelius's line "that neither a
posthumous name is of any value, nor reputation, nor anything else."

From Paris on May 25, 1899, Glasgow expressed her shock to Horace
Traubel, Walt Whitman's Boswell, that her lunatic family had allowed the
Richmond Dispatch to publish one of her private letters describing a visit to the
Old Seraglio in Constantinople.[65] Glasgow's friendship with Traubel, which
began with his writing to praise *The Descendant,* lasted for the next sixteen
years. Although she chided him about his eternal optimism, she also found
him to be a generous reviewer of "pessimistic" books, such as *The Voice of the
People* (1900). It surprised Traubel to learn how little she knew of Whitman,
and he went about educating her. Soon Whitman became her favorite poet,
probably more for the cadence of his verse than its sexual content.[66]

Glasgow's letter from Constantinople, which her family so proudly published, shows her responding to the city's sensuality, its "dazzling effect of
gorgeousness." The glasshouse atmosphere of despotism and emeralds the
size of eggs thrilled her as they did other Westerners.[67] Remembering her
study of political economy, she also saw the unnamed minions who produced this hybrid atmosphere: "It is a palace belonging to oriental fairy tales,
not to real life — the lives of thousands of workmen."[68] Her almost visible response to place could make her ache with the burden of imagined lives.

The idea of the East never fully engaged Glasgow's imagination. Perhaps
her understanding of antebellum myths made the "Orient" seem too familiar or uncomfortable, the past too palpable. Unlike Rebe, she could not wait
to get to England, where she always felt a strange but reassuring sense of
déjà vu. Of all English places, she felt most at home visiting the Brontë par-

sonage in Haworth, Yorkshire. The sisters toured the house and the family graveyard, which seemed to exude history and memories she associated with Hollywood Cemetery. Rebe decided that Rochester had to be the most attractive man in fiction, one she might have loved: "Certainly he is a hero I think I should rather spend an evening talking to than any I can think of." [69] Glasgow drank in the utterly lonely and somehow comforting atmosphere. Thinking of her own relationship to Richmond, she could understand why Emily Brontë would want desperately to escape the place of her birth and still find herself homesick anywhere else.

In comparison to Constantinople, the small towns in Yorkshire, and the few places they then toured in France and Norway, London seemed pale and sterile. It had, however, other compensations. Glasgow cared neither for the music hall nor the play *Cyrano de Bergerac*. She had her heart set on meeting William Heinemann, whose publishing house she considered the most respected in England. Heinemann looked, as the playwright Clemence Dane described him, exactly like a picture of Pepys, twinkling, tubby, and disarmingly kind. He and his wife, Magda Stuart Sindici, had just married that past February. The author of *Via Lucis* (1898), the 20-year-old Magda had great charm and a mind like Mary Stuart's, "hard as a diamond and as clear." [70] Together they made a formidable team that few people, including Glasgow, could resist. The meeting with the Heinemanns seems a fitting end to Glasgow's grand tour. Serving as her imagined audience, they recalled her real purpose, which awaited her at home in Richmond.

Glasgow arrived back in the United States in September 1899, stronger and more ready for the work of completing the last chapters of *The Voice of the People*. In December, she began to worry about the status of its publication, having heard from Walter Hines Page that Harper's was in receivership. "I like the Messrs. Harper," she wrote, "they have always been kind to my interests, and I do not wish to leave them unless it is true that the business is not really under their direction, or unless I might reap greater advantages for my book" (AA, 189). Glasgow considered giving the book to the new firm of Doubleday, Page, & Company, but first she wanted to learn their standing, "financial and otherwise." As always, she emphasized that the editors' opinion of her work concerned her most (AA, 189) while arranging the best possible terms.

In July 1899, J. P. Morgan had asked Frank Doubleday and his partner S. S. McClure to take charge of Harper & Brothers for a few months before deciding whether they wanted to run it permanently. They sought Walter Page's help, and after the probationary period all three decided to withdraw and leave the management to George Harvey, who rescued the firm for several more decades. Page and Doubleday almost immediately founded Doubleday, Page, & Company,[71] and one of the first authors they sought to attract was Ellen Glasgow.

As the turn of the century approached, the course of Glasgow's future seemed set. She had published two novels and written a third. She had begun to break away from Richmond and her father, and she had limitless ambition. Torn by conflicting desires and contradictory sensations, she felt "wounded and caged" as well as young and hungry for experience. To be filled with yearning, to want to throw herself into writing as a man might fling himself "into a hopeless battle" (WW, 152), hurt so exquisitely it might have been pleasure.

CHAPTER 4

HEART HUNGRY

1900–1905

To have had one emotion that was bigger than you or your
universe is to have had life.

> Ellen Glasgow, *The Deliverance*

I

THE WINTER AFTER her return from Europe, Ellen Glasgow fell in love
for the first time. She was months shy of her twenty-seventh birthday. "One
moment," she writes, "the world had appeared in stark outlines, colorless
and unlit, and the next moment," it felt "flooded with radiance" (*WW*, 154).
The occasion of this transformation seemed inauspicious enough. Cary and
Rebe had accompanied Glasgow, who wanted to meet with her new publisher, Doubleday, Page, and Company, to New York City. After a matinee,
they stopped for tea at a friend's house, and Glasgow's life—to use her own
word—would be forever "transfigured."

In Glasgow's telling, she entered the drawing room and almost immediately sensed someone looking at her. No matter how uncomfortable or
immodest she felt, she could not resist returning the man's gaze. She grew
aware that a circle of attraction divided them from the other guests, and
"aware, too, of his tall thin figure and his dark . . . face, with hair which was

slightly gray on the temples" (154). Her perception, however, failed to encompass one important fact about the man she called in her autobiography
Gerald B: he had a wife and two college-age sons.

When the two finally talked, a miracle occurred: Glasgow had no trouble
hearing his voice. The one man in a whole world of men "who knew, by sympathy, or by some other instinct, the right way of approach," he responded to
her sporadic requests to repeat a remark as if she was endearingly dependent.
His simple presence helped past fears recede. "Here, now," she thought, "this
is my moment!" (155). On the way home, Cary recounted the gossip about
Gerald. He worked for a firm near or on Wall Street, and he and his wife
lived together as strangers for the sake of their children. Cary's disclosure
may have made him more romantic to Glasgow. The next day, she replaced
her wardrobe of half-mourning with vividly colored dresses and smart Pari-
sian hats.

When Gerald B met Glasgow, he had already read her first two novels, *The
Descendant* and *Phases of an Inferior Planet*. "There is something [in them],"
he told her, "I don't know what, but there is something" (155–56). Unlike
Hamlin Garland, he found the "something" intriguing rather than disturbing. Gerald may or may not have been a ladies' man. He may or may not
have attended the tea hoping to get a glimpse of the attractive author whose
photograph he had probably noticed when reading *The Descendant*. On her
1899 passport application, Glasgow had described herself as brown-eyed,
round-faced, and—contrary to friends' memories of her diminutive size—
5' 5" tall. Glasgow's exaggerated notion about her stature did not extend to
her appearance. "Although I was not beautiful," she conceded, "I created the
semblance of beauty for everyone [male or female] who has ever loved me"
(158). Often a spellbinding talker, she created that image with words.

Glasgow felt that while she and Gerald lacked any common intellectual
interest, they possessed kindred natures. She saw herself through his eyes as
funny, valiant, and mysterious. Nothing short of "a compelling physical mag-
netism" (157) drew them together. The affair deeply troubled her. On one
hand, she couldn't have found a better way to get back at her father, whom
she believed to have been an adulterer. On the other, she found herself repeating what she believed to be his behavior.

The meeting with Gerald came at a crucial time for Glasgow. The "successful failure" of her second novel had undercut her faith in herself. Love
proved to her that she could overcome almost anything, even the terror associated with deafness. The stricken look vanished from her eyes, and she

became reborn. A friend told her that just a month before she had seemed half-alive. Now she radiated life. The razing of inhibitions, the great discovery that she could triumph over circumstances, had destroyed and then recreated her very consciousness. She resolved to make herself well, happy, and beautiful. Glasgow willed a new self into being, one who refused to be "another victim of the world's superstitions about women" (163). The chapter with Gerald "transfigured" her life by converting the virginal woman, whom her culture tended to patronize or pity, into a femme fatale. The secret of a hidden life may itself have given her a sense of power or amusement over those who thought of her strictly as a maiden lady.[1]

Because Gerald left, as far as we know, no record of the relationship, Glasgow's version of their perfect accord remains again *the* version. What were his real feelings? Did his death in 1905, no matter how painful for her, offer a form of escape? The guilt and recriminations, the shifting balances of power and commitment common to such affairs, belong to another story. Glasgow wrote or coded that story in the margins of her books: in Venice, May 3, 1899, "Thou shalt renounce!" (underlined twice); by the Gulf of Saint Lawrence, August 20, 1901, "*Thou shalt renounce!*"; two days later, August 23, again by the Gulf of Saint Lawrence, "*Thou shalt renounce!*" this time written next to a passage from *The Thoughts of Aurelius* that reads: "Aiming, then, at things so high, remember that it is no moderate passion wherewith you must attempt them, but some things you must utterly renounce, and put some, for the present aside." For Glasgow, love proved to be a short madness of joy — to paraphrase Nietzsche — in the most sorrowful experience.[2]

Glasgow confided her feelings about Gerald to no one, except perhaps Cary and Rebe. Rebe later denied his existence: "I was with Ellen day and night as we shared the same room for 29 years," she wrote Marjorie Rawlings. "It was I, not Carrie [Coleman, her childhood friend] who took all the trips with her to Europe and for months in spring and fall in New York. I can declare in *positive* terms that Ellen did not have a love affair of any kind in her youth." Rebe's testimony has to be suspect.[3] After all, she barricaded herself in Glasgow's study following her sister's funeral, destroying or removing anything that might damage Glasgow's reputation, including books on the psychology of sex.

According to Glasgow, she and Gerald managed to see one another during her visits to New York. Their relationship may well have excited speculation beyond their immediate circle, for the couple liked to dine in small, ethnic restaurants, favoring a Hungarian establishment reminiscent of the

"Chat Noir" in *The Descendant*. Tucked away at the end of an unfrequented street that smelled of crushed apples, the restaurant seemed alien and remote. The two especially loved the boat ride to Coney Island, the night and the elements making them feel anonymous and aware of one another. Glasgow cherished the feeling of being isolated yet protected, not only in a world within a world but in a world unto itself. The times with Gerald mirrored the secret world she entered when writing. Like the professor in Willa Cather's novel, *The Professor's House* (1925), Glasgow worked in her upstairs bedroom, while downstairs the everyday realities of life continued. Behind her locked door, she became "immersed in some dark stream of identity, stronger and deeper and more relentless than the external movement of living" (*WW*, 41). In both life and art, she preferred to be suspended between dreaming and waking, all reality, as she said, concentrated "into a solitary brooding power, a solitary brooding emotion" (160). She became a connoisseur of the prolongation, rather than the fulfillment, of desire.

For Glasgow, the years with Gerald culminated with a single moment of absolute communion. During the summer of 1903, they met at the foot of the Jungfrau in the Bernese Oberland. The two climbed, holding hands and scarcely speaking or breathing. "Earth and sky met and mingled," she remembered.

> We stood . . . alone with the radiant whiteness of the Jungfrau. From the mountain, we turned our eyes to each other. We were silent, because it seemed to us that all had been said. But the thought flashed through my mind, and was gone, "Never in all my life can I be happier than I am, now, here, at this moment!" (*WW*, 164)

The margins of Glasgow's books proclaim the intensity of this experience. The date, August 2, 1903, and the place, "Before the Jungfrau," mark a mystical, possibly even sexual, union. Glasgow used the date as a stamp of truth, writing it next to telling comments, such as the *Bhagavad-Gita*'s Fourteenth Discourse on wisdom and perfection. "Live as on the mountain" became a personal standard, a reminder of past risks worth taking, a retort to those other admonitions to renounce.

For years people have been debating the identity, even the existence, of Gerald B.[4] Candidates have included Walter Hines Page, Pearce Bailey, a New York doctor, Holbrook Curtis, another doctor, Hewitt Hanson Howland, an advisory editor at Bobbs-Merrill, and, most recently, William Riggin Travers, a wealthy man of leisure.[5] Evidence that any of these men was Gerald B remains slight, though Irita Van Doren's assertion that Glasgow had been Howland's mistress gives pause. Glasgow might have confided in her literary executor, as she read aloud sections on Gerald from her autobiography.[6] However, the facts of his life, and those of the other candidates, do not coincide with Glasgow's version of Gerald's marriage or his death. Of course, she may have invented such discrepancies to mislead. Reverting to the values of her Victorian upbringing, she could have chosen to present Gerald as a devoted father to cancel husbandly remisses. How could she explain to either her readers or herself, for example, why she and Gerald did not marry? Without serious impediments to the union, the rebel against convention begins to resemble the heroine of a seduced-and-abandoned novel or the predatory vamp of post–World War I fiction.

Opinions about the identity of Gerald have all led to dead-ends. The case for Travers illustrates the gulf between intriguing coincidences and solid evidence. Born in 1861, Travers was twelve years Glasgow's senior. He graduated from Columbia in 1882 and divided his time between a winter home in Aiken, South Carolina, and a summer place in Newport, Rhode Island. At the time Glasgow would have met him, Travers had been married for about ten years to Lily Harriman Travers, a first cousin to Averill Harriman's father and an heiress. The couple had no children, contrary to Glasgow's account in The Woman Within (157). In 1905, the year of his death, Travers and his wife were estranged, and Town Topics implicitly blamed him: "Newport society has decided," it proclaimed, "that Bill Travers, as a husband, had grown impossible."[7] The report so incensed Travers that he conferred with the district attorney about beginning an action for criminal libel against the editor. Friends said nothing about the cause of the separation except that at one time he had drunk excessively. No breath of scandal touched Glasgow.

Notwithstanding the attraction of opposites, Travers seems an unlikely lover for Glasgow.[8] A noted Newport whip and an animal lover make strange bedfellows, not to mention that he belonged to the world of Old New York she despised. His father, William Riggin Travers, had amassed a fortune, estimated at well over a million dollars. Known affectionately as "Stuttering" Travers, he helped to found the popular Racquet Club in 1873, and much later the Metropolitan. Edith Wharton, who satirized him as the gossipy Sillerton Jackson in The Age of Innocence (1920), was a childhood friend of his daughter, Matilda Travers Gay. At the time of his death the younger Travers had increased his father's estate to several million dollars. No one could account for his suicide, except to cite despondency over his wife's filing for an uncontested divorce the previous month. Travers himself had spoken of his depression to friends and even joined the firm of Huhn, Edey & Company, hoping that work would shake off "the blues." The prescription had appeared to be working. He passed the previous season at Newport, gave and received social invitations, and built a Japanese tea house. Despite his melancholy, his death came as a surprise and excited some speculation. During his examination of the body, the coroner had observed the portrait of a very handsome woman hanging over Travers's bed: "The picture," Mr. Travers's partner admitted, "was not of the former Mrs. Travers."[9] No one knows the identity of the woman or the location of the picture.

The publication of Travers's obituary in the Paris edition of the *Herald Tribune* matches Glasgow's account (in *The Woman Within*) of reading about Gerald's death. However, his case is no stronger than that of another man whose death the *New York Times* also reported on September 30, 1905: Herbert Valentine, a New York lawyer. A member of the Bar Association, the American Numismatic and Archaeological Society, the New York Genealogical and Biographical Society, and the New York Botanical Gardens, Valentine had interests that Glasgow would have respected. On August 29, Valentine killed himself in his room at the Hotel St. Andrew on Seventy-second and Broadway, where he had been living since July 20. After removing his coat, he put one cartridge in his revolver, stood before a mirror, and fired a bullet into his brain. The suicide might have been prevented. In the late afternoon, a chambermaid had inadvertently opened the door of his suite and seen him pacing up and down with a revolver in hand. She notified the manager, who stationed bellboys near the room. They heard nothing. At about 8:30 P.M., the manager sent two employees to the room with ice water to see if they could discover what was happening. They found the door locked and Valentine's body inside. He had been dead for about an hour. His room contained photographs of exotic places and luggage with many foreign labels. If Travers seems a candidate for his involvement in high finance, so does Valentine for his probable connection to a prominent Richmond family and his sojourns (or rendezvous) abroad.[10]

The one piece of evidence that links Glasgow and Gerald, a letter dated March 23, 1901, and signed "Gray," remains no less problematic:

Elaine, My darling—Again my heart is desolate and I have left you (after three years of weary waiting, *why* have these unhappy circumstances repeated themselves in my life[)]. This is just a little wail I am sending I can't write. The

train is so shaky. Those few fast fleeting hours, how they sped! But they are as pearls to me. Ah! my sweet you little know the preciousness and sweetness of yourself—and weren't you so cunning to let me see you—and I know I made your dear head ache—but I don't really believe I have seen you—it is a dream —was I actually there and could put out my hand and touch you. I could say so much but you will think I have lost my reason. I am longing to see you with all my heart—and I would have stayed until Monday—but really was afraid my elation and perfect delight at being with you might make you ill. How I hate to think of you having those suffering headaches it cuts me to the core of my heart to see you pale. You must get strong and well for *Nova Scotia*, for I am surely going with you. Such writing! My darling I must stop. Did you catch any *one* of those kisses sighs and looks I cast—as I passed you by this morning. And you promised to think of me when you were awake—but I—I was think- ing *all* night of you—and still you taunt me with indifference. O! would that I had stayed over—but even then the parting had to come—Don't let *Cary* laugh at this letter—does she read them? I hate N. Y. only I love Richmond— it is now the most *perfect* stop, hallowed by my Elaine's presence. My darling good-bye a kiss, another, and yet another! And that makes my three. *I* am not content but I shall have to be—with my thoughts and my tenderest greeting Ever Elaine
Love
Gray

Arguments for thinking that Gerald wrote the letter are sketchy. True, Gray may have been a nickname that Glasgow gave the lover she described as having graying hair on his temples. In the late spring of 1901, she, Cary, and Rebe vacationed at Prince Edward Island, and Glasgow may have preserved this letter as a form of evidence, much as Wharton saved the journal she ad- dressed to her lover, William Morton Fullerton. The nicknames intimate a certain playfulness and posturing, which the tone of the letter, at once sexual, parental, and beseeching, supports. In the tradition of courtly love, the writer seeks to serve his chaste mistress who inspires him to altruistic acts. Glas- gow's headaches keep him at a distance *and* under control. This pattern would be repeated in her correspondence with the last love of her life, Henry Anderson. The letter also insinuates that while the relationship had not been consummated, Glasgow allowed her lover certain liberties: the three kisses. It expressly captures the come-hither quality of the affair coyly described in her autobiography, which teases: Did they or didn't they (*WW,* 163)?

However much the letter teases biographers and critics, its tone suggests that a woman, not a man, wrote it. Glasgow had, for example, a female friend named Gray who married in 1906. Not only does the style of the letter match that of existing correspondences between late nineteenth-century women, as the historian Anne Scott Frior has observed,[11] but its ungrammatical nature suggests someone without much education. The underlining of Cary's name seems reminiscent of the kind of emphases a young woman might use.

The identity of Glasgow's lover may always remain a matter of speculation. Some people think Gerald her greatest fiction.[12] Lives always contain elements of fiction, whether they are recounted in autobiographies or autobiographical novels, such as George Borrow's *Lavengro,* D. H. Lawrence's *Sons and Lovers,* Virginia Woolf's *To the Lighthouse,* or Glasgow's own *Barren Ground* (1925). When Glasgow looked at the welter of her own life in *The Woman Within,* she may have been confirming only a small part. Can any autobiography or biography ever corral the slippery monster we call "life"? "Writing lives *is* the devil" because we can never wholly know ourselves, never mind another.[13] By its very nature, biography approaches but cannot penetrate the mystery of a person's life. Intriguing personalities resist summation. When it most matters, biography—which registers human yearning, suffering, and creativity—seems greater than a compilation of facts and dates. We must read Glasgow's story about Gerald B with this idea in mind. The question of his identity matters far less than Glasgow's sense of the relationship's meaning and its import for her fiction.

Glasgow never wholly defined herself by her relationship with Gerald. She said that she wanted "happiness" without ever claiming that she wanted marriage. The day-to-day intimacy of marriage has daunted other hearing-impaired people with fewer resources. The specter of children and the demands of career concerned Glasgow. An affair—requited if probably unfulfilled—had its advantages, making her the heroine of her own drama, while reinforcing the complex and romantic vision she had created of herself: a woman at once desirable, rebellious, and plagued by tragedy. Glasgow's lifelong search for truth encompassed her posthumous admission of an affair with a married man. Though no one can confidently name Gerald B, her admission seems less designed to shock, or prove her femininity, or her heterosexuality, than to set the record straight.

II

At the turn of the century, Glasgow became—in the words of the author of *The Mind of the South*—the first Southerner "to approach the material of her world almost exclusively from the viewpoint of the artist."[14] Excepting

Joel Chandler Harris's stories of Uncle Remus, George Washington Cable's chronicle of the racially mixed Grandissime family, and Mark Twain's *Puddn'-head Wilson*, Southern fiction tended to glorify a legendary antebellum past. Glasgow's impatience with sentimentality, her faithful rendering of her region's customs and manners, changed the direction of Southern letters for the next three decades.

We might stop for a minute and consider how Glasgow not only acquired but also defined an artist's perspective. Before the turn of the century, she saw her world partly through the lens of a sociologist. The narrators of her first two novels (much like those of George Eliot) help us to understand the different, often competing systems of belief shaping characters and situations. When Glasgow approached her personal, much more inchoate world, she chose another medium, poetry—almost as if she believed ideas belonged in novels and feelings in poetry. Glasgow considered herself a novelist rather than a poet, yet she wrote poetry (as do many people) to sort out, heighten, or commemorate her feelings. *The Freeman and Other Poems*, a collection she wrote in the 1890s, refers, for example, to the major tragedies of her life: her mother's breakdown and Walter McCormack's suicide. Of the earliest episode, she writes:

> At the street's sudden end a shining square,
> The sunny threshold of an open door
> Thick with the dust of an untrodden stair
> That leads beyond me to the upper floor—
> Then memory halts—it dares not enter there.[15]

In "Love Has Passed the Way" she opens another door, this time to McCormack's New York hotel room:

> Ah, what means the vacant room?
> Ashes where the flames were red?
> What the shudder in the gloom?
> What the corpse upon the bed?
> Break my heart as best it may,
> Love has passed along the way. (*Poems*, 35)

The individual poems function like links in a metaphorical chain. Lying close to the bone, they reveal the incidents and unresolved feelings that held Glasgow to the past. When Doubleday published the poems in 1902, readers found them depressing to the point of "ghastliness" (*Reviews*, 72). They did not want to accept, as the speaker of "The Sage" declares, that the only refuge "is within" (Poems, 29). Glasgow later protested to Howard Mumford Jones that her book of poems had never really been in print, and, indeed, just nine copies had sold.[16]

As her poetry suggests, Glasgow envisioned her own life as a process "of mutability and of development" (CM, 60). This view informs her histories of Virginia. Glasgow had come to think of Virginia as more than a place. It was an intimate province of mind and matter inseparable from herself. Having set her first two novels in New York (55), she now felt capable of approaching her immediate world with the detached eye of a novelist and the idiosyncratic vision of a poet.

During the years of her affair with Gerald, Glasgow published three novels, The Voice of the People (1900), The Battle-Ground (1902), and The Deliverance (1904). Together they chronicle the South from before the Civil War to the end of the century, redefining in the process the genre of historical fiction for future Southern writers. Glasgow wrote Walter Hines Page that the popularity of the first book would determine whether she would write an entire series.[17] The idea for a "series" or "trilogy" may have come to her as early as August 1897, when she paid a clandestine visit to the state's Democratic convention. Smuggled by one of the doorkeepers into the Roanoke opera house, she watched from backstage a thousand sweltering men argue the merits of free silver. That experience—along with the memory of her tobacco-chewing great uncle, William Glasgow, a member of the Virginia General Assembly from 1881 to 1884—found its way into The Voice of the People.

The Voice of the People outlines what would become Glasgow's major theme: how social and political upheavals following the Civil War affected the layered tiers of Southern society, including landed gentry, independent farmers, and freed blacks. Published at the end of the century, the book captures the ethos of the South as well as the moral climate of the entire country. This was, of course, an era of great change. Glasgow's own brother could be counted among the entrepreneurs who made fortunes in coal, oil, and gold, while a new generation of monied aristocrats rose to political prominence. The industrial explosion that had followed the completion of the transcontinental railroad in 1868 fueled the exodus from the country to cities like New York, the population of which grew to 3.5 million by 1900. The small family farm that Thomas Jefferson had praised for its distinctively American spirit of self-reliance struggled to survive in the South as well as in the Northeast.

The Voice of the People (its title borrowed from a column in the Richmond

Times-Dispatch) encompasses the period following Reconstruction, 1867–77, an era that Glasgow compared to the fin de siècle. In her portrayal of both the old and the new Souths, Glasgow portrays and then criticizes a way of life that claimed 600,000 lives in the Civil War and left the region economically and ethically spent. This first book of her "social history" captures the passing of the old agrarian culture and the rise of the new industrialism, which made the middle class (composed of people like the Glasgows) a "dominant force in Southern democracy" (*CM*, 4). *The Voice of the People* marked a radical shift in Southern literature from romance to realism. Glasgow may have been the first novelist, man or woman, to look at the South as a region constantly in transition. Van Wyck Brooks credited her with taking "the South out of the South," and giving it "in fiction a touch of the universal." To his mind, "her Virginian scene was, in fact, a wider scene, the all-American scene of two generations."[18]

Glasgow set *The Voice of the People* in Kingsborough, a town modeled after Williamsburg and hovering upon the "outskirts of modern advancement" (*Voice*, 13). She made her protagonist, Nicholas Burr, the son of a perennially unsuccessful peanut farmer, whom a prominent citizen, Judge Battle, educates as a gentleman. The plot follows Nicholas's rise to governor of the state and ends with his sacrificial murder when he tries to stop a mob intent on lynching a black man. Glasgow's analysis of post-Reconstructionist politics focuses on the alliance between former masters and slaves against the rising middle class, represented by Nicholas himself.[19] The alliance had, in her mind, devastating effects for blacks and women. The voice of the people dies with Nicholas, assassinated by the very people he represents. Freedom of speech becomes a sign of oppression, granted to servants who have exchanged the "devotion of their lives . . . in extenuation of the freedom of their tongues" (*Voice*, 349).

Glasgow's depiction of black characters, her use of racial stereotypes and dialect, has led some readers to accuse her of racism. Oddly enough, contemporary British reviewers saw Glasgow's black characters as touchingly humane and her story "a strong commentary on the lynching practices which are the disgrace of certain States of America" (*Reviews*, 45). One American reviewer, William Morton Payne of *Dial*, even thanked her for her message of practical idealism:

> Shocking as was the murder [of Nicholas], it was less shocking and less permanently demoralizing than the success of their lawless undertaking [the

lynching of a black man] would have been. In describing this scene, the author rises to the true dignity of the situation, and leaves a deep impression upon the minds of her readers.[20]

Just how much Glasgow was writing against the national grain of racism can be seen in the tremendous popularity of Thomas Dixon's pro–Ku Klux Klan novel *The Leopard's Spots: A Romance of the White Man's Burden — 1865–1900* (1902), published two years after *The Voice of the People*. Dixon's 1905 novel *The Clansman* would be made into a Broadway play and then D. W. Griffith's 1915 movie, *The Birth of a Nation*.[21] *The Leopard's Spots* triumphantly ends with the lynching of a black man who raped a white woman. "Can the Ethiopian change his skin or the leopard his spots?" its epigraph asks. While Glasgow's characterization of Nicholas might seem to align her with conservatives who called for civilization's "recommittal to masculine hands,"[22] it never aligned her with racists like Dixon any more than Mark Twain's politics blinded him to Jim's humanity in *Adventures of Huckleberry Finn* (1884).

Glasgow dedicated *The Voice of the People* to her younger sister, Rebe, but it bears a kind of shadow dedication to her populist brother-in-law, Walter McCormack. Glasgow's advocacy of Jacksonian notions of democracy reflects her sympathy for people whom she felt were dispossessed. The political vision that informs her novels — including *The Builders* (1919) and *One Man in His Time* (1922), the title of which recalls a section title of *The Voice of the People* — did not, however, lead to changes in her life. Glasgow guarded the doors to One West Main more fiercely than Andrew Jackson guarded those of the White House. As a Southerner, she may have been born with a love of politics in her blood, yet she never really loved "the people" whose views she represented in her novels.

III

By February 1900, Doubleday and Page had *The Voice of the People* in press.[23] By June it had sold over 12,000 copies. Aside from complaints about its length or excessive descriptions of landscape, the reviews lived up to Glasgow's expectations. True to her word, she decided to write *The Battle-Ground*, the second novel in her trilogy of Virginia. By March 1901, Glasgow had a draft, which she gave to a public stenographer, Julia McCrae, to type a clean copy. McCrae left the only copy of *The Battle-Ground* in the Jefferson Hotel the day an electrical fire burned the building nearly to the ground (March 1901). What the flames didn't destroy, smoke and water damaged. Glasgow had to reconstruct the novel from notes.

The Battle-Ground reflects Glasgow's sense of the dictates of the historical genre. She envisioned her book, with its battle scenes, in the tradition of Stephen Crane's Red Badge of Courage (1894) and bragged that British officers read it for its military accuracy. When Thomas Nelson Page died, she may have been the only Richmonder to cast a skeptical eye on the flag flying at half-mast over the Capitol. He wrote exactly the kind of romances she disdained. To research her book, Glasgow studied old newspapers, diaries, and letters, and toured battle sites from one end of the Valley of Virginia to the other. "What a mountain of endeavor," she later joked, went into the making of realistic novels (CM, 21).

Glasgow never wrote about the Tredegar Iron Works, this arsenal of the Confederacy so close to her house, so intimate to the life of her father. The Tredegar nevertheless shapes the background—and helps to explain certain ambivalences—of The Battle-Ground. To someone who thought herself the South's only realist, the received history of the Works would have resembled a Confederate romance. Her father managed his uncle's company with the same benign paternalism that governed Robert Owen's or Sir Titus Salt's self-made manufacturing towns in England. If Tredegar's rolling of the Merrimack's armor and recasting of Lee's bronze ordnance before Chancellorsville improved the military prospects of the Confederacy, their faulty cannon at Port Royal, Yorktown, and Fort Fisher worsened morale and performance. The company's difficulties in manufacturing adequate numbers of iron field pieces in advance of Gettysburg, its inability to deliver gunboat armor and machinery speedily, and its failure to adopt the Rodman method (in which cannon were cast around a hollow core rather than in a solid tube) all contributed to the South's defeat.[24]

The Battle-Ground highlights Glasgow's uneasy relationship to a past tied to the destructive powers of the Tredegar. Seeking a truth beyond that of external surroundings (CM, 63), she used the war as a backdrop for all human suffering—as "old as the Devil" himself (TB, 5, 13). The novel's opening scene—slave women and children singing mournful farewells to family and friends as they are carted off to a new plantation—locates the true battleground in acts of oppression. While the novel offers a utopian vision of a new, more egalitarian South, it also continues myths enshrined in Margaret Mitchell's Gone with the Wind (1936) and Glasgow's own family. " 'Even in the midst of the horrors,'" Glasgow quotes her mother, "'a wave of thankfulness rushed over me when I heard that the slaves were freed.' The few servants we inherited were happy. But there were others" (*WW*, 40). The last two sentences, in which the voices of mother and daughter merge, belong to Glasgow. They suggest that Glasgow's criticism of cultural myths did not prevent her from fostering them. In *The Battle-Ground,* the squares cut from the hero's regimental flag will gain a similarly dangerous nostalgic meaning as they pass from generation to generation.[25]

Glasgow herself realized the difficulty of approaching "the Confederacy without touching the very heart of romantic tradition" (*CM*, 24). She lived in the city that had housed the government of Jefferson Davis, along with the Tredegar, and at least one of her sisters had belonged to the Daughters of the Confederacy. She may have despised the principles of the Confederacy, but she also found something heart-rending about the veterans who survived the war. On one Memorial Day, for example, she served fried chicken, mint juleps, and after-dinner cigars to a whole company of Texans, who in gratitude presented arms to her in the street.[26] She told Rebe that she liked to do for soldiers what other people did for the officers.

In the first two weeks, *The Battle-Ground* sold over 21,000 copies, firmly reestablishing Glasgow's reputation by holding its own against such bestsellers as Owen Wister's *The Virginian,* which then went on to sell over 1.5 million copies. Her treatment of the Civil War anticipated, if not prompted, a spate of later novels, including James Boyd's *Marching On* (1927), Evelyn Scott's *The Wave* (1929), Stark Young's *So Red the Rose* (1934), William Faulkner's *Absalom, Absalom!* (1936), and Allen Tate's *The Fathers* (1938). In fact, *The Battle-Ground* proved so popular that years later an Englishman, writing under an assumed name, H. Grahame Richard, copied its plot for his 1917 novel, *Shadows.* A committee for the Authors League found him guilty of plagiarism—after he had disappeared.[27]

Thrilled by the book's success, Glasgow expressed her gratitude to Page for convincing her not to serialize it: "The share of the sympathetic publisher in the author's success—the true success so different from the ephemeral—is apt to be overlooked in these blatant days, so it is just as well that some of us keep it in mind."[28]

Whether it was the affair with Gerald B or the revising of childhood stories, Glasgow reached out to people in ways that she had not since her mother's death or the onset of deafness. She felt more sanguine and at peace with the world than she had in years. The day after New Year, 1902, she wrote Lizzie Patterson that though they seldom saw one another, "the past is quite as strong as the present and much more sacred. You are bound up, my dear, with some of the happiest memories of my life, and the older I grow the more earnestly I feel that the few intense joys of childhood are the best that life has to give." [29] For a brief time life did not threaten to belie myth.

IV

During the next two years, Glasgow found herself living in and through the hero of *The Deliverance* (1904). Christopher Blake appeared to her in the center of a ploughed field, dropping tobacco plants into the earth. She conceived the novel, which examines the effects of social transition upon ordinary people from 1878 to 1890, like Millet's painting, *The Man with a Hoe* (1863). She may have been influenced by Edwin Markham's enormously popular poem "The Man with a Hoe" (1899). Glasgow consciously chose to work in "two strongly contrasting tones of light and darkness," knowing that the impressions of the scene would be as primitive as the mind and heart of her leading figure, "which were controlled by violence, and by the elemental motives of desire and revenge" (*CM*, 33). The inception of this novel suggests one way in which Glasgow's hearing loss possibly shaped her creative process. Many writers recount how their characters stride into their studies and insist on talking, but Glasgow's characters appeared to her as part of a visualized scene. In these initial encounters, which reflect one adjustment to deafness, they wait for her to speak for them.

Glasgow set *The Deliverance* (1878–90) immediately following the end of the era of Reconstruction. She realized that turn-of-the-century Richmond had not lost many of its antebellum sentiments about women or blacks. They could only experience a new millennium by hereditary patronage, not political right. As one character in *The Deliverance* observes: "Dat's de tribble wid dis yer worl'; w'en hit changes yo' fortune hit don' look ter changin' yo' skin es well" (*D*, 59). No reader in 1904 could deny the truth of this statement. In the years following Reconstruction, local governments supported a tacit policy of general intimidation, as Southern states rewrote their constitutions to rescind most of the rights of black citizens. By the turn of the century, three-quarters of the black population had become tenant farmers or domestic workers, their economic condition not substantially improved since antebellum days. Literacy laws, designed to prohibit or delay blacks from voting by asking them endless, meaningless questions, led people to line up outside polling places as early as midnight. The *Richmond Times-Dispatch* editorialized in 1904, for example, that education is the "curse of the negro race" because there was less criminality among illiterate black citizens.[30] On April 22, the same paper reported the whipping of a black man for insulting young (white) ladies.

Glasgow's vision of Reconstruction—a period she considered worse than the war itself—dismisses popular stereotypes of the rape of the South. Instead she redefines the very concept of "reconstruction" by ignoring its political and emphasizing its spiritual dimension. The plot of *The Deliverance* follows a campaign of revenge that ends in death. When Blake realizes his moral culpability in the murder of a former overseer who defrauded his family, he confesses to the crime. Upon his release, he marries the murderer's sister, who also happens to be the overseer's granddaughter. Her pride chastened by a disastrous marriage, and his by imprisonment, they can forge a new South based on an alliance between the aristocracy and the rising middle class. One reviewer declared that Glasgow did for the South of Reconstruction what Harriet Beecher Stowe had done in *Uncle Tom's Cabin* for the antebellum South (*Reviews,* 90). She had brought a particular era—its struggles, failures, and violence—to life with the same sort of moral intensity.

Glasgow dedicated *The Deliverance* to her doctor, Holbrook Curtis, "with appreciation of his skill and gratitude for his sympathy." The dedication led Marjorie Rawlings to believe that Curtis was Gerald B. Glasgow had known Curtis since the winter of 1902, when she rented an apartment in New York and took treatment from him for her ears. Lizzie Jones, who had never traveled outside Virginia, accompanied her and did the cooking. Considerably older than Glasgow, Curtis became a kind of substitute father, if not lover. His patients attributed to him miracle cures, but as Glasgow's dedication makes clear, her gratitude lay in his kindness and "sympathy," one of the major themes of her novel.

At the new year, 1905, Glasgow wrote Walter Hines Page, remembering the previous Christmas she had spent at his home in Englewood, New Jersey. Her letter, which thanked him for making her life seem worthwhile, also reveals the tenuous nature of Glasgow's feelings. She may have found happiness in love, but she also experienced long stretches of doubt and misery. "In the highest sense you have given me encouragement," she wrote her publisher, "even when you did not dream that I needed it, when you did not know how bitterly I wanted to throw it all away—and life with it. The years have brought a good many things to me, but they have taken them all away again except my work."[31] As the letter suggests, nothing was as it appeared. No amount of recognition sufficed in retrospect, a futile operation on her ears had left her terribly depressed, and she had begun to feel that the affair with Gerald was slowly killing her.[32] From 1896 to 1905, her copy of the *Bhagavad-Gita* had become as dog-eared as her copy of *The Thoughts of Aurelius*. Its pages provide a map of her emotional life that highlights her efforts to end the relationship with Gerald. "Before the Jungfrau, Aug 2, 1903," she wrote alongside the passage: "The wise grieve neither for the living nor for the dead."[33] The port of Bremerbad and the date, August 8, 1905, would come to signify the time and the place where she finally abandoned desire, felt satisfied in herself and stable in mind.[34]

The years with Gerald rank among Glasgow's most productive. At home in Richmond, she kept to a rigorous schedule, writing from 11 to 12 every morning and for three or four hours every evening. She liked to sit in a rocking chair with a large pad of paper on her lap. She did not yet use a typewriter. In between periods of work, she rested or walked. Looking back on this period in her life and on her novel, *The Deliverance*, Glasgow thought that she may have overemphasized the importance of romantic love and its ability to triumph over revenge. She wondered whether any love—including perhaps her own for Gerald—"could have conquered the triumphant hatred in Christopher's heart and mind" (*CM*, 44). At the time, however, love did seem to offer a partial deliverance from past hatreds. "The substance of anybody's house [or soul]," a character notes, "is a large price to pay for a single feeling" (*D*, 201). Like her hero, Glasgow could hate twice as long as most people could love, and love twice as long as most could live (205). She, too, had grown cold to human sympathy while simultaneously craving and resenting its expression.

The depth of Glasgow's struggle for self-possession and the extent of her passion should not be minimized. Even as a child, she had intense likes and dislikes. For example, she had a crush on a friend of the family named Munford. On the day of his marriage, she threw herself on the floor kicking and screaming. He managed to assuage her grief with a small gold ring that she kept all her life.[35] As a woman, Glasgow was no less fervent. The marked sections of the *Bhagavad Gita* articulate her desperate efforts to be strong by extinguishing desire. Writing offered escape and solace, but frequently it proved not enough. Fate had bound her to a wheel she called "life," which spun her where it willed.

CHAPTER 5

THE WHEEL OF LIFE

1905–1908

Was love, when all was said, merely a subjection to the flesh
instead of an enlargement of the spirit?

Ellen Glasgow, *The Wheel of Life*

I

IN MARCH OF 1905, Glasgow needed all the courage she could muster. Cary had cancer. Over the last five years, she had grown increasingly ill and nervous. After the necessary and apparently successful operation, she seemed, as Glasgow wrote Arthur in London, "already at least fifteen years younger than she did before she went to bed."[1] She would, however, need to be very careful for a long time. Glasgow thanked Arthur for his concern and felt that in the last year she had grown to know his value. Like their father, he exuded tenderness in a sickroom.

Cary's illness, whose symptoms would recur within shorter intervals during the next six years, had overwhelming consequences for Glasgow. Not only did she have to confront the prospect of Cary's death but also her own possibly from the same disease. In 1905 (and until recently), cancer also had a social stigma. People spoke the word in hushed voices, and a patient's family could find themselves isolated less by the burden of care than by fear. Glasgow worried most that the disease would destroy Cary's sense of identity, and she did her best to have their lives pick up where they had left off before the operation. Afternoons almost always included visits to and from friends, cups of tea and glasses of sherry. On nice days, she and Cary might drive to an afternoon concert of Beethoven and Tchaikovsky or a Shakespeare comedy in the old Adams garden on Church Hill. The family agreed to think that rest and care would permanently restore Cary's health.

During this difficult time, Glasgow relied on the friendship of two women who happened also to be writers: Mary Johnston (1870–1936) and Amélie Rives Troubetzkoy (1863–1945).[2] In them, she sought both models for living and a way to repair her devastated family. As Cary convalesced, Glasgow saw Johnston almost daily. Before long, Johnston assumed Cary's role as confidante. In Johnston, Glasgow found another sister, while in Rives she found a substitute mother. Each friend gave her the courage to claim her own life. Johnston wrote despite severe health problems. Rives had survived a bad first marriage and, by her account, an addiction to drugs, which she had injected from a sterling silver syringe.[3] Possessing Anne Glasgow's gentleness and Ellen Glasgow's irreverence, Rives now seemed to have it all: an enviable career and an adoring second husband.

Johnston became the first woman writer with whom Glasgow had a sustained and intimate friendship. Here was someone who spoke her "language" and who occupied similarly concentric worlds: the immediate world of Richmond and the larger world of New York publishing. How many people did Glasgow know who also felt the pressures of the "blank" page, or to whom she could reveal so many selves? Before Johnston moved to Richmond in 1902, Glasgow knew her as the best-selling author of *To Have and to Hold* (1900). Together they shared an interest in foreign places and a fascination with metaphysics. Beyond this, Johnston came to love Cary nearly as much as Glasgow herself did.

Johnston and Glasgow felt that they came from curiously similar backgrounds. Glasgow's father brought knowledge of the law to his job as manager of the Tredegar Iron Works. Johnston's father, John William Johnston, practiced law after the Civil War and presided over concerns important to the Tredegar: the James River–Kanawha Canal Company and the Georgia Pacific Railroad Company. Johnston's mother, Elizabeth Dixon Alexander Johnston, came, as did Glasgow's father, from Scotch-Irish ancestry. She died two years after the birth of her sixth child when Johnston was 19 (1889). Glasgow, as we know, lost her mother at 20. Both friends believed that childhood tragedies had influenced their personal and artistic development.

Acutely introspective, Johnston described herself as having been a "diffident and sensitive" child, whose eye problems and migraines kept her from
attending school. Her formal education lasted a mere three months. Johnston began writing as a form of therapy, but when her father suffered financial
reverses in the Panic of 1895, writing became a necessity. Of that time, she
recalled, "We were living comfortably in an easy Southern fashion in New
York. In a week all was changed. There was a sharp need of retrenchment
and even when retrenchment was accomplished need remained."[4] Johnston
set to work with a vengeance, writing and rewriting and burning, as did
Glasgow, every returned story. Her apprenticeship spanned three years. After
the popularity of *Prisoners of Hope* (1898), set in seventeenth-century Virginia,
publishers began to court her, and soon she made enough money to support
her family more than "comfortably." Johnston differed from contemporary
writers of historical romance in her subjugation of "romance" to "history."
Prisoners of Hope and the novels that followed had a social, religious, and racial
scope that Glasgow, with her own "historic imagination," appreciated.[5]

The friends took genuine delight in one another's successes. Glasgow congratulated Johnston when *To Have and to Hold* sold over half a million copies
and praised *Sir Mortimer* (1904), an Elizabethan romance, as "full of colour
and poetry and quick action."[6] For her part, Johnston most admired *The
Battle-Ground* (1902), the book closest in spirit to her own work.

Glasgow sought to understand herself through Johnston. Their personal
points of correspondence and difference intrigued her. "I feel that I shall be
as glad as possible to know you better—to stand within the gate," she had
written at the beginning of their friendship in 1904. "Yes, I dare say we are
different in many ways—it will be interesting, don't you think, to learn how
different. And the main thing [talent or spiritual insight], perhaps we both
have."[7] By February 1905, Glasgow's tone had turned confidential:

> I shall never forget the last talk I had with you the afternoon before you
> went. You looked so much like a little child, and there are moments when
> one seems almost to see the soul of one's friend shining through the delicate
> flesh. The people I love best, I love for this spiritual quality, for it shows me
> God, somehow, & I hunger for him even when I am least positive of his being
> underneath us all.[8]

Glasgow thought herself the more impulsive of the two and confessed her
initial suspicion that Johnston's natural reserve would inhibit real frankness.

With Johnston, Glasgow tried to sort out questions about religion, which
had preoccupied her since childhood. Even then she had wondered why God

let people and animals suffer when He could prevent it by either a word or a gesture. She prayed constantly, asking Him to let her die before school opened again or to make her ailing mother well. At 12, she accompanied her Aunt Bec, her father's sister, to the Armory to hear the famous evangelist Dwight L. Moody. Despite rumors that he had criticized Robert E. Lee and Stonewall Jackson, he preached for ten days to a full audience. Glasgow sat on the front bench, immediately beneath the preacher's eye. Moody singled her out — a little girl dressed in blue — for special praise, and she experienced a short-lived religious conversion. Glasgow and Johnston discussed books such as *Modern Philosophy, The Imitation of Christ, The Garden of Allah,* and one of Glasgow's perennial favorites, the *Bhagavad-Gita.* "A little of the same spirit is lighting each of us on our way," Glasgow told her, "and it is this that draws us, I hope, together, and will keep us friends until the end." [9]

Glasgow had first become curious about Buddhism after her extended trip to Egypt, Scandinavia, and Europe in 1899. With Cary and Rebe, she tried to look upon all being as "having the nature of space . . . without essence, without substantiality." [10] In a poem written in the 1890s, she expressed the belief that "Decay cannot unmake me, I am part/Of an eternal whole." [11] By 1906, she defined God in terms of love: "There's so much of the child in me yet," she wrote to Johnston, "and life to me means love just as it does to a child — love of many kinds and degrees, but each and all helping us on our way and bringing the journey's end a little nearer the knowledge of God." [12] Finally, she decided that Buddhism failed because it proved "too lofty for the human mind, and the metaphysical doctrine too profound for the human heart which craves a future of unbroken identity." [13]

Glasgow may have characterized herself as "the last unwilling scapegoat of Predestination" (WW, 275), yet she still longed passionately for a God whom she could love. That longing never abated. The phases of her life can be seen as loosely falling into overlapping, rather than distinct, religious chapters: the first marked by her rejection of her father's Presbyterian faith; the second by her belief in science; the third by her affinity for the Stoics; and the fourth by a turning to mysticism. In the 1920s, she came full circle, by acquiring a new respect for certain values she associated with the Presbyterianism of her childhood.

In Glasgow's mind, Johnston's intellectual and spiritual pursuits made her only slightly less unorthodox than Amélie Rives. Like Glasgow, Rives had built a reputation on being a literary rebel. So beautiful that people cut and displayed pictures of her printed in magazines and illustrated papers, she lived as unconventionally as any of her own heroines. Ten years older than Glasgow, she had been born in Richmond, the daughter of Sarah Catherine Macmurdo Rives and Alfred Landon Rives, a Confederate colonel. Her godfather, General Robert E. Lee, had to be the South's most fabled son. In 1888, she married a great-grandson of John Jacob Astor, John Armstrong Chanler, and published her first novel *The Quick or the Dead?* The book sold over 3,000 copies and caused a furor that made the reception of *The Descendant* look tepid. Its author, who had thought nothing of having her recently widowed heroine contemplate a second marriage, found herself accused of immorality. The charge gave her a certain cachet in England, where she was living. Oscar Wilde befriended her, as did a loosely structured group of friends known as the "Souls," led by George Curzon, a young member of Parliament who eventually became governor-general of India and chancellor of Oxford University. The Souls defended themselves against charges of snobbery and aestheticism. During this period of her life, Rives said she became addicted to laudanum and, with a determination Glasgow could appreciate, had kicked the habit "cold turkey."

Rives, who possessed a piquant blend of sentimentalism and sexuality, expressed her feelings for Glasgow in the emotionally extravagant language of nineteenth-century women: "All my love and sympathy has been with you, but it has necessarily been an abstract sort of love and sympathy because I could not express it to you with warm, living lips and glances and embraces. . . . I take you in my arms and love you dearly, dearly." [14] At the same time, she believed that heterosexual "passion is perfume and flame . . . its own excuse and raison d'être." [15] A self-made woman, she rose phoenix-like from the ashes of her first marriage. A year after her divorce in 1895, she married Pierre Troubetzkoy, an artist who also happened to be a Russian prince. At the time Glasgow and Rives became close friends, Rives lived at Castle Hill, a red-brick, eighteenth-century mansion that could have been a model for Tara in *Gone with the Wind*. Glasgow loved to bring guests to Castle Hill, where Pierre would greet them at the end of a long drive bordered by a double wall of dark green box bushes, and Amélie would entertain them in her green and gold drawing room furnished with French treasures. Glasgow cared for the Troubetzkoys individually but also as a couple. Their accord belied her own distrust of marriage and made her wonder about the absences in her personal and creative life.

Throughout their long friendship, Glasgow and Rives shifted roles according to need. In the beginning, Glasgow sought a kind of literary mother, with whom she could discuss her work and topics as varied as spiritualism and face creams. Later she reassured Rives, who tended to deprecate her own achievements, about the value of her work. To no one did Glasgow express more tenderness: "Do you remember those lovely nightgowns you had made for me in Italy so long ago?" she wrote Amélie after Pierre's death. "I have just found six that I have never worn and I am sending them to you . . . and I shall like to think of you with my monogram on your dear, loyal heart." [16]

Glasgow's friendships with other women allowed her to express a range of feelings and thoughts that her clandestine and conflicted relationship with Gerald made impossible. Glasgow kept many of her friends for life. Her love for childhood companions, such as Carrie Coleman and Elizabeth Patterson, reveals a capacity for friendship few people have recognized. Glasgow found in her women friends, if not a Virginia version of the English Souls, a community of like "souls." These women led tangential yet intertwined lives, and that arrangement allowed them whatever degrees of intimacy and freedom they needed. As Glasgow told Johnston, "Love me, as much or little as you can, and I shall love you back in my own measure." [17]

II

By July 1905,[18] Cary had recuperated enough to accompany Glasgow and Rebe to Europe. Strangely enough, they sailed (on the SS *Bremen*) with the purpose of consulting an aurist, Isadore Müller, about Glasgow's deafness and not a specialist about Cary's cancer, which everyone thought in remission. "It may be that he can do nothing for me," Glasgow had told Arthur, "but my ears interfere so with my enjoyment of life that I should like to feel that I have done all in my power to make them hearable." [19] The sisters planned to go directly to Carlsbad, where Müller summered. Rebe had learned some German and intended to serve as translator. Glasgow worried that if she needed extended treatment or an operation, the doctor's costs might exceed the thousand dollars she had set aside. She thought about selling Tredegar stock until Arthur agreed to advance her any additional monies. She promised to repay him as soon as her next novel, *The Wheel of Life* (1906), saw print. Unfortunately, the elaborate planning proved futile. The doctor could do nothing to restore her hearing or her peace of mind.

After Carlsbad, the sisters went to Nordhausen, Germany, to see a repatriated Richmonder, Otto Plotz. Plotz's new home lay in the Harz mountains, not far from the haunt of Faust's witches. Glasgow loved the landscape, which seemed to her a forested version of the Yorkshire dales. She did not mention the daughter whom Plotz and his wife had nicknamed for her, but Rebe assured friends at home that "Baby Ellen [Hermine Willamine Inger-borg Plotz] is really beautiful."[20]

In late August, the sisters returned to Mürren, Switzerland, a tiny village next to the Jungfrau, where Glasgow had experienced her happiest moments with Gerald. They stayed in a hotel catering to middle-aged English gentle-women and clergy. Glasgow spent her days taking scenic walks and her evenings reading by the wood fire. The hotel library housed the complete Tauchnitz edition of Trollope—over ninety tiny volumes—including her favorite, *Framley Parsonage*. When standing with that very book in hand, she received her last letter from Gerald. Reconstructed from Glasgow's memory, it bears no stylistic similarities to the letter from the mysterious Gray:

> I am in the hospital. They have told me what I suspected. I have only a few weeks at worst, a few months at best. I waited too long for the operation. But what was the use? They couldn't cure me, and God knows, I wouldn't have lingered on as an invalid. My first thought was of you. . . . It meant giving you up. (*WW*, 165)

Gerald died before Glasgow sailed for home.[21] She learned of his death, as if he was a stranger, from a front-page obituary published in the Paris edition of the *New York Herald*. It merely confirmed the inevitable. Her life with him had ended on the Jungfrau.

After reading Gerald's letter, Glasgow fell into a kind of stupor. "Could she never escape from death?" The days seemed to bleed one into another without leaving any telltale marks. Though she retained no memory of what passed, at some point Glasgow went up the hillside outside her hotel and lay down in the grass. She remembered thinking, "If only I could lose my-self in nothing or everything!" Then, with every ounce of strength, she tried to will it, to make herself "part of the grass and the wind and the spirit that moved round them, and in them." She tried to imitate the mystics, "who had attained Divine consciousness" by "extinguishing their innermost core of identity," but nothing happened. Exhausted, she felt herself sinking deeper and deeper into the earth (*WW*, 165).

At that moment of surrender, she experienced a revelation. The golden August light streamed through her as if she became something outside her-self: wind and grass and air. "Spirit? Matter? Imagination?" she asked (166–

67). It didn't signify. For an instant, she had shed the onerous garment of self. She felt an ecstasy born of agony, the absolution, as she described it, of forget-fulness. The vision sustained her a lifetime. Glasgow experienced something akin to the religious fervor that inspired eighteenth-century Calvinists, such as Jonathan Edwards during the Great Awakening, as well as contemporaries like William James, who explored similar ineffable moments. Glasgow woke not so much from grief but from the moral lethargy of her relationship with Gerald.

III

In the year following Gerald's death, Glasgow returned again and again to her vision on the Jungfrau. "What sorrow, what trouble can there be to him who has once beheld that unity?" she asked. From 1905 to 1907, she could be characterized as a believer more than a skeptic. In a North German church, before sailing home in 1905, she had received a "message," which was "ful-filled" six months later (February 3, 1906) in Boston. There once again she experienced religious rapture. Like her Puritan forefathers, she had begun to read life as a series of divine signs.

Glasgow hinted to friends such as Johnston and Page about a period in her life when she "was brought back to some kind of acceptance and reconcilia-tion" through her reading of Schopenhauer and Eastern philosophy. During the last year, she told Johnston, she had been happy for the first time in her life — happy not in the outward shadow called a "self," but in her soul, now "clear and radiant." [22] When Page warned her not to "take metaphysics too seriously," she responded that the soul remained the one subject upon earth "which a human being can take seriously." [23]

Glasgow's "metaphysics" had a marked effect on her fiction. Trying to find fictional equivalents for her experiences, she began to write a different kind of novel: one that eschewed the marriage plot in favor of the spiritual quest. The books written immediately before and after Gerald's death, *The Wheel of Life* (1906) and *The Ancient Law* (1909), while considered artistic failures by many critics, nevertheless paved the way for *Virginia* (1913) and *Barren Ground* (1925), the books that changed Glasgow's career because they universalized — to use her word — the personal. By then, the First World War had made relevant stories of devastation and renewal. The poor critical reception of *The Wheel of*

Life, including a tepid review in the *Richmond Times-Dispatch*, did not seriously hamper its sales. At the end of the year, readers who liked *The Deliverance* had bought enough copies to secure it tenth place on the list of bestsellers.[24]

The most mystical and openly autobiographical of all Glasgow's novels, *The Wheel of Life* details the spiritual growth of a poet, Laura Wilde, whose commanding intellect and instinct for truth make people either worship or loathe her. Laura's journey parallels Glasgow's description of her own life from 1905 to 1906, in a letter written to Mary Johnston. Glasgow hoped that her confidences would comfort Johnston, who was recovering from depression and ill health after the death of her father:

> I *know* it all [she wrote], for a year ago I passed through exactly the same awakening of myself, though from different causes. Mine was not physical, but spiritual—mental—what you will! For a year I was so dead that I couldn't feel even when I was hurt because of some curious emotional anaesthesia, and, like you, I had to fight—fight, a sleepless battle night and day, not for my reason but for my very soul. Then at the end of a year—at Bremerbad last summer I came out triumphant, and for three whole months it was as if I walked on light, not air.[25]

The Wheel of Life reproduces this struggle, which recalls Kate Chopin's novel of sexual discovery, *The Awakening* (1899), almost verbatim. Unlike Chopin, Glasgow claimed to have taken her novel "directly from experience," and for that reason she felt that it proved less successful than her Virginia books. She had been "too close" to her subject.[26]

The idea that Glasgow intended *The Wheel of Life* as a disguised autobiography is disturbing. Perhaps her harshest book, it presents "life" and "art" as absolutely exclusive choices. Laura, wanting "to be, to know, to feel" (*WL*, 238), to *live*, falls in love with a charming sensualist who makes her realize her own capacity for jealousy and deceit. The novel's section titles—"Impulse," "Illusion," "Disenchantment," and "Reconciliation"—mark the stages of her journey from romantic to divine love. Realizing that she "never wrote a sincere line" (464), Laura abandons art in favor of an idiosyncratic, mystical version of stoicism. While Glasgow ostensibly criticizes whatever shields people from "reality," she finally celebrates "a love so sexless, so dispassionate that its joys were like the joys of religion" (177). The novel ends with a scene reminiscent of its author's "awakening" on the Swiss hillside: "Love which had recoiled from its individual object overflowed her heart again until she felt that it had touched the boundaries of the world" (469).[27] That love includes female friendship, which Glasgow presents as another kind of sacrament (349), paying, in this way, tribute to her own friends Rives and Johnston.[28]

The Wheel of Life marks a shift in Glasgow's philosophy. Inspired by Darwin, her earliest novels, The Descendant (1897) and Phases of an Inferior Planet (1898), analyzed the social forces that shape our inherently narcissistic natures.[29] In contrast, The Wheel of Life advocates such total self-renunciation that one reviewer compared it, this most Christian of Glasgow's novels, to Tolstoi's Resurrection. Although Glasgow's friendship with Mary Johnston enriched her life, it had negative consequences for someone whose genius lay in apprehending the concrete, those details that reveal both individual character and a particular social milieu.[30] Glasgow had a much harder time trying to convey the "immaterial" sense of unity she experienced on the Jungfrau. When she tried, she found herself talking to the already converted.

IV

The experience on the Jungfrau had reconciled Glasgow—at least for the time being—to what Whitman calls "the Me myself." Several times a week in 1906, Mary Johnston and her cousin Coralie strolled over to One West Main. There they found Cary, despite some obvious discomfort, bright and animated. The friends gossiped about fellow Richmonders, travel to foreign countries, and books, books, books. In November alone they discussed Alcott, Emerson, Twain, Kant, Schopenhauer, Aurelius, and the Brownings. Extrapolating from the Brahminical idea of colors, in which red meant the earth, Cary pronounced Amélie Rives's soul gold, Johnston's mauve, and Glasgow's clear pink.

The women also watched Rebe, who would marry Cabell Carrington Tutwiler a few short weeks later, address wedding invitations. The December fifth wedding had to be a quiet affair because Tutwiler's brother had recently died. The thirty guests who attended the ceremony and breakfast found One West Main decorated with chrysanthemums and palms and lighted by white candles, much as it had appeared the day Cary wed Walter McCormack fourteen years earlier. Frank Paradise,[31] an Episcopalian minister whom Rebe and Ellen had met during an October vacation in the Adirondacks, performed the service.

Sensing the minister's interest in Glasgow, her friends did their best to make his ten-day stay memorable. On the Sunday following Rebe's wedding, he preached at St. Paul's. The next few days evolved around his entertainment: tea at Johnston's house, a trip to the Confederate Museum, and a tour of a tobacco factory because Glasgow wanted him "to see and hear the negroes." They saw, in fact, 1,400 men and women at work. Johnston described the scene as a blur of color: "brown workers, brown leaf, brown walls and beams, now and then a note of red." The workers wore handkerchiefs or paper caps over their heads and stood at long tables stemming the tobacco or bearing it in crates to a great belt. The air was warm and clogged with the scent of tobacco. As people worked, they sang "Roll, Jordan, Roll, Happy Land."[32] None of the party thought it odd or impolite to watch people perform as though they were actors in a play.

Glasgow certainly exerted herself to entertain, even charm, Paradise. In his honor, she invited Governor Andrew Jackson Montague to a sumptuous supper where guests feasted on raw oysters, sweetbreads, pheasants, salad, ham, ice cream, sherry, and champagne. The minute she returned from taking Paradise to the station, Glasgow wrote Rebe: "After you went, I don't know what I should have done if he hadn't been here. He wasn't like the man at Hurricane somehow, for on this visit he seemed to say always the right thing & everybody found him very entertaining."[33] Glasgow began to think that he might fit into her life as easily as he had fit into the community.

After the festivity of the wedding, Christmas promised to be bleak. Glasgow missed Rebe, whom she addressed as her "own darling child." "I never knew what you were or how much I loved you until these last few days," she wrote the day after Rebe's marriage. "You have always been the most perfect thing on earth and I love you with every bit of my heart."[34] One West Main seemed unnaturally still, with Cary often too sick to come downstairs for meals and Frank recuperating from appendicitis. After Lizzie Jones came by to help pack the remainder of Rebe's things, the house seemed to assume a forlorn air. Everything upset Glasgow, who felt the greater share of household burdens, from the "imbecilities" of servants to the frustrations of temporary writer's block. The dueling between Glasgow and her father wore on her nerves. She predicted, and probably hoped, that on Christmas day he would as usual eat mince pie and get sick.[35] Living with him made her feel 14 again—and vulnerable. She still hid stray dogs from him, and his displeasure predictably brought on a migraine. His word ruled. When he had one of his "economical streaks," the household might subsist on rabbit for a week. He also had little respect for his children's privacy or economic independence.

For Christmas, Arthur had sent each of his sisters twenty-five dollars, and Francis had confiscated five of Cary's without explanation. Glasgow donated hers to the SPCA before he could claim it. On Christmas day, she and Carrie Coleman took presents to several needy women, and Glasgow treated the servants to plum pudding and whiskey—at her own expense. She sent dinner and presents to the residents of Richmond's Afro-American Old Folks Home because the community fund did not provide for them. Mary Johnston remembered her with a series of small, antique French engravings of the heads of philosophers, but the best that she could say of the day was that it ended.[36]

The situation at home probably convinced Glasgow to enter into an "experimental" engagement with Frank Paradise. The engagement lasted three years, and though she liked him, she realized that she had never known anyone, not even Gerald, whose companionship she could enjoy all the time (*WW,* 178). The romance with Paradise, who wrote books on religion and politics, had everything the one with Gerald did not: poetic sympathy and easy rapport—everything except sexual excitement. It was the kind of love she thought she had wanted her entire life and learned she did not. To her, madness or abandon represented the essence of love. Glasgow felt mostly gratitude for Paradise's attention. Later she wondered whether there might be an "intimate relation between desire and the sense of inadequacy" (179) that had led her to accept his proposal. Unlike Gerald, Paradise gave her no cause for jealousy. The balance of power resided with her.

After the engagement ended, Glasgow did not hear from Paradise again until 1924, when Louise Willcox met him and his wife, a fresh-looking young Englishwoman, on a train. He had lived abroad since his marriage in 1914, and Willcox couldn't tell whether he had remained a minister. "Give Ellen my love," he instructed her, "and tell her it's the same love." "So there it is for what it's worth,"[37] Willcox told Glasgow, who responded by sending him a copy of *Barren Ground* (1925). "I suppose I must draw your portrait in your books," he replied, "but one may have memories." He obviously did not read the character of embittered Dorinda Oakley autobiographically, for he imagined Glasgow glorying in her powers and honors. "All these I felt," he wrote, "and something else, something more." After nineteen years, the "more" must have been flattering. His letter also contained a picture of himself looking tan, trim, and prosperous, with, in his own words, his not very pretty (albeit gifted) wife, Dorothy Pyman.[38] Glasgow later told Irita Van Doren that she had been engaged to a minister who had fathered thirteen children. The idea of thirteen children made her laugh. (In fact, Paradise had six children from two marriages.)

The new year, 1907, seemed to bring more troubles. Glasgow had finished four chapters of her next novel, *The Ancient Law*, with five more in rough draft, and hoped to do twenty before she went on vacation in the beginning of July. But holidays and household cares—the hiring of a new cook, the cleaning and renovating of the servants' quarters, the ongoing battle with dust from the unpaved road—consumed much of January. When Glasgow woke up in the morning, she felt as if her bedroom were situated near a volcano,[39] and to make matters worse, the servants had all decamped after the new year. One had absconded with the bed linen, including Cary's, and what the first had left behind, another took.[40] Glasgow could not work with the household in constant chaos. She felt "so little of the natural happy instinct for life" that she sometimes wished just "to lie down quietly and give it up." Any of the thousand lives she saw beyond seemed preferable to her own.[41]

Home felt more and more like a tomb, for Cary's poor health and continuing depression saddened Glasgow and imperiled their old comradery. Cary could no longer function as her sister's ears, picking up missed threads of conversation. For the first time in years, Glasgow had to mediate her own safe passage through the world. She, Cary, and Rebe had always had a triangulated relationship that seemed, in Rebe's mind, to make her the odd person out. Now the balance of affection shifted, for Glasgow confided to Rebe that she wearied of being careful of every word around Cary.[42] With Rebe gone, Cary ill, and Frank withdrawn, Glasgow had to assume responsibility for the entire family. She did not accept the role gracefully. Aside from her hearing impairment, she had neither the temperament nor the desire to serve.

At the end of February, Rebe returned home for a visit. It began well enough. The sisters visited with old friends, including Mary Johnston, Carrie Coleman, and Roberta (Berta) Wellford, a close friend of Glasgow and Cary. Their talk centered mostly on books. No one liked Nathaniel Hawthorne's *The Marble Faun;* and excepting Johnston everyone preferred Jane Austen's *Pride and Prejudice* to *Mansfield Park*. Glasgow and Johnston argued the merits of Henry James's *The Turn of the Screw*, which Johnston called a "putrescent thing."[43] Glasgow thought James wonderful, though "a constitutional spinster."[44] Little did she know that she would soon be involved in negotiations as delicate as any found in a James novel.

Before Rebe left on the sixth of March for Philadelphia and Glasgow for Castle Hill, more than discussion went awry. The timing of the visit may have precipitated the argument that ensued. Glasgow felt overtired and anxious about her book, and Rebe, now a married woman, no longer played the role of her "dear child." From the extant correspondence, it seems that Glasgow chastised Rebe for leaving her to shoulder all the burdens of One West Main. She felt that she had treated Rebe, her childhood "shadow," as a surrogate daughter, building her confidence and encouraging her to marry. Rebe's new independence, as well as Glasgow's own worries about a nonhearing future, the loss of inspiration, and the time to work, led to recriminations over Rebe's desertion and the character of her husband. Rebe accused Glasgow of jealousy, and Glasgow countered that if she could believe her well and cheerful (which she could not), she wouldn't mind giving her up.

Cary took Rebe's part and thoroughly upbraided Glasgow, who resented the interference but realized its necessity. For Rebe's sake, she promised that she would try to feel at home with her husband. "Men, however, are so different from women," she forewarned, "that I don't know how it will be. But I'll try for your sake." [45] Playing one sister off against the other, Glasgow wrote that quarreling made her lose all balance:

> I suppose it's silly to get upset by what Cary says, but she made me feel that I never wanted to see any members of my family again. Of course you are the only one that has ever come in any vital way near to me, & it was because I cared more for you than for myself that I was always eager for you to marry, because I realized that my work took up so much of my time & you had nothing in your life that corresponded to it. I shall always love you in this way, but I have a terrible temperament to deal with. [46]

The letter, both plea and insult, reveals a side of Glasgow that few people saw. Frequently and for days, she would find herself "unstrung, quivering with sensitiveness, and vaguely exasperated with people and circumstances" (WW, 178). She could as a result be unreasonably petty.

The sisters did not make up until May, when Glasgow wrote Rebe that she had kept her alive for years, that she loved her more than anybody. Glasgow sent a poem as a partial apology. After Glasgow's death, Rebe wanted Marjorie Rawlings to publish the poem so that Arthur would understand just how close she and Ellen had been:

To Rebe

Where Love and Hate have died at birth
And Fame has fared from view,
Ah, What remains of any worth
To consecrate to you?

The shadow where the sun has shone,
Where right has been the wrong—

Dear heart, I pledge to you alone
The silence after song.[47]

The poem echoes Walter Savage Landor's well-known "Rose Aylmer": "A night of memories and of sighs I consecrate to thee." An elegy to missed love, it acknowledges Glasgow's own failings of sympathy.

V

In the summer of 1907, Glasgow came home from West Virginia ready to finish the final chapters of her novel, *The Ancient Law*. Arthur had treated his family to a vacation at "the White," where Ellen, Emily, and Frank shared a five-room cottage with their father. Surprisingly, Glasgow complained more about the sitting room's wallpaper, scarlet peonies on a bright blue background, than its occupants. Frank, who had planned to stay most of the summer, contracted typhoid fever and had to return to Richmond. His father accompanied him.[48] In their stead, Glasgow invited Louise Willcox, whose brother had rejected her first novel, and Julia Sully, a Richmond socialite who promoted the arts. Avoiding the young matrons sauntering in white muslin with babies in tow, Glasgow threw herself into vigorous physical exercise, riding horseback every morning no matter the weather.[49]

Once home, she finished her novel on schedule, Doubleday, Page publishing it in the spring of 1908. Its dedication read to "Effendi," a nickname for Frank N. Doubleday formed from his initials F. N. D. Like Rebecca Harding Davis's *Life in the Iron Mills* (1861), Elizabeth Stuart Phelps's *The Silent Partner* (1871), Mary Wilkins Freeman's *The Portion of Labor* (1901), and Edith Wharton's *The Fruit of the Tree* (1907), *The Ancient Law* analyzes the rise of industrial capitalism and its attendant social ills. Through her novel, Glasgow continues the tradition of nineteenth-century women whose social consciousness led to the organization of women's exchanges, sewing schools, day nurseries, infirmaries, relief agencies for the unemployed, and homes for "fallen" women.

However much the novel pays tribute to women of conscience like her sister Cary, it focuses on a subject closer to her father's heart: prison reform. Francis Glasgow had served on the board of the Virginia Penitentiary before becoming chair in 1891. The penitentiary, which had been designed by Benjamin Henry Latrobe in 1796, opened by the turn of the century. From its conception, it reflected progressive ideas on reform that grew from a belief in the environmental, rather than the genetic, roots of criminal behavior. The prison housed both men and women, whose products were sold in a prison store. Cheap prison labor made an impact on the local economy. In 1886, for example, the Knights of Labor went on strike for six months, hoping that Haxall flour mills would stop using barrels made by the convicts. The male prisoners also maintained country roads and labor for the Virginia Manufactory of Arms. During Francis Glasgow's tenure, the board approved the costs of running the prison and inspected the facilities, particularly the hospital. The minutes of the board's meeting do not discuss specific reforms, though they do show the members' approval of additions to the penitentiary for the superintendent and clerk and better quarters for the guard.

For all her dislike of her father, Glasgow admired his work on the board of the penitentiary. Her protagonist, Daniel Ordway, illustrates the principles of rehabilitation that Francis supported. Released from prison, he dedicates his life to improving the lives of others. After the death of his father, he invests his entire inheritance in a mill that will be run cooperatively. The novel ends with his preaching a democratic version of the Golden Rule from town to town. He has no wish to return to his family and the well-appointed prison they call a home.

The critical reception of *The Ancient Law* proved more disappointing than that of her previous book—and without the huge sales. A review in the London *Saturday Review* particularly rankled: "The story is founded on a basis of false sentiment and false psychology [elements Glasgow herself hated] and is constructed throughout on sentimental sensational lines" (*Reviews*, 129). She should, according to the *Bookman*, have known better (125).

Glasgow decided that a change of scene might give her a fresh perspective. In 1908, Cary still felt well enough to sightsee. Arthur again acted as his sisters' fairy godfather. From the middle of July to October 1908, Glasgow, Cary, and Roberta Wellford, their Richmond friend, traveled in Italy. The women landed in Venice and went on to Rome, Assisi, Borca, and Naples. In Assisi, they met a Franciscan monk from Florence named P. G. Geroni who acted as their interpreter and showed a decided preference for Glasgow, maybe because she so obviously respected his spiritual commitment. The friends could not get over the idea that his aristocratic family had simply "given" him to the church. Geroni told them that when he realized what that meant, he had suffered and then accepted his fate. He later served as head of the Franciscans in China and died in North Africa around 1912 or 1913. In Richmond lore, he became one of Glasgow's suitors, last seen trying to gain entrance to One West Main. People wondered if he, like Homer Baron in Faulkner's "A Rose for Emily," had also been murdered and entombed by the woman he jilted.

Despite the compatibility of the travelers, the trip generated tensions reminiscent of the sisters' 1899 tour of Egypt and Europe. This time Glasgow felt left out: Cary and Berta "enjoy each other & everything together," she wrote Rebe:

> Berta thinks her thoughts & waits on her assiduously. As for me, I, of course, would have a better time if I had a fourth person, who was congenial, to pair off with me. I see everything by myself, but the astrologer told me that to be always alone was [the] inevitable fate of one with my horoscope.

She reminded Rebe of their own earlier journey together, which took on the quality of a shared dream. Someday she and Cabell would see Italy, and "enjoy that more."[50] As her letter to Rebe suggests, Glasgow's sense of exile had reasserted itself in Europe. The revelations and comfort she had experienced in Bremerbad seemed far away and, worse, the depression that marked the completion of her novels returned.

VI

By early December of the next year, 1908, Glasgow had made up her mind to seek a new publisher. The decision had not come easily. Her friendships with Frank Doubleday and Walter Hines Page mattered to her. She told herself that her work mattered more. Understandably she preferred to think that the public's response to The Wheel of Life and The Ancient Law resulted from marketing decisions her publisher had made and not from the novels themselves. Already angry with Page for not doing enough to insure favorable reviews, she became more so when he sent her an article published in his journal, The World's Work. Page seriously mistook his audience. "Life of a Monkey Against the Life of a Man" discusses the use of animals in medical research. The author, Dr. Simon Flexner, having himself developed a serum for meningitis, which saved countless lives, labeled advocates for the monkey sentimental, ill-informed agitators.[51] "Personally," Glasgow wrote Page, "I have not the slightest objection to being branded as either 'sentimental' or 'emotional,' since it puts me in a very respectable class from Christ to the first sentimentalist who suggested that truth might still prevail though the pursuit of it through the rack and the thumbscrew should be abolished."[52] She could not understand why vivisectors would object to giving animals anesthetic before killing them or having laboratories open for inspection. "Please don't think that I mean to be harsh," she ended. "I realize that you have heard

only Dr. Flexner's side. Ask for Mark Twain's—or for Robert Browning's—
or Tennyson's, or a thousand others of equal heart and brain." [53]

Glasgow's annoyance with Page grew from her fear that her career might
be in decline. When she thought of leaving his firm, she remembered that
the president of Macmillan, George Brett, wanted to atone for rejecting *The
Descendant*. "Now, quite frankly," she asked him, "how much do you wish [to
atone]?" [54] Brett wanted to atone enough to accept her next novel, *The Romance of a Plain Man* (1909), sight unseen. In return, Glasgow promised not
to be a nagging author.

Glasgow had a hard time keeping her promise, for after Brett read the
manuscript, he insisted on a total revision of the second half. One of its
major themes—the need of love in a woman's life—had been "badly and in-
conclusively developed," and "the climax should *color the entire narrative.*" [55]
Beside herself, Glasgow consulted Page (who might be excused if he saw her
dilemma in terms of poetic justice). Then she asked Brett to void their contract. Brett refused, saying that he would only release the book to another
publisher in its present form. Much as Glasgow thought Brett mean and un-
trustworthy, her almost belligerent confidence in her power to write both
popular and lasting books faltered. After Brett had apologized for any un-
intended discourtesy, she agreed to his terms. When *The Romance of a Plain
Man* (1909) appeared in May, she complained about the small sales (slightly
over 23,000). [56] He justified the sales by reminding her that his firm had managed to overcome the reluctance of booksellers, who still had unsold copies
of *The Ancient Law*, to stock the novel. [57] Needless to say, he chose the worst
argument to placate her. She informed him that it had been a mistake to
separate her books. By January, she owned the plates to *The Romance of a
Plain Man*, which she gave to her old firm, Doubleday, Page, her publisher
for the next twenty-three years. Glasgow's relationship with Macmillan had
lasted less than a year. [58]

The Romance of a Plain Man seems to reflect Glasgow's own vacillations of
mind. Set in Richmond from the years after Reconstruction to the present
day (from 1875 to 1908), *The Romance of a Plain Man* chronicles the rise of
a Horatio Alger figure, Ben Starr. Glasgow probably modeled him after her
financier-lover, Gerald B. As in *Silas Lapham* (1885), the protagonist's material gains mark his spiritual decline. By seeming to advocate Starr's point of
view, Glasgow places herself in the awkward position of defending behavior
she usually denounced. She excuses Ben's insensitivity to his wife, Sally, for
example, because he must concentrate on "larger" (urbane rather than do-

mestic) problems. Glasgow treats Sally, who cannot live without Ben's love, harshly. Sally loves her husband more than her child and more than herself. Her feelings, which may comment retrospectively on Glasgow's own for Gerald or Cary's for Walter McCormack, are unnatural, if not suicidal. They cripple Sally, who suffers from a diseased spine (another name for a weak backbone), and corral Ben, who must care for her. In a novel full of abusive and alcoholic fathers, Sally has created an ideal father, ever attentive and asexual. The novel's conclusion harks back to the sentimental tradition, for Ben awakens to his wife's inner spirit, the fineness of her sympathy, and the quickness of her understanding. The novel replaces what he worships — material things that can be grasped in the hands — with a new, feminine aesthetic, which Glasgow vaguely defines as "the finer beauties of life" (Romance, 442). Male reviewers especially found Ben's domestication incredible. They complained that even a "great" woman novelist like Glasgow cannot discern what a man feels or how he behaves.[59] Six years later (1915), she proved them wrong by writing a jingoistic poem entitled "Albert of Belgium" under the pseudonym of John J. Newbegin, Esq. The poem, which Glasgow sent to three well-known poets (George Sterling, Edward Robeson Taylor, and Edwin Markham), met with general approval.[60]

If her masquerade as John J. Newbegin sounds amusing, Glasgow's adoption of a male voice in The Romance of a Plain Man seems at once defiant and desperate. Opposition made her even more determined to work on. She felt that something had come between her and her single-minded devotion to her craft. Surveying her past and contemplating the future, she wondered where she stood. When art failed, nothing seemed to matter. The emotional awakening she had experienced ended in spiritual crisis.

CHAPTER 6

BEYOND HEARTBREAK

1909–1914

A tragic irony of life is that we so often achieve success or
financial independence after the chief reason for which
we sought it has passed away.

Ellen Glasgow, *The Woman Within*

I

IN THE SPRING of 1909, Glasgow sailed again for England. The situation at
home made a respite necessary. As Cary grew thinner and weaker with each
day, Glasgow found it harder and harder to pretend that she would improve.
Glasgow's own health, especially her difficulty hearing, made it impossible
for her to travel alone. Cary could no longer accompany her, and though
her brother Frank might have been a welcome companion at one time, he
too seemed consumed by some hidden affliction. Glasgow suspected that in
Frank's case the disease had psychological roots, but she had given up trying
to identify them. He had shown signs of depression for years and received
no treatment. The trip to Europe became feasible when Elizabeth Patterson,
Glasgow's childhood friend, agreed to go.

On the voyage over, Glasgow never felt free from the pressures of home or the constraints caused by her deafness. She refused to sit by herself for fear that one of the other hundred first-class passengers might engage her in conversation. Although Glasgow had finally accepted the fact that no medical procedure would restore her hearing, she had not resigned herself to using the unwieldy and often inadequate hearing machines available. She saw her adulthood as falling into two phases: the first marked by her search for a cure, and the second by her search for a better hearing device (WW, 183). At their best, these devices were obtrusive. "It was so touching," one friend recalled, "when at last she heard the birds sing." When she got a hearing aid, the first sounds she wanted to hear were the sounds of nature. Glasgow finally settled on a device that fit into a little silver mug about the size of a child's christening cup. The instrument was so crude, however, that when dining with friends, she had to keep one hand to her ear to hold the attachment in place. With the other, she ate like a "hummingbird," [1] in the only way she could manage. On trips abroad, Glasgow found it difficult to avoid the "ignorant kindness" of strangers (183) who wished to help her with information she could not hear.

Glasgow and Patterson arrived in London the first week of April. Within days, they received news of Frank's death. It seemed an ugly portent of what awaited Cary. No matter how far she traveled, Glasgow could not escape the burden of home. On April 7, 1909, Frank had shot himself in his office at the Tredegar Iron Works. With its usual charity toward prominent citizens, the local paper attributed his death to despondency over his continuing symptoms from typhoid fever. On the day of his death, Frank added two codicils to his will: the first left each of his sisters an income of $1,000; the second gave his one friend, Frank Hobson, a gregarious neighbor and distant relative, his watch and chain. The year before, Arthur had created a trust of $49,000 for the benefit of his brother and sisters. As originally arranged, Frank's death increased that trust by $35,000.[2]

Ellen Glasgow's niece Josephine Clark remembers visiting her grandfather on the day of Frank's death. He came into the room where she and Cary were sitting. They noticed that he had tears in his eyes and seemed to be cradling something in his arms. It was his son's suit, impeccably folded. "Frank has killed himself down at the Works," he announced. "I don't know what to do with his clothes." Cary cried, "Burn them! They'll have blood on them." "No," he said, caressing the jacket, "the material is too fine. Some poor person can get some wear from them." [3] Francis had his way, and the man who received the suit wore it to seek employment. When Francis Glasgow died, the man wrote a condolence letter telling how the possession of a decent suit of clothing had changed his life. He saw his benefactor—unlike Francis's own daughter, Ellen—as the kindest of men.

Glasgow decided not to return home from London. There was nothing she could do except try to hold herself together. She felt sad and old and haunted by "something so terribly pathetic about poor Frank" that overnight her face appeared to develop lines and furrows.[4] Trying to forget herself, try-ing not to think of Cary's inevitable future, she sought the company of other women who had dedicated their lives to a cause greater than themselves.

Glasgow found those women in the suffrage movement. Since the death of Gerald B in 1905 and her friendship with Mary Johnston, Glasgow had be-come increasingly involved with woman's suffrage as well as animal rights. Like her British counterparts engaged in the women's movement and anti-vivisectionist demonstrations, Glasgow saw little distinction between cruelty to people and cruelty to animals. By May 1908, she and Cary had become "bound up heart and soul in Woman Suffrage."[5] That year Glasgow devoted much time to both. In March, for instance, she addressed a large audience at the Richmond Women's Club, dedicated to promoting self-culture and study, on "The Moral Responsibility of Man to Animals."[6] Mary Johnston, enlisted to pour tea, thought she appeared frightened but in earnest. The next day, Glasgow entertained Johnston and Laura Clay, a Kentuckian who lectured on woman suffrage. "Nothing could have been more ridiculous than the timid yet courageous air with which the few bold spirits arrived, glancing around to assure themselves that no strayed male was watching" (WW, 185).

One of the reasons that Glasgow had wanted to go to London was to meet leading figures in the suffrage movement. After Frank's death, she determin-edly kept to her itinerary. She met the poet and novelist May Sinclair (1863–1946), who worked with the Women's Freedom League and the Women Writers' Suffrage League, a nonmilitant organization. More different than alike, the women did have common interests. Sinclair had a domineering and puritanical mother, the equivalent of Glasgow's father, and had educated her-self in Greek, German philosophy, and English literature. An early advocate of the importance of psychological theories on art, especially those of Freud and Jung, she later worked for the Medico-Psychological Clinic of London and promoted the careers of poets such as Robert Frost, Ezra Pound, T. S. Eliot, and Hilda Doolittle (H.D.).[7] At the time she made Glasgow welcome, Sinclair had established a salon in Kensington, where she entertained intellectuals and artists such as Ford Madox Ford, Edith Wharton, and now Ellen Glasgow, who departed more amused than flattered.

After a party at Sinclair's, Glasgow told her sister Cary, she needed the consolation of bread puddings:

> In a circle of chairs arranged in the centre of the room there sat about 20 women and two men—all drinking tea & eating bread & butter in a funereal silence. She greeted us in a whisper & placed us with our backs two inches from the stove where we sat with the perspiring falling from our faces, in a silence as profound as that about us. In the middle of the room a sullen, handsome . . . coloured girl sat all alone on a high chair, with a stolid & angry look on her face, drinking tea & eating plumcake as hard as she could & nobody addressed a word to her from the beginning to the end of the performance. Behind her a very large man entered & stood perfectly still, clenching & unclenching his fists. At the end of 20 minutes an idea seized him & he darted over, took up a plate of plum cake & handed it about.[8]

Glasgow left the party feeling that Sinclair, who resembled a "frightened mouse," had ignored her. She had no idea that the event had been held in her honor.

Despite the misunderstanding, Glasgow admired Sinclair. Sinclair had joined an army of women ready to march, even to die, for the very cause Mary Johnston, Cary, and she herself ardently espoused. With Sinclair's probable intercession, Glasgow met with Emmeline Pankhurst, the leader of the Women's Social and Political Union, and Lady Lytton, whose politically driven hunger strikes eventually left her partially paralyzed. The example of these women inspired Glasgow to accept Sinclair's invitation to march in a suffrage parade. Because of likely arrests, Sinclair warned her to drop out before the end. Glasgow found the experience exhilarating—the ranks of women, sometimes in the thousands, moving like a single body fixed on one goal. The previous year, for example, 13,000 women marched from the Embankment to Albert Hall and the next summer, on June 18, 1910, the members of the Women Writers' Suffrage League, including Sinclair and Alice Meynell, marched four abreast to the music of forty different bands. Each woman carried a goose quill and a black-and-white banner emblazoned with the name of a female predecessor, such as George Eliot, Fanny Burney, or Elizabeth Barrett Browning.[9]

For Glasgow, these marches approximated her wish for communion with an "Absolute" (WW, 166). In this she differed from veterans of other wars and virtuous causes perhaps only in the degree of her irony. Her objectivity made her a poor soldier—as *The Battle-Ground* might have suggested—and a disappointed mystic. While her sympathy lay with "those militant suffragists" (186), she understood the complex lines of allegiance that could unite women politically if not socially. Her most outspoken advocate for women's suffrage, Miss Motoaca Bland (*The Romance of a Plain Man* [1909]), works for the emancipation of women who oppress women, and women who love oppression (206).

In spite of new friends and worthy causes, the trip to England marked a low point in Glasgow's life. She later thanked Patterson for her forbearance: "Dear Precious," she wrote, "the further I get from England the more I realize what beautiful patience & sympathy you showed me every minute. I don't believe anybody else in the world would have been—or could have been— as understanding as you were there." [10] Glasgow wondered what awaited her at One West Main. Because Frank had gone so quickly, would she have to remind herself that he had not just stepped out for a walk? She could imagine his footsteps echoing on the long upstairs staircase (*WW,* 183), his presence asserting itself more strongly in death than in life.

II

When Glasgow returned to Richmond in the middle of July, she found her father grown old and irascible. She also found Cary, who seldom left her new bedroom on the southwest corner of the first floor, gradually succumbing to cancer.

Every room in One West Main held perturbing memories. Glasgow could barely wait to leave again, and in August she and another friend, Julia Sully, vacationed in Colorado Springs, Colorado. The resort was the kind of place, she informed Patterson, where husbands brought "delicate wives" and a cowboy sporting a sombrero served the guests breakfast in bed. [11] Other guests teased Glasgow after the local paper declared, "Now that Miss Glasgow has come, the Rocky Mountains will have their Boswell." Evenings she and Julia sipped cocktails presented to them by a Chicago millionaire who enjoyed listening to their conversation. An avid reader of detective books, Glasgow even got the chance to solve a mystery of her own. She and Sully tracked down a reclusive Englishman living in the mountains. According to the locals, he had hidden himself away after a blighted romance and amassed a collection of prints.

Glasgow recounted the adventure to Patterson:

> We found him at last buried absolutely alive, a fine looking old man, wearing peasant clothes, & without a human being within miles & miles. He showed us a box of perfectly worthless pictures, with a dazed look, as if he hardly knew we were there. We discovered from pictures that his people were English publishers . . . with a house in the Strand.[12]

Neither the company of strangers nor the majestic landscape kept Glasgow from feeling anything but "very, very unhappy at times." The thought of Cary's sad life and her own circumscribed future depressed her "terribly." "Life is over for me, my Lizzie," she wrote. Glasgow could not get out of her mind the image of an old woman she had seen in England, probably when touring an almshouse. To her, the woman's isolation had loomed worse than death. "*That*," she told Patterson, "is the end."[13] The old woman in England and the old man in Colorado represented for Glasgow a future she did not want but felt she could not escape. Whatever One West Main held this time, she had to confront it.

III

Determined to support Cary as Cary and Walter had supported her, Glasgow returned to Richmond ready to do battle. In November, she granted an interview to advance women's suffrage. She later claimed to have spoken "the first word ever uttered in Virginia in favor of votes for women" (*WW*, 185). The interviewer, Carter W. Wormeley, assured the readers of the *Jewish Record* that no matter how pronounced Miss Glasgow's views, they could not be considered radical.[14] In Colorado, after all, women enjoyed the full privilege of franchise. Glasgow wanted readers to understand that other women, especially those in England, shared their concerns about political and economic equality. She made her argument along class lines: "I was impressed with the fact that the most ardent and enthusiastic advocates of woman's suffrage were to be found among the most exclusive, retiring, brilliant and intellectual literary circles and among the most representative classes of society." Regardless of station, no American woman could compel proper pay for her work without the vote. That fact rendered her "without voice in political or governmental affairs."[15] Woman's suffrage, she insisted, concerns itself with justice, right, and truth, the keystones of a democratic society. Finally, Glasgow assured her audience that proponents for woman's suffrage were not lesbians or anarchists.

The interview appeared one week after the formal organization of the Virginia League for Woman Suffrage. Meeting at the home of Mrs. Dabney S. Crenshaw on November 20, 1909, the group elected Lila Meade Valentine (1865–1921) president, Mary Johnston honorary vice-president, and Ellen Glasgow third vice-president. Lila Valentine had considerable experience in public health and education. By focusing attention on rat-infested classrooms, for example, she had almost single-handedly forced the city of Richmond to build a new high school.

Despite Glasgow's recognition that suffrage affected all women, the league's members came from Richmond's self-designated "best" families. Their first, as yet unofficial, meeting had occurred in the Victorian drawing room of Carrie Coleman's mother. The women sat on carved rosewood furniture as their hostess, known as the former "beauty of Winchester," served tea in china cups and sugar with silver tongs. The league found an immediate friend in the editor of the *Richmond Times-Dispatch*, Henry Sydnor Harrison, a cousin of James Branch Cabell and an admirer of Mary Johnston. When Johnston sent him a long editorial in December entitled "The Status of Woman," he barely blinked before granting her forty-eight column inches.[16]

Much of Glasgow's winter, apart from a trip to New York at the end of January, centered around the league and what Johnston called "suffrage talk." Whenever Cary felt well enough, she and Glasgow attended meetings together. Though Glasgow now spoke before the league and participated in marches (when it didn't rain and the route promised to be untaxing), she had no desire to endure the public abuse that Valentine and Johnston had begun to incite. It was a long-standing joke among her friends that she would never have considered marching in suffrage parades at all except to show that she had an "exquisite figger."[17] In 1901, the league, now called the Equal Suffrage League of Virginia, presented a petition to the state legislature for a federal amendment. Its impact can be partly measured by the formation of a rival male organization called the Anti-Suffrage League.[18] The Anti-Suffrage League had little to fear, for in 1912 the resolution for a federal amendment failed by a vote of 84 to 12.

Glasgow either spent time with her sister or worked on her current novel,

The Miller of Old Church (1911). The spring of 1910, she and Cary planned one last trip together to visit friends in Constantinople. Cary especially wanted to see recent excavations of Troy, and everyone hoped to add some joy to her life after the hardships of the last year. The sisters never got to Constantinople. Cary became so sick in Naples that they started back to New York, stopping first in Paris and then resting in Italy and Switzerland. The voyage home had some restorative effect, but not enough. A few days after reaching Richmond around the end of May, Glasgow waited as Cary prepared to leave for the hospital. Looking out a second-story window, she saw the carriage, drawn by a pair of pure white horses "with flowing silvery manes and tails" pull up to the house. To her, it seemed "the carriage of death" (*WW*, 189).

The next day Cary underwent surgery. Glasgow believed the operation had been successful until her sister Emily, visiting from West Virginia, burst into her room and cried, "Do you know that Cary is dying? Dr. Willis said I wasn't to tell you, but I have to tell somebody" (189). This was more than Glasgow could bear. She could not bring herself to enter the hospital. Berta Wellford finally told her that she had to pull herself together or Cary would know the truth. The family had agreed to shield Cary until the pain made any secret futile. Then she could make her own choice. Like Ellen and Frank, Cary saw suicide as an acceptable option.

Cary came home from the hospital that summer in an ambulance, accompanied by Anne Virginia Bennett (1884–1956), the nurse who would become Glasgow's secretary and companion. Her equanimity won the respect of all the members of the household. When any of the staff had a question, they went to her instead of Glasgow. Glasgow was too much of a perfectionist, and the smallest mishap could make "Dicey"—as the staff called her—go "on the warpath."[19]

Bennett was a handsome, efficient woman who loved fashionable clothes, especially cashmere and black chiffon. Supposedly jilted by a doctor, she developed an unwavering contempt for men. She couldn't understand why the "good Lord hadn't created all women as strong-minded as herself."[20] After 1916 Bennett became a permanent member of the Glasgow household and devoted her life to making Glasgow's more comfortable. "A.V." (as Glasgow called her) came to love One West Main and the woman who lived there more than her own nine brothers and sisters. When Glasgow traveled, Bennett insisted that she never felt lonely because the house seemed to hold Glasgow's presence in its very woodwork. If Glasgow became depressed, so did she. Bennett came to live through Glasgow, who depended on her and appreciated her without ever forgetting that she was the employer and Bennett the employee. Glasgow often entertained friends without her, for example, and after Glasgow died, no one treated Bennett as the chief mourner. Glasgow herself had not arranged for Bennett to be buried in the family plot at Hollywood Cemetery, and very few of her friends even invited Bennett to lunch or for a drive.

Bennett proved indispensable during Cary's illness. Like Eva Birdsong in *The Sheltered Life*, Cary suffered from uterine or possibly breast cancer: "She had all the horror Mother and so many women felt, of this particular malady," Glasgow explained. "But for this instinctive horror, as several physicians told me afterwards, she could easily have been saved in the beginning" (*WW*, 190). Cary lived for a little more than a year longer, first as an invalid, then slipping in and out of consciousness over the last seven months. No one told her—or needed to tell her—the inevitable. Glasgow coped by trying to make Cary's summer as happy as possible. She rented the old Rose Cottage in Warm Springs and stocked it with her sister's favorite foods and European wines. At home, she made certain that Cary had around-the-clock care. It tells us something about Glasgow that above all she wanted Cary to assert her femininity against an illness that seemed to assault it. Dressed in tea-rose chiffon gowns and lace-trimmed bed-jackets that Glasgow selected, Cary looked, through her sister's eyes, lovely to the end: "She was so thin and frail that she seemed scarcely more than a child asleep. Her small child's face was of a delicate pink, and so transparent that it was like porcelain with a light shining through" (192). During this time, Glasgow confided in no one except Berta Wellford and Anne Virginia Bennett. She hated the thought of people knowing more about her sister than Cary knew herself. Even Glasgow's father had not been told the truth about his daughter's condition for fear he would tell any casual acquaintance. Cary died on August 19, 1911. Glasgow selected a verse for her gravestone from the *Bhagavad-Gita*, a book they had studied together: "The unreal has no being," it reads. "The real never ceases to be."

IV

Despite all odds and clearly as a gift to her dying sister, Glasgow finished writing her new novel, *The Miller of Old Church*. The book's dedication—"To my sister Cary Glasgow McCormack in loving acknowledgment of help and sympathy through many years"—were the last words Cary ever read.

Inspired by Cary and maybe by her work with the Virginia League for Woman Suffrage, *The Miller of Old Church* pays tribute to the women who helped Glasgow while her sister lay ill: Mary Johnston, Berta Wellford, and Elizabeth Patterson. "The relation of woman to man," one of Glasgow's characters observes,

> was dwarfed suddenly by an understanding of the relation of woman to woman. Deeper than the dependence of sex, simpler, more natural, closer to the earth, as though it still drew its strength from the soil . . . the need of woman for woman was not written in the songs nor in the histories of men, but in the neglected and frustrated lives which the songs and the histories of men had ignored. (*Miller*, 410)

The novel's underlying feminism — or its heroine's assertion that the touch of a man's hands made her want to strike out and kill (69) — may have inspired H. L. Mencken's pronouncement that even trying his "honest darndest" (*Reviews*, xxv, 153) there were novels like *The Miller of Old Church* he simply could not read.

Mencken aside, *The Miller of Old Church* received a much warmer reception than the three preceding books. Glasgow had conceived the novel, set in Brunswick County at the turn of the century (1898–1902), as a companion to *The Deliverance*, which spanned 1878 to 1900.

The Miller of Old Church raises questions about sex and violence that Glasgow would return to after the First World War, but its primary focus centers on class. Glasgow frames her discussion of class as many nineteenth- and early twentieth-century African American writers did about race. Her heroine, Molly Merryweather, has a choice, what the nineteenth-century African American writer Frances Harper called "two offers." Under the terms of her father's will, she stands to inherit a small fortune if she lives with either her cousin Jonathan or his mother, Angela. Or, she can marry Abel Rivercombe, the local miller interested in politics. Molly eventually chooses the miller, who represents the future of the South's rising middle class. Like many Glasgow protagonists, Molly is the product of opposites. Unlike them, she does not have to choose between father or mother or Calvinism and Anglicism. Rivercombe promises that their marriage will not violate the "integrity" of her personality (*Miller*, 256). Although this is the idea that had most concerned Glasgow about Cary's illness, she levels her most scathing criticism at women of her own class, exemplified by Angela Gay, a despotic invalid who rules through sentiment: "She had surrendered all rights in order to grasp more effectively at all privileges" (72). The efforts of Angela's family to preserve her illusions end repeatedly in misfortune. While Angela represents the myopia of the Old South, she more specifically conjures the ghosts of invalid Glasgow women. *The Miller of Old Church* heralded Glasgow's return to a more immediate and less ethereal past. Her next novel, *Virginia* (1913), would mark a recognition of the intersection of personal and cultural histories.

V

Cary's death ended a chapter in Glasgow's Richmond life. She needed a place to breathe, a place where she could lose herself in the crowd. New York City beckoned. In August, she and Carrie Coleman looked at apartment after apartment until Glasgow found one "high up on Central Park" (*WW*, 194). Her niece Josephine remembered it being on the then-unfashionable side of the park behind the Metropolitan Museum of Art.[21] The New York that Glasgow knew remained a circumscribed world. In a city teeming with life, with ethnic neighborhoods each with its own customs, foods, and fashions; with museums, music, and theater, she lived almost like a recluse. She needed the time and the distance to mourn her sister and to make decisions about her own future. The city did not speak to her as it does to so many writers. If Walt Whitman roamed its every corner and Theodore Dreiser looked in every shop window (between his so-called sexual rounds with women), Ellen Glasgow enjoyed the luxury of being anonymous. She felt none of the wonder of her fellow Southerner, Thomas Wolfe, who reveled in the city's sheer immensity and imagined millions of lives enfolding. For obvious reasons, Glasgow dreaded the noise and jostling of crowds.

Like other American writers, Glasgow felt the need to escape the demands of her hometown, sometimes of the United States itself. Unlike Henry James and Edith Wharton, however, she did not have the choice of expatriation. Her disability limited her movement, both physically and emotionally. New York was a compromise, a place close to Richmond by train but a world apart. Glasgow settled there, much as Gertrude Stein, who never learned French and yet settled in France. An exquisite stranger, Glasgow lived among its people, sympathizing but never truly understanding their inner lives or the ministrants of their many faiths. She lived, as she herself reminds us, in exile.

It took Glasgow months to get situated. She chose a color scheme of soft dull browns and greens, and one reporter noted that she seemed to emanate from her surroundings themselves: "Her gown is a tone deeper than her brown cushions and catches a sheen from the Japanese gold wall behind her. More brilliant still is her burnished nimbus of red-brown hair" (*RD*, 21). Glasgow had brought with her much of the drawing-room furniture from One West Main—a small painted fire screen, a Chippendale desk, and Queen Anne chairs. Consciously or unconsciously, she had recreated her house in Richmond, the place that had taken possession of her—or she it. No doubt the room gave her a needed sense of continuance.

During this time in New York, Glasgow cemented her friendship with the testy Kentucky writer James Lane Allen (1849–1925). The pair had begun corresponding in 1910 when she sent him a volume of her poetry, and he responded by saying she must be his friend. Glasgow's move to New York made that possible, though her bereavement and ill health confined their friendship largely to an exchange of letters. The two should have been comrades. Instead, they had a knack for irritating one another. Neither could ever say the right or soothing thing. She unerringly affronted his dignity, and he couldn't tease without hurting. Allen came from a well-to-do family impoverished by the Civil War and had earned a living as a college professor before becoming a writer. In the same year that Glasgow published *The Descendant*, he published his most popular book, *The Choir Invisible* (1897). It and *The Reign of Law: A Tale of the Kentucky Hemp Fields* (1900) concerned themselves with evolution, a subject always close to Glasgow's heart. When Glasgow began their correspondence in 1910, he had recently published two novels after a six-year hiatus, *The Bride of the Mistletoe* (1909) and *The Doctor's Christmas Eve* (1910). The public liked neither.

In a sense, Glasgow replaced Allen's lost audience, though she had never had a very high opinion of his Kentucky romances. To her, he appeared lonely and resigned, while the "grand manner, so much admired in his youth, had become slightly pompous."[22] Allen was pompous and needed reassuring. "I take it for granted that you, as the rest of us," he wrote, "suffer from the feeling that the book sent forth into the world is hardly more than the shadow of that substance which remains within us."[23]

From the beginning Allen's humor had a flirtatious, slightly aggressive note that recalls Henry James's attitude toward Edith Wharton: "When you have won the fight against vivisection in favor of the lower animals," he told the future vice-president of Richmond's SPCA in January 1910, "please write a book on the manner in which ladies try to vivisect all higher animals that disagree with them! And in this book, please enter a plea for the world-wide organization of women against needless torture of each other."[24] Allen's humor held Glasgow at a distance. He liked nothing better than for her to take offense. After visiting her sickroom, he taunted, "I am glad that the hair hangs down the back and not from a nail! I *had* had my doubts about *that,* too." Another visit assured him that her illness did not stop her from being perverse.[25]

At the same time that Allen challenged Glasgow, he also sought her praise and advice about revisions. Glasgow told his would-be biographer that she had tried to do "what was required of her in the way of adulation—and invariably failed."[26] Still she hoped (as she might have of her own biographer) that he would stress Allen's "courage, his tenderness of heart, his patience, his fidelity, his fortitude in affliction and disillusionment."[27] That he had supported and cared for his invalid sister excused, in Glasgow's mind, much of his unpleasantness. Though she had begun by matching Allen's banter, she soon learned that silence worked best. He could not stand to be ignored.

Their waspish correspondence continued intermittently over the next thirteen years until they had a serious falling out in the summer of 1923: "Your letter has just come," he informed her. "There have not been any 'indignations': I have merely offered 'passive resistance' to your indifference! In your last letter you rather laid down the conditions in which you would continue to write, and I was excluded at birth from having conditions laid down to me—*any* conditions by *anybody:* a terrible way to be born but my sole way!" Allen died two years later, still wanting to talk to Glasgow but unable to do so without alienating her. "Have you ever realized that I greatly care?" he asked.[28] Glasgow did, and despite her feeling that he was impossibly sensitive and misanthropic, she knew that he had offered her real friendship.[29]

Glasgow's relationships with men tended to fall into one of two patterns: the first reminiscent of her relationship with Walter McCormack, where she romanticized and respected the man; the other reminiscent of her agonistic relationship with her father. Her friendship with Allen fell into the second category, but it also foreshadowed and to some extent paralleled her on-again-off-again friendship with James Branch Cabell. She had yet to find a man who could love her as she was, appreciating her peculiar blend of moonlight and iron. The older she grew, the harder she found it to behave—as she phrased it—in the "classic feminine manner."[30]

VI

Allen's antagonism toward Glasgow's feminism may have contributed to the cooling of their friendship in 1912. That year and the next Glasgow actively, if less fervently, supported the cause of woman's suffrage. Neither "woman's acknowledged intuition nor woman's unacknowledged intelligence," she believed, "would change so much as an atom in man's practical politics" (*WW*, 187). Nevertheless, she still marched in an occasional parade with old friends like Johnston and Willcox and new ones like Bennett. On May 4, for instance, Johnston led the delegation from Virginia. Many of the 20,000 participants who walked from Washington Square, up Fifth Avenue, to Carnegie Hall in New York City dressed in white. The women who rode on horseback reminded spectators, including 1,000 male supporters, of an army of Joan of Arcs.[31]

Glasgow contributed to the cause by writing a poem entitled "The Call." It appeared in the November 1912 issue of *Current Literature* as well as the July issue of *Collier's Magazine*. "Woman called to woman at the daybreak!" it begins:

> When the bosom of the deep was stirred . . .
> Queen or slave or bond or free, we battled . . .
> Hidden at the heart of earth we waited,
> Watchful, patient, silent, secret, true;
> All the terrors of the chains that bound us
> Man has seen, but only woman knew!
>
> Woman knew! Yea, still, and woman knoweth!—
> Thick the shadows of our prison lay—
> Yet that knowledge in our hearts we treasure
> Till the dawning of the perfect day.
>
> Onward now as in the long, dim ages,
> Onward to the light where Freedom lies;
> Woman calls to woman to awaken!
> Woman calls to woman to arise![32]

The poem did not adequately reflect Glasgow's present feelings or politics (or for that matter her literary talents). Since her move to New York, she told Lila Meade Valentine, she hadn't had much heart in anything—not even women's suffrage. "I used to once," she wrote, "but I haven't now."[33]

Apart from a few publications, Glasgow almost seems to have disappeared from the world during 1911 and 1912. While close friends visited her, she still felt unready to return to Richmond. In March 1912, for example, she wrote Lizzie Patterson that she would spend a few days in Richmond at the beginning of May unless she could not make up her mind to go back. She dreaded seeing the place again.[34] From Glasgow's extant medical prescriptions, we know that during this time she suffered from stomach and skin ailments, headaches, and neuralgia.

Despite recurrent health problems and worries about money, Glasgow continued to work on *Virginia* (1913), the novel that had pushed its way into her distracted mind during Cary's illness. In January 1912, she told her agent that she expected to finish the book in a year and that it would be "an analytical story" of about 150,000 words. The writing of *Virginia* marked a new phase in Glasgow's method of composition. Apart from her first book, *The Descendant* (1897), she had read every subsequent book aloud to Cary, discussing it chapter by chapter. *Virginia* was the first novel Glasgow wrote without her sister's silent collaboration. That change marked, in her mind, the end of her long apprenticeship. She now had the novelist's full command of her subject.[35] Almost by default and with great unease, she had become the sole authority on whose "word" her work stood or fell. Glasgow completed *Virginia*, published in May 1913, on schedule. Its dedication read: "To the Radiant Spirit who was my sister Cary Glasgow McCormack."

While Glasgow sat day after day and month after month, brooding on Cary's lamentable past, she saw how one life could represent a whole system of failed beliefs and behaviors. If Glasgow found, with Cary's passing, an independence she had not sought, she also found a form best suited for her talents: the novel of manners. When novels of manners are "great," she realized, they do not record superficial behavior, but examine the codes that govern people's lives. And like most codes or philosophies, they surrender to other manners and ideas in the making. Glasgow had learned (as Henry James noted) that what we call experience is our apprehension and our measure of what happens to us as social creatures. In this way, *Virginia* became her most directly autobiographical book to date, for she inverts the form of her previous "social histories" by subordinating the broadly historical to the intensely personal.

Glasgow had an imagination ruled by the tyranny of place. As its title suggests, *Virginia* is the story of a woman and a place, the one place where Glasgow discovered she could write. It shows her trying to make sense of a past she fled in Richmond, of her sister's death, and her feelings for her father. These feelings underlie *Virginia*, but at the same time they intensify a larger vision. Glasgow localizes the whole history of the South in the state of Virginia. In this respect, she was the kind of regional writer Marjorie Rawlings called "accidental." She used a specialized locale as "a logical or fitting background" for "particular thoughts or emotions" crying out for articulation.[36] This brand of "regionalism" presupposes a consciousness that a given locality generates its own legacies of thought and conduct. With this idea in mind, Allen Tate argued that literary artists make poor colonials. Glasgow came to understand that regionalism may be "limited by geography but not in time." She saw the present growing out of the past, and responded by "offering as an imaginative subject the plight of human beings as it has been and will doubtless continue to be, here and in other parts of the world."[37] She believed both in an old-fashioned "universal" and in the intrinsic value of art for life's sake.[38]

Originally Glasgow intended *Virginia* to be a candid and ironic portrait of a Southern lady and the Victorian tradition (*CM*, 77). As she wrote, however, "the simple goodness of Virginia's nature had turned a comedy of manners into a tragedy of human fate" (79). She could not deny the reality or the significance of her sister and mother's lives. Ill-educated, sentimental, and submissive, Virginia sacrifices youth and beauty in the service of a husband and children helpless not to outgrow her. Once the feminine ideal, Virginia gives way to the new woman, represented not only by her husband's lover, a woman of burning vitality and intellect, but by her own daughters, Lucy a pre-flapper and Jennifer a young Jane Addams and possibly a lesbian.[39]

Because Glasgow envisioned "the Problem of the South" as one of race as well as gender,[40] she has little sympathy for the young Virginia, who can gaze nonchalantly past a man beating a mule toward the sight of the old slave market. Virginia does not have the imagination to feel the horror of people having been sold there. With a slight adjustment of vision, however, "Virginia" could realize that the barriers of knowledge and race obscure our common humanity. Virginia's philosophy of what Glasgow would call in a 1916 interview "evasive idealism" has negatively determined the status of women,[41] the plights of black Southerners, and the state (or state of mind) of Virginia.

Glasgow argues that the problem of the South—and of Virginia—will only be corrected when the spirit of "patriarchal tyranny" passes (*Virginia*, 272). She posits that spirit in Cyrus Treadwell, the town's leading patriarch. Though Cyrus represents the new economic order, he claims the social privileges of the old. He does nothing to provide for Mandy, his former mistress, or his mulatto son, Jubal. Eighteen years later, he has trouble recognizing her as the woman now doing his family's laundry. In turn, Mandy has learned the lesson of the master. When Cyrus responds to her sexually, she tries to turn the situation to her monetary advantage. In Cyrus's mind,

> there came [into her face] an expression which was half scornful, half inviting, yet so little personal that it might have been worn by one of her tree-top ancestors while he looked down from his sheltering boughs on a superior species of the jungle. The chance effect of light and shadow on a grey rock was hardly less human or more primitive. (*Virginia*, 129)

Mandy's references to their shared past as well as her assumption of equality infuriates Cyrus. "It's a pretty pass things have come to," he thinks, "when men have to protect themselves from [the claims of] negro women" (130). Dismissing Mandy, he rushes off to rescue his impecunious nephew, thinking, "I'm not one to let those of my own blood come to want" (131).[42] Glasgow's ironic juxtaposition of the two incidents supports the claim Cyrus wants to deny while undercutting any sense of his inherent racial superiority. He has made the women in his life what they are, and his refusal to recognize either his culpability or his mulatto son eventually leads to civil unrest. Jubal's murder of a white policeman, a kind of social patricide, functions as a warning.

Glasgow saw the soul of Virginia much as she saw her own, torn between hereditary opposites. She patterned Cyrus, an industrialist, after two male family members: her uncle Joseph Reid Anderson and her father, Francis Glasgow. The *Tread*well Tobacco Factory evokes the *Tred*egar Iron Works not just in name but also in its riverbank location and deadly business—the production of cigarettes, already suspected of causing respiratory diseases. Anderson and Francis Glasgow believed that every individual had a predetermined place in life. Cyrus's affair with Mandy and his wife's subsequent illness replicates Glasgow's memory of her parents. Her inability to make Virginia wholly ironic or tragic highlights the problem of autobiographical fiction, in which the author's ambivalence rebels against reductive summation. In the future, Glasgow's genius would lie in extrapolating from the autobiographical. She had realized that fiction calls not for the supposedly dispassionate eye of the historian or scientist but for passionate engagement.

VII

The mixed reception of *Virginia* disheartened Glasgow. The *New York Sun* summed up the world of the novel as a place where "every woman suffers and every man is vile," while the *Sewanee Review* lauded Glasgow for her contribution to the feminist movement. The *Richmond Times-Dispatch* alluded to the polemical nature of the novel, noting that in late April Glasgow had spoken in behalf of suffrage in Norfolk, Virginia, where she was a guest of Judge and Mrs. Louise Collier Willcox. Forever contrary, H. L. Mencken, in an essay called "Various Bad Novels," showed the first signs of succumbing to a Glasgow story. The book may not be a masterpiece, nor even a secure second-rater, he told his readers, but he found it "well written, as far as novels go in our fair land." [43] Whatever the critics thought, Glasgow knew that the ironic overtones of *Virginia*, "the relentless logic of events, and the application of modern theories in psychology," made it the most "modern" of her books to date (*CM*, 94). Not for a moment did she doubt that Cary would have loved it.

As Glasgow worked on her next novel, *Life and Gabriella* (1916), a story that contains dissimilar sisters, she might have thought of her relationship to her own sisters. For all her compatibility with Cary and Rebe, they also had experienced hurt feelings and jealousies. Glasgow's relationship with her niece Josephine warmed her toward Josephine's mother, Annie, but in truth the sisters had little in common except good will. With her oldest sister, Emily, she had even less in common and a fair measure of ill will. Glasgow still resented Emily's championship of their father and her part in disposing of their mother's dog. Eighteen years her senior, Emily had seemed the wicked sister of fairy tales, censorious and prudish enough to conceal a copy of *Moths*, Ouida's risqué romance, beneath her shirtwaists. When Emily returned home after Cary's death to care for their father, her relationship with Glasgow did not improve. The servants wondered if she drank secretly, and her alleged rages used to send the daughter of James Anderson into hiding. Although Glasgow thought she remained afraid of life, her death from cancer in 1913 came as a shocking reminder of her family's accursed luck. If Glasgow refused to pretend to false sentiment, she also mourned the past.

Glasgow hoped that time and distance could create forgetfulness. In the spring of 1914, she and Louise Willcox decided to go to Europe before world events would make it no longer possible. This trip differed from the last, for now Glasgow went as a recognized novelist intent on meeting writers whom she had long admired. The women began their vacation in London and stayed near Arthur's house at the Hotel Curzon. Although Glasgow thought his friends fashionable, rather than literary, she was flattered that they claimed to have read her books. They particularly amused Willcox, a respected editor and critic, by confusing her with the sentimental poet Ella Wheeler Wilcox. Willcox joked that she would have liked the poet's fame without being held responsible for her verse.

Glasgow and Willcox did what most tourists do: they lunched at Windsor, attended Shaw's *Pygmalion*, and went shopping. Glasgow, who liked to talk about patterns and materials for the latest fashions, bought a "ravishing" dress and cape of brown crepe,[44] which she might have worn when Walter Hines Page, now ambassador to the Court of St. James, invited her to dinner at the American embassy. For the most part, Glasgow preferred visits to the countryside. From the Stoke-Poges churchyard near the tomb of Thomas Gray, she sent Rebe a forget-me-not.

Glasgow's real adventures began in June when she visited Thomas Hardy, the "great" English writer she had so long admired. Glasgow arrived at Max Gate, the home of Hardy and his second wife, for afternoon tea and instantly fell in love with Wessex, Hardy's wire-haired terrier. She found her host wistful and kind, immaculately neat in his appearance, with a face small and worn to sharpness (*WW*, 197). The two writers talked frankly about their work. Hardy, who had long been writing poetry instead of fiction, told Glasgow that he thought his poetry would outlive his prose, which his wife had first read when she was 12 years old. "Of all the human beings I have known," Glasgow wrote in her autobiography, "none could have been more natural and less pretentious" (198). Their philosophies of life seemed in accord, especially, in Glasgow's mind, their sympathy for the "inarticulate agony" (198) of animals. But of course they shared a temperamental pessimism and a belief in the inevitability of human suffering.

Besides Hardy, Glasgow met Joseph Conrad, Arnold Bennett, John Galsworthy, and Henry James. Glasgow and Willcox visited Conrad and his family at Capel House in Kent, where they were then living. Glasgow, who admired *Heart of Darkness* and felt herself familiar with almost every line he had written, found Conrad capricious and fascinating. She may have been the only person ever to describe him as having a "lovable personality" (201). Conrad treated her with courtesy. He showed her manuscript drafts with hardly a word left unchanged. Before they left, he told Louise Willcox that Glasgow was "doing better work than any other American woman novelist"

(201). Missing the condescension, Glasgow repeated the remark. She thought him a natural innocent.

Glasgow had a charming naivete about these male writers. She perceived Galsworthy to be a perfect gentleman of the old school, though she later faulted him, as she did William Dean Howells, for a failure to divorce sex from sentimentality. Glasgow compared Ada Galsworthy to the woman her husband had "idealized in *The Patrician,* lovely and passive, with the consecrated air that so frequently invites martyrdom" (202). Ada might have seemed like her own Virginia come to life. Galsworthy gave Glasgow autographed copies of *The Country House* and *The Purple Land,* and on her return to Richmond she sent him and Ada *The Battle-Ground* and *Virginia.* He complimented her portrayal of Betty Ambler and the Major, while Ada, noticing the dedication to *Virginia,* wondered if Cary could have been any more radiant than they found her sister Ellen to be.[45]

Glasgow and Willcox continued their literary tour of England at the home of Arnold Bennett, whom Ada Galsworthy had described as "a bit of a bounder" (*WW,* 203). Glasgow liked him and his "very French" wife, Marguerite. Her remark that *The Old Wives' Tale* ranked among the six greatest English novels flattered him, and he too gave her an inscribed copy.

Glasgow had a less successful meeting with Henry James, a writer whom she had early admired. Through the intercession of a friend, she and Willcox received invitations to a reception given by Margaret Brooke, the Ranee of Sarawak. James also attended, and Willcox's brother, Price Collier, introduced them. Unaware of Collier's role in the rejection of her first novel, Glasgow considered him a friend or at least someone she could understand more than she could understand James. James's "hesitating, polysyllabic, and endlessly discursive soliloquies" (206) made him unintelligible to someone with a hearing impairment. Sensing his kindness, Glasgow nevertheless criticized him for his snobbishness. He appeared less real than Hardy or Conrad and more foppish. Incredibly, she praised him as a simple man—as, without words, he might have seemed.

We can only guess what would have happened if Edith Wharton in the hopes of seeing her friend James had also attended the Ranee of Sarawak's reception. Certainly James would have enjoyed the spectacle of his hostess and old friend skirting the topic of William Morton Fullerton, a bisexual journalist whom all three—Brooke, Wharton, and James himself—had loved. Or he might have garnered a *donnée*—a kernel for a story—in the meeting of two grand dames of American letters. Probably the women would have found a cozy corner to chat about books and dogs and writing, but most likely Glasgow would have interpreted Wharton's shyness as coldness or class snobbery, and Wharton would not have been above a sly murmur to James, "Glasgow? a Scottish writer?" Wherever Glasgow went that summer, she sensed a slight disdain for American letters, even from Americans themselves.

On June 18, 1914, Glasgow and Willcox sailed home on the German liner *Imperator.* Like other wealthy tourists, Glasgow enjoyed crossing the Atlantic in a kind of floating hotel, whose appointments, from mahogany paneling to crystal chandeliers, matched those in the lobbies of the *nouveau luxe* hotels springing up in Europe. Glasgow was not above asking her publisher to alert the crew to her presence. This time, Walter Hines Page asked his friend Theodore Roosevelt, who was returning from Africa, to look after Glasgow and her companion. The former president, an intimate of Edith Wharton, duly invited them to tea in his imperial suite. He proved the perfect host. Even when speaking to another person, he turned carefully in her direction or spoke at exactly the right pitch. The most literary of politicians, he had read her books and, even better, he could talk about them intelligently. Had anyone told her that she would have liked this "roving barbarian of the West," this "big game hunter" (208), she would have laughed. Yet, like him she did. In retrospect, it seems strange that Glasgow, who had a lifelong interest in politics, left no record of speaking to America's best-known politician about current affairs in Europe or Asia. Roosevelt's second term as president had ended just five years before in 1909, and three years earlier he had received the Nobel Peace Prize for mediating the end of the Russo-Japanese War. Roosevelt, who enjoyed the company of artists as much as cowboys, prizefighters, and explorers, seems to have kept the conversation gratifyingly focused on her. She left most impressed by his enormous energy, something she would later admire in her fiancé Henry Anderson.

Just weeks after Glasgow's arrival in New York, the First World War broke out. It seemed incredible to her—especially considering her encounter with Roosevelt—that they heard no rumors of war, except a feared uprising in Ulster. In August, an era ended, for the world at large and for Glasgow herself. Within the next two years, fate would obey Amélie Rives's command to fill Glasgow's arms with *all* that could satisfy her. "You were made for love," Rives assured her.[46] Now it seemed about to happen—a comedy of errors that would consume twenty years of Ellen Glasgow's life and all her illusions, including—as she wrote—the illusion of her own disillusionment.

CHAPTER 7

NEW BEGINNINGS

1915–1922

Oh, life is a glorious cycle of song,
A medley of extemporanea;
And love is a thing that can never go wrong;
And I am Marie of Rumania.

Dorothy Parker

I

ELLEN GLASGOW'S FATALISTIC RESPONSE to the First World War differed from that of female contemporaries such as Dorothy Canfield and Edith Wharton. Canfield, for example, wrote home from the front,[1] and Wharton marshaled her tremendous powers of organization to establish and superintend the American Hostel for Refugees. In contrast, Glasgow withdrew and fretted. Human beings, she thought, would never cease to kill one another for the highest possible motives. Images of the war replaced girlhood nightmares of a dog run to death or a child abducted and murdered. Night after night she awakened from dreams of "gangrened flesh on barbed wires, the dead stiffened in horror, the eyeless skulls and the bared skeletons, the crosses and the poppies" (*WW,* 233). Neither volunteering for Red Cross service, as did Anne Virginia Bennett, nor raising money for humanitarian causes, Glasgow almost sat out the war. The war, however, would affect her in ways she could not imagine, making her desirous of new beginnings and drawing her back to the home where she had suffered. Above all, it linked her fate with the fate of a queen and a country thousands of miles from Richmond.

II

In the summer of 1915, the war might not have existed for Glasgow. Having resolved to suppress thoughts of the horrors in Europe, she looked forward to traveling west to California, a state known for new beginnings. Like Huckleberry Finn, she yearned to begin again in the territories. It was almost as if Glasgow intuited something good about to happen, as if the world held out its hand and she just had to step forward. Her childhood friend Carrie Coleman had agreed to accompany her to California. Carrie, whose first name makes it easy to confuse her with the other Cary in Glasgow's life, had become a sister more than friend. She wore the world, according to a Coleman family servant, "like a loose garment."[2] Glasgow always associated Carrie with Jerdone Castle, the magical place both their families had owned and where Carrie had been born. Carrie's father had been a surgeon in the Confederate Army, caring for General Lee's wounded. After the war, he worked as a government engineer, at one time involved in the construction of levees on the Mississippi River. Carrie also grew up in a religious household, for her mother had converted to Catholicism three months before her birth. But unlike Glasgow, she continued to practice her childhood faith throughout her adult life.

For her part, Carrie loved and humored Glasgow. She readily admitted to not understanding or even finishing her friend's books—a fact that amused Glasgow. While not intellectual, Carrie had a rarer gift: people felt better, even special, in her presence. One friend commented that when she wore yellow and blue, she resembled an Easter egg, full of sweet surprises. Customers who visited her antique shop across from the Jefferson Hotel went away feeling that she had given them a gift from her own home. When Carrie married late in life, at the age of 43, four years after the friends' trip to California, Glasgow insisted on having the ceremony take place in the front drawing room of One West Main. The room, filled with antiques, such as a large mirror originally ordered by James Madison, reflected a sense of continuity the First World War had temporarily interrupted. By symbolically giving the bride away, Glasgow demonstrated the centrality of her role in Carrie's life. She knew better than to repeat her mistake with Rebe and had only kind things to say about Carrie's new husband, Frank W. Duke.

Glasgow could not have had a better traveling companion than Carrie, who assumed the social responsibilities and the burden of good talk that had previously fallen to Cary, Rebe, and other friends. Her often ceaseless chatter created a space where Glasgow could rest from the constant burden of trying to hear and perform. Carrie could make Glasgow laugh as uncontrollably as she had decades ago at Jerdone Castle, especially when they teased each other about "beaux." Watching Carrie polish her shoes and don pale gray stockings for a lunch date, Glasgow declared the symptoms "serious." Carrie only half-joked about Glasgow falling for a colonel in the army. "I'd love to live out here," Glasgow coyly told Rebe, "for the air and the flowers." [3]

Both women thought of California as "a land of perfect enchantment." It appeared everything that Virginia was not: raw, vigorous, and free. Glasgow felt immediately at home in San Francisco, where everyone—from the members of "The California Branch of the Society of Americans of Royal Descent" to the commissioner of the Virginia Building at the Exposition— greeted her. In California, she took pride in her heritage without resenting its demands. When the commissioner of the Virginia Building asked her to serve as his "official hostess," she readily agreed. She and Carrie alternately felt they were visiting royalty and ordinary tourists. One day, they had passes to the fairgrounds; another they saw *A Midsummer Night's Dream* performed under the stars. On Mount Tamalpais, Glasgow walked among the redwoods, escorted by one of what seemed a gratifying gaggle of reporters and photographers seeking interviews. The ex-mayor of San Francisco and vice-president of the World's Columbian Commission, James Duval Phelan, invited them to his home.[4] Through him, they met the prolific novelist Gertrude Atherton (1857–1948), remembered today, if at all, for *Black Oxen* (1923) or her historical books like *The Conqueror* (1902). Everything seemed larger than life out West, from the towering redwoods to elephantine daisies and hollyhocks growing in Phelan's garden.

California never figured as a setting in Glasgow's novels, but it offered an imaginative alternative to New York and Virginia. Like many travelers, Glasgow expected that a shifting of scene would effect a cure for the soul. She had lost, for the time being, her obsession to write. Unlike so many travelers, however, she left scant account of her transcontinental trip. Where are the descriptions of the Great Divide, the salt flats of Utah, or the cosmopolitan port of San Francisco and its breathtaking views of the Golden Gate? Glasgow did not associate Yosemite, which inspired painters like Albert Bierstadt and William Keith, with the sublime majesty of the Jungfrau. Rather, she experienced a landscape already tamed. Shutting out the sheer vastness of the West, she might have been taking a garden tour or a stroll in Kensington Gardens. The West did not take root in her imagination as it had that of Brett Harte and Mary Austin. She gave barely a thought to its diverse peoples or its history alien to her own. The same can be said of Glasgow's tours of Europe, which she experienced largely through her reading of novels and *Baedeker*. She traveled in Europe as she had crossed the Atlantic, in an expensive cocoon. Glasgow's disability and her temperament led her to experience these places from the outside. To this extent, she remained a provincial Southerner. It did not matter whether she went west or east. Defining all places by Richmond, she lived like a tourist everywhere else.

III

Glasgow described *Life and Gabriella*, a "new woman" novel subtitled *The Story of a Woman's Courage* (1916), as her "final departure" from the Victorian tradition (*CM*, 97). Originally she thought of the novel as a sequel to *Virginia* (1913) and the second book in an uncompleted trilogy of "American womanhood." She intended to argue that a woman's influence would always remain subtle and indirect.[5] More androgynous than her other heroines, Gabriella is, like Glasgow, a belle without beauty and a romantic without blinders. In some ways she succumbs to the male plot Wharton manipulated so well in *The Custom of the Country* (1913). Having fallen passionately in love with a pretty face, Gabriella soon discovers that her husband's "prolonged silences covered poverty of ideas rather than abundance of feeling."[6] *Life and Gabriella* echoes much of Glasgow's earlier criticism of marriage, neurasthenic women, and altruistic mothers of selfish children. It differs in its frank treatment of female sexuality. Unlike Edna Pontellier of *The Awakening* (1899), Gabriella refuses to protect her children from the consequences of her passion. Her attraction to her first husband allows Glasgow to explore the force and amorality of sex—a topic no longer forbidden in fiction. Praising the shape of its narrative, Joseph Conrad pronounced *Life and Gabriella* to be of "the very first class order."[7]

Because Glasgow made it obvious that Gabriella and her second husband would enjoy more than a companionate marriage, Richmonders wondered how a maiden lady could write so realistically about sex. Friends who knew nothing about Glasgow's relationship with Gerald remained surprised that she never married, "if only to have the experience. She had so much curiosity, it would be reasonable to expect her to do it just to know what it was all about."[8] Berta Wellford believed that she "felt free to do things in New York" that she would not have done in Richmond. "Only two or three of us knew about the men in New York," Wellford confided, including her landlord, a Mr. Mulhern, whom Glasgow used as a model for her male protagonist in *Life and Gabriella*.[9] In Richmond, Glasgow always acted discreetly.

IV

Glasgow spent the spring of 1915 in New York, returning to Richmond in October. James Lane Allen couldn't believe that she had left New York without saying goodbye: "It was not very kind," he complained, "it was not very friendly, it looked very indifferent, and it left me with seemingly no assurance that my letters might not be as my visits had been—of no noticeable impact."[10] The reasons for Glasgow's departure—whether economic or personal—remain obscure. Certainly the change would circumscribe her freedom. But Glasgow had greater concerns. Her father had been in poor health since his 1912 retirement from the Tredegar Iron Works, a firm he served for more than sixty-three years. Every morning he had walked the dozen or so blocks from his house on West Main to his job as manager of the Works, accompanied by the son of his cook. Behind yellowing lace curtains, elderly women lingered to watch him pass. Now there were rumors, which may have influenced Glasgow's decision to return home, that he had proposed marriage to Anne Virginia Bennett, who had remained at One West Main after Emily's death in 1913. Bennett had no interest in marrying her employer, though in later years she enjoyed reminding Glasgow that she could have been her stepmother. Whatever the reasons for Glasgow's decision to scurry home, the fact so pleased her father that he changed his will: she was to inherit all the household furniture after she paid for packing and shipping the items her sisters had selected.

Francis Glasgow lived only a month after Christmas. On January 29, 1916, he died, his final illness precipitated by a fall on the icy front steps of One

West Main. Glasgow's sister, Annie Clark, who was visiting at the time, described his death to her son, Glasgow: "Grandfather was sitting in his big arm chair in the library. He seemed very weak, but not like any one near death. His mind was perfectly clear." He went to sleep downstairs on a bed they had made for him so he wouldn't have to climb the stairs and he never woke up again. Neither Ellen, who had gone to New York for treatment of an abscessed tooth, nor Rebe, at the hospital with her son, was there. Arthur watched with Annie. "He wants Ellen to continue to live in this house," she explained, "it belongs to him, you know—but nobody knows what Ellen will do, & it is going to be a hard problem for her to decide. She cannot live here in this big house alone—but I think she will probably arrange to stay in here for a while, any way." Annie ended her letter by assuring her son that he had inherited outright his grandfather's watch and his collection of Walter Scott novels. She thought that Ellen would let him have any other books he wanted.[11]

Francis's children respected his request that at his funeral the elders of the Second Presbyterian Church would serve as honorary pallbearers. They buried him in Hollywood Cemetery next to his wife. The death of Francis marked the end of an era for his daughter. If there was "no permanent escape from the past" (WW, 209), there need not be perpetual imprisonment. The headline of Francis's obituary perhaps best captured the distance she had traversed: "Iron Works' Manager was Father of Ellen Glasgow, Novelist."

V

In the end, Ellen Glasgow had no choice but to settle in Richmond. Her sense of identity remained inseparable from place: "I feel as if I were rooted in the soil," she told an interviewer. "Whenever I go away I feel that and whenever I come back I feel as if I were returning to my own."[12] Bennett agreed to stay on as her secretary: "She was, and is," Glasgow wrote in The Woman Within (1954), echoing her description of Lizzie Jones, "a woman of much character, and of great natural intelligence. . . . More than anyone else since I lost Cary, Anne Virginia has had my interests at heart; and she has shared my compassion for all inarticulate creation, and even turns that compassion upon me" (216). Like Carrie Coleman, Bennett had little interest in reading any books except romances or mysteries, and Glasgow felt that she looked with suspicion upon "people who wrote" (216). Yet Glasgow felt close to Bennett, who by nursing three members of her family (Cary, Emily, and Francis Glasgow) had herself become family, a kind of poor relative.

It suited Arthur, who did not intend to sell the old house, to have his sister living at home. Though in London, he did what had to be done to make it more habitable, footing the bills for everything from white-tiled bathrooms to electric lights. Workmen painted and papered every room. For her new study on the northeast corner of the second floor, Glasgow chose a pattern with red-roofed houses and green trees against a dark background. "I haven't a particle of interest in the house," she wrote disingenuously to Rebe before the renovations began, "and don't care a hang what it is like."[13] She did, however, want everything done properly, despite the constant disruptions that made it difficult to write. As costs mounted, misunderstandings inevitably followed, testing the relationship between brother and sister. Glasgow took offense when Arthur questioned her about expensive changes, such as crystal chandeliers and blinds. She could care less about them. They looked "cheap and common." The fresh walls and paint had obliged her to spend money on furniture, and if Arthur wanted she would reimburse him $657 for wall coverings. "I am perfectly willing to sell my Norfolk and Western stock," she wrote,

> and pay for anything else you think I ought to pay for. It was so good of you ever to want to do over the house that I feel dreadfully about your thinking I wanted to be extravagant. . . . Yes, as far as I am concerned, I have felt all along that it is a mistake for you to repair this house. My hold on life is so light at best that I have felt of late—for the last year—that a breath might blow it away. All summer I have been haunted by a feeling that after the house was finished I should not live to get the benefit of it.[14]

Arthur did not question her about the expenditure again. By Christmas, the dust had literally settled, and Glasgow looked forward to his visit. "I am so alone in the world now," she wrote, "that it means a great deal just to think of you as not being so far away."[15]

Emotionally and aesthetically, Glasgow found it more difficult than she had anticipated to adjust again to life at One West Main. Decay had touched neighboring houses, and the noise of streetcars shrilled in the front room. As she would write in The Sheltered Life (1932): "One by one, they saw the old houses demolished, the fine old elms mutilated. Telegraph poles slashed the horizon, furnaces, from a distance, belched soot into the drawing-rooms" (5–6). Everywhere the familiar had become strange. Even her mother's old house at Needham, which Arthur had once thought of buying, now belonged to another family. When Emily died, Glasgow had moved into her larger bedroom on the northwest front corner. After the death of Francis Glasgow, Bennett took Emily's old room, and the southwest bedroom, which Glasgow had once shared with Rebe, became the guest room.[16] Against anyone's expectations, Ellen Glasgow claimed her father's room on the southeast side of the house. Maybe the symbolism of the move amused her, for, after all, she had willed out. More likely, she still associated the space with her mother—or the convenience of the bedroom adjoining her study overrode personal distaste.

As Glasgow assumed her father's role and responsibilities in 1916, she began to sound less like a rebel and more like a conservative. The women's movement continued to interest her, but with increasing reservations. Doubting the assumption that women would make wiser voters than men, she argued for the development of women themselves—and here, too, with a caveat. She cautioned that the growing intellectuality of women had its undesirable side: "There was a tranquility, a graciousness about the old order," she reminisced, "and I hate to see our women lose their qualities . . . of sympathy and softness."[17] Like most of us, her opinions were influenced by her personal situation. She could not entirely dismiss the myth of the old South, which had come to encompass the memories of her mother and Cary.

Living in One West Main, Glasgow began to imagine time blurring and curving back on itself. "I was living with ghosts," she explained in her autobiography:

> The house belonged to the dead. . . . One after another, they went continuously by me in the lonely evenings—Mother, Walter, Frank, Cary, Emily, Father—but the only shades that stopped the beating of my heart were those of Mother, Frank, Cary. . . . Even the creative impulse was disintegrating within. (*WW,* 222)

The solitude, which Glasgow felt necessary for creative work, had become a burden.

VI

When Henry Anderson (1870–1954), robust and confident, walked into Ellen Glasgow's life on Easter Sunday, just before her forty-third birthday, the timing could not have been better. Maude Williams, a friend whom Glasgow had met the previous year, had invited her to lunch. Maude, a large and rather flamboyant woman, wanted her to meet her husband's law partner. She knew that Glasgow would find him "compatible."[18]

Richmonders thought Anderson, an Anglophile and a Republican, something of a maverick.[19] Three years older than Glasgow, he had been born in Dinwiddie County, Virginia. His mother came, as did Glasgow's, from Virginia's aristocracy. His father barely earned a living as a country doctor. Anderson's parents had enough money to educate him at home with private tutors, but not enough to send him to college. He began his career on a railroad in Crewe, Virginia, then worked his way through law school at Washington and Lee University, where he served as secretary to the president. In 1916, Washington and Lee granted him an honorary doctorate of laws.

In 1898, Anderson moved to Richmond, and in 1901 he became a partner in the law firm of Munford and Anderson. Within five years (1906), the Virginia Railway and Power Company named Anderson, who specialized in corporate law, its vice-president and general counsel. Two years later, Anderson helped Frank Gould reorganize the International & Great Northern Railway. He also tried and failed to deliver Virginia's electoral votes to William Howard Taft, a Republican from Ohio. Taft remained a friend, a fact that Anderson's enemies said he advertised by prominently hanging Taft's portrait in his library over the mantlepiece.

At the time he met Ellen Glasgow, Anderson no longer resembled his impecunious, if ambitious, younger self. The friend of presidents, he lived opulently at 913 West Franklin Street, attended by a staff of English-trained servants, including a butler, valet, cook, chauffeur, and chambermaid. Richmonders mocked Anderson's English accent, the last remnants, they whispered, of his affair with a certain Lady Hadfield. Also an acquaintance of Glasgow, Lady Hadfield (the former Frances Wickerham) had, in their minds, turned a country boy into a gentleman.

Gossip had prepared Glasgow to dislike Anderson, and considering her ambivalent feelings toward her brother Arthur, no one would have imagined her attraction to a similar man. Of the Glasgow children, however, she and Arthur were most alike: "I can never understand," she told him, "the way you and I appear to have exhausted all the ambition in the family."[20] Energy and initiative never failed to impress Ellen Glasgow, and in Henry Anderson she recognized someone as opinionated and unyielding as herself.

Anderson's abrupt and pretentious manner masked, as did Arthur's, a sense of familial responsibility. To his nieces and nephews, Anderson seemed larger than life. At Christmas, his exotic-looking foreign car became Santa's sleigh, laden with fancy foods and wished-for presents, and at least one nephew received a college education.

A bachelor in his mid-forties who shied away from marriage, Anderson had, like Gerald, a history with women. As a young man he had fallen in love with a cousin of Maude Williams, who would have accepted his proposal had she received it. When Frances Shield, Anderson's niece and Lady Hadfield's namesake, asked him why he had never married, he implied that he had experienced an early disappointment. His precarious financial position at the turn of the century had made his union with a wealthy debutante impossible. Anderson's explanation is, at the least, misleading. In a city still recovering from the economic panics and crises of the 1890s, Anderson's partnership with some of Richmond's most respected and wealthy citizens would have appeared to secure his financial future. By 1902, for instance, he earned one-third of his firm's growing profits.

Though clearly liking the company of women, Anderson's actual relations with them remain ambiguous. He thought of himself as a gentleman and believed in keeping a woman's secrets to the grave. At the same time, he cultivated the rakish impression of having secrets to keep. Anderson paid court to women with titles and honors that made them public personalities. Usually he chose women who were unavailable or unmarriageable, women who have traditionally screened men with sexual secrets of their own.[21] If nothing more, Anderson liked the image of being a ladies' man, and, in Glasgow's sardonic recollection, one could always identify his current infatuation as the woman wearing the "latest thing in orchids" (WW, 226).

Glasgow responded first and foremost to Anderson's physical vitality. Recently back from vacationing in Florida, his skin had burned, like his hair, to a deep sand color. He glowed with health, and Glasgow thought: "Here is reality, here is life itself, solid, eager, active, confident, and undefeated" (224, 225). She felt, as she had with Gerald, a mysterious communion that defied analysis. She meant, if she didn't say, "sex." Glasgow soon received her own orchids from Anderson, and by June he addressed her as "dear Vardah"—a nickname she had been given by an astrologer. While the name has no meaning, it probably reminded Glasgow of a Hindu goddess.

Anderson enjoyed playing the part of a courtly lover. He persisted in seeing Glasgow as a woman of "strict principle," one who believed in restraint and tradition; yet her refusal to see him alone rankled—no matter how much he wanted to worship and serve, "to respond in a way worthy of the beauty and nobility" of her call.[22] She believed that her opposition attracted him, but it might have been something more conventionally feminine: the art of making another person feel the center of your universe. "She gave you her *undivided* attention" is how one friend phrased it.[23] When Glasgow chose, she could speak exactly as she wrote. Anderson found her intellectually challenging and immensely entertaining. "Say that again, Ellen," he would beg, the idea had been expressed so "beautifully."[24]

Their courtship hit a snag in June when her trip to New York, to consult doctors and to shop, caused Anderson some concern. He did not like her friendship with another new friend, Pearce Bailey, a founding father of that city's Neurological Institute. Bailey had agreed to help Glasgow with the clinical details of a story about a male psychoanalyst who chooses to accept a university chair rather than run away with his lover, a philosopher who has just turned down a college presidency for his sake. Casting an ironic eye at marriage, Glasgow wondered whether "the professional instinct"—the story's title—had evolved to any great degree in the female of the species.

Bailey could not have been more enthusiastic about their collaboration. In March 1916, he had written Glasgow and enclosed some more "dope":

> It seems to me that Estbridge's review of his life should follow the scene with Tilly [his wife]. Won't you write the scene right in & get it back to me before Wednesday. I think you might go right on from where I stop. . . . Have given no other thought to the other stories—want to keep the characters of this one clear in my mind. . . . what I sent you is merely dictated & you are free to cut it up or do away with it altogether as you please.[25]

Despite Bailey's obvious fondness for Glasgow and their mutual interests in psychology and literature, Anderson attracted her more. In July, Glasgow sent him a poem she had published four years earlier entitled "The Song." Anderson rightly saw the poem as an amorous gesture:

> Long, long ago upon another star
> I heard your voice and looked into your eyes;
> The worlds are many and the way is long,
> Perchance I may have missed you in the skies
> But still the memory beckons from afar,
> And still I search the face of the earth
> For one I loved upon another star.[26]

Anderson sat up all night writing his own response. Playing with Glasgow's own words, his "answer" seems a prelude to an offer of marriage or a cautious man's version of Marvell's "To His Coy Mistress":

An Answer

I

As in the shadow of the dark'ning night,
I turned from the ways of the passing throng
Your hand came forth as a flash of light
Bearing a message—'twas just a "Song."

II

It speaks of the days of the long ago,
The aching dreams of another world;
Of the mystic stars our souls did know,
Ere they went out through gates of pearl.

III

To yield themselves to the Greater Will,
To bear new life to forms of clay,
To play their part, though dreaming still,
In God's great scheme of destiny.

IV

Perchance 'twas there our souls were one
Back at the dawn of Earth's young day
When fate stepped in, and this was done—
Our souls were parted and launched away.

V

To roam the world, as the Hindu dreams,
Haunted by joys of the beautiful past,
To seek its mate by hills and streams,
And when united find Heaven at last.

VI

Then only do we look or sigh again,
For sweet dream dews of the earlier star,
To quench the thirst of the weary strain,
Or cool the fever of the "things that are"?

VII

The search is over, for this we know
That Love is God, and "God is Love,"
That through its power e'en here below,
We compass the realms that were above.

VIII
And yielding our all, our souls may claim,
The perfect joy, the endless youth,
And find in Love's Consuming flame,
That the Hindu's dream is really truth.[27]

Glasgow received the poem while she was vacationing at Pearce Bailey's house in Bar Harbor, Maine. Anderson hoped that she would not come to like the house — or its owner — too much. "I can take care of you, and a chaperon too," he wrote, "*if you* need one."[28] Plans for Anderson to visit Bar Harbor or for Glasgow and Carrie Coleman to meet him in New York never materialized.

On September 7, Anderson, depressed and irritable over President Wilson's handling of the striking railworkers, sailed for England on board the *Adriatic*. A farewell letter that Glasgow sent had comforted him, "starting into a world at war," and he loved both it and the sender: "I miss your little hands." He would not return until Christmas. "I confess I am seeing red [about the current political situation] and about ready for revolution," he complained to Glasgow. "Nothing could be worse than Wilson for President."[29]

During Anderson's absence, Glasgow contemplated what marriage to him might mean. The emotional, if not financial, burden of supporting One West Main had become almost intolerable. The monies from Doubleday and the family trust gave her about $11,000 a year. She could not count on any royalties from Harper's. Her May check from sales of *The Descendant* (1897) had totaled $1.44. Still, many families would have envied Glasgow her income. To Glasgow, as to most people, money signified independence and control. She remembered how after her mother's funeral her father had sold her mother's mare, and she did not have "so much as a penny" (*WW*, 86) to stop it. She never wanted to be in that position again. An advantageous marriage would allow her to write solely for "art's sake."

Meanwhile Glasgow had to meet expenses. Following Bennett's suggestion, she asked Paul Revere Reynolds to get the largest possible price for a new story about a haunted house. "Of course," she told him, "I cannot let my work appear in the second rate magazines," nor did she care to take less than $1,000.[30] In December, *Scribner's* published "The Shadowy Third." A delighted James Lane Allen congratulated her. "You pretend [in your newspaper reviews, or interviews], that you are a realist," he wrote:

You may even imagine you are one. But a realistic novel of yours I have never read — yet!

You get the facts: therein and so far you are a realist. But out of real things you make, nothing could keep you from making, something that lies beyond the boundaries of what people know as life. Because to do that, namely, to live beyond the boundaries of what people know as life is *you!* Your imagination has the wing that flies over the fences.[31]

The title of "The Shadowy Third" refers to the ghost of a little girl, murdered by her stepfather who can then inherit his wife's millions. The child appears only to those possessing sympathetic imaginations: her mother, Mrs. Maradick, an elderly black butler, and the nurse, Miss Randolph, hired to confirm the mother's madness. The most Jamesian of Glasgow's stories, it explores other contemporaneous realities open to the dispossessed. The narrator, despite her obvious infatuation for Dr. Maradick—a character modeled after the Philadelphian nerve doctor S. W. Mitchell—aligns herself with her patient, thereby subverting social and professional dictates. Her efforts prove ineffectual, however, and Mrs. Maradick's death in an asylum leaves her husband free to marry his former love. The nurse sees the child only one more time, on the day of Dr. Maradick's reckoning. Summoned by an emergency, he trips over a child's skipping rope lying coiled on the stairs and dies. A misstep in the darkness, Glasgow asks, or an invisible judgment?

The success of "The Shadowy Third" inspired Glasgow to publish two more stories in February 1917, "Thinking Makes It So" and "Dare's Gift." "Thinking Makes It So" presents its plain, 43-year-old heroine, Margaret French, as a cross between Glasgow and Elizabeth Barrett Browning. Like Browning, she begins a secret correspondence with a man who admires her poetry. Margaret fears that their meeting will end the relationship. Instead her lover declares, "My beautiful, I should have known you among a hundred women, for you are just as I dreamed you."[32] If Glasgow wanted to be loved for her soul, Anderson wanted to be loved for himself: "I would that I were better and bigger," he pleaded, "but just see me as I am."[33]

The third story that Glasgow published, "Dare's Gift," should have given Anderson pause. The title refers to a house that shares some characteristics with One West Main. Since the first Dare betrayed his leader in Bacon's Rebellion and Lucy Dare surrendered her Northern lover to Confederate soldiers, Dare's Gift has housed voices urging betrayal. Notwithstanding the horror that Lucy Dare inspires, Glasgow presents her as "one of the mute inglorious heroines of history" (*CSS*, 106). The recovery of her story, which "failed to arrest the imagination of her time" (106), acts as a warning. Antigone lurks beneath the belle's complaisant exterior. "There are many

More than one childless couple offered to adopt young Ellen Glasgow

Anne Gholson Glasgow, Ellen's
mother, in middle age

Francis Glasgow, the family
patriarch

Cary Glasgow McCormack,
Ellen's favorite sister

George Walter McCormack,
Cary's husband and Ellen's first
intellectual mentor

Rebe Glasgow Tutwiler, Ellen's youngest sister

Frank Glasgow as a student at
Virginia Military Institute

Arthur Glasgow receiving his honorary L.L.D. Arthur supported his sister throughout her career

Green Forest, the childhood home of Francis Glasgow and the setting of Ellen Glasgow's *Vein of Iron*

Ellen Glasgow spent the happiest times of her childhood at Jerdone Castle Farm, some thirty miles from Richmond

One West Main, Ellen Glasgow's home for over half a century

Ellen Glasgow's study, the one place she could always write

The garden at One West Main

Ellen Glasgow vacationing at White Sulphur Springs

Ellen Glasgow (*left*) and friends, probably Mary Johnston and Cary Glasgow, gathering flowers at the White

In the grand tradition, Ellen Glasgow recorded her spiritual awakening in the Swiss Alps

A recuperating Cary Glasgow McCormack at Warm Springs

Ellen Glasgow, the South's first realistic novelist, in a conventional pose

Ellen Glasgow at 40

Ellen Glasgow, as always in the latest fashion

Ellen Glasgow with Joseph Conrad, 1914

Henry Watkins Anderson. Glasgow never married Henry Anderson and never broke off their engagement

Queen Marie of Roumania, the other woman in Henry Anderson's life

Along with Henry Anderson, Marie of Roumania devoted herself to helping victims of the Great War

A pensive Ellen Glasgow in later years

Anne Virginia Bennett, Glasgow's secretary and companion, who worked with Glasgow for the RSPCA

James Branch Cabell, the novelist, with whom Glasgow had a long but troubled relationship

Ellen Glasgow cared deeply about the design of her books, from the weight of their paper to the cloth for their covers

such women among us," a character cautions. They move "in obscurity—reserved, passive, commonplace—and we never suspect the spark of fire in their natures until it flares up at the touch of the unexpected" (108). An anti-war story, "Dare's Gift" ends with a chilling example of the cost of preserving illusions. The elderly Lucy Dare spends her days knitting mufflers for the Allies, stitching together the present that has yet to learn from the past.

Anderson did not, of course, recognize Lucy Dare's streak of ruthlessness in the woman he courted. Nor did he see Margaret French's vulnerability. To the last, Ellen Glasgow would make him pay for his oversight.

VII

During the spring and summer of 1917, Richmond could not have seemed farther from the flooded, rat-infested trenches of Europe. Glasgow and Anderson sat on the back porch of One West Main, dining on oysters, lamb hash (his favorite), or split-down-the-back chicken (her favorite). They created their own oasis among the microphylla roses and ferns, the potted geraniums and shrubs. Long into the night, they talked about life and literature, the plot of her new novel, *The Builders* (1919), eventually serialized in *Woman's Home Companion,* and the politics of its hero, David Blackburn.[34] Not surprisingly, Blackburn's politics reflect many of Anderson's own beliefs, including an impatience with American isolationism.[35] He and Glasgow's heroine, Caroline Meade, a nurse modeled after Bennett, practice the altruism Anderson thought crucial to international peace.[36] A Republican who denounces, like Anderson, the League of Nations, Blackburn nonetheless dreams of the "perfectibility of human nature." "If we look back over history," he argues, "we find that the sublime moments with men and with nations" involve "a new spiritual voyage of discovery" (*Builders,* 356). This can only be accomplished, Glasgow explains, when the United States (and particularly the South) outgrows its provincialism.

In early June, Glasgow had to put work on her novel aside. Her sister, Annie Clark, suffered a stroke and no one expected her to live. After Cary, Glasgow cared for Annie the most among her older sisters. Her sympathy for Annie's daughter, Josephine, brought aunt and niece closer together. Now she and Rebe would be the only sisters still living. Glasgow remembered how she had spun romances around her sisters' beaux, especially the young man whose "blue blood" did not offset the fact of his poverty or his ungainly limp

(*WW*, 58). She remembered also the days she spent with Annie's family after her mother's death. All these deaths and the ones in Europe—her immediate world seemed to reflect the chaos of the world at large.

The war did not leave Glasgow untouched either. Anderson, who had been turned down for active service, planned to leave for Roumania, where he would chair the Red Cross Commission. The appointment recognized his having raised over a quarter of a million dollars for the Red Cross. On July 18, 1917, Lieutenant Colonel Anderson wrote Ellen Glasgow: "I *want to see you.*" The following evening, Glasgow penned a note to herself: "Thursday the nineteenth of July 1917. I became engaged to Henry this evening." [37] Anderson parted from Glasgow—as he would the next year from another woman—by dropping to his knees and kissing the hem of her skirt. The next day he left for Europe.

Anderson traveled from New York, to Chicago, Vancouver, across the Pacific to Japan, then to Russia, and finally into "the silence" of Roumania (*WW*, 231). His daily notes and telegrams to Glasgow dwindled. How could he integrate his current experiences with those of the past few months? The conditions in Roumania defied description. By November 1916, 40 percent of the country's original army had been killed or wounded, and the royal family had fled to Jassy, the former capital of Moldavia, ten miles west of the Russian border. Five hundred thousand refugees, needing food, clothes, fuel, and shelter, poured into the province in time to face the worst winter in recorded history—with temperatures often 30 degrees below zero. Members of the diplomatic community had to compete for resources, and the royal family evidently survived on beans. In December, typhus and smallpox broke out and over 300,000 people, more than the population of wartime Jassy, died from starvation, disease, and exposure. Horse-drawn carts piled with bodies regularly rode up and down the streets. [38]

When Henry Anderson arrived in Jassy in September 1917, leading forty members of the Red Cross—doctors, engineers, hygienists, and sanitation experts—Queen Marie, the granddaughter of Queen Victoria, greeted him. Known as the most beautiful, and thought to be the most promiscuous, woman in Europe, Marie immediately realized the value of courting a man in Anderson's position. Such men came, she wrote, "with full hands and a magnificent supply of provisions of every kind." [39] If Anderson responded to Marie's film-star beauty and latent sexuality, her genuine vulnerability made him a latter-day knight. "It is," she told him, "always a lonely thing to be a

Queen."[40] Since the outbreak of the war, she had worked tirelessly. To raise money for British Red Cross work in Roumania and to raise the consciousness of the West, she published a book of sketches called *My Country* (1916).

It could be said that by accepting, even encouraging, his natural obeisance and strong sense of "unworthiness,"[41] Glasgow had prepared Anderson to fall in love with the queen of Roumania. With Marie, Anderson continued the relationship begun with Glasgow. Against a backdrop of death and destruction, they exchanged daily notes and costly presents, and together they toured hospital wards where the queen, dressed in a white Red Cross uniform, distributed food, candy, and cigarettes. Marie's rhetoric—"I am no more at all a selfish woman, I certainly in this war have learned to live for others, entirely and uncomplainingly"—reinforced his notions of true womanhood.[42] She saw herself as a fictional character, as lovely, if not as misunderstood, as Angelica Blackburn in Glasgow's *The Builders*: "A Queen if she is worthy of the name must live in beauty," she wrote Anderson, "but I live also in eternal and almost terrible hard-work. . . . Occasionally I groan, wonder if *one* heart can be strong enough, rich enough, brave enough, large enough for so many always increasing wants!" In fact, when Anderson gave Marie a copy of the novel, she sympathized with the pampered and manipulative Angelica, who had "an unfair amount of what she does not deserve."[43]

Ellen Glasgow heard almost nothing from Anderson during this time and could not understand why he did not return with the rest of the commission in October. Friends and neighbors in Richmond assumed that Anderson and the queen were lovers. But in fact this is highly unlikely. Marie enjoyed a long relationship with her adviser Prince Barbo Stirbey, known for his wealth and fatal charm for women. The rumors about Anderson nevertheless placed Glasgow in an untenable social position, for close friends either suspected or knew of their engagement. Even Glasgow's brother Arthur, who liked to avoid emotional tangles, thought it judicious to apprise her of the rumors. "I seem to grow nearer to you every time that we are together," she responded.

> Whatever comes in the future I want you always to remember that no one could have been better or kinder to me than you have been in the last few years since father's death. . . . One thing more has been on my conscience too, my dear. Never for a moment regret our last conversation, for I understood that you talked to me as you did because you really had my interest at heart. If things are right what you said will not make any difference, and if things are wrong, you will have said far less than the truth.[44]

The slow mails and censorship made any meaningful communication between Glasgow and Anderson impossible. She accused him of treating her
lightly and found gossip about his diverting an unfair share of Red Cross
funds to Roumania humiliating. By the time Roumania fell to the Germans
in March 1918 and Anderson had made his way home through Odessa into
Ukraine,[45] Glasgow had changed as much as he. To her, the war, if not her
love for Anderson, had become an "obscene horror" (WW, 229).

VIII

Despite her remove from the war, Glasgow felt constantly assailed. Not only
did she worry about Anderson's well-being and the status of their relationship, she also worried about the safety of Anne Virginia Bennett, whose
departure left Glasgow feeling despondent and overworked. Bennett's Base
Hospital (No. 45 in Richmond) had been called to active duty and sent to
France in March.[46] According to army reports, the building that housed Bennett's unit had no central heat or plumbing and the food, mostly canned
corned beef and hash, was inedible. Nurses like Bennett worked around the
clock as sick, wounded, and gassed soldiers streamed into the ready-made
hospital. Bombs fell just twenty miles away at Saint-Mihiel, where French
troops held the Allied line and U.S. troops attacked the German flank. From
this assault alone, casualties numbered over 20,000. Crude surgical proce-
dures and lack of supplies prompted one doctor to describe their work as
"scientific butchery conducted under the rules and regulations . . . adopted
for the guidance of the military surgeons by the Medical Department of the
Army." [47] Everyone, even the wounded, helped carry patients from one room
to another in a building that had four floors and no elevators. Bennett shared
a sense of comradery with her fellow workers, many of them fellow Richmonders, and during this time formed a special friendship with Nan Quailles
Gibson, the one person who was solely her friend and not Glasgow's.

However unreasonably, Glasgow felt deserted. When Anderson returned
home, he found his fiancée withdrawn and angry. He could not diffuse her
jealousy of Marie, and on July 3 they quarreled openly. He asked her to listen
to the text of a speech he intended to make the next afternoon. He particularly wanted to include a sentence that had impressed the queen. Glasgow
thought the phrase — "Happiness comes only from the sacrifice of self in the
crucible of service" (WW, 237) — ironically infelicitous. Piqued, Anderson did

not bother to disguise his admiration for Marie. Glasgow may have been willing to concede Marie's greater beauty, but not her being a better writer.[48] Behind Anderson's every remark, Glasgow heard an implied comparison to Marie's advantage. She accused him of enjoying the war. After they parted at midnight, she slowly climbed the stairs to her bedroom and locked herself in. There she took an overdose of sleeping tablets. Glasgow was, as her friend Berta Wellford testified, always having violent love affairs that never went anywhere. This one had obviously gone too far. In the morning, she woke nauseated, more sardonic than ever, and still engaged to Anderson.

Anderson's narrative of their troubled courtship survives only in an undated poem entitled "The Confession":

> I own it now, I own it at thy feet
> That I have survived against my love and then
> That vaunting strength, I blindly could not see
> My weakness 'till passion's burning wind did beat
> My spirit to the earth, at last to flee
> In outer darkness; for at the judgement seat
> Of thy pure soul, what hope was there for me?

Anderson asks how it came to be. He then details their first meeting, the "treasures" of Glasgow's mind and heart, his growing love, and his dream of their life together:

> Then came my fall, I know not how or why,
> — like the Ancient God with reckless pride
> In newfound joys, with wings as yet untried
> I dared to boldly rise unto the sunlight high
> Of thy sweet soul, unheeding of a voice that cried
> The warning— My strength did melt before thy
> Fire, and passion loosed, drove me from thy side.

The poem ends with the hope that a new morning will dawn.[49]

The poem could not, however, affect an already predestined course of events. In November 1918, Henry Anderson left again to supervise the Red Cross relief effort for the entire Balkan region. On the eve of his departure, he visited his mother in Farmville and confided his engagement to Ellen Glasgow. "Learning of this gave me great pleasure," Laura Anderson wrote Glasgow, "as I have always wanted him to marry and have the association of a confiding, trusting wife to make his nice house a *home* such as cannot be when alone."[50]

IX

In Paris, Anderson organized an entirely new unit of personnel and arranged, during January 1919, for massive amounts of supplies to be shipped from Marseilles to Roumania. The war had maimed so many civilians that an artificial-limb factory had to be built. Anderson, who thought of himself as a cultural ambassador, had found his calling: "If we can plant that one seed [of justice and friendship] in the hearts of these simple Balkan peoples, then our task will have been achieved." In spite of his partisanship, Anderson had an understanding of ancient antagonisms in the region and cautioned that the "idea of the rights of minorities and of individuals . . . is a living, essential thing, and the extent of the recognition of these rights regardless of nationality is the test of our civilization." [51] At the end of twelve months, Anderson could claim astonishing success. They had, he wrote his law partner Randolph Williams, accomplished the impossible. Over 500 personnel and 25 million pounds of supplies from points all over France and Italy had been transported to the various ports of the Balkans, "where transport was and is more a name than a fact." [52]

Anderson later maintained that he had been offered the crown of Albania but decided instead to return to Richmond. Once home, the ongoing argument with Glasgow continued. He tried to divert her with tales of social occasions — a topic he thought of interest to all women. Glasgow was not impressed. Nor could she simultaneously digest tales of starving peasants and details of a ball he had given in honor of Queen Marie. Chivalric to the last, Anderson did his best to reason with her. "Let's try being just two human beings and stop plaguing providence for a while," he begged. "I even should like just being a child for I am tired of problems. We *might* try at being children!" [53]

Ellen Glasgow refused to behave. Anderson knew of her suicide attempt and felt always "under the shadow" of her terrible threat. When he called at One West Main, Bennett, who had recently come back from France, could barely bring herself to speak to him. She predicted that if he and Glasgow married, she would divorce him after twenty-four hours. Anderson's failed attempts to live by Glasgow's standards ended in what he called their "monthly climaxes." [54] Because his impotence matched his good intentions, Glasgow was able to keep him in thrall for the next twenty-seven years. The power struggle extended beyond the grave with the publication of Glasgow's autobiography and its damning portrait of Anderson, whose own letters present a much more compassionate man: "Yet you are surprised that my letters are sometimes such as I might write to any acquaintance!" he answered Glasgow.

> You take a phrase and twist it with meanings which never occur to me. . . . We parted one week ago in an unusually good humor, both of us, and with a better outlook than for months, even yours. Instead of going forward from that new starting point with courage and faith, you go back to reading all letters, get your thoughts and worries all started again, find in them something irritating, then start writing, and we have again torn down the whole business. . . . If we have no faith in each other or ourselves let's say so and part; if we have let's use it — For myself my faith has never wavered even in the face of events and of some letters which seemed to me harsh beyond the possibility of belief — So I am coming to supper tonight not because of your last note but in spite of it, and because I know it is not *you*. . . . You see my faith is hard to destroy.[55]

When Glasgow asked Anderson if he still considered them engaged, he prevaricated:

> Of course I do, and there has not been a word or suggestion to the contrary. Even when in your last letter you said I could do as I pleased . . . any change in status should be by mutual agreement. The only difference between us seems to be that you seem to regard it as irrevocable while I feel that if circumstances arise which would render unwise the carrying out of the agreement, we should change or end it — but by mutual consent in a dignified and proper way.[56]

Discussion about marriage continued until about 1920 when Anderson suggested that they both take (psychological) "treatment" to prepare themselves. Glasgow, who had long ago begun shopping for her trousseau, pushed Anderson to the boundaries of endurance. He wrote:

> I am wondering if it ever occurred to you that your judgement might be wrong. . . . Your judgement seeks not only to cover the present but to sweep back over the past and to wipe out my character, my sincerity, everything, in one sweeping decree — a decree as tragic as it is sweeping, and as wrong as it is tragic. I have made no decision, but must, of course, accept yours. You wrote me a letter, which from anyone else would have been unbearable, even offensive. From you it just hurt — hurt me as I have never been hurt — I could in self-respect and out of respect for you make but one reply. . . . I am not asking and have never asked help in my material affairs — such as John Branch

and others you mention could give — What you have done, and it is much and highly valued, you have done of your own accord. It is the more appreciated for that reason. The help I have asked of you, and which you can give so splendidly when you will is intangible, and therefore more potent. It is the help of understanding, and sympathy even for my errors or weakness, of encouragement when I am discouraged, the help of the Spirit — the help which trusts even with death, and is seeking to cheer the lonely path. This help you have often given, and can give when you will in such wonderful measure.[57]

The reasons for Glasgow's fierce tenacity remain obscure and complicated. Did she think that winning the argument would repair the misunderstandings and recriminations of the last year, or was she forcing his hand? She may well have wanted to humiliate Anderson by destroying his view of himself as a gentleman. He instead cast himself in the role of the forsaken lover: "Since you have 'turned away forever,'" he told her. "I accept it, and go forth to face life as best I can shadowed by one great failure!"[58]

Anderson's regret sounds hollow. As the relationship progressed, he may have realized how seriously Glasgow's hearing impairment would affect their daily lives. For a man who thought that sickness was "ugly," marriage to someone with Glasgow's health problems would have appeared daunting. Queen Marie, beautiful, active, and altruistic, represented his feminine ideal. Glasgow was, in Anderson's words, Marie's opposite: a woman writer, he told Rawlings, "lives such a secluded life." Richmond reduced the situation to the formula of one man and two women: one woman was "in the fullness of her youth and beautiful; the other one not young, and deaf." In truth, all these "romantic comedians" — to borrow Glasgow's 1926 title — were middle-aged. Henry Anderson, as one friend explained, put something into Glasgow's life, and also "took something out." She was "so fine that it didn't occur to her that he wasn't in earnest."[59] Neither did it occur to Anderson until it had become too late. He kept miniatures of both Marie and Glasgow until he died, though Marie's portrait replaced Taft's in his library.

The death of Laura Anderson in January 1921 brought them together briefly, but ultimately freed him from marrying to please his mother. Anderson thanked Glasgow for her "loving consideration," consisting of a telegram, flowers, and letters. He hoped that his mother would be with him more now than before since her love, care, and example would strengthen and encourage him along the road of life.[60]

Glasgow assumed Laura Anderson's role during Henry Anderson's 1921 campaign for governor. Anderson had many friends in the Republican party.

The previous year the Virginia delegation had nominated him for vice-president, a vote he lost to Calvin Coolidge, who after Harding's death became president. Anderson's political ambitions reached beyond the crown of Albania to a seat on the U.S. Supreme Court, and his campaign platform spoke to a national audience. In addition to the usual call for better roads, schools, and more accountable government, Anderson advocated a reform of election laws that favored Democratic candidates and a repeal of poll tax that excluded black voters. "It must be recognized by any fair-minded person," he bravely (and suicidally) argued, that white people should insist on "one standard of justice in Virginia which shall be applied to rich and poor, white and colored, without discrimination. No free government can be founded upon two standards of justice."[61] "The essential purpose of a free government," he asserted, is to protect the right of minorities.[62]

The Democrats immediately attacked Anderson's platform by raising the specter of black rule. The tactic, which had earlier helped to defeat Populist candidates like Walter McCormack, outraged Glasgow, who interrupted work on *One Man in His Time* to come to his defense. In a speech entitled "My Fellow Virginians," she compared the "menace" of black enfranchisement to her childhood fear of Mr. Mugglewuggle: "Whenever my conduct was not becoming in a perfect lady of the age of three or four, I was solemnly warned, just as politicians are warning us today, that if I 'didn't look out and behave,' Mr. Mugglewuggle would 'pop up and get me yet.'" The race question, she continued, "has been the Mr. Mugglewuggle of Virginia politics" (FV, 60). Glasgow asked people to see beyond party politics to the heart and mind of the candidate. To those who know her history with her father, she then set an extraordinary example by praising the efforts of Governor Westmoreland Davis in the area of prison reform: "For many years — all through my Father's life," she practically eulogized, enlightened Virginians worked to make good citizens out of former criminals (64). Glasgow's father had presided over the board of the Virginia Penitentiary beginning in 1891. Eventually Anderson insisted that she not sacrifice any more time away from books for speeches, and she complied.

Receiving 30 percent of the vote, Anderson lost the election to the Democratic candidate Lee Trinkle. He had little support from black voters, who rejected the Republican platform calling for an exclusively white — or "lily-white" — party in Virginia. A third party that called itself the "lily-blacks," led by John Mitchell Jr., a banker and editor of the *Richmond Planet,* had siphoned 5000 expected votes for Anderson. Sporting a pince-nez and campaigning in a chauffeur-driven car, Anderson had appeared to embody the principles of benign patriarchy. After his November defeat, he went on to serve three presidents: Harding, as special assistant to the attorney general; Coolidge, as the U.S. agent on the Mexican Claims Commission; and Herbert Hoover, as a member of the National Commission on Law Observance and Enforcement, in which he outlined a system for the repeal of Prohibition that would grant liquor profits to the government. With his law partner, Jennings C. Wise, Anderson became Hoover's chief Southern strategist. Their advice that Hoover remain silent on race as he reformed the Republican leadership backfired by wedding both blacks and whites more steadfastly to the Democratic party.[63]

Glasgow's ambivalence toward politics can be read in her 1922 novel, *One Man in His Time*. The novel evolves around two political rivals, John Benham, a Virginia aristocrat, and Gideon Vetch, an upstart who made it to the governor's mansion. Benham misses the best because, "with every virtue of mind, he lacked the single one of the heart." He possesses, as Glasgow came to think of Anderson, "every grace of character except humanity" (*Man*, 306).

Vetch, in contrast, seems too human, a reformer who can countenance the ends justifying the means. Between them stand representatives of the South itself, Corinna Page and Stephen Culpepper. They, like their region, suffer from ennui. Both side with Vetch and the future: Corinna breaks her engagement to Benham and sends him back to a former lover; and Stephen will marry Vetch's adopted daughter Patty. "What can one build a world on," Corinna asks, "except human relations—except relations between men and women?" (*Man*, 306). Resembling Faulkner's Joe Christmas in *Light in August* (1932), Vetch seems uncategorizable. Glasgow suggestively describes him as racially "other": "With his gaunt length, his wide curving nostrils, his thick majestic lips, he looked . . . a rock-hewn Pharaoh of a man" (182). Sacrificed to the general will, Vetch dies (much like Nicholas Burr in *The Voice of the People*) from an assassin's bullet. The future remains in the hands of Stephen and Patty, in the relations—Glasgow wrote, obliquely criticizing Anderson—between men and women.

Despite their troubled history, neither Anderson nor Glasgow could quite imagine life without the other. "Dear, *Dear*, DEAR!" Anderson joked. "If I am as bad as your last note says why bother with me at all? Anyhow, the withered and stricken remains of me will come down tonight and be converted into a metaphorical grease spot on the rug."[64] Anderson felt a sense of obligation toward Glasgow, and whenever possible, they continued to meet for dinner on Sunday evenings. Anderson's chauffeur would deliver a note naming the time of his arrival, and Bennett would ask James Anderson to prepare three breads for dinner.

Although both Anderson and Glasgow had other flirtations, they agreed to a kind of companionate marriage, which gave them no real pleasure. Glasgow remained bitter and indignant to the end, and Anderson loyal and severe. When interviewed by Marjorie Rawlings, he described Glasgow as a "brilliant conversationalist" who always dressed in good taste. She was not beautiful or pretty, despite her lovely eyes. She was overly sensitive, and he impatient: "there are two elements," he believed, "one, emotional, which is the feminine and the affirmative, the other, the mind or the intellectual, which always says 'Be careful.' This is the negative and the male. She represented the emotional and I the intellectual." [65] Anderson had obviously absorbed his mother's ideas about a woman's role. "My own belief," he wrote several years before his death, as if he was continuing the old argument with Glasgow, "is that women are happier where the dominance of the man in the relationship is recognized. . . . I do not like weak men, nor do I like women who are too aggressive." [66] He flatly denied that he and Glasgow had ever been engaged, though their engagement had never been formally dissolved.

Whether Anderson was in love with Marie or simply afraid of Glasgow, he remained the love of Glasgow's life. She kept several pictures of him, including one that shows Anderson wearing the full dress uniform she hated. After her death, Anne Virginia Bennett destroyed his photographs, each and every one.

CHAPTER 8

WHAT ENDURES

1923–1930

When the Lord let me be born in America in the Nineteenth
Century, He gave me a skin thick enough to survive it.
Ellen Glasgow, *The Romantic Comedians*

I

ELLEN GLASGOW REMAINED FRIENDS with Henry Anderson until her death in 1945. For seventeen months of those twenty-one years, they made one another happy. In the immediate aftermath of their war and the Great War, she could do nothing but sleepwalk through time. Yet her creativity continued to grow, for what she called the whole Anderson "episode" exercised a profound and pervasive influence over the next stage of her artistic development (*WW*, 227). The relationship had forced her to sacrifice her ironic perspective, to enter into an alien and uncomfortable point of view, and it taught her much about emotion and change. She recognized that two things, and two things only, were requisite to her identity as a human being and as a writer: direct experience and the opportunity to translate the intensity of that experience into art (*CM*, 109–10). If experience—to use her words— had crumbled "in the end to mere literary material" (*WW*, 226), it also led to what she considered her finest work.

Although Glasgow disliked the "patter of Freudian theory" (*WW*, 227), she read extensively in psychology and came to think of her writing as a version of the "talking cure." From about 1916 to 1924, she experimented once again with shorter fictional forms, especially the ghost story, whose elastic boundaries permitted the exploration of a wider emotional terrain. Glasgow had always believed that a writer should follow his or her conscience. If her most autobiographical novels had ultimately failed, they failed because they kept the outline of experience without communicating its essence. For Glasgow, the short story functioned like literary études or exercises culminating in the performance of *Barren Ground* (1925).

In October 1923, Glasgow published a volume entitled *The Shadowy Third and Other Stories*. All but one of the stories, "Jordan's End," had previously seen print. The book contains four ghost stories: "The Shadowy Third" (*Scribner's Magazine*, December 1916), "Dare's Gift" (*Harper's Magazine*, February and March, 1917), "The Past" (*Good Housekeeping*, October 1920), "Whispering Leaves" (*Harper's Magazine*, January and February, 1923), "The Difference" (*Harper's Magazine*, June 1923), and "Jordan's End."[1] Of the stories written from 1920 to 1923, one, "Whispering Leaves," nostalgically returns to the worlds of Needham and Jerdone Castle; and three, "The Past," "The Difference," and "Jordan's End," explore a lover's defection, whether to another woman as in "The Past" and "The Difference" or to madness as in "Jordan's End." Examined chronologically, they may reveal Glasgow's increasingly angry response to Anderson.

Drawing on Glasgow's recent history, both "The Past" and "The Difference" cast two women as rivals for the same man. In "The Past," the second Mrs. Vanderbridge competes with the ghost of her predecessor. The first Mrs. Vanderbridge died in childbirth and assumes the form of her husband's guilt and sorrow. Through an act of renunciation similar to Glasgow's at Bremerbad, the heroine banishes the past and confirms herself: "I give him back to you," she tells the ghost as Glasgow must have dearly loved to tell Marie of Roumania. "Nothing is mine that I cannot win and keep fairly. Nothing is mine that belongs really to you" (*ST*, 138).

More cynical, "The Difference" denies its heroine her moment of triumph. Margaret Fleming loves her husband enough to offer him a divorce to marry his mistress. He indignantly refuses: "Anybody would think that you are angry because I am not in love with her!" (259). In fact, she is, for the tawdriness of his passion cheapens her past also. The heroine of "Jordan's End" is far more ruthless. When her husband retreats into another kind of madness, a family legacy from intermarriage, she kills him.

While the stories offer an overview of Glasgow's response to Anderson, they also reflect the mask she assumed for the world. Blithe and defiant, she mocked herself and pretended to laugh at life. Supposedly nothing could defeat a person without illusions. She wondered how any love, unless it was the "biological imperative" (WW, 245) of first love, should seem so important.

II

In the 1920s, Glasgow rededicated herself to her career. She considered the gift of her imagination — the source of creativity and the repository of memories — a "divided endowment." And still she knew it would not fail her. For someone who considered place and self intertwined, it seems only fitting that her rejuvenation paralleled that of her native city. With the organization of the Virginia Writers' Club in 1918 and the Cabineers, a group that supported local artists,[2] Richmond entered a new cultural epoch.

Nothing marked this epoch more than the birth of *The Reviewer*, a "little" literary magazine published in Richmond from February 1921 to October 1924. Founded on a whim, *The Reviewer* had four midwives or editors: Hunter Stagg, Emily Clark, Margaret Freeman, and Mary Dallas Street. Hunter Stagg and Emily Clark, who later married the very wealthy and elderly explorer Edwin Swift Balch, had experience reviewing books for the city's leading newspapers. Margaret Freeman, destined to be James Branch Cabell's second wife, drummed up advertising and collected manuscripts. And the future novelist Mary Dallas Street became the chief fundraiser, bringing order, and sometimes her own cash, to the loosely structured magazine always teetering on bankruptcy. They were an odd crew. Street's mannish appearance excited comment,[3] and Clark's acid tongue alienated friends and foes alike. Hunter Stagg needed all of his substantial charm to keep the peace.

The editors conceived the magazine as a direct response to H. L. Mencken's criticism of Southern letters in his "Sahara of the Bozarts" essay. Mencken argued that the South had "lost its old capacity for producing ideas." It had become intolerant and ignorant.[4] Cabell quipped that a lynching party awaited "King Mencken" at points south of Maryland. Nevertheless Mencken's aesthetics, what might be called a poetic version of realism, would inform *The Reviewer* and also influence Glasgow in *The Sheltered Life* and *Vein of Iron*.[5]

When Emily Clark and friends founded *The Reviewer*, they sought the help of both Mencken and Ellen Glasgow. Glasgow signed the decree announcing its creation in the fall of 1920. "With sufficient youth and ignorance to assist you," she remarked, "you *may* accomplish the impossible."[6] For a few years, they did. Contributors included leading authors of the day—Mary Johnston, Henry Sydnor Harrison, Amélie Rives, Joseph Hergesheimer, Agnes Repplier, Louis Untermeyer, and Carl Van Vechten—as well as those yet-to-be discovered: Allen Tate, poet, novelist, and essayist, and Julia Peterkin, who would win the 1928 Pulitzer Prize for fiction. The magazine received kudos from the *New York Times* and the *Herald Tribune,* causing Amy Lowell to complain that she had been the only prominent writer not asked for a piece.[7]

Glasgow sent an article for the third issue of *The Reviewer,* entitled "The Dynamic Past." Gently rebuking Mencken and echoing Ralph Waldo Emerson, she emphasized the need for "correct standards of art and life—standards of our own—not those we have copied from others." "The past and the present and the future are the same endless stream," she wrote, "and with all our efforts we can merely change the course a little—we can never break the eternal continuity of race" (*RD,* 52–53).

Glasgow's connection to *The Reviewer* and her growing friendship with Cabell, a courtly, shy man who edited three of its issues,[8] brought her into direct contact with many new authors and critics. After the New York Society for the Suppression of Vice banned *Jurgen* (1920) as indecent, Cabell gained a national platform. Writers everywhere, including Glasgow, rallied to his defense. "After eighteen years of unsuccess," Cabell joked, "I had become temporarily famous through accident."[9] *The Reviewer,* which people identified with Cabell, seemed an oasis for believers in the First Amendment.

With the rise of *The Reviewer,* Richmond buzzed with intrigue. To the chagrin of other hosts, Emily Clark monopolized visitors like Irita and Carl Van Doren, an ex-pedagogue and editor of the *Nation,* or the novelist Joseph Hergesheimer, who told Mencken not to look at Clark's face (the "ugliest" he had ever seen) but at her legs ("they are perfect").[10] Hunter Stagg, known for pursuing friendships with noted or avant-garde writers, raised eyebrows by entertaining the black poet Langston Hughes. Hughes might have thought a repast of anchovy paste and biscuits a poor recompense for being on display, or what he called "the Negro in vogue."

As Richmond's literary grande dame, Glasgow inevitably became the subject of gossip. Younger writers wanted her approval even as they needed to see her as part of a waning tradition. Her relationship with Hunter Stagg provides an example. When he retailed some scandal about Frances Newman, a former librarian whose novel, *The Hard-Boiled Virgin,* raised eyebrows, he could not believe that Glasgow got up to shut the doors. He wrote Carl Van Vechten that the anecdote made her nearly "[pass] out with joy." [11] At the same time, he worried that Glasgow might be ignoring him after he wrote a qualified review of *One Man in His Time*. Her reserve did not prevent his criticizing her "false position" at a dinner the Cabells gave for Mencken, her nemesis as a reviewer. When Glasgow met Mencken, newspaperman, essayist, and cultural critic, he "personified the national spirit of iconoclasm." [12] He delighted and angered readers with his prejudices. Younger writers took his declaration that American culture had become second-rate as a challenge. Mencken celebrated Cabell as a writer who transcended regional limitations and whose novels continued an interrupted but once great tradition of Virginia letters. One of his country's most famous bachelors, Mencken also had a streak of gallantry. To everyone's surprise, Mencken found Glasgow charming, so charming that he began to modify his tone when reviewing her work.

Stagg and his friends coveted invitations to One West Main where they could meet visiting celebrities, such as Van Vechten, Blanche and Alfred Knopf, and Elinor Wylie, whose multiple marriages allowed Glasgow to remark that she preferred kleptomania to nymphomania. At the party Glasgow gave for the British novelist Hugh Walpole, the drink flowed—to Emily Clark's amazement and approval—endlessly. Guests wandered from one flower-filled room to another or ambled in the backyard among the jessamine and magnolia trees. Later in the evening, they listened to Negro spirituals.

Although Glasgow came to dislike Walpole, their relationship shows her reaching beyond the boundaries of Richmond. Glasgow shared the general public's view of Walpole as a second-rate writer, scorned by such proponents of the New Novel as Katherine Mansfield, Dorothy Richardson, E. M. Forster, and Virginia Woolf. She may or may not have heard rumors that he was a "sodomite," who, by his own account, had admired Henry James to the point of offering him his body. (James refused on the grounds that he was too old for this kind of experiment.)

Glasgow invited Walpole to stay with her during his 1920 lecture tour of the United States. Bennett, who hated male writers even more than men in general, did not strenuously object because he loved dogs almost as much as she did. Walpole returned to One West Main in 1922, 1923, and 1926. On these subsequent visits, Glasgow slowly realized that he preferred Cabell's company to hers. The one-sided nature of their friendship began to annoy her. She had not known that Walpole's benign, schoolmasterish exterior masked a prejudice against blacks and women writers. [13] In general, he predicted that literary women, such as May Sinclair, Mrs. Ward, J. O. Hobbes, and Ethel Mayne, couldn't "stand the pace . . . they can't last out."[14] Specifically, he accused Glasgow of fiercely clutching her reputation.[15] If Walpole's feelings for women tended toward disdain, his attitude toward Glasgow became further complicated by her deafness. Walpole's mother, whose character he described as diffident and sarcastic, had been partially deaf since childhood.

Despite the hidden tensions in their friendship, Glasgow still expected him to entertain her in England. When she arrived in 1927, he could only spare her an afternoon. Glasgow recognized his portrait in the following newspaper story and wrote above it "Hugh Walpole":

> I know of a distinguished English novelist who came to the United States on a lecture tour and in the six months he spent here, since he stayed with friends wherever he went and his railway fares were paid for him by the lecture agency, he is currently reported to have spent ten cents.[16]

Though the two continued to correspond intermittently until 1930, she now held him in contempt. He had proved himself no gentleman.

Through the 1920s, Glasgow continued to emerge as a public figure, accruing honors and exciting envy. She protested that the minor dramas of her life, including the one with Walpole, seemed less real than those she wrote. Except in futile moments of anger against cruelty, she claimed to have disliked no person she knew well. Because, she adds, no one she knew well had ever been "willfully or deliberately cruel" (WW, 245). This generosity, however, belongs to retrospect. Another fiction perhaps, but one that left her pride intact.

III

Declaring (perhaps disingenuously) that it was easier to suffer yourself than to make others suffer, Glasgow shrank from any act that would increase the totality of pain in a world already miserable (WW, 271). Since childhood, she had felt a special affinity for dogs, and her reading in Eastern philosophy reinforced her belief that every living thing had a soul. She liked to debunk hierarchal notions of human beings' superiority to animals, which she called "anthropomorphic pomposity" (CM, 119). A member of the Richmond SPCA since 1893 and its vice-president from 1911 on, Glasgow assumed the presidency in 1924. She saw her work for the SPCA as extending civilization.

Among her papers, for example, she kept an account of the infamous "Mary Ellen" case that led to the formation of the Society for the Prevention of Cruelty to Children. In 1875, Mary Ellen had been rescued by the ASPCA.

Glasgow changed the course of RSPCA's history by making it politically active. The society opened an animal shelter after she donated half of the required $6,000. In three years, contributions made it possible to provide a home for cats, build kennels and runs, purchase a Ford to use as an ambulance, and hire a part-time assistant. Agents roamed the streets of Richmond recording abuses to animals and arresting the worst offenders.[17] Glasgow showed more than her share of the family's business acumen when she organized a rotating board of directors of Richmond's influential citizens, among them Henry Anderson and Douglas Southall Freeman, then editor of the *Richmond News Leader.* The society campaigned against the inhumane treatment of mules used in highway construction, and Glasgow even enlisted her old friend Alexander Weddell in the battle to end the torture of horses in Argentina, where he served as ambassador. Weddell in turn suggested that John Stewart Bryan, the president of the College of William and Mary and chairman of the board of trustees of the Richmond Public Library, help the Virginia legislature pass a law to protect horses used in construction.[18] Meanwhile the Richmond chapter's protest against vivisection proved successful enough to alarm local doctors and to prompt Dr. William Porter's charge that Glasgow's interest in animals made her abnormal. In his mind, all maiden ladies, especially those who loved animals, suffered from sexual repression.

Some of Glasgow's friends thought that Dr. Porter might have a point. After all, she claimed that as a child she had loved, after her mother, her dog best.[19] Glasgow appreciated Byron's tribute to the memory of his beloved Newfoundland buried at Newstead Abbey:

> Who possessed Beauty without Vanity,
> Strength without Insolence,
> Courage without Ferocity,
> And all the Virtues of Man without his Vices.

Her love of dogs seemed to increase in direct proportion to the diminishment of her hearing. Visitors to One West Main found the license that Glasgow allowed her pets, jumping up on laps and under full skirts, disgusting. One friend called her affection for dogs a kind of "fetish."[20] She began to collect ceramic figurines of dogs, including an eighteenth-century Crown Derby given her by the English publisher C. S. Evans.[21] Eventually she owned over a hundred pieces, which adorned her study and covered mantlepieces and table tops. Arthur Glasgow thought his sister's love of dogs an affectation. "*What* obsessive affection for animals," he snapped. "It was always for some special one."[22]

To Glasgow, no dog could have been more special than Jeremy, a pedigree Sealyham terrier named after the protagonist of Hugh Walpole's 1919 novel. "I doubt," Glasgow wrote, "whether any other living creature ever came quite so close to me" (*WW*, 247). Jeremy had been a 1921 Christmas present from Henry Anderson, who had himself received a similar gift from Queen Marie: a Russian wolfhound named Tania. Marie wanted him to have a living creature of hers beside him. "It formed a very real link."[23] (Most likely, Anderson said the same to Glasgow without attributing the remark to Marie.) Those who knew Glasgow tended to talk about the dog as though he were a person, someone with extraordinary intelligence and a vital personality. A friend recalled,

> On one occasion, when a caller who was not liked by a certain member of the household came to the house, "Jeremy" treated him with his accustomed cordiality, but when he went back upstairs, he crawled apologetically into the presence of the person who disliked the visitor, for his remarkable intuition had told him of that dislike. . . . He was always cordial but he was always apologetic when the caller had left.[24]

Within a year, Jeremy acquired a companion, for Glasgow bought Billie, the small white poodle with whom he played.

However excessive Glasgow's affection, it scarcely matched that of Anne Virginia Bennett, who treated Jeremy like a newborn baby. "Jeremy was *my* darling dog," she declared after Glasgow's death. "I took care of him."[25] (That care extended to wiping his bottom on their morning walk in full view of anyone passing.)

In Richmond, Glasgow was almost as well known for her work with animals as she was for writing novels. During "Be Kind to Animals Week" in 1952, Bennett gave permission for the *Richmond News Leader* to publish Glasgow's poem, "The Plea." It ends:

> I stood for sorrow and I knew
> The cry of every hunted hare.
> The cowering mole beneath the dew,
> The struggling bird within the snare.
> Judge Thou, my doubt, O faith that sees,
> As one who pity had on these![26]

IV

Ellen Glasgow's favorite novel, *Barren Ground*, incorporates her personal philosophy of suffering.[27] Of herself and her heroine, Dorinda Oakley, she confirmed: "We were connected, or so it seemed, by a living nerve" (*CM*, 163). The writing of *Barren Ground* led Glasgow to a liberating creed of fiction (213), one that honored the world within over the one without. "I wrote *Barren Ground*," she recalled, "and immediately I knew I had found myself. . . . I was at last free" (*WW*, 243–44). Finally she had found what she had been seeking since her teens: a code of humane stoicism "sufficient for life or for death" (271), a code that she herself understood to incorporate many of her father's Calvinist values.

Barren Ground signaled the beginning of her finest work.[28] The title points to the literal and spiritual inheritance of Glasgow's heroine, Dorinda Oakley. Seduced and abandoned, she plows her hatred of her former lover into the land, finding in the process a version of Glasgow's own humane stoicism. Like her author, Dorinda has always lived with Calvinism, either as an ethical principle, represented by her grandfather John Calvin Abernethy, or as a nervous malady, personified in her mother. Fashioned after Francis Glasgow, Abernethy is a retired missionary who embodies what Max Weber called "the Protestant ethic and the spirit of capitalism." The same uneasy alliance that fueled the Tredegar Iron Works during the Civil War allows him to view slavery—one of "the strange gestures of divine grace"—as a preordained form of submission to legitimate authority. Tenets such as election and predestination absolve the individual of personal responsibility. The fifty slaves on which Abernethy founds his fortune, if not his "estate," constitute "a nice point in theology." His conscience finds ease in the material success that indicates probable election. Later he sees no irony in selling "black flesh" to redeem "black souls in the Congo" (*BG*, 7–8).

The doctrine of social, cultural, and sexual predestination entitles Abernethy, in his roles of patriarch and minister, to colonize natives in Africa and women at home. Glasgow's equation of slavery and marriage condemns Calvinism's not-so-benevolent paternalism. Dorinda has as little place in this tradition as Glasgow had in the tradition of Southern plantation novels or, for that matter, in the tradition of legendary Southern belles. Mrs. Oakley's thwarted ambition finds shape in neurotic dreams of "blue skies and golden sands, of palm trees on a river's bank, and of black babies thrown to crocodiles" (44). Her dream, both sexual and maternal, is in truth little different from her father's reality in foreign countries, or for that matter, Pedlar's Mill, Virginia, where he peddled black flesh.

Glasgow sees the domestic ideal, with its emphasis on religion, as one of women's ancient antagonists. She does, however, have some sympathy for Mrs. Oakley's mania because it allows her to survive. Glasgow connects "this dark and secret river of her dream," flowing "silently beneath the commonplace crust of experience" (121), with creativity. The artist, as she writes in *The Woman Within*, is also "immersed in some dark stream of identity, stronger and deeper and more relentless than the external movement of living" (41). Mrs. Oakley's recurrent bouts of madness, which emanate from her frustrated creativity, seem to comment—like Charlotte Perkins Gilman's story "The Yellow Wallpaper" (1892)—on the imprisoned female imagination.

In *Barren Ground*, Glasgow details what she called "the blissful tranquility" of "falling out of love" (*WW*, 244). The outline of Dorinda's plot—an awakening to self, nature, and artistry (landscaping the wilderness)—parallels that of *The Woman Within* and effects in fiction what Glasgow, who maintained a relationship with Henry Anderson, found more difficult in life. Lacking a sense of original sin or outraged virtue, Dorinda stands as Glasgow's critique of mid-Victorian heroines, whose minds "resemble a page of the more depressing theology" (*BG*, 198). She refuses to take what God wills. By choosing celibacy, she ensures a future free from any form of social-sexual predestination. But while Dorinda's choice may be necessary, admirable, and—to the extent that it is a form of repression—abnormal, nothing shields her from the realization that she is ultimately alone.

Dorinda finds meaning in life from work and in nature. She sculpts the land that in turn nourishes a series of her evolving selves. Unlike her Calvinist forefathers, she neither eroticizes the wilderness of Old Farm nor sees it as a psychic territory that must be crossed to reach the promised land.[29] Her relationship with Nature is personal and self-reflective:

> Kinship with the land was filtering through her blood into her brain; and she knew that this transfigured instinct was blended of pity, memory, and passion. Dimly she felt that only through this emotion could she attain permanent liberation of spirit. (*BG*, 299)

This mysterious unity with the land becomes the guiding principle of the novel. Embracing her grandfather's personal beliefs (divorced from their religious context) of firmness and frugality, Dorinda grows to resemble Glasgow as she appears in *The Woman Within*. Dorinda's "deep instinct for survival" becomes "a dynamic force" (*CM*, 160)—indicated by the section titles "Broomsedge," "Pine," and "Life-Everlasting"—that transforms, as does art itself, barren ground into Elysian fields. She comes to grace or experiences, in secular terms, what Calvin termed a "quickening." By recovering herself, she begins the journey that ends for Glasgow in a vision of Everything or Nothing or God.

Glasgow struck a chord, for *Barren Ground* began selling at over 1,000 copies a week. Although Mencken found the novel's seduced-and-abandoned theme melodramatic,[30] most critics recognized its importance and compared its author to Thomas Hardy, George Eliot, and Knut Hamsun. Glasgow's publisher announced that realism had finally "crossed the Potomac." Despite its Southern setting, reviewers saw *Barren Ground* making an important statement about national life. (Glasgow would herself echo this view of regional literature at the Southern Writers Conference in 1931.) Cabell, whose *Straws and Prayer-Books* she had favorably reviewed in the *New York Herald Tribune Books* the previous year, commended her "portrayal of all social and economic Virginia since the War Between the States" (*Reviews*, 254–55). Later he claimed that Glasgow stole this idea from him, but for the present he remained friendly. Other critics took the opportunity to summarize and reevaluate the body of her work. Such retrospectives led Glasgow to think that she had a real chance of receiving the Pulitzer Prize, already granted to Wharton for *The Age of Innocence* in 1921 and Willa Cather for *One of Ours* in 1923. Her competition included F. Scott Fitzgerald's *The Great Gatsby*, John Dos Passos's *Manhattan Transfer*, Theodore Dreiser's *American Tragedy*, along with the eventual winner: Sinclair Lewis's *Arrowsmith*.

Certainly *Barren Ground* marked a triumph for Glasgow. Its evocation of nature won her friends among the Southern agrarians, while her poetic realism influenced the work of other novelists, including Robert Penn Warren (*Night Rider* [1936]), Eudora Welty (*A Curtain of Green* [1941]), and William Faulkner (*Go Down, Moses* [1942]).[31] Glasgow's relationships with Edwin Mims, then finishing *The Advancing South* (1926), Stuart P. Sherman, a critic for the *New York Herald Tribune Books*, and Carl Van Vechten, the impish patron of the Harlem Renaissance, date from this time. Glasgow had a partiality for Van Vechten. An imposing man—tall, silver-haired, and square-jawed—Van Vechten had dancing eyes that could look sightless when he was preoccupied or angry. Friends remember him in a perennial position, leaning back in a big armchair with a decanter by his side, smoking one of his endless procession of cigarettes.[32] Van Vechten knew and photographed prominent artists, including Glasgow (and her dogs). He cared for all kinds of people, such as Langston Hughes and Gertrude Atherton, or, for that matter, Gertrude Stein and Ellen Glasgow, who had little in common except his friendship.

Many people thought that Glasgow sought out men who could help her career. But they did the larger share of courting. "You are a great artist and at the same time a great thinker," Edwin Mims wrote her.[33] Stuart Sherman met Glasgow at the Van Dorens, where he fell in love with her "spirit": "Don't let your 'fighting spirit' devour your charm!" he warned in the earlier manner of Walter Hines Page. "Now you, if you will let me say so, seem to brim with a certain sort of Happiness. Let us have it—under tension."[34] They wondered how such a philosophical and sanguine, even blithe, personality could write a book like *Barren Ground*. "This book is so remote from anything I know of you," Van Vechten wrote, "[that] it makes me feel, indeed, how little I must know you at all!"[35]

In truth, few people did.

V

Anyone who met Glasgow the summer of 1925 would have thought her life full of laughter. For eight weeks, she rented a house in Barnstable on Cape Cod. Because Bennett had refused to leave Jeremy, Glasgow traveled with her niece Josephine Clark. She played golf almost every day and claimed that it improved her health more than any medicine. Eventually she had to give up the sport because she could not hear players calling "Fore!"

Success agreed with her. Arthur took an almost personal pride in his sister's growing reputation and at Christmas rewarded her in the usual way with a grayish-blue Buick sedan that cost almost $2,000. He reasoned that since she now had a chauffeur, a man named Nathaniel Martin, she needed a better car. Carrie Coleman also benefited from Arthur's generosity by purchasing the old Essex at "a good price." Arthur helped to maintain his sister in a style that intrigued reviewers, who repeated the old stories about her Tidewater background. Neither she nor the critics entertained at One West Main saw anything sexist or gratuitous in describing the taste of her creamy eggnog or her debut at St. Cecilia's Ball. Writer after writer exulted over the Chinese Chippendale chairs, the old mahogany, the drawing rooms' blue silk brocade curtains, or the fire screens "embroidered by the delicate hands of gentle ladies long since dead and gone."[36] Northern visitors especially liked to think of her as a Southern aristocrat surrounded by faithful servants—from the maid who drew the morning baths to the cook known for his diamondback terrapin. When one friend asked her if she had a servant as loyal as Dorinda Oakley's friend, Fluvanna, she replied, "It is true that I have a Fluvanna, but 'she' is a man [James Anderson], who has been in our family for nearly thirty-five years. . . . There are few of his generation left anywhere, and least of all, I believe, among the colored younger servants in the South." [37]

The triumph of *Barren Ground* so revived Glasgow's energy and spirits that the following summer she wrote in a frenetic few months the first of her Queenborough trilogy, *The Romantic Comedians* (1926). She may have gotten the idea for *The Romantic Comedians*, which pokes fun at Henry Anderson, [38] from Emily Clark. In July 1923, Clark had published a satire in *Smart Set* called "Lustre Ware" that ridiculed Anderson for his noted pomposity. Clark had enough doubts about the piece to publish it under a pseudonym, "Priscilla Hale." She alternated between glee at its warm reception and anxiety that Anderson, who served on *The Reviewer*'s board of directors, would learn of her "purely literary exercise." Many Richmonders believed Glasgow the author: "It was the most brilliant thing she ever wrote," said one, "but it wasn't very kind." [39] Clark confessed her role to Glasgow, whom she feared offending as Anderson's best friend. "She was lovely about it," Clark wrote Joseph Hergesheimer. "She seemed to understand that I wasn't malicious . . . but just used him as I would a lump of clay, and became entranced with my own idea." [40]

Anderson, who in the twenties acquired a reputation for flirting with young flappers and dancing to dawn at "the Hot" (Springs), fared better in Glasgow's hands. She ostensibly wrote *The Romantic Comedians* for her private diversion, though Richmonders could not help recognizing Henry Anderson in her characterization of Judge Honeywell, with his English valet, wire-rimmed glasses, Victorian pomposity, "international attitude toward life" (*RC*, 5), and twin sister. Glasgow situates the newly widowed 65-year-old Judge Honeywell between duty and desire, that is, between Amanda Lightfoot, the woman who has waited over thirty years for him, and Annabel Upchurch, a young flapper. The judge bitterly resents his twin, Edmonia Bredalbane, for reminding him of his age. He reasons that a man in his prime appears distinguished, a woman preposterous. The judge thinks that Edmonia's four marriages and numerous lovers makes her a woman of liberal views and loose behavior.

Like Virginia Woolf did in *Orlando,* Glasgow lampoons conventions of gender by designating Honeywell the weaker "sister." The next generation, which scorns his romantic idealism, views Edmonia's "scarlet letter" as if it were a "foreign decoration for distinguished service" (*RC*, 84). As she explains to her brother:

> Behavior as much as beauty is a question of geography, and that my respectability increases with every mile of the distance I travel from Queenborough. In France, my reputation is above reproach; by the time I reach Vienna, I have become a bit of a prude; and contrasted with the Balkan temperament, I am little more than a tombstone to female virtue. (310)

There is no fool like an old fool and, despite Edmonia's warnings, Honeywell marries his Annabel. Annabel does not believe in suffering (never mind in silence) and within a year of the exhausting honeymoon leaves her husband for a man her own age. Honeywell has a nervous collapse and seems resigned until he notices his nurse — "younger than his memory of his mother, younger even than Annabel" — and thinks, "There is the woman I ought to have married!" (345). Although Glasgow spoofs American culture after the Great War, she refuses to condense experience into any formula, sentimental or otherwise. No matter how much she laughs at Honeywell, she evokes our shared recognition of the amoral will to life and happiness. In this way, *The Romantic Comedians* resembles *Virginia* (1913), for it too begins as a satire and ends, if not as tragedy, as a poignant tale of lost youth and renewal.

The first novel to impress H. L. Mencken unequivocally (likely for its sexual emphasis), *The Romantic Comedians* sold, within a few months of its September publication, over 100,000 copies. Glasgow's contract had stipulated that her 10 percent royalty would retroactively increase to 12½ percent when the book sold over 30,000; after 35,000 copies her share would increase to 15 percent. In November, the Book of the Month Club offered *The Romantic Comedians* to its subscribers. Even with over 141,000 copies sold, it nevertheless failed to make the list of top ten bestsellers, in which Anita Loos's *Gentlemen Prefer Blondes* ranked second. Glasgow would have liked the additional publicity such sales generated, but she no longer needed to worry about making ends meet. In July, Arthur had a deed of trust executed in her name and that of Josephine Clark. The trust, which totaled well over $100,000, contained tax-free securities. He hoped that it would insure her an additional $300 a month (and Josephine an additional $100).[41]

As Ellen Glasgow looked forward to the new year, she prided herself on having survived love, ecstasy, and anguish. She had, in her own words, "come, at last, from the fleeting rebellions of youth into the steadfast—or is it," she asked, "merely the unseasonable—accord without surrender of the unreconciled heart?" (WW, 296).

VI

In June 1927, Glasgow and Carrie Coleman Duke sailed for England on the SS *Olympic*. Once more, Arthur Glasgow helped finance the trip, and (once more) Henry Anderson said goodbye with his trademark orchids. Through fall and winter, Glasgow had suffered again from difficulties with her ears and from nervous exhaustion. Iron tablets helped her lethargy no more than exercise. She originally planned to take the "cure" in Carlsbad and then check into a sanitorium recommended by Arthur in Paris, but by the date of the actual trip she had recuperated physically, if not mentally.[42]

Glasgow arrived in Southampton on a gloriously sunny day. Arthur met her and Carrie at Waterloo Station and brought them to Moncorvo House, the home he shared with his wife and daughter in Ennismore Gardens. In 1902, Arthur had married, despite Ellen's warning to the bride that "the Glasgows make bad husbands." His wife, Margaret Elizabeth Branch, came from a wealthy and connected family, her ancestor Christopher Branch of Abingdon-on-Thames having settled in Virginia before the Pilgrims landed at Plymouth Rock. A beautiful woman, Margaret had caught the roving eye of King Edward VII. She had, according to her own testimony, kept her virtue by refusing to dine with him without her husband. Glasgow never cared for Margaret—perhaps because of her good looks, perhaps because she seemed to fritter away her time raising orchids and serving on the boards of charities. She told friends that Margaret, suffering from milk leg, spent most of her life "between the sheets,"[43] and many people believed that Glasgow had used her as a model for *The Builders'* neurasthenic Angelica Blackburn. What Margaret thought of her sister-in-law we can only guess.

The First World War had made Arthur, who had developed an economical process for converting waste gas into fuel, an even wealthier man. Like other American entrepreneurs of middle-class origins, he had gone about acquiring culture. His home contained works of art by Donatello and Romney, a ballroom decorated with rare tapestries, and a wine cellar that gladdened his sister's heart. Nothing, Glasgow wrote Rebe, lifted her mood more than escaping from prohibition! Given her choice of all the guest rooms, she ran "true to form" and "chose the best & most luxurious," with an attached bath-room. Carrie settled for the adjoining room.[44]

The return to England invigorated Glasgow. She couldn't wait to explore London and turned Carrie out of bed early. Their adventures consisted of simple pleasures, from breaks in routine and little incidents that seemed to have great import. One rainy morning, for instance, the friends stole through the sleeping house like naughty youngsters and hailed a taxi to take them to the Foundling Hospital. The occupants of the hospital had all been removed to the country and a "For sale in freehold lots" notice hung on the gate. The sign suggested, to Glasgow's mind, a whole story about societal changes and the advancing of economic order. During the day, Arthur and Margaret left them to themselves, and the friends went sightseeing, shopping, and for a course of beauty treatments that included facials, hairstyling, and manicures. Glasgow liked to shop at Selfridge's and bought Bennett a coat and herself a new set of golf clubs. Her sister-in-law introduced her to the duchess of Hamilton, a crusader against vivisection, who had come to enlist Margaret's help—much to Glasgow's surprise—in organizing an international humane congress: "the only one of Margaret's friends I ever felt drawn to," she told Rebe. The duchess did not eat meat and refused to wear fur.[45]

At the end of July, Glasgow left London for a tour of Yorkshire. She and Carrie had reservations at the Majestic in Harrogate, a turn-of-the-century hotel designed to provide "refined" accommodation for those visitors want-ing to benefit from the "rejuvenating" sulfur waters of the Pump Rooms and Royal Baths. By the time Glasgow arrived in Harrogate, her blood pressure had dropped to an abnormally low level, and her doctor prescribed hypoder-mic injections of arsenic and strychnine.

Glasgow could still go sightseeing, and with a hired driver she and Carrie took day trips to towns such as Whitby and Durham. In Durham Cathedral, the friends stood in the nave whispering in unison: "Why did no one ever tell us how magnificent it is?"[46] Glasgow's tour of northern England's past included literary sites such as Tintagel, associated with King Arthur and his knights, and Shandy Hall, the home of Laurence Sterne. It also took a more predominantly spiritual, if not religious, route. Time and time again she thanked Henry VIII for his destruction of monasteries and abbeys because, like a century of tourists before her, she found nature's slow reclamation of ruins more sublime than the finished monuments.

Unlike John Ruskin, Glasgow believed that nature framed civilization, making its remnants more humane: "First man did everything," she told

Rebe, "and then Nature beautified and softened and embellished the ruins to the last delicate touch." For this reason, the empty spaces and walls of Fountains Abbey not far from Harrogate stimulated her aesthetic and spiritual senses. Straining miraculously upward without any support, the abbey seemed a microcosm of all human yearning, and its history—from eminence to dissolution to transformation—a paradigm of life's predestined cycle. The remote abbeys at Easby, Bolton, Byland, and Rievaulx, as well as Richmond Castle and Saint Agatha's Church at sunset, seemed holy places. "Places usually give me more than people," she confided in Rebe, "and because of this I have been able to open my mind to this beauty and interest as I was never free to do when I travelled before the war." [47]

On her return to London, Glasgow learned that she had the use of her sister-in-law's car and the chauffeur, Halsey. Halsey drove so fast that she lived in fear of his running over a dog. As a talisman perhaps, they drove miles to visit the Animal Rescue League in the poorest part of London, and Glasgow wrote Bennett that in comparison to Virginia, "England is a paradise for dumb things." [48] It was not, however, a paradise for the elderly. Glasgow visited several almshouses: one founded in 1437, where the men wore blue coats and the women red capes, and another in Dorchester that housed six men and one woman who complained that she felt married to them all. [49] Glasgow found these places "pathetic but full of human interest." [50]

Glasgow's visits with old friends disheartened her: May Sinclair had suffered a stroke, and Joseph Conrad's wife, Jessie, had become enormously stout and complacent. It troubled Glasgow that Conrad's widow had inherited nothing except the shadow of his fame. The Hardys, both of whom Glasgow liked, had changed little, though Wessex, their wire-haired terrier, had died a few weeks earlier. Glasgow, who had hesitated to disturb them, took comfort in knowing that age had not deadened his sensibilities. [51] They reminisced about her visit in 1914, when she had pleased him by reciting his own lines from The Dynasts, and Glasgow perhaps remembered these lines again in 1928 when Hardy himself died:

> O Immanence, that reasonest not,
> In putting forth all things begot,
> Thou build'st Thy house in space—for what? (WW, 197)

Glasgow had hoped to meet Virginia Woolf, whose experiments with point of view in Mrs. Dalloway (1925) she admired. Instead she lunched with Woolf's friend and lover, Vita Sackville-West, and toured Knole, the 365-

room manor that had been a present from Henry VIII. Beside Sackville-West, new friends included Frank Swinnerton, whom she found more interesting than his countless books. Radclyffe Hall—soon to cause a furor with her lesbian novel *The Well of Loneliness* (1928)—returned to England expressly to meet her.

Looking forward to beginning work again, Glasgow sailed for New York on September 7, 1927. Anderson sent gardenias in lieu of the usual orchids and met her at the dock. He then returned to Richmond, where she arrived three days later. Once home, Glasgow found Richmond as provincial as ever.

VII

Glasgow had hoped to devote herself to writing *They Stooped to Folly* (1929), the next novel in her Queenborough trilogy. Instead, she became involved in a battle against censorship involving the Richmond Public Library's policy toward Sinclair Lewis's *Elmer Gantry*. Glasgow unequivocally opposed censorship in a public library. No one, she observed, obliged people to read a particular book: "Any book that is written by an author of established reputation and treated seriously by the leading reviewers should be at the call of mature readers." In *Elmer Gantry* she failed to see anything "more harmful than a shrewdly observed and badly written study of crude emotionalism" that ran for "four hundred and thirty-two unalluring pages"—a hundred pages under Glasgow's own average. "Indeed," she concluded, "this book is so poor a novel that it may prove to be good propaganda." Glasgow believed that discussions about censorship should focus on what constitutes "art" and not on questions of morality.[52] She tried to resign from the library's board of trustees, but a satisfactory end to the controversy made her resignation unnecessary. Remembering her own book-starved youth and how much a subscription to the New York Public Library had meant, Glasgow retained a great respect for the service that librarians provided. When she and James Branch Cabell attended a convention of librarians, for example, she made it a point—despite Cabell's impatience—to stay until she had shaken the hand of every participant.

In Richmond's literary history, the names of Ellen Glasgow and James Branch Cabell seem unalterably linked. Their friendship, which began years before, flourished in the late twenties and thirties. Glasgow had a soft spot for the grave young man she remembered from that long-ago visit to Williamsburg. It worried her when he was sick, and she once sent him a bottle of Harvey's Bristol Cream with the admonition to drink a glass of sherry with lunch. For his part, he found her mixture of gossip and pessimism more diverting than spirits.

Cabell had a low voice, and his speech to some sounded painfully deliberate. To Glasgow, it rang clear and concise. Scholarly and every bit the gentleman, Cabell teased and flirted with her. Above all, he put her at ease. She thought he wore his disillusionment "very much as an explorer adventuring into the jungle wears his mask of gauze" — as a protection against things. She found him, like most cynics (herself included), a romantic, and thanked him for giving "this democratic Age of Concrete the manner of The Primrose Way rather than of Main Street."[53]

Like Glasgow, Cabell had created a space for himself to write. Having married a woman of means, he spent a large part of his day in his study, which contained more than a hundred brass and china animals and two maps of "Poictesme," his fictional equivalent of Glasgow's Queenborough. Cabell shared Glasgow's distaste for music—and for most novels by Willa Cather (who, for her part, could not get through a Glasgow book). He especially appreciated Glasgow's concern for his wife, Percie, whom some Richmonders thought too social or pushy. In 1929, Cabell dedicated his novel *All about Eve: A Comedy of Fig-Leaves* to "Ellen Glasgow—very naturally—this book which commemorates the intelligence of women." Glasgow, who teased that his tributes were written "in dust upon mauve or purple jackets,"[54] returned the favor with *They Stooped to Folly: A Comedy of Morals,* a book that honors the chivalry of men. The dedication reads:

> To James Branch Cabell
> . . . In Acknowledgment of Something
> About Eve . . .
> This Book Commemorates the
> Chivalry of Men.

Glasgow and Cabell differed less in their visions than in their chosen forms: his a self-described "epic" of men torn between eros and spirit, materialism and culture, and hers a "social history." In the end, she came to find her reality barely distinguishable from his dream.

Glasgow believed that Cabell's novels captured the Southerner's eternal dilemma. Why, she asked in "The Novel in the South" (*Harper's,* December 1928), has the South remained so hostile to thinkers and artists? To her, the answer lay in the Southerner's pleasure-seeking nature (*RD*, 70–71) and fear of offending. Before the Civil War, only the slave, the poor white, or the immodest woman might have felt inclined to protest, and no one would have listened. After Reconstruction, a "mournful literature of commemoration" (72) perpetuated sentimentalism. Glasgow cites *Uncle Remus*, Joel Chandler Harris's collection of folktales written in black dialect, as a notable exception, for "whenever the Southern writer escaped into the consciousness of a different race or class, he lost both his cloying sentiment and his pose of superiority" (73). Foreshadowing her speech to the Southern Writers Conference in 1931, Glasgow claimed that Southern novelists could stimulate a new national literature if they turned inward for inspiration. Those now leading the way— James Branch Cabell, DuBose Heyward, Paul Green, Julia Peterkin, Burton Rascoe, and Frances Newman—fearlessly scrutinized life to re-evaluate the past and the present (79).

At the end of the decade and almost forty years after her examination at the University of Virginia, Ellen Glasgow's stature took an academic turn. In February 1929, the University of Rochester offered her an honorary doctorate of letters, which she deferred; in June of the following year, the University of North Carolina awarded the same degree for helping "to develop in the South the habit of self-criticism."[55] These tributes highlight Glasgow's increasingly active and vocal role in defining not only Southern letters but the South itself. To others, she had come to be the logical ambassador for Southern literature.

VIII

Glasgow's 1929 novel, *They Stooped to Folly*, can be read as an extended commentary on the mores of her region. In this satiric comedy of manners, Glasgow uses the trope of the "ruined woman" to survey Southern, if not American, provincialism, from the Victorian to the modern period. Glasgow spares no one: not her protagonist Virginius Littlepage, who lusts after a divorcée returned from service in the Balkans; not his wife, Victoria, worn out with the strain of being a good "influence"; not the truth-seeking younger generation as self-deceived as their elders; nor least of all Virginius's brother Marmaduke, an artist. Maimed, isolated, and an "enemy to society" (*TSF*, 273), Marmaduke spends his time painting nudes no one wants to see and telling truths no one cares to hear.

Glasgow analyzes what Mencken liked to call "the Southern attitude toward fornication" (Reviews, 31). The topic of "fornication," of course, allows her to expose the tenuous nature of civilization. Debunking Freud's characterization of women's friendships as "unnatural" or lesbian, she nevertheless links, as he does, the continuance of civilization with sexual sublimation. In They Stooped to Folly, A loves B who loves C who loves A. The book begins and ends in the consciousness of its male protagonist, entering in the interval that of his wife and would-be mistress. By shifting the novel's central consciousness, Glasgow refigures reality while insisting that myths of mother love and chivalry never die, any more than ingrained attitudes about class or race. The seduction of a woman constitutes some sort of claim on a decent man, for example, until one confronts "the fact of colour," which makes "a difference in the moral, as well as the legal, angle of vision" (TSF, 259). Glasgow would explore this idea more fully in her next novel, The Sheltered Life (1932), by giving Eva Birdsong and her black servant, Memoria, the same plot with different consequences. In They Stooped to Folly, Glasgow finds little difference between Victorian spirituality and postwar materialism, yet she sympathizes with the next generation's fierce need to find something worth loving, "not love alone, but something worth loving" (350).

When she negotiated for the publication of They Stooped to Folly with Doubleday (now Doubleday, Doran, and Company), Glasgow could point to the success of her last two novels. She particularly wanted her books well advertised and insisted on a substantial increase (from $10,000 to $15,000) in the advertising budget. A rival publisher, Alfred Harcourt, understood the importance that Glasgow placed on marketing. In November 1929, he attempted to lure her away from Doubleday by promising her the same terms he had granted Sinclair Lewis: a $20,000 advance, a royalty of 15 percent, and a guaranteed advertising expenditure of $15,000. Although tempted, Glasgow refused. The Literary Guild had chosen They Stooped to Folly as one of its selections, and she credited her publisher with their choice. The novel immediately sold 120,000 copies. Arthur sent his congratulations on her unsurpassed "epoch-making work": "I am more than ever proud of you," he wrote without any irony, "which is superlative praise, considering . . . [my] previous feeling for you." [56]

Despite the enthusiasm of friends and family, the book received mixed, though largely positive, reviews. The naysayers saw its theme as essentially old-fashioned and its tone as too piercing. At once feminist and antifeminist, They Stooped to Folly defines social and moral constructs in terms of male privilege and criticizes women "because they have embraced sacrifice as an ideal," turning the "American Republic into an oligarchy of maternal instincts" (*TSF,* 130).

Writers such as Sara Haardt and Stark Young, a reviewer for the *Herald Tribune* known for his extremely popular Civil War novel, *So Red the Rose* (1934), openly acknowledged their debt to Glasgow. "I wanted to tell you . . . the part your 'Barren Ground' played in 'Heaven Trees' and even in the other book, though that was two years later," Young wrote her in 1928:

> I was at my father's house in Mississippi in the summer of 1925, when I read the book. The last shreds of the life there, my father and all, you know what it was, were all round me. The comment that your book was on all that, is evident. My father died in October and I began to work on my book, and much of that tenderness or whatever it is in "Heaven Trees" that people seem to love so, is related to this visit, your book, his death and so on.[57]

Glasgow responded to these overtures with advice and practical help. Sometimes she even allowed excerpts from her letters to be used in advertising circulars. The admiration of younger writers flattered Glasgow, reassuring her that she had not become old-fashioned.

In the late 1920s, Glasgow also developed friendships with two New York doctors, Ward A. Holden and Joseph Collins, who saw a close connection between psychology and literature. With Collins in particular, she could continue the discussions about psychological motivation she had enjoyed with Pearce Bailey before his death. The author of such books as *The Way with Nerves* (1911) and *The Doctor Looks at Literature* (1931), Collins had compared Glasgow to Maupassant in his study of American women writers, *Taking the Literary Pulse* (1924). Glasgow enjoyed his sexual banter and salacious sense of humor—perhaps because she understood that his amorous adventures lay elsewhere. His prurient interest in her sex life amused, rather than offended, her. The two took pleasure in pushing one another to the limits of their tolerance. When discussing *Of Mice and Men,* for instance, Collins argued that Lennie had an orgasm every time he squeezed anything, whether a rat or a woman. Glasgow ended the conversation by calling him "a dirty old man, with your French boys and reading things into a book that . . . [aren't] there!"[58] By discussing topics not considered proper in Richmond, Collins helped Glasgow to step out of the role she had played for the last fifty years. Several of Glasgow's friends found Collins offensive, but he stood by her to the end with offers of emotional and financial support.

Just as Glasgow had met Collins through Pearce Bailey, she met Ward

Holden through Collins. Holden, who addressed Glasgow as "Cara mia," did not share Collins's interest in French boys. He pursued her, yet whatever attraction she might initially have had for him faded almost immediately. Holden assumed a greater intimacy than she wanted to concede after they passed the good part of one night trying to save the life of a sick dog by feeding it a mixture of milk and whiskey. When the dog died, Holden comforted her with a kiss. Holden, who measured his life by "affectionate friendships with fine women," thought Glasgow to be a woman of the world. His letters to her alternate between bursts of sensuality and descriptions that could come from *Women's Wear Daily*:

> Your expressive mobile face, your wonderful waved black hair, your exquisite white shoulders and arms and tiny hands, your trim aristocratic legs, your black gown with the metal ornament applied to the left of the skirt and the varicolored soft batik scarf that trailed behind you—all made up a picture not to be forgotten. And it was indeed lovely to hold you in my arms, and indeed delicious to kiss your sweet lips—sophisticated certainly, but not primitive.
>
> I shall remember, dear, though with your present-day philosophy you refuse to take romantic experiences seriously.[59]

Glasgow chided him for mistaking the color of her hair, and politely but firmly tried to distance herself. She made it clear that she wanted friendship, not love, and Holden, who had begun to sound like Henry Anderson by "trying to write acceptable replies" to her "beautiful letters," shifted his tone: "Our discussion on the superiority of affection to love has unsettled my ideas, dear, and I, like you, am wondering."[60]

In August, Glasgow had no compunctions about leaving Holden to take what would soon become her annual trip to Maine. She did, however, worry about leaving her Jeremy, who was recovering from the second of two gall-bladder operations, one in December 1928 and the other in July 1929. Glasgow had not trusted local veterinarians. Instead, a Richmond surgeon, Dr. James Galloway, supervised the case, sitting up nights with his patient to no avail.

Glasgow returned to be with Jeremy in his last hours. Despite Galloway's solicitude and consultations with specialists from New York and Philadelphia, Jeremy eventually succumbed to pneumonia. "Not only are Miss Glasgow and Miss Bennett grief-stricken over his death," wrote Virginius Dabney, a respected historian with a wicked sense of humor, but 'Billie,' Miss Glasgow's little French poodle, wanders about the house distracted." Dabney had gone to pay his respects and had been roped into writing the obituary. As he tells the story, he quivered with fear that he might offend Glasgow by remembering Jeremy as, well, as a dog. His tongue-in-cheek obituary, published in the *Richmond Times-Dispatch* on September 2, 1929, must have amused Glasgow's friends, who found her love of Jeremy abnormal. Dabney presents Jeremy as belonging to both the FFVs through Glasgow and the FFDs (First Family of Dogs) through his sire, the great champion Barberry Hill Gin Rickey. Dabney fails to state that Jeremy had become a local celebrity in his own right and that friends from all over the world, including Hugh Walpole, commiserated with Glasgow over her loss. Joseph Collins told her that "intense love has terrible exactment";[61] and Radclyffe Hall, another animal lover, assured her that dogs had an afterlife and that Jeremy would greet her in heaven.[62] Amélie Rives wrote that she had dreamed of Glasgow, awake in a lighted house, "sorrowing for Jeremy."[63] Jeremy was embalmed and buried in a baby's casket in the backyard of One West Main, his grave marked with a marble stone.[64] (When Billie died of heart failure nine years later, he was buried next to Jeremy.) Of all Glasgow's acquaintances, Carl Van Vechten best understood her feelings: "There is no good telling you, dear Ellen, that you will get over it because you won't. . . . That is the permanent comfort that animals give us, the power to *remember* & feel. I understand, dear Ellen, but I cannot help you."[65]

Jeremy's death left Glasgow heartsick. From Rebe's home in Chestnut Hill, Pennsylvania, she wrote Bennett that she had an unabating, stabbing pain in her heart. "I know it is far harder on you," she acknowledged, "because he was much closer to you than to me, & I don't see how you get any peace."[66] Glasgow mourned Jeremy for an entire year. His death served as an emblem, focusing all the pain and loss she had felt throughout her life, including the dream of a marriage with Henry Anderson.

The following summer, in June 1930, Glasgow, accompanied once more by Carrie Duke, embarked on another trip to England.

> I may be better physically [she wrote on board], but my state of mind is as depressed as ever, and I do not take the slightest interest in going to England again. Life seems to have worn on my nerves until I cannot escape any part of the past. Yesterday was the anniversary of Walter's [McCormack's] death & I lived over all those horrors again. But I believe that Jeremy's loss has shaken me deeper than everything else. I don't know how or why, but it was just as if the last living roots of my being withered and died that day when I came home from Maine and saw him. If I had not gone away it might have been

easier. I don't know,—but that moment seemed to epitomize all life to me. Nothing has mattered since—all I have wanted is to have everything over.[67]

Glasgow grieved for Jeremy as if he had been a child. Friends who understood her pain had filled her stateroom with flowers and, true to form, Henry Anderson took his leave with a corsage of orchids, which she wore each night.

Once in London, Carrie urged Glasgow to visit Harrogate, where she could undergo a "cure." The moment Glasgow arrived there in July, she collapsed, and Carrie had to arrange for round-the-clock nursing. It took a full month for her to recover sufficiently to travel. When she did recover, however, she made up for lost time by touring the Lake District, where she stopped at Windemere and Grasmere, the home of William Wordsworth. Glasgow's spirits began to improve during the Scottish leg of their tour. Thinking of her own father, she marveled at the imagination of the Scots: How could the same mind, "nurtured on the dry bread of Calvinism," conceive a war memorial (in Edinborough) that honored carrier pigeons as well as fallen soldiers? Here was no irony or attempt to demean the dead. Glasgow made two pilgrimages of sorts: the first to Dryburgh, the burial place of Walter Scott; and the other to Greyfriars, where she had no success locating the grave of John Grey's faithful dog, Bobby.[68] She distrusted the story that an old sexton had secretly buried him in the center of a flowerbed near his master, whose grave he had guarded until his own death. "Ah, human nature!" she wrote Anne Virginia. "And, ah, dog nature!" Although Glasgow spent a cozy evening with Una Troubridge and Radclyffe Hall, she wrote Bennett that she had not had one hour—or even one moment—of genuine pleasure during the entire trip. "The best (of the bad)," she decided, happened when she unexpectedly discovered a "field of flaming poppies."[69] In an elegiac mood, she perhaps thought them a remembrance for all the dead.

Before sailing home, Glasgow spent a few weeks in Paris, where she roamed parks and museums, while Carrie looked at fashions and drank champagne cocktails at the Ritz. In September, the friends returned to Richmond. Glasgow liked the conceit that she had given up on life, but once again it had gathered her back into its net. She would feel younger as she approached 60 than she had at 20. Without her knowing it, the best years lay ahead.

CHAPTER 9

BLOOD AND IRONY

1931–1932

*We are, I think, less interested in any social order past or present
than we are in that unknown quality which we once called the
soul and now call psychology of mankind. Into this world of
psychology we may look as into a wilderness that is forever conquered and yet forever virgin.*

Ellen Glasgow, opening speech of
the Southern Writers Conference

I

ELLEN GLASGOW LIKED to pun that the South needed blood and irony—
blood because it had strained too far from its roots, irony because it believed
its own myths (*CM*, 28). As her declaration highlights, she felt herself attracted to apparently opposing traditions: one associated with "realism"; the
other with "legend," which she defined as the dynamic "living character of a
race" (12). This blend of romanticism and realism, practiced by Glasgow and
championed by that enemy of the "Bozarts," H. L. Mencken, became in the
1930s one of the distinguishing marks of Southern literature. It informs Glasgow's earliest work and finds full expression in *The Sheltered Life* (1932).

Although the next generation of Southern writers, including William

Faulkner and Julia Peterkin (known for her sketches of Gullah blacks), remains indebted to Glasgow for her challenge to contemporary views of history, her greatest contribution to literature lies in her frank treatment of race, an issue that remained complex in her own life. In the late twenties, for example, Glasgow appeared at her niece's coming-out ball in Richmond as Mme. Paradise, the alluring and literary friend of Samuel Johnson who also happened to be a slaveowner. As Mme. Paradise, Glasgow came sheathed in a colonial gown of brocaded cream silk. Everywhere she walked, a black child trailed with her hat and prayer book. If Glasgow wished to make the point that an intolerable, immoral system supported "paradise," it would have escaped most of the assembled company. This is exactly the idea Glasgow emphasizes in her fiction, yet how are we to interpret her comment to Carl Van Vechten after reading his novel *Nigger Heaven* (1926), which she approved? Only in the father of Mary, "a very appealing character," did she find the slightest trace of the blacks she knew: "The serene fatalism, the dignity of manner, the spiritual power, all these qualities decayed, it appeared, with the peculiar institution [of slavery]."[1] In her daily life, Glasgow puzzled over the issue of race, wavering between her feelings, often obscure and inherited, and her reason. In her fiction she sought to forge a "dynamic tradition" that recognized the individual and integrated histories of white and black Southerners.

At 57 years old, Glasgow had been writing novels for over three decades. At times, she had felt discouraged, even bitter, about her own career, but as the new year approached she determined to reach out to the next generation. Glasgow mentioned to James Southall Wilson, the editor of the *Virginia Quarterly Review* and the Poe Professor at the University of Virginia, an idea that had been brewing in her mind for two years: a gathering of Southern writers that would define the direction and scope of Southern, indeed American, literature and draw attention to unsung regional talent.[2] Wilson immediately saw the importance of such a "pow-wow."[3] It would tell the rest of the country that the South was no longer a "lost province, to be governed, in a literary sense at least, by superior powers" from the Northeast and Middle West.[4] Wilson arranged a February meeting with DuBose Heyward, the author of *Porgy* (1925), and Archibald Henderson, the biographer of George Bernard Shaw, to discuss the idea. Illness prevented Glasgow from attending this and subsequent planning sessions. Heyward and Henderson suggested that Cabell join their committee, and he agreed to let them use his name with the provision that Stark Young, then a drama critic originally from Mississippi, and Paul Green (a North Carolinian best known for his Pulitzer-

Prize-winning play *In Abraham's Bosom* [1927]) be added to make the group more representative. Cabell contacted Willa Cather, who flatly declined, and Heyward and Henderson presented the idea to John Crowe Ransom and Thomas Wolfe. Wolfe humbly accepted the "honor." The final committee consisted of Glasgow, Heyward, Henderson, Cabell, Young, Green, and Wolfe. Wilson circulated a master list from which they each picked twenty to twenty-five names. The committee then selected those writers they wished to invite, essentially formulating Southern letters for the next decade. Stressing the informality of the meeting, Wilson assured the would-be participants of absolute privacy, something that William Faulkner warned he needed: "You have seen a country wagon come into town, with a hound dog under the wagon. It stops on the square and the folks get out, but that hound never gets very far from that wagon. He might be cajoled or scared out for a short distance, but first thing you know he has scuttled back under the wagon; maybe he growls at you a little. Well that's me."[5] The weekend proved that Faulkner knew himself well.

For the first annual Southern Writers Conference, October 23 and 24, 1931, writers descended on Charlottesville from Arkansas, Kentucky, Mississippi, North Carolina, South Carolina, West Virginia, and, of course, the host state Virginia. Wilson housed them at the Monticello Hotel and the Farmington Country Club, located a few miles west of town with a view of the Blue Ridge Mountains. Originally designed by Thomas Jefferson for an Albemarle County family, it was, wrote Emily Clark, "the loveliest club in Virginia." Guests occupied former slave quarters now converted into rooms with baths.[6] Other faculty members, including the historian Stringfellow Barr, acted as chauffeurs. In addition to Faulkner and the members of the committee, a partial list of those attending includes tried-and-true Southerners such as Struthers Burt, Caroline Gordon, Mary Johnston, Josephine Pickney, Alice Hegan Rice, Cale Young Rice, and Allen Tate (whose mother came from Virginia gentry), as well as those with more tenuous ties: John Peale Bishop, Herschel Brickell, Emily Clark, William E. Dodd, Isa Glenn, Irita Van Doren, and Sherwood Anderson, who jokingly declared himself a Southerner by virtue of his Italian blood. Conrad Aiken, Irvin Cobb, Julia Peterkin, Burton Rascoe, Elizabeth Madox Roberts, T. S. Stribling, Stark Young, and (to everyone's disappointment) Thomas Wolfe were among those who declined or withdrew at the last minute. Mencken, now married to Sara Haardt, an author whose style and philosophy of resolute fatalism show Glasgow's direct influence, begged off: "Going to orgies at universities is very far out of my line."[7] It was not, however, out of Faulkner's, whose first and last remarks were reported to be "Know where I can get a drink?"[8]

The two-day conference, centering on "The Southern Author and His Public," began with an eleven o'clock welcoming address by Ellen Glasgow, followed by an open discussion. The rest of the day consisted of a lunch hosted by the editors of the *Virginia Quarterly* at Wilson's home, and an afternoon motor trip to Castle Hill, where the 68-year-old Amélie Rives Troubetzkoy, ailing with rheumatic gout, received visitors in her room. After Prince Troubetzkoy escorted his guests down the tree-lined drive, they returned to the Farmington Country Club for dinner. Faulkner sat next to Glasgow, who daintily cut his meat into small pieces and fed him bits from her plate as if he were one of her pet dogs.[9]

The next day was just as busy: a tour of Monticello in the morning, a roundtable discussion at noon, a late lunch at the home of Isa Glenn's brother, the attorney who had represented Cabell during the *Jurgen* controversy, another roundtable discussion in the afternoon, and a goodbye tea sponsored by the Colonnade Club on the lawn of the university at sunset. As twilight deepened, the participants might have imagined Edgar Allan Poe, once a student at the university, standing among them.

For Glasgow, the conference validated a lifetime of struggle. She believed that she, a born novelist, had formed herself into a writer (*WW*, 41). However much she felt that she deserved the respect of all assembled, the idea of addressing her peers caused her considerable consternation. She revised and fretted over her speech to the last. Her listeners may in some ways have considered themselves "Southern" writers, but in her audience sat agrarians such as Tate,[10] and proponents of the machine age such as Green. Furthermore, Glasgow's courtesy to Faulkner did not preclude her resentment at the "Raw-Head-and-Bloody Bones" school of writers he and Erskine Caldwell seemed to represent. To her, those men remained "incurably romantic": "Only a puff of smoke separates the fabulous Southern hero of the past," she would soon argue, "from the fabulous Southern monster of the present."[11]

Glasgow's actual remarks show her at her best—wise, witty, and generous. "When I was asked, as the only woman on this committee, to bid you welcome to Virginia," she opened,

> I modestly replied that women come before men only in shipwreck. But Mr. James Cabell, who imposes his duty upon me, is constrained to illustrate that after fifty the only thinking worth doing is to decline to do anything. I, on the contrary, believe quite firmly that the longer one lives in this world of

hazard and escapes disaster, the more reckless one should become — at least in the matter of words. (*RD*, 91)

Glancing around the room, at people like Irita Van Doren and Isa Glenn who lived in New York City, she then observed how "elastic" and, in truth, how meaningless the epithet "Southern writer" had become. Faulkner, who had already begun drinking, raised his head every time she paused and muttered, "I agree. I agree," though he later announced that he "didn't give a damn about Ellen Glasgow."[12]

Glasgow assured her audience that their work brought "diversity to life" and that quality made them "world," rather than regional, writers. Expressing a lifetime of pent-up passion about her true vocation, writing, she spoke extemporaneously as well as from her typed text. More impressionistic than formally structured, her speech moved with slight transitions from one topic to another and of course emphasized her conviction that art united history and fiction (*RD*, 95, 92). Yet she must have surprised her listeners with the exhortation (given her response to Faulkner) to be brutal: "If you have a genius, be brutal. If you have not genius, be more brutal. For the only safe substitute for genius in American literature is brutality" (96). Be brutal in the service of truth, she urged, but also have pity.

The address won her the undivided respect and affection of at least one member of her audience, Allen Tate. Before the conference Tate had described her as among "the worst novelists in the world," "an incredible old snob," and a writer of "abominable prose."[13] He thought that her books sold by the hundred thousand because she convinced outsiders that all Southerners were pretenders. After the conference, he wrote Stark Young that

> the more I think about grand Ellen Glasgow, the more I fall in love with her. None of her books is as grand as she is. . . . Miss Ellen — I feel like calling her Miss Ellen because she's first of all a grand person without any of this spurious literary mystery about her all those Middle West lady writers assume — well, Miss Ellen . . . has one of those fine impeccable consciences that live entirely alone; that's what I feel about her — she has something deep and indestructible in her character which was possible to her generation but not mine.[14]

From this time, Glasgow counted Tate among her friends. Teacher, critic, and novelist, Tate was also a political poet in the sense that he thought art measured contemporary culture against enduring standards, and like Glasgow, whose influence he recognized, he concerned himself with philosophical systems. When a student at Vanderbilt University, he had become associated with the Fugitives, a group of poets that included John Crowe Ransom and Robert Penn Warren, Tate's roommate. Tate brought an understanding of literary modernism to the Fugitives' discussions of poetry and a belief in the transcendent power of the creative imagination. He and Glasgow both insisted that an artist must be responsible to his or her conscience.

Tate's infatuation with Glasgow did not prevent him from feeling disappointed in the conference itself. The amiability of the conference had made real discussion not quite in good taste. Henderson concurred, calling it a "glorified house party": "This first conference leaves all the major problems, and even the minor problems, but unattacked or even undiscussed. . . . I am afraid this was a by-product of luxurious and vapid femininity."[15] Faulkner was, as Stark Young noted, "in absentia in many ways,"[16] and Cabell refused to talk publicly, observing that he wrote to compensate for this deficit. The second conference in Charleston the following year floundered for a lack of focus, and the original committee, of which Glasgow had been a member, disbanded.

When Glasgow took the stage at the Southern Writers Conference, she made herself an emblem of Southern letters, and critics such as J. Donald Adams of the *New York Times* and Howard Mumford Jones (whom Mencken called "a third-rate pedagogue")[17] began to lobby for the region, as well as for the woman whom they felt was equally neglected. "We have been intimidated by northern propagandists, disguised as critics, who tell us to be national," Tate wrote her in the rhetoric of Reconstruction; "yet when they reveal their own nationalism, we are left out of it, permitted to come in if we consent to be like them: they, at any rate, dictate the terms of association."[18] To Tate, Ellen Glasgow represented a particular period in American literature mostly of his own imagining, and as such she became—to use her own phrase from *The Sheltered Life*—less a flesh-and-blood woman and more a "memorable occasion" (6).[19]

Who could reconcile this articulate and passionate woman with the secretive teenager scribbling the first pages of *Sharp Realities?* If Glasgow's vision of a world literature, in which individual truths form part of a collective whole, sounds today both conservative and prophetic, it struck many of her contemporaries as a call to arms.

II

Of all Glasgow's books, *The Sheltered Life*, which spans the Civil War to the First World War, best captures her preoccupation with the tension between public and private lives. By 1932, the year she published *The Sheltered Life*, Glasgow had long considered herself what we might call a "new historicist" or a revisionist historian. From the turn of the century, she had worked on novels that composed, to use her words, a "social history" of Virginia, chronicling "the rise of the middle class as the dominant force in Southern democracy" (*CM*, 4). The "truth" of these earliest novels depended, in her mind, on their historical accuracy. Thirty years later, when Glasgow came to write *The Sheltered Life*, her thinking about history had changed as much as she had herself. She felt that the person who had conceived *The Battle-Ground* had died. Then her "historical conscience" had dominated her "developing literary instinct." Now she could "break fresh ground, and at least . . . lay the foundations of a more permanent structure" (*CM*, 63, 5). Influenced by nineteenth-century German thinkers, especially Johann Fichte, she saw every moment of duration affected by all past moments and determining all future moments. Glasgow had come to believe that history was nothing more or less than personal memory writ large. Instead of emphasizing the sociological or Darwinian theories that drive the storylines of her earlier novels, she offers a more complexly organic and troubling vision of human experience.

In *The Sheltered Life*, Glasgow explores the cultural evolution of memory by analyzing the education—or miseducation—of a girl not unlike herself. The year is 1906, the place once again the city of Queenborough, and the girl nine years old. "When is time?" Jenny Blair asks. "When is eternity?" "Now and forever," her grandfather answers. A prototype of the woman artist, she exists in a world of sounds, rhythms, and images that Glasgow calls "make-believe." "I'm alive, alive, alive, and I'm Jenny Blair Archbald" (*SL*, 1), she has chanted longer than she can remember. The poem tells her she is this and not that. A kind of mantra or mnemonic prompt, it places her in time, in history itself.[20]

Jenny Blair's education comes from a cast of adults who represent, in Glasgow's mind, the major forces that have shaped the South's character and history. Jenny's "teachers" include her grandfather General Archbald, her neighbors George and Eva Birdsong, and a black woman named Memoria. The novel's reigning patriarch, Archbald represents a system of beliefs associated with the Old South. To preserve appearances, he fought in a war he could not support and married a woman he could not love. His successor, George Birdsong, cares for nothing except sensual pleasure, while George's wife, Eva, epitomizes the purity and pretense of "true womanhood." [21] For the sake of protecting legions of women like her—as toast after Southern toast declared—the Civil War had been fought. Eva houses an unnamed cancer, which seems to be nowhere and everywhere—in breast and womb and mind—as ubiquitous as the air she breathes or the myth she lives. Glasgow commemorates the history of black women through the character of Memoria, who testifies to the impossibility of separating her history from that of Jenny Blair and the other women of Queenborough. In the characterization of Memoria, who embodies (as her name suggests) memory itself, Glasgow intertwines social history and private lives. By conflating the lives of Memoria and Eva, specifically through their sexual relationships with George Birdsong, she reveals the arbitrary and despotic character of racial division.

Jenny learns to read the South's forgotten and forbidden history in Memoria's white features as well as in those of her apparently fatherless son. Jenny's initiation into womanhood coincides with her knowledge of George Birdsong's double life. Her decision to keep George's secret ironically traps her in the childlike world of make-believe. After tripping over a loosened brick outside Memoria's door, she loses both consciousness and conscience. "Nothing was important," she reflects as George Birdsong bends over her,

> except this queer sense of his belonging here, of his being at home in Canal Street, in Memoria's house. For he stood there, in the centre of what Jenny Blair thought of vaguely, as "a coloured room," with an unchanged air of physical exuberance, of vital well-being, of sanguine expectancy. (SL, 40)

Before Jenny's eyes, the customary hierarchies of gender, race, class, and age have dissolved. The very room seems "colored"—not only with taboo but by George's unlawful sense of proprietorship.

Jenny's awakening to sexual and racial difference heralds the first step in the anesthetizing process of becoming a Southern lady, a process that Glasgow herself weathered and withstood. Jenny must separate herself from the female poetic that Glasgow associates with Memoria and African American culture. The prosaic future holds no more adventures in Canal Street, where "women of dubious color" speak a strange and exciting tongue (SL, 37). Hereafter her genuine poetic gift for imitation will serve the status quo, in which, as Mary Boykin Chesnut had observed: "Any lady is ready to tell you who is the father of all the mulatto children in everybody's household but her own."[22] Like the ladies of Chesnut's era, Jenny, whose flirtation with George Birdsong ends in murder, must learn to deny the truth of her own experience —the "burden of tragic remembrance" that Memoria symbolizes (CM, 203). For Ellen Glasgow, as for Emily Dickinson, "remorse is memory awake."

In The Sheltered Life, Glasgow spares no one. She criticizes Southern women, who have typically derived power from motherhood and femininity, for continuing sentimental traditions that rob them of autonomy and individuality. She obliquely criticizes Memoria for her passive collusion in their public "fabrication." (As the Birdsongs' laundress, Memoria sanitizes or whitewashes their dirty linen.) Not least, Glasgow criticizes General Archbald, who repeats the novel's last lies. "Eva did not mean to shoot her husband. Jenny Blair is innocent." The "truth" becomes his property, bits of knowledge he can share or withhold, idiosyncratic scraps of a past that give the appearance of whole cloth.

Glasgow's portrayal of Archbald—which incorporates her belief in a kind of historical determinism as well as a mystical reality "profounder than the depths of experience" (WW, 125)—highlights again her ambivalent relationship to the past.[23] She assigns him three memories that illustrate successive stages in the cultural evolution of memory that shapes individual personality. The first memory marks his bloody initiation into manhood and exposes the deforming power of tradition. The second memory, of Archbald aiding a fugitive slave, shows the considered gaps in history. The slave's story forms no part of present history: did he escape or was he caught? The memory upholds the myth of the old South in which plantation owners were either slaves to their slaves or secret abolitionists. Archbald conveniently forgets that he won his title defending the Confederacy. Continuing the fiction into the next generation, Jenny Blair regrets that her grandfather never did what he pleased. "I suppose," she adds, "colored people do" (SL, 229). The third memory confirms Archbald's complicity in a manufactured history.[24] Erotically refiguring the underlying violence of the first two memories, this memory centers on the suicide of Archbald's married lover, whom he did not fight to keep.

Glasgow's vacillating tone toward Archbald grows from her own conception of the artist. She believed that creativity originated in an ahistorical place where "an underlying force in life" abides.[25] Fiction, itself both an act of memory and creation, parallels what she considered the "accommodating processes of evolution" (CM, 23) because it reflects human beings' changing views of themselves and the universe. She realized that no matter how much we imagine ourselves freed from time or place or history, these factors have

nevertheless determined the nature of our rebellion, the scope of our emancipation.

Of all her novels, *The Sheltered Life* most reflects (and replicates in the section entitled "The Deep Past") her own process of composing. The design
of Archbald's life, which runs "forward and backward," matches that of her
own—woven, as she writes in *The Woman Within*, of recollections that had
no part in the remote, hidden country of her mind. Glasgow envisions memory working on several levels, one visceral (with "the skin of the mind"), the
other deep (with "the arteries"). The second form of remembering plunges
one down a dim vista of time where fragments of scattered scenes flicker and
die and flicker again (*SL*, 108). Here, as Glasgow writes in her interpretation
of prose fiction, characters appear too real for "dismemberment" (*CM*, 201).
The artist has a responsibility to listen and to remember.

Time remains "stranger than memory" (*SL*, 109) because it simultaneously
orders and estranges experience. The self can never live in the time that en-
closes it. As experience unfolds, the "time" has already passed. This thinking
partially explains Glasgow's pessimism. Loss becomes a natural part of the
human condition, "a twisted root . . . an ugly scar" at the source of being
(118). As she grew older, she claimed her suffering as only a survivor can: it
brought her closer to the realities that imparted "the spirit of things." [26]

When Glasgow turned to her own life in *The Woman Within*, she continued to ask, "Why and what is human personality?" (*SL*, 120). Despite the
claim that she never believed in the separate ego, Glasgow did believe that
the "homely texture of life . . . [was] woven and interwoven of personalities" that cross "without breaking, without bending, without losing their
individual threads of existence" (195). She advised her readers to "always preserve, within a wild sanctuary, an inaccessible valley of reveries" (210), a place
where one could escape like Archbald or be renewed. For Ellen Glasgow, this
place harbored the enemy of the sheltered life. From it streamed the well-
spring of her memory, the source of her creativity.

Along with Cooper's *The Last of the Mohicans*, Wharton's *The Age of Innocence*, Cather's *The Professor's House*, Faulkner's *Absalom, Absalom!*, and Mor-
rison's *Beloved*, *The Sheltered Life* stands among America's great novels of
remembering. In it, memory and Memoria, the past and the present, the august and the petty, live synchronically and possibly most completely. If Glasgow's earlier books at times sounded notes of intellectual discord, *The Sheltered Life*—its "vast significance of remembrance" outlasting all "monuments
of experience" (112, 113)—rises to the harmonics of a national requiem.

III

A chorus of contemporary critics hailed *The Sheltered Life* as Ellen Glasgow's crowning achievement. Fanny Butcher of the *Chicago Daily Tribune* wrote that Glasgow had produced "another of her memorable pictures of the social order which is, like Boston, more of a state of mind than a geographical section." [27] Other leading critics concurred: Henry Seidel Canby of the *Saturday Review of Literature*, J. Donald Adams of the *New York Times Book*, and Isabel Paterson of the *New York Herald Tribune Books*. Sara Haardt wrote a favorable review, and Glasgow dined with her and Mencken in late October: "I felt instantly at home with your Henry," she wrote, "and very congenial." [28] For his part, Mencken liked to tease Glasgow—supposedly a vehement disbeliever—about being "an earnest Christian lady who saved his wife from . . . the heresies of Darwin, Nietzsche, and Clarence Darrow." [29] With his usual sensitivity, he recorded his impression of the Saturday lunch:

> The old girl is deaf and carries a loud speaker, but she uses it adroitly, and is pretty good company. She drank two stiff sherrys before lunch, got her full share of a bottle of claret, and then topped off with a big drink of brandy. These stimulants made her garrulous. . . .
>
> She pretended to loathe the literary teas and other such parties to which she has been going in New York, but it is well known in publishing circles that she really enjoys such things vastly, and is keenly alive to their advertising value to her books.[30]

Friends like Mencken make a reviewer like Clifton Fadiman of the *New Republic* seem tame. Fadiman published the one scathing and entirely wrongheaded review of *The Sheltered Life*, arguing that her allegiance to her own class blinded her to "the obvious fact that the machine and the plantation are merely two forms of exploitation. . . . Nor is there any indication that she is aware of the salient feature of Southern social and economic life—the continuation of black chattel slavery under the guise of the industrial hire-and-fire system" (*Reviews*, 337–38). Glasgow had worried about someone like Fadiman reviewing her book: "I was radical myself once and I am still in spots," she told a staff member at Doubleday, Doran, "but the manners Communism breeds have about cured me." [31] Fadiman not only attacked what Glasgow saw as the heart of her continuing argument with the South, he made her life seem pointless. She had always put the best into her books, as she wrote Stark Young, "to compensate, in a way," for the way she had lived.

Above all, she felt that she had not exhausted the creative part of her mind, and now, when everything else seemed to matter so little, she wanted to give her whole self to it.[32] Fadiman's review angered Young, and he decided to submit a second review for the *New Republic*. "Will you be sensible," he admonished, "and write me something you want to achieve. . . . This would make the review more useful and it does seem we are good enough friends not to go mincing around all such matters."[33] Not surprisingly, his review stressed Glasgow's own views about the universality of her vision, which expanded beyond the code of Virginia to "the conventions of the world we call civilized."[34]

Stark Young's friendship with his "Cousin Ellen," a title of respect and courtesy that did not have the antebellum or spinsterish overtones of Tate's "Miss Ellen," benefited each. The friendship certainly involved their writing positive reviews of one another's work, but it also gave each a platform for their shared aesthetics. Young, who rejected art for art's sake, believed that art could mold, if not recreate, contemporary society. A scholar, translator, teacher, and accomplished painter, he admired Glasgow's intellectual vitality and "profound inner energy."[35] He placed her in the role of a surrogate cousin, emotionally as well as professionally. Although Glasgow had never wanted children, she was not without maternal instinct, especially when it could be exercised infrequently or through the mail. For his part, Young cast himself as a dragon, standing between her and the malice of others.[36] In turn, he sought her sympathy, first when he lost his nephew and namesake, Stark Young Robertson, and then when his beloved housekeeper died.

Young was just one of the ever-widening circle of people who valued Glasgow's friendship. Increasingly housebound and almost entirely deaf, she found it easier to speak to people in letters. Letters allowed an intimacy that her deafness made almost impossible in person. Her "Scottish strain of mysticism" made her feel that with certain people, including Tate and later the playwright Clemence Dane, she had been "predestined" to be friends.[37]

From the 1930s until her death, Glasgow corresponded with critics like Edwin Mims, Allen Tate's nemesis as an apostle of the New South, Howard Mumford Jones, respected (despite Mencken's estimate) for his many books on American literature, and Van Wyck Brooks, author of *The Flowering of New England*, who called *The Sheltered Life* "the turning-point in the literary history of the South."[38] From them, Glasgow sought reassurance and advice about prominent reviewers known to be sympathetic to her novels. Her relationships with male critics tended to follow a certain pattern. She usually initiated the friendship with a note complimenting the receiver on a particular article or point of view, then cemented it with gifts of her books. When the man happened to be married, like Howard Mumford Jones, Glasgow made friends with the wife—or in J. Donald Adams's case, wife and mistress—often inviting the couple to Richmond. "Howard showed me your note to him," Bessie Zaban Jones wrote, "in which you make such overwhelming statements about me, so that it is almost more my letter than his. I suppose it would be ungrateful to ask you to write directly to me so that I could have the fun of finding my own name on the envelope."[39] The relationships were mutually beneficial. Bessie Jones wanted to write an article about Glasgow in the Middle West and her husband shared Glasgow's desire to promote Southern literature. As something of an institution, Glasgow began to find herself exempt from most criticism. With time, even Clifton Fadiman became less hostile.

Glasgow's new friends, particularly someone from a similar background like Young, allowed her to see her own past in ways that she had not before, while linking her to the future. She would live in their minds as well as her books. The work, which had begun by making life bearable, now made it harmonious. She had not only survived, as she wrote of Dorinda in her preface to *Barren Ground*, "she had lived some desperate daily life of her own . . . [and] had become the center of a universe that expanded" (*CM*, 162).

In 1932, Ellen Glasgow once again expected to win the Pulitzer Prize for fiction. *The Sheltered Life* had dominated the front pages of the *New York Herald Tribune Books* as well as the *New York Times Books*. Cabell wrote that her splendid reviews made him regard her with "low envy" and advised her to mention the title at least three times in any conversation.[40] Her publishers could not contain themselves. Never before had one of Doubleday, Doran's books received that kind of attention,[41] and they began printing the second edition before the first achieved general circulation. Eventually the book went into seven printings. At the year's end, *The Sheltered Life* ranked fifth on the list of bestsellers, and Glasgow was tirelessly signing copies of the first volumes for *The Old Dominion Edition of the Works of Ellen Glasgow: They Stooped to Folly, The Battle-Ground, The Deliverance*, and *Virginia*. Cabell, engaged in autographing his own eighteen-volume *Storisende Edition*, trusted that she exacted a royalty of 25 percent on all signed copies.

In May 1932, the Pulitzer Prize committee announced its recipient for fiction: T. S. Stribling's *The Store*, which chronicles the unscrupulous rise of a poor white, Miltiades Vaiden—exactly the kind of "bloody bones" approach that Glasgow deplored in Faulkner. If she felt disheartened, friends such as Henry S. Canby, J. Donald Adams, Lewis Gannett, William Soskin, Allen Tate, and Cabell were incensed. Isa Glenn wrote, "I am very indignant, honey. I hold, and I'm sure all of us hold, that *The Sheltered Life* should have got it. Well—damn it!" [42] Glasgow put on a brave front: "After more than thirty years of this," she told Tate, "one becomes accustomed, if not entirely reconciled, to the national apotheosis of the average." [43]

VEIN OF IRON

1933–1937

Yet something stronger than joy, the vein of iron far down in her inmost being, in her secret self, could not yield, could not bend, could not be broken.

Ellen Glasgow, *Vein of Iron*

I

IN 1932, THE PULITZER PRIZE committee's decision was just one of several setbacks for Glasgow. Over the past few years, slumps in the market had seriously depleted her income from stocks. In June 1931, for example, Dan River Mills informed its stockholders that they would not receive a July dividend on preferred stock. As Glasgow and Bennett recuperated from influenza, she joked with Cabell: "It seemed to me that we needed only this to complete our despondency—I had almost written 'ruin,' but I remembered in time that, though fallen in spirit, we are still perfect ladies!"[1]

Glasgow felt pinched enough to forgo a visit to Glen Springs until the heat finally drove her and Carrie Coleman Duke to Nantucket for July and August. When Arthur asked her for an account of her situation, she explained,

If you hadn't asked, I should not have told you how deplorable it is. All the money I saved from my latest book seems to have gone for good, except the part I spent on going abroad twice and taking Carrie. Radio B preferred, for which I paid 74 is down to 9; Kennicott, for which I paid 92 to 11; Penn. R.R. for which I paid either 76 or 84 is down to 17. . . . I had to sell the only thing I could sell without heavy loss, 14 shares of Appalachian. You cannot conceive of greater depression, though, I imagine, life in England is none too cheerful.[2]

Arthur responded with a check for $6,000, which repaid a bank loan of $4,000 as well as Anne Virginia Bennett's salary for the previous five months. Arthur's generosity made it possible for Glasgow to get through the winter without reducing her standard of living. He also helped Rebe, whose husband, Cabell, had experienced huge losses. Rebe scoffed at her husband's believing "in the country" enough to invest in anything.[3] Despite his own troubles (including an ill wife and recurrent eye problems that at one time required daily injections), Arthur never failed to come to his family's financial rescue. His sense of responsibility extended to his nieces and nephews as well as the husband of his deceased sister Emily. In 1931, in addition to sending a generous check to Glasgow, he also sent his brother-in-law, now remarried and the father of three children, $1,000 as a kind of payoff which he hoped would extinguish future responsibility.[4]

Glasgow's needs and manner of living kept her dependent on Arthur, who supplemented her income until she died.[5] Her dependency corrupted their relationship. No matter how much she respected his position, she found her own humiliating. At Glasgow's funeral, Arthur told a friend, "I've always given to my family generously but not graciously. The result is not one of them has any use for me."[6] In her 1941 novel, *In This Our Life*, Glasgow's protagonist declares of his benefactor, "I ought to be grateful to him. I despise having to be grateful" (43). The criticism of Arthur that Glasgow voiced to friends grows from a certain degree of displaced revulsion at herself. "I love you dearly," she confessed, "and I am deeply grateful, though I seldom show what I feel."[7] In this, brother and sister were well matched.

Glasgow's anxieties about money continued for the first part of 1932. Although she sold many books, she made most of her money on advances. From her income, she supported the staff at One West Main and covered her own large medical bills, including rest cures, whether at expensive hotels in Europe and New York or at an occasional hospital, such as Watkins Glen Sanitarium. Despite an income that would have easily kept a middle-class family comfortable, Glasgow could not live on her royalties, which often amounted to paltry sums after the first sales of a new book; in 1935, for example, she earned around $600 from Doubleday, which did not have to report on income under $1,000. Glasgow's publishers refused to understand her financial position or credit what they would likely have credited in a man: her right to make the best deal for herself. "I confess that wherever business is involved, I am at a singular disadvantage," she told them, "and I realize more and more that every author needs either an agent or a lawyer. It always depresses me profoundly to find that even your best friends think only of grinding your profits down to the edge of starvation when they cease to feel as your friends and begin to speculate as your publishers."[8] Doubleday saw her demands for higher royalties, movie rights, books in stock, unremaindered copies, and second serialization rights as excessive: "She was"—according to her Doubleday editor—"a helpless steel trap."[9] One year, they even paid half her Christmas card bill. With some justification, they saw her requests for free books, often eight to ten a week, as extortion—especially after she refused to write squibs that would help sales. Glasgow saw these "perks" as a sign of her importance to the firm.

What Glasgow knew of the stock market and read in the financial section of the Sunday *New York Times* did not make her feel any more sanguine about her economic future. For that reason, it seems astonishing that she did not leap at the chance to have *The Sheltered Life* serialized in the *Cosmopolitan*. Not only had the magazine offered to pay her the enormous sum of $32,000, but publishing in the *Cosmopolitan* would make her work known to a wide audience of potential readers. Glasgow rejected the offer out of hand. It angered her to think of "all the beautiful trees that have been sacrificed to make our many horrible and hideously cheap magazines."[10] Her publishers were stunned and exasperated by what they considered her snobbery. What made the readers of *Redbook* any more desirable than those of the *Cosmopolitan*? Did you have to have a certain pedigree to read a Glasgow novel? Glasgow, of course, interpreted her refusal differently: "At a sacrifice," she wrote her editor Daniel Longwell, "I have stood against the commercialization of my work—for my work is the only thing in the world that makes life endurable. If I lose that integrity, I am lost indeed."[11] (Arthur Glasgow could have been forgiven a slight smile at his sister's "principles," for he literally supported them.)

Glasgow's finances became more secure in June 1932 when Arthur's wife, Margaret, agreed to relinquish to Glasgow her two-sixths share from a trust that Arthur had established in 1926. Glasgow could draw on those additional funds, which, at her death, would revert back to her sister-in-law.[12] "In your place," she told her brother again and again, "I doubt if I should be nearly so generous; and in my own mind I have never been about to see what return it ever brings you. The reward of virtue has always seemed to me to be vastly exaggerated."[13] Glasgow had acknowledged her debt to Arthur in her dedication to *The Sheltered Life*. It reads: "For Arthur Graham Glasgow whose affection is a shelter without walls." It is her only dedication that begins "for," rather than "to." She especially wanted this tribute to appear in the English edition, which Arthur could give to friends.

In the autumns of 1931 and 1932, Glasgow experienced physical illnesses that left her feeling despondent. Whatever their emotional origin, they were also related to chronic ailments. Glasgow seldom found herself free from pain associated with her ears, sinuses, or respiratory system. She feared being left alone, especially during trips to New York when Bennett visited a sister living in Brooklyn. Her impairment made her what she never wanted to be: the object of pity and the subject of anecdote. One friend, for instance, recalled her trying to talk to an elderly deaf man. "Do you hear me?" she asked. "Do you hear me?" he echoed. Abandoning words, they stood holding hands.[14]

Glasgow's doctors tended to diagnose her condition as "just nerves," and one liked to tease that "it won't be long!"[15] No one fully credited how hard she tried to lead a normal, active life. When the son of a friend killed himself in December 1931, she understood this most terrible of tragedies: "The mystery to me is not why a few are unable to bear life," she told Arthur, "but why the whole world doesn't end its existence."[16] Glasgow hated her physical and economic dependency, yet whenever she tried to share her worries with friends and family, they turned a "deaf ear" to feelings they wanted to deny.

The beginning of the new year, 1933, saw Glasgow struggling to regain her health and spirits. After finishing the last prefaces to the *Old Dominion Edition*, she went in March to New York City to visit doctors. The remaining four volumes of the edition — *The Voice of the People, The Miller of Old Church, Barren Ground,* and *The Romantic Comedians* — came out in April, later than expected because Doubleday, Doran was trying to conserve resources. Glasgow had mostly used the opportunity to prune her earlier work, deleting what now seemed infelicitous phrases or excess dialogue. It mystified her editors, who thought her a born complainer, that small changes would mean so much to her. She had, she told Tate, revealed more of herself than usual in the one-to two-page prefaces, which, when expanded, would form the nucleus of *A Certain Measure* (1943).

In view of the previous year's reception of *The Sheltered Life*, a novel

"too good to win the Pulitzer,"[17] the *Old Dominion Edition* received surprisingly little attention, though Cabell, Stark Young, H. L. Mencken, and
James Southall Wilson wrote omnibus reviews. Probably the reviews that
meant most to Glasgow were those written by Mencken and Cabell. Now
that Mencken had married Sara Haardt, Glasgow considered him a good
friend. Nonetheless, she treated this cigar-smoking literary pugilist more gin-
gerly than she treated other friends who also happened to be critics. Glasgow, knowing his reputation for prickliness and independence, recognized
in Mencken someone who, like herself, stood for certain absolute principles.
In deference to his wife, Mencken managed to write a review of Glasgow's
edition that did not require him to praise her directly. Most critics, he repeated, would probably agree with Glasgow herself that of all her books
Barren Ground (1925) deserved "first place" (*Reviews*, 362). Privately, however,
he had called it "poor stuff" and opined that in comparison to Ruth Suckow
"La Glasgow" treats her yokels as if "they are simply animals in cages." [18]

Critics tended to think they should like Glasgow's books either more or
less than they did. She was too popular to be "great" and too "great" to be
popular. If the academics had trouble categorizing her work, imagine the
struggle of Cabell, who wrote such different books. In his review of the
Edition, for example, he analyzes himself as much as Glasgow. At once con-
descending and uneasy, the tone of his review bares the complex nature
of their relationship. He considers Glasgow his foil. While she writes her
"salty reams about chivalry," Cabell says, he sprinkles "sugar upon the same
topic." [19] Why, he asks, did her literary coin rise with each novel and then fall
almost as far as a Confederate dollar? Because each of her books showed the
influence of current trends, which explained their immediate appeal. Subsequent shifts in literary fashions tended to hide their "real merits as a work of
art" (*Reviews*, 355). Cabell's assessment has held true ever since.

The disappointing reception of the *Old Dominion Edition* did nothing to
improve Glasgow's spirits or health. In the summer of 1933, she placed herself
under the care of Dr. Bordley at Johns Hopkins Hospital in Baltimore, Maryland. She received thirty-three treatments to correct a sinus problem that,
in her doctor's opinion, had been poisoning her for years. They should have
cured or killed her, she quipped. In the end, they did neither. Bordley advised
a minor operation that Joseph Collins cautioned against. The time in Baltimore was not wholly wasted. Glasgow visited with Haardt and Mencken,
whom she believed wise and fortunate in his love.[20] At the beginning of August, she had intended to go to Rebe's house in Philadelphia, but Rebe said

it might as well be quarantined. The servants were sick, and her son had eye problems, which threatened to end his hopes of an academic career (a career Glasgow thought fit only for the unambitious). Instead, Rebe joined Glasgow and they slipped away to the seaside resort of Atlantic City. When the treatments ended, Arthur offered to send Glasgow for an "after cure" to Blowing Rock, North Carolina. Eager to get back to work, she declined.

Glasgow's mood did not lift until September when she visited Green Forest, the family homestead in Rockbridge County, in preparation for her 1935 novel, *Vein of Iron*. Now rebuilt after an 1820 fire but with many of its original rooms intact, the old house seemed peopled with her past. "What a spirit those pioneers had!" she wrote Allen Tate.[21] The same spirit, she realized, lived in her brother, named for their family's first American patriarch. "You are the only one," she told Arthur, "who seems to have carried on the strain."[22] Glasgow stayed in western Virginia just four days, motoring through the mountains and strolling among graves in the Falling Springs churchyard.

Always attuned to past times and places, Glasgow also had an ear for new voices. In the next year, she extended her friendships with the biographer Douglas Southall Freeman, and other "literary" figures: J. Donald Adams, Bessie Zaban Jones, and Irita Van Doren. An editor for the *New York Herald Tribune* and an insatiable gossip, Van Doren became one of Glasgow's most trusted friends. She had great personal charm and a renowned sense of humor. At the Southern Writers Conference, Sherwood Anderson could not get over that fact that despite her hair, which tended to stick straight up everywhere, she still managed to be chic. Van Doren advised Glasgow on her career and paved the way for Alfred Harcourt to publish her next novel. Before she died, Glasgow made Van Doren and another editor, F. V. Morley, her literary executors.

With Van Doren's blessing, Alfred Harcourt visited Richmond in August 1934 and invited Glasgow to write her own contract. He realized that her long association with Doubleday had begun to wear thin. Glasgow resented the disappointing sales of *They Stooped to Folly*—well under the 100,000 she had expected. Somehow Doubleday had the impression that she had expected them to secure the Pulitzer for *The Sheltered Life*. When Harcourt offered her an advance of $20,000 on a basis of 15 percent for the first 25,000 copies sold and 20 percent thereafter, along with a guaranteed ($15,000) advertising budget, she was ready to be wooed. Daniel Longwell, a senior editor at Doubleday, did his best to dissuade Glasgow from switching firms by arriving at One

West Main with a blank contract—a fact that Glasgow strategically passed on to Harcourt. "It is just as well," she said smugly, "that Harcourt, Brace should realize that, good as their terms are, I am able to command them elsewhere."[23]

The drama did not end. After receiving a telegram announcing Glasgow's defection, Nelson Doubleday dashed to Richmond and offered to buy her contract from Harcourt. He came to upbraid but stayed instead to lunch, for Bennett had calmed him at a critical moment with a pitcher of mint juleps. Doubleday conceded that many of the books his firm produced might seem cheap to Glasgow. She must understand, he pleaded, that as the employer of 1,100 people he had to make choices, which sometimes placed people above aesthetics. Glasgow sympathized without changing her mind: "I do not want to make my living out of the mass mind," she told Van Doren.[24] She had been particularly miffed at Doubleday's sale of her books at a reduced price to the Dollar-a-Month Club.

Glasgow never regretted the change to Harcourt. She liked *Vein of Iron*'s large, clear type, the creamy tone of the paper, and the feel of its weight in her hand: "Only a book of substance would take that rich, dark cover."[25]

II

Sometime in 1934, inspired perhaps by her trip to Rockbridge, Glasgow also began writing her life story. She rejected Carl Van Vechten's suggestion for a working title, "A Virginia Lady," preferring "Autobiography of an Exile." In preparation she read James Joyce's *Portrait of the Artist as a Young Man*. She would continue to labor on the manuscript—kept in a locked black-leather briefcase and labeled "Original Rough Draft"—over the next eight years.

Glasgow had reached a stage in her development where she could take—borrowing Whitman's phrase—a backward glance. When she turned the other side of 60, she entered a period of more intense personal reflection. Looking back on the course of her life, she could not help but note changes in her culture. They made her feel, as always, at odds with the universe. She despised "the machine age" and thought its youth had chosen "futility" over "fortitude" (*RD*, 226). Paradoxically, Glasgow's inward turn, her self-conscious writing, confirmed her public mask. She reveled in the role of public crank. "You'll never really *write*," she told a niece who worked as a journalist and wanted to write novels, "as long as you love people so much."[26] Glasgow gave her views free reign in a 1933 essay for the *Nation* entitled "What I Believe." The essay opened with a return to the world of her unhappy childhood and the writing of her first novel. It includes a potpourri of political economy—the conviction that private ownership of land should be curbed, for example—along with home truths. "I believe," she declared, "that the approach to a perfect state lies not without but within, and that the one and only way to a civilized order is through the civilization of man."[27]

Glasgow's analysis of contemporary society informs her nostalgic re-imagining of her Scotch-Irish ancestors in *Vein of Iron* (1935). Her profound change in attitude had been gradual. Only a few years before, for example, she had engaged in a bitter argument over religion with the rector of St. Bartholomew's Church. He expressed his acceptance of Divine Love and a guarantee of immortality, while she took delight in denying both his premise and conclusion. "No holds were barred," another guest remembered, "the sparks flew, even the fur. . . . Ellen was gay, flashing, and barbed. He was suave and persistent." Everyone else was embarrassed. Glasgow later declared him "a dreadful man." He thought her the most unhappy woman he ever met, and one of the most charming.[28]

In *Vein of Iron*, Glasgow tried to articulate the importance of altruism in a "world that has surrendered to the worship of things."[29] A fictionalized version of the beliefs outlined in the *Nation*, the novel also served as a rebuke to the rising generation of Southern writers, such as Faulkner, whose *Absalom, Absalom!* (1936) she would read, envy, and resent: "All I ask him to do is to deal as honestly with living tissues as he now deals with decay, to remind himself that the colors of putrescence have no greater validity for our age, or for any age, than have—let us say, to be very daring—the cardinal virtues."[30] As she grew older, Glasgow sometimes forgot that her own first novel dealt with illegitimacy, degeneration, and free love—topics aimed to shock and that she continued to explore. Although she described herself as more defiant than ever, she cherished civility, a virtue she tended to confuse with class.

Recalling *The Voice of the People* (1900) or *The Deliverance* (1904), the first books in Glasgow's social history, *Vein of Iron* presents the cardinal virtues as faith and love. Once again Glasgow re-evaluates and maternalizes the influence of her father, Francis Glasgow. She sets the novel, which follows the fortunes of the Fincastle family from the turn of the century to the present day (1901–33), in Ironside, Virginia, the fictional name for the area originally comprising the ancestral home at Green Forest. Through each individual character, she tries to trace the hidden motive or the vein of iron, which held the generations together: "Religion. Philosophy. Young love. Simple human relationships. Or the unbreakable will to live that we call fortitude."[31] In *Vein of Iron*, Glasgow conflates major systems of belief and reduces them to the single trait of fortitude.

For the three years that Glasgow worked on the novel, she projected her consciousness "into that resolute breed" from which her father had sprung, in an attempt to analyze the primary elements of the Presbyterian spirit and theology (*CM*, 168, 169). The main strength of the book lies in the contrasting figures of the old Presbyterian grandmother and her "pagan philosopher" son (174). Grandmother Fincastle embodies the "vital principle of survival" (169).[32] With her bright, ageless eyes, she reminds her granddaughter, Ada, of the enduring rock profile at Indian Head. If Mehitable Green, the black midwife modeled after Rhoda Kibble in *Barren Ground*, has an equivalent in any Glasgow novel it is Grandmother Fincastle, the Scotch-Irish matriarch known for her curative powers. Like Mehitable Green, Grandmother Fincastle mediates between worlds divided by class and race.

Positing civilization, no matter how mean, in the small town of Ironside, and nature, raw and unbridled, in Thunder Mountain, Glasgow characterizes those worlds much as Edith Wharton had in *Summer* (1917). Unlike Wharton, however, Glasgow exposes the futility of distinguishing between "nature" and "civilization" or the "sacred" and "profane." Thunder Mountain changes its "nature" with every successive epoch of the Fincastles' personal or the community's collective history. Originally a Shawnee hunting ground, claimed by white settlers, it now houses idiot children born from generations of incestuous unions. Where others see squalor, Ada Fincastle and Ralph McBride see an earthly paradise in which every tree and blade of grass seem to celebrate their forbidden love. In Grandmother Fincastle's imagination, the mountain rises like an altar to the heavens.

All her life, Glasgow had been familiar with, though far from sympathetic to, her father's faith; yet the trip to Rockbridge had fired her imagination enough for her to reread the Confession of Faith, as well as the Larger and Shorter Catechisms.[33] When she transposed her father's beliefs to a female protagonist, she could view them more sympathetically. Grandmother Fincastle does not question the "cruel doctrine" of predestination. Neither can she understand her son John's heretical stance against the divine birth. Nevertheless, the rigid Presbyterianism, which so repulsed Glasgow in her father, yields to love in Grandmother Fincastle. Despite her convictions, Grandmother Fincastle cradles Ada as she gives birth to an illegitimate son.

Through the arms of her grandmother, "firm as the roots of an oak," Ada feels "the steadfast life of the house, the strong fibers, the closely knit generations" gathering "above, around, and underneath" (*Vein,* 260-61). In the next generations, Grandmother Fincastle's faith becomes secularized. Her son craves truth as another man might crave drink (51), and Ada craves love enough to overlook Ralph's history of infidelity.

Glasgow conceived *Vein of Iron* as the story of an era as much as a family. Chronicling the Fincastles' precarious fortunes during the Great Depression, she notes the sweeping changes outlined in her article, "What I Believe." The Depression serves as a metaphor for the spiritual malaise she thought a legacy of Calvinism. Glasgow objected to any suggestion that *Vein of Iron* defended a social order, old or new. However, Ralph and Ada's hopeful return to Ironside does indeed mark their recovery of "a continuing tradition" (461). There they will feel the dead generations reaching out to them in adversity; there they will regain some of the lost certainty associated with a previous age. Whether Glasgow liked to admit it or not, she inherited more from her father than a share of the family trust and the color of her eyes. As the original title of *Vein of Iron,* "The Will to Live," suggests, she could also claim a code for being.

The novel, selected by the Book of the Month Club, placed second on the year's list of bestsellers. Glasgow sometimes disliked the thought of book clubs, yet she knew from Alfred Knopf that Willa Cather, for example, had dramatically increased the sales of *Shadows on the Rock* through book club subscriptions. Objecting to the absurdly low price that clubs paid for the books, she advised Alfred Harcourt to let them take a small edition. She was still incensed that the Literary Guild, which had bought 70,000 copies of *They Stooped to Folly,* had tried to sell remaindered copies to a magazine for prizes.[34] Cabell wrote what he called a "thousand word eulogy on her book" for the *Book of the Month Club News,* saying that if she wanted anything changed, she needed to tell him: "Now that the riffraff is out in full force armed with corncobs, we have to wear the label of aristocracy whether we like it or not; so let's carry it off defiantly." For his efforts on her behalf, Cabell wanted his "pound of flesh"—a Glasgow review of his next book, *Smith,* in the *Saturday Review.*[35]

Glasgow found nothing odd in Cabell suggesting how she should describe his book. She did the same when Stark Young reviewed *Vein of Iron,* pointing out the quality of writing, especially the use of different rhythms for retrospection, narrative, and dialogue. Without a trace of false modesty, she hoped Young would highlight these distinctions, which "only a mature art could have dared."[36] Glasgow did not have to worry about the reviews of *Vein of Iron*. Even Mencken, who had recently lost his wife from tubercular meningitis, wrote that he thought *Vein of Iron* her best book. Glasgow responded that she knew Sara would have liked it. "I should love to talk with you of Sara," Glasgow responded, "and I think she would have liked our talking of her."[37]

There's no denying that Glasgow wanted friends, such as Stark Young and Allen Tate, to promote her novels publicly. Privately, however, she could admit her works' shortcomings. When Tate criticized her early books for their point of view, she readily concurred. "It astonishes me," he admitted, "that an author who has written some twenty books should suddenly write an entirely different kind of book."[38] Viewing each new book as a new self, Glasgow rejoiced in his bewilderment that the same person could have written *The Battle-Ground* (1902) and *The Sheltered Life* (1932), thirty years apart: "I have always wanted to put my best into my books," she told Young,

> to make them compensate, in a way, for the kind of life I have had. Strangely enough, I have a feeling that my best work is ahead. . . . Now, when everything matters so little, I may give myself to that. The only thing I have saved out of the wreck is the gift of work, and I shall cling to this as our ancestors clung to the Rock of Ages.[39]

III

If Glasgow ended the year with the literary triumph of *Vein of Iron*, she had begun it with a triumph of another kind: making Gertrude Stein's February visit to Richmond an unforgettable occasion. Richmonders primarily knew Stein from the *Atlantic Monthly's* serialization of *The Autobiography of Alice B. Toklas* (1933). Carl Van Vechten summarized the general opinion when he informed Stein that he had heard "nothing but praise for it." Sherwood Anderson agreed but admitted to feeling a bit "sorry and sad" for "Hemmy" (Ernest Hemingway) as she flayed him with a "delicately held knife."[40] Such responses to the *Autobiography* had convinced Stein that she could find audiences in the United States interested in her work as much as in her personality.

Stein hadn't returned to the United States in over thirty years, and one friend cautioned that she and Alice would be like "two Rip van Winkles." On the contrary, she enjoyed the trip tremendously—the Yale-Dartmouth football game in New Haven, parties with James Weldon Johnson, Mary Pickford, and the Fitzgeralds, a meeting with Eleanor Roosevelt at the White House, and, on February 5, a dinner arranged by Carl Van Vechten at One West Main.

Van Vechten proved the ideal impresario for Stein, whom he had known since they met at a 1913 performance of Stravinsky's *Le Sacre du Printemps*. The music that horrified most listeners, soft sounds giving way to crashing chords, intrigued them. The boos, hisses, and whistles of the rest of the audience served to cement their friendship. Because Stein effected with words what Stravinsky did with music, Van Vechten thought her a genius and committed himself to promoting her career in the United States.

Stein looked forward to the Richmond leg of her tour. She had already met Hunter Stagg in Paris in 1923, and asked him if *The Reviewer,* like other magazines, feared publishing her work. Stagg had replied that *The Reviewer* feared nothing, and Stein rewarded him with a controversial piece entitled "An Indian Boy." Published in January 1924, it generated much discussion and lost *The Reviewer,* to the glee of its staff, some conservative subscribers.

Carl Van Vechten must have looked forward to the meeting between Gertrude Stein and Ellen Glasgow, two equally imperial women. The contrast in personal and artistic styles could not have been more dramatic. Stein, with her close-cropped gray hair, tended to wear loose-fitting Roman robes and sensible shoes. Glasgow, on the other hand, enjoyed black-sequined gowns and swaying ostrich-feather fans.

Glasgow told Van Vechten that she would be glad to entertain "visiting royalty": "If you think I shall like Miss Stein," she told him,

> I am sure to do so. And even if I shouldn't like her, I should still be polite, because I was so unfortunate as to be born that way. I can be as rude as anybody if I am prepared; but it takes me at least twenty-four hours to make ready. Usually I avoid modern Fads and People Who Lecture. However, I have nothing against G. S. except her "influence." My private opinion is that the people she has influenced (especially Hemingway) couldn't have been much worse if she had left them alone.[41]

Without being able to think of literary people for Stein to meet other than James Branch Cabell, she would do her best.

Glasgow did better than her best. When guests entered the front high-ceilinged hall of One West Main, they left their coats with Mattie Coleman, who, like all of Glasgow's servants, from the chambermaid to the chauffeur, wore a uniform (blue, gray, or black). That night the select company included Mark Lutz, a young friend and occasional lover of Van Vechten who had arranged for Stein to lecture on "Plays" at the University of Richmond and on "Pictures" at the Woman's Club, just a few blocks from Glasgow's house. To the guests' delight, Stein played Stein played Stein, remarking everything "Southern," which was not so Southern as she had expected and not so Virginian,[42] and expounding on "inner" and "outer" reality.

Cabell marveled: "Is Gertrude Stein serious?"

"Desperately," Toklas answered.

"That puts a different light on it," he said.

"For you," Toklas answered, "not for me." [43]

Carl Van Vechten remembers Glasgow "presiding over the lace and silver and porcelain, the shad roe and Smithfield ham" and at least six different hot breads.[44] Bright pink apples boiled in grenadine decorated the overabundant platters of meat, and for dessert whole cooked oranges that had been stuffed with nuts and cherries and then served with endive and cheese. Glasgow sat at the head of the table, where she could survey her guests. Despite her own sparse appetite, she took real pleasure in watching people eat. When a glass needed refilling or a plate removed, she stepped on a small bell that rang in the kitchen, and a waitress quickly appeared.

After dinner, other guests came to meet Stein and sip eggnog reputed to be the creamiest in existence. The party had its moment of overt drama when a strange woman pranced up to Glasgow and asked her to sign a book. Before departing, the gatecrasher kissed Glasgow goodbye and declared, "No one had a more delightful time than I." [45] Glasgow told Cabell that this person had not been crushed, as she should have by the laws of poetic justice. Rudeness being "the better part of morality" notwithstanding, she could not be rude to someone in her own house.[46]

Glasgow enjoyed watching Stein hold court. She and Stein tactfully avoided dangerous literary topics by talking about dogs. To Richmonders, Glasgow and Stein could not have seemed a more incongruous couple. Both had—as Hunter Stagg said of Glasgow—short tempers, biting tongues, and a large share of vanity. They also had hearts "full of kindness and generosity," which many people never appreciated.[47] Similarly, the relationship between Glasgow and Bennett oddly mirrored that of Stein and Toklas, who no doubt speculated about Glasgow's sexuality as she did about theirs.

The self-proclaimed mother of modernism never recorded her response to her regal hostess, though Toklas found her "quite extraordinary, very brilliant—and gracious and attaching . . . and fearless and all with an incredible smile and charm. I've never known anything suggesting it and was not prepared for it—even after meeting her that lovely night at her house. She was transcendent."[48] Stein seemed more taken with the city of Richmond and the Jefferson Hotel: "I was not disappointed it was a nice place to walk in and the hotel had baby alligators in it and we liked everything."[49] Glasgow privately recorded her skepticism in pseudo-Steinian prose: "Gertrude Stein," she wrote in her journal, "a wise overgrown child, as obvious as an infant. Likes obvious things. Barnum discovered that people are always willing to pay for the pleasure of being fooled. 'Alice, Alice, Gert is eating chocolate.' "[50] Glasgow felt that Stein lectured people who could not read a line of her writing. To her mind, Stein kept repeating, "A rose is a rose, is a rose, is a rose." While she thought Stein a "freak writer," she also thought her a "genuine person—An example of American gullibility Americans They believe anything you tell them three times."[51]

In retrospect, Richmond did not think so kindly of Stein. The Daughters of the Confederacy bristled at her characterization in *Everybody's Autobiography* (1937) of Robert E. Lee as a "weak man":

> He acted like a man leading a country in defeat, he always knew it but and this why I think him a weak man he did not have the courage to say it, if he had had that courage well perhaps there would not just then and not so likely later that Civil War but if there had not been would America have been as interesting.[52]

Stein didn't care what Richmond thought. She liked the fuss and found a Mrs. Leigh Tyree's remark that General Lee never really surrendered "charming": "He said the Confederates would lay down their arms if their implements were returned to them, so they could go back to work."[53]

Stein's lecture tour may have inspired Glasgow to try her hand again at lecturing. In April, she agreed to speak to the Friends of the Princeton Library because they had assured her she could say what she pleased and "not merely pay after-dinner compliments." "It isn't worthwhile to leave the South," she wrote Alfred Harcourt, "in order to make or hear compliments."[54] Accompanied by Carrie Coleman Duke, Glasgow arrived in New York City, where Harcourt, Brace and Company paid for her accommodations. Glasgow, who experienced some of Stein's stage fright before large audiences, delivered her speech on April 25 to 450 people. In it, she objected to the current taste for violence and singled out Faulkner for being as unrealistic as the romancer James Lane Allen. Few things are more certain than this, she warned: "The literature that crawls too long in the mire will lose at last the power of standing erect. On the farther side of deterioration lies the death of a culture" (*RD*, 166). Acknowledging that it is "as useless to run away from the past as it is to run away from what we call life" (164–65), she pleaded for a different kind of revolution: one that renews the spirit. To applause and with aplomb, Glasgow returned to her seat. Because of her deafness, noise tended to disorient her, and when she found her place she missed the seat and landed on the floor. Stark Young assured her that she had fallen stylishly—with her hat still on.[55]

In May, the Pulitzer Prize committee finally did something she could approve: they honored Douglas Southall Freeman for his biography of Lee. Freeman, whose obsession with Southern history even excelled Glasgow's, graciously recognized his friend's help in having secured Stephen Vincent Benét as a sympathetic reviewer: "The judges made a lamentable mistake last night for the PP should not have gone to me but to the gracious lady whose generosity assured for the Lee [biography] a reception it could not otherwise have received along with my profound admiration you will always have my deepest gratitude."[56] That gratitude extended into the next generation. Freeman's daughter remembered Glasgow as she herself would have liked to be remembered: a woman as alive and warm as her most charming heroines.

IV

Glasgow would have looked back on 1935—which included trips to Barnstable, Massachusetts, in July and to Ventnor, New Jersey, in October—with pleasure, if it hadn't been for the young writer Julian Meade. Meade published a gossipy memoir entitled *I Live in Virginia,* which included portraits of Amélie Rives, James Branch Cabell, and Ellen Glasgow. He informed his readers that Rives's first husband had been an inmate of Bloomingdale Hospital and implied that Cabell had married a wealthy woman to support his career. Glasgow was sentimental about dogs (*and* deaf). His "portraits" incensed both Rives and Glasgow. "I know it is silly to be sensitive about such a thing," she told Freeman, "but I can't help wincing when anyone speaks of my deafness."[57] Glasgow had more cause for complaint. "She was not beautiful," Meade wrote,

> and I think it was silly of some of her friends and reporters to say that she was. God had given Ellen Glasgow enough without anyone needing to add a schoolgirl complexion or glorious bronze hair. . . . Her voice in conversation was emphatic and her patrician A's were pronounced with a marked precision. Sometimes her voice was higher or more metallic than she intended it to be. There was a reason for this which many of her readers did not know. Although America knew that Booth Tarkington had trouble with his eyes, that Laurence Stallings had been badly wounded in the war, that various literary figures had various afflictions, few readers knew that Miss Glasgow was quite deaf.[58]

He added insult to injury by lumping her opinions with those of other "lady novelists," suggesting that she was a hypochondriac, and repeating a now-forgotten critic's opinion that she did not belong among the "Big Six" of American women novelists.

Glasgow felt betrayed. Here was a young man she had entertained at One West Main belittling her in print. "Of course," she told Stark Young,

> I would rather you would not review that book unless you say in a brief press notice that [it] is trivial gossip and not worth publishing. . . . He is as clear a case of arrested mental development as I have ever encountered, and he is simply trying to exploit hospitality—or rather kindness to what appeared to be discouraged and unhappy youth. . . . I wasted several hours on him, and I was never able to convince him that he should learn to write and to record accurately before he tried to make a sensation.[59]

The controversy escalated in 1937 when Meade told Margaret Mitchell that Young supposedly went into a rage at the mere mention of *Gone with the Wind*. Mitchell assured him that no one had helped her more than Young. Meade then told the entire story to Young, thinking he would find it amusing or complimentary. Needless to say, Young found it neither—especially after he received a letter from Mitchell describing how the rumor of his "holy rage" had made her "very ill," both for him and herself. "I have been the victim of so many ridiculous and sometimes vicious rumors," she wrote Young, "(as, for instance, that I am now in Reno divorcing my husband) that I become enraged whenever I hear anyone repeat a rumor about anyone else." Young sent Glasgow a copy of Mitchell's letter as well as Meade's, which he critiqued paragraph by paragraph for infelicitous and pretentious prose.

Young's reply to Meade mimicked Meade's letter to him, recycling the very phrases—such as "people who like books"—that Young had derided in his letter to Glasgow.[60]

For his part, Meade felt that Glasgow and her friends, including Emily Clark and Amélie Rives, had conspired to prevent his book from being reviewed. Young clearly enjoyed the intrigue and called Glasgow (who thought Young's response to Meade "milk and honey") "a beautiful fiend."[61] Meade probably could have saved the situation by apologizing to Glasgow. Instead, he went on the attack and threatened, in the most opportunistic manner, to sell her letters. "People have even offered to buy these letters," he wrote, "and there have been times when I needed to sell anything I could. . . . I shall think the matter over and perhaps I shall return them all for *you* to destroy but, unless something very unforeseen occurs, I shall not dispose of them." Glasgow assured him that she was ready to go to court. Not intimidated, he asserted that he owned any letters he had received, hers as well as those from other writers, such as Edwin Arlington Robinson.

> It must be comforting [he wrote] never to have failed in compassion—I envy you the peace it must bring you. And it must be a great consolation not to have offended a friend or acquaintance. You are the only person I know who hasn't. Since this is, what I think one calls, a swan song—I'd like to say this. I never wrote a line which I believed would really *offend* you. But I knew that you would never *approve* of anything I wrote about you and that you would not *like* any effort I made. . . . I cannot wish you success, for you have had as much success as any one gets in this life. A Nobel prize would not alter your status. . . . But I can wish you good health and I would say happiness, if I did not know that word is an unknown quantity for so many of us.[62]

In Glasgow's mind, the quarrel with Meade came to foreshadow the end of her career. "No one in the modern world," she told one friend in 1936, "is more lonely than the writer with a literary conscience."[63] The honors and accolades seemed to herald signs of her decline, so many bouquets to a diva passed her prime. More than ever, she tried to increase her readership, even enlisting Arthur's help in entertaining the critic Edwin Mims and finding English editors and reviewers for *Vein of Iron,* published in England in 1936. She still believed that the English notices made a positive impression on American reviewers.

The summer, with a June vacation by the sea in Ventnor, New Jersey, visits to friends in New York and Connecticut, motortrips though the Berkshires and Housatonic Valley, and a stop at Bread Loaf, the writers' community in Vermont, passed almost before Glasgow felt it had begun. At Bread Loaf, Glasgow taught several classes in English and thoroughly enjoyed the sound of her own voice saying unorthodox things.[64] Now 63, she wanted to leave her mark on the next generation.

V

Glasgow was not a woman to let an opportunity to ensure her reputation pass. One presented itself in December 1936 when Donald Davidson, a poet and perhaps the most political of the Fugitives, approached her about giving an address to an assembly of scholars containing a few chosen souls interested in pushing the "special purposes in which we"—and he thought she—were interested. "Take my word for it," a friend teased, "you could make even a Modern Language meeting . . . come alive" (WW, 271).

Glasgow, whom James Branch Cabell described as candidly exclusive and intolerant of dullness, made an exception when she agreed to entertain the Modern Language Association at One West Main. Glasgow wanted to invite every academician attending the conference until Donaldson told her she would be deluged with bewhiskered Chaucerians, specialists in Old Gothic and High German, French, Italian, and Spanish, who had not even a speaking knowledge of the English language. As an alternative, he asked her to designate a time at which the members of his committee and their wives could call.

It was to have been a glorious moment in Glasgow's career, the academy at her feet. But on the day of the address, she came down with laryngitis. Glasgow's indisposition did not stop the show. On the last day of December, Bennett ushered the selected professors into the drawing room, where Allen Tate—a dapper little man with an enormously high brow and a monocle—delivered Glasgow's speech entitled "Elder and Younger Brother." The speech articulated the relationship between scholars (the elder of the brothers) and the creative artist. Glasgow described the assembled academicians as few would have defined their colleagues—earnest seekers after the good and true, lovers of wisdom, and preservers of truth (RD, 167). Because she understood the academy's role in determining the shape of a national literature, she pleaded for standards: "We need insight; we need integrity and audacity . . . we need really to live in the modern world we inhabit" (172). Surrounded by antique furniture and blue damask, Tate spoke for Ellen Glasgow:

I began my literary work more than thirty years ago [he read] as a rebel against convention. I am still a rebel, but the conventions [as Tate himself illustrated] are different. . . . No longer would I make a revolution for the melancholy privilege of calling things by their worst names. . . . Yet, I still believe that the mood, if not the manner, of revolution is the most fertile of soils. (170–71)

Ellen Glasgow's spirit could be said to have possessed Allen Tate that day. For a few magical moments, she, the writer, and he, the speaker, spoke with one voice. If that voice seemed to link their generations, it also seemed a happy omen for Glasgow's future.

CHAPTER II

THE RAGGED EDGE

1937–1941

Faithful for a lifetime to a voice.
Ellen Glasgow, *Phases of an Inferior Planet*

I

ALTHOUGH ELLEN GLASGOW had always craved recognition, it too often seemed a tribute to her longevity. The rebel had become an entrenched member of the establishment, if not a living memorial to past causes and lost values. In December 1938, for instance, Glasgow became the sixth woman admitted to the American Academy of Arts and Letters. Two years later, she received the *Saturday Review of Literature* Award and guarded the gates, as one of the electors, to the Hall of Fame. Serving as a juror for the Book of the Month Club Fellowship, Glasgow had the near-impossible task of ranking the work of John Steinbeck, Katherine Anne Porter, Zora Neale Hurston, Robinson Jeffers, and Henry Steele Commager—her favorite for his biography of Theodore Parker. Time has proved a kinder judge than Glasgow, who decided that Porter lacked "vitality," Steinbeck exhibited "an obvious disdain of all craftsmanship," and Hurston promised only more and more of the same thing, "good Negro folklore."[1] Like many writers, Glasgow could be overly generous to friends and extracritical of strangers whom she inevitably saw as rivals. Having earned a reputation as a "stylist," she had also become an arbiter of literary standards and a maker of careers.

The public performance of being Ellen Glasgow took its toll. She had cultivated an "ironic mood" and a "smiling pose" and held them, "without a break or a change" (WW, 139), for almost forty years. In a slim book, entitled Of Ellen Glasgow (1938), Cabell tried to capture the "miracle" of Ellen Glasgow. Instead, he gives us the caricature that has become myth: her revolt against tradition, her exclusiveness, "fortified, not veiled by the tradition of aristocracy," her jealousy of other women writers, and her love of epigrams, gossip, and dogs.[2] Resembling many public memoirs, Cabell's portrait did not convey his subject's nuances and quirks, what she called her "humanity."

Glasgow coupled "humanity and distinction, reality and art,"[3] in her characterization of both people and places. On the fifteenth of May, she and Carrie Duke sailed on the Conte di Savoia for Italy, a country that represented to generations of tourists these very attributes. As usual, Henry Anderson saw her off with champagne (we have no record of orchids), his presence marking, like Banquo's ghost, Glasgow's endings and beginnings. The short trip, the most restful in years, passed uneventfully and without ill health. As a precaution, Glasgow brought along a list of names of Florentine doctors, none of whom she had to consult. In Fiesole, she and Carrie stayed at a friend's villa, which Lorenzo de' Medici had originally bestowed on Marsilio Ficino for his translation of Plato (WW, 264).[4] The house had gardens overflowing with lush, almost painfully exquisite flowers—blues that looked like swelling bruises and pinks like bleeding hearts. Around her she felt the art of Italy, the remains of ancient civilizations, "Etruscan places," and the silent company of writers, like the Brownings, who had been here before. Every evening the friends sat on the terrace overlooking a hillside of olive orchards and the white road, bordered by cypresses, that ran up to Fiesole. Glasgow spent her days mostly reading, interrupted by short excursions into Florence, where she liked to sit before Botticelli's "The Birth of Venus" or listen to organ music in the cool dark of some deserted church. She seems to have made no contact with her nearby neighbors at I Tatti, the museum-like estate of the Renaissance art critic Bernard Berenson, or with Percy Lubbock, whose Craft of Fiction (1927) she had assiduously studied.

The company she did seek tended to be religious. After visiting the friars of the Little Poor Man's monasteries, she tried to analyze the quality of their solitude so like and unlike her own: "I cannot write of the bliss and the agony the human soul must pass in its supreme hour of miracle — or of illusion. For the air in that solitude was still brushed by the passing, centuries ago, of that miracle — or of that illusion. Outward or inward vision?" she asked. "What does it matter? In that place, at that unforgotten moment, 'the only Christian since Christ' had found his Christ. Or had he found, instead, [what Matthew Arnold called] 'the flight of the alone to the Alone'?" (*WW,* 265–66). Glasgow had begun to prepare herself for her own final flight.

II

At the end of the summer, Glasgow came home eager to work on her next novel, *In This Our Life.*[5] She had, however, promised Scribner's that she would first supply prefaces for a subscription issue of her novels. Maxwell Perkins, a preeminent American editor best known perhaps for his collaborations with Thomas Wolfe and F. Scott Fitzgerald, wanted to publish the book immediately. Perkins appreciated Glasgow's "urbanity" and her technique.[6] He suggested that they begin with three prefaces and follow them after a month with two more, until the set was complete. Each volume would sell for ten dollars apiece. Scribner's agreed to pay one-third royalty to Harcourt Brace for *Vein of Iron* and one-third on the other volumes to Doubleday, Doran. After all the sets sold, Glasgow stood to make about $8,000.[7]

The prefaces gave Glasgow the opportunity to argue her importance, not just to the general public, but to posterity. If the chance seemed too good to miss, the actual design and writing proved difficult. Following Cabell's advice, she planned to expand the earlier essays included in the *Old Dominion Edition.* They were delightful as far as they went, he told her, but the new ones should be longer "so that your customers may see, and cannot miss seeing, the plain and ponderable addition. When I next see you I shall submit a simple formula by which you can do a 2,000 word preface without the least mental strain."[8] When Glasgow gratefully asked for the "formula," Cabell explained:

> There are just four points, I think, to be covered always, the place and the significance of the book in your complete work, that social history of Virginia; your own personal view of the book nowadays, as well as, if you like, of the dead person who wrote it; the book's origin and the circumstances in which it was written; and how, and when, and what happened after, the book was published — which of course gives you a free hand with its reviews and the acquaintances you may have made through it.
>
> With this formula once firmly fixed in mind, and with a little juggling

about of its four parts, the writing of a 2000 word preface is really no intellectual effort at all, as you will soon find.[9]

Cabell read and commented on the prefaces in progress—as did Carl Van Vechten—before they went off to Perkins. Although the "formula" gave Glasgow the blueprint she needed, it did not help her with questions of tone. Did she sound too conceited? Should she remove a paragraph about Edith Wharton, which stressed the collaborative nature of Wharton's work while underscoring the independence of her own?[10] (She did not.) Glasgow, who felt uncomfortable speaking directly to her readers, sought assurance from Cabell. She had difficulty articulating what had made her an artist and why her books should be read.

For any writer, rethinking previously published work can be agonizing, and Glasgow resisted Perkins's admonition that the set should have as much new material in it as possible.[11] In September 1937, she revised the preface to *The Miller of Old Church,* and followed it two months later with the one to *Barren Ground.*[12] By December she had finished writing the introduction to *Vein of Iron,* received the proofs for *The Romantic Comedians,* and begun thinking about sending advance copies to possible reviewers, among them Henry Seidel Canby of the *Saturday Review of Literature* and J. Donald Adams of the *New York Times Books.*[13]

Cabell held her hand through the production of the edition from beginning to end. He advised her about small matters, such as word substitutions, as well as larger issues of organization. He even consented to proofread. "I wonder why you are always so good to me," she told him. "I know I do not deserve half of it. Still, I wish to encourage such generosity wherever I find it, and especially in high places. Thank God the final preface has gone!"[14]

The edition, 810 handsomely produced and signed sets, appeared just after the new year—January 20, 1938. Glasgow arbitrarily arranged the novels not according to their chronology but to their locale: novels of the countryside: *Barren Ground, The Miller of Old Church, Vein of Iron;* novels of the city: *The Sheltered Life, The Romantic Comedians, They Stooped to Folly;* and novels of the Commonwealth: *The Battle-Ground, The Deliverance, Virginia, The Voice of the People, The Romance of a Plain Man, Life and Gabriella* (a book that Cabell had suggested including in the *Old Dominion Edition*). Glasgow had felt compelled to warn Scribner's that they would lose every penny invested in the series. They didn't lose every penny, but they were slow to recoup their investment. At the beginning of 1940, for instance, they had sold 259 sets and asked Glasgow, who had immediately seen the advantages of compiling the prefaces in a separate volume, to delay the prefaces until they had sold 200 more of the Virginia edition.[15]

Despite assurances by Perkins to the contrary, Glasgow claimed that reviewers would ignore this edition as they had the last. To prevent that happening, she began to lobby friends. In April 1938, she wrote Bessie Zaban Jones that she would "of course" like Howard to do "something":

> What do you think of this suggestion? Don't pass it on to Howard unless you approve of it. I feel sure that George Stevens, the new editor of the *Saturday Review*, would be glad to have Howard write a review of this edition. In that way, George might get a set from Mr. Perkins, and then Howard and you would have it for your own. Does Howard ever suggest books he would like to review? Anyway, George is a good friend of mine, and has a strong liking for my work.[16]

Because Henry Canby wrote a notice for the *Saturday Review*, Glasgow devised another plan for Jones: he could write a review for the *New York Herald Tribune*, which reached a much larger audience anyway. Glasgow first passed the idea by Irita Van Doren, who thought Jones "penetrating," if sometimes "difficult" (meaning negative), in his reviews. "So will you put it gently," Glasgow wrote Bessie, "and with wifely tact, to Howard that if he has not the time and the sympathy, it would be better for him not to accept the offer." With some pride, she added that "whoever wrote the article would have a set of this really lovely edition."[17]

Jones eventually wrote the ideal review, calling Glasgow's prefaces "the most important pronouncements upon novel writing since Conrad and Henry James." Her wit rivaled that of George Meredith, while the reality of her fiction—and perhaps its chronicle of parochial family histories—matched that of Thomas Mann. With tongue in cheek, he found "something humorous about reading Ellen Glasgow in the chilly glory of fine printing. The liveliest mind in Virginia," he told his readers, "is not yet ready for a typographical tomb. The tribute of beautiful format is richly deserved, but the implication that she is about to become the youngest daughter of the skies must be emphatically repudiated" (*Reviews*, 401–2).

Glasgow especially liked Jones's observation that her style uncannily reproduced the flow of time, but she took exception to his statement that as a Virginian she trapped herself in family and matters of "heredity." "No, my friend," she disingenuously chided, "I have not, and have never had the Virginian 'family complex.' I don't care a continental about 'family' in that sense." Jones might have reminded her of her repeated boast that she had the inheritances of 300 years in her blood. Her quibble about heredity aside, she had one more, "that the article could not be longer." [18]

This monumental edition of her work further canonized Glasgow. Tastes and styles would, of course, inevitably change, but she had done her best to insure future readers and to guide their judgment of her novels. From the beginning, she had sought more than temporary acclaim, and now she could survey the solid body of her work in matched bindings lined up like soldiers of fortune (*CM*, 117). What other American novelist had lived to see two representative editions of her work?

III

In 1938, Glasgow accepted honorary degrees from Duke University and the University of Richmond, where her friend Douglas Southall Freeman served on the faculty. She wanted to attend the ceremonies; however, she feared that her "damnable deafness" would make her a poor guest. She did not want to cause any "embarrassment" and began to dread an occasion she would have otherwise enjoyed.[19] Freeman understood her concerns and did his best to make the ceremony more like a private convocation. He assured her that she would not be bothered by loudspeakers and cameras, which added to her sense of disorientation. Nor did she have to march in the procession. The ceremony, which went without mishap, exceeded her hopes.

Unfortunately, the occasion at Duke, which also honored Norman Vincent Peale, realized Glasgow's worst nightmares. Before agreeing to accept the degree, she had asked expressly for a doctorate of laws rather than of letters. In her mind, the difference acknowledged her lifelong interest in philosophy and "truth." The university agreed, and Glasgow, despite reservations about sitting for hours with a "heavy cap" on her head,[20] promised to follow directions. She also asked, as in Richmond, that no photographs be allowed. Whatever its generous intentions, the university could not control every proud parent in the audience. In the split second when Glasgow reached out her hand to accept the degree, someone snapped a picture. The flash upset Glasgow, who managed only to retreat to her chair without falling. Either from confusion or for protection, she sat during the rest of the ceremony with her back to the audience. By making herself conspicuous and causing embarrassment, she had done exactly what she had hoped to avoid.

The degree itself offered no consolation, for when Glasgow unrolled the diploma, it pronounced her a doctor of letters, not laws. After the president, William P. Few, heard of the mixup from the dean of the women's school, he asked Freeman to award the correct degree at any time Glasgow found acceptable. The Freemans duly invited a few friends along with the presidents of the University of Richmond and the College of William and Mary to another ceremony at their house. Everyone, Glasgow included, wore full academic regalia. This time the occasion went smoothly.

Glasgow ventured one more time onto the academic stage to accept a degree from the College of William and Mary in Williamsburg. The long ceremony, in June 1939, took place on the lawn under stately old elm trees that sheltered mockingbirds. The birds' chatter nearly drowned out the opening prayers and hymns, but Glasgow, liking her purple hood, ornamented with gold, silver, and green, enjoyed being part of the spectacle.[21] Years before, when she poured over Walter McCormack's books on political economy, Glasgow had doubted whether any object could reflect the amount of labor that had gone into its creation. Now she could count her years of labor in academic regalia, such as the American Academy's gold key and small button for "informal wear." Could these tributes ever compare to the thrill of holding the books themselves? If Glasgow thought public honors empty, she would have resented their being withheld.

IV

Glasgow might be said to have lived both in and not in Richmond. No writer embodied the city more, and no writer erected as many barriers to protect what she called her "native country of the mind" (CM, 31). In the last years of her life, Glasgow found another country, which matched the lost and remembered fields of her earliest memories, in — of all places — Castine, Maine, a small coastal town that she called (after Sarah Orne Jewett's novel) the Country of the Pointed Firs.

Glasgow learned of Castine from Effie Branch, a Richmond neighbor and Arthur Glasgow's sister-in-law. Branch had a house in Castine high above Penobscot Bay. Originally built in 1924, "The Play-House" (or Guerdwood, as it is now called) had a facade of pink stucco. With its dark-wood trim, red-tiled roof, balconies, terraces, and formal garden, it seemed more in keeping with California than New England. Locals had doubts about the quality of its construction and placed bets that the stucco would crack "come winter."

Glasgow had visited Castine as early as 1914. Beginning in 1938, she made it her home each year from June to October. Castine sits on a high, green peninsula surrounded by granite cliffs, which most people call "pink" but with her usual pessimism Glasgow called "gray." Below, a tidal river widens into the bay. The village, which spreads out from the harbor, has some of the same characteristics that Glasgow appreciated in Richmond: tree-lined streets with old white colonials and mustard-colored Victorian houses, and a long, rich history.[22] In the 1870s, adventurous souls tired of the circus-like atmosphere of "the White" and other summer watering places discovered the Maine coast. Painters from James Whistler to Marsden Hartley were to paint its rugged granite and breaking surf. Castine had bracing air, footpaths by the sea, and a golf course Glasgow regretted not being able to use.

The townspeople saw Glasgow, who farmed out the household's washing and ironing, as a potential source of income.[23] They wondered at the size of her household, which included a companion (Carrie Duke or Josephine Clark), a secretary (Anne Virginia Bennett), a chauffeur (Nathaniel Martin), and a cook-chambermaid (Mattie Coleman). The local fishermen, boat builders, farmers, and shopkeepers knew Martin, who recounted his daily battles with cantankerous skunks and crafty raccoons, better than they knew Glasgow. He might have been the first black man some of the townspeople had ever seen.

Glasgow's first rental in Castine, Littleplace, belonged to the artist Allen Tucker. It had a studio where she would write, unless the fog drove her back into the main house. According to local legend, she prepared herself by pacing from one end of her bedroom to the other reciting passages from Keats, Shelley, Browning, and Shakespeare. The exercise supposedly attuned her ear to the music of words.[24] Littleplace had delphiniums "as blue as the heavens and nearly seven feet high,"[25] but the house she came to love best faced the harbor and sat at the bottom of the long hill from the Branches. Appledoor's large yard had beach roses, locust trees, cedars, and a perennial garden, where Glasgow read or played with her favorite dog. Every October, to insure their return, Bennett saw that the owners came back to a house filled with flowers, fresh towels, and bars of exotic soaps.

Glasgow attended Effie Branch's musicals and cocktail parties in the evenings. During the day, she walked for miles, often along a path known as the Indian Trail, which follows the coastline through the Witherlie Woods beyond Fort George and the town's golf links. The general practitioner in Castine remembered her as a short, slightly plump woman, with waved hair, who "went about strutting like a little partridge" in bright-colored clothes and a large, red floppy hat.[26] He kept her going on aspirin and phenacetine.

Glasgow thought that in Castine she had discovered the "ideal life" for herself, a life of working, walking, resting, driving, and almost "complete isolation." She wrote a friend that "if there were no fogs in Maine," the place would seem perfect.[27] Hunting wildflowers, blueberries, and mushrooms, Glasgow could have returned to her childhood world of Jerdone Castle. She didn't name any trees, as she did then, but when a full-grown willow tree fell victim to the saw, she commiserated with the house's original owner: "You needn't say a word," she told her. "I know exactly how you feel. How could any man do such a thing!"[28] At One West Main, Glasgow had two birdfeeders, a House of Lords, for pigeons, and a House of Commons, for sparrows. Here she liked to watch the goldfinches alight on the green pines like so many Christmas ornaments or feed the ruby-throated hummingbirds birdseed and water mixed with honey.

Glasgow was not the only—or as far as residents were concerned, the most famous—writer who summered in Castine. Katherine Butler Hathaway, the author of *The Little Locksmith* (1942), felt as if she became an entirely new person when she bought a house there. Like Glasgow, Hathaway suffered from a disability, in her case a diseased spine that affected her growth and limited her activities. Hathaway thought of herself and all the other summer boarders as

a race of people whose lives are finished, and who therefore are treated by the real citizens with patient compassion, as though they were not quite normal or else victims of a disaster . . . a mild sort of nuisance and responsibility which good-hearted normal people must look after in exchange for small sums of money . . . [because they apparently have] no homes of their own, no occupations, and, I hate to say it but I am afraid it is true, in their being people whom nobody anywhere overwhelmingly wants or needs.[29]

Oddly enough, no record of Glasgow and Hathaway meeting exists. Whether they did or didn't meet, the two women sought in Castine a similar space to write and a substitute community that supported them without intruding.

Glasgow admired her year-round neighbors, those "sturdy Maine folk," from a distance. "They have advantages over us of the South," she reasoned:

For one thing, they live in a thinly settled country, and, in Maine at least, they have the inestimable blessing of belonging to a single race. Unless you have lived in the South, I suppose you could never understand how thoroughly I enjoy the simple cleanliness of the Maine villages and farms and roadsides.[30]

Although Glasgow's comment verges on racism, it reflects her wish to escape the legacy of Southern history. Because she knew so little of ordinary life in Maine, especially its poverty, she swallowed its myths whole. Independent, thrifty, self-respecting, and proud, Mainers were first cousins of her own fictional family, the Fincastles. Bred to fortitude by a harsh climate, they constituted a breed apart. And Glasgow, herself in exile, felt at home. To Edwin Mims, she described Castine as a place with "no waste paper, no offensive billboards, no refuse heaps, no unsightly trash by the roadside. And, best of all, no miserable ill-treated animals. Many times I have thought, 'If only when they conquered us, they had civilized us as well.'"[31]

V

Although Maine may have been the only place Glasgow could write outside of Richmond, work on her next novel proceeded slowly. In October 1938, she went to New York, where she spent a miserable three weeks hospitalized with a back injury. She had a large, airy room, a private nurse, her own linens designed with Italian cutwork, and bouquets of flowers from thoughtful friends. When feeling well enough, she held court. Carl Van Vechten remembered visiting her one time after a manicurist had just done her nails. "I have never seen you look so lovely," he told her. "Carl," she replied, "you've never seen me in bed before."[32]

At the end of October, Glasgow left Doctor's Hospital, slightly improved after having shortwave electric treatment. Once home, history seemed to repeat itself. She grieved for her childhood friend Lizzie Patterson, whose husband had been murdered by their chauffeur. People whispered that the chauffeur had found his wife and his elderly employer in a compromising situation. After her husband's death, Lizzie refused to step foot in the garden, except to get in and out of her car.[33] "They were completely happy," Glasgow insisted, "and she had no other life."

Over the years, Glasgow's own losses had made her especially sensitive to those of friends. She knew, for example, when Amélie Rives would be

mourning with "every breath, every heartbeat" the anniversary of her husband's death: "Dear, dear Amélie!" she asked. "Is there not that moment that
exists somewhere beyond time? Which is more sure for you, the lost happiness with Pierre or the present anguish of separation? . . . when one has had
perfection, it is there forever, while the heart is alive and remembers."[34]

The loss of her husband and the ravaging of age and illness had left Rives
seriously depressed and suicidal. Either by accident or design, Glasgow had
a stroke of genius when she asked the celebrated beauty to share the secret
of her youthful appearance. Questions about the best and simplest skin-care
products made Rives, who had intermittently considered writing a book on
the subject, almost girlish again. Roused from a debilitating mourning, she
debated the use of hot water for washing (never), the correct application of
lipstick (heavier on the upper than on the lower lip), and the desired con-
sistency of *rouge en crème* (attained by slowly warming the jar between your
thighs). "I think it is glorious," Rives wrote, "for two sadly intelligent people
like us to be silly together."[35]

Glasgow's sympathy, while affected by issues of race and class, also embraced members of Rhoda Kibble's family. After Roberta ("Birdie") Richardson, one of Kibble's granddaughters, died, she informed Rebe: "Poor Aunt
Roberta Richardson died yesterday, the grandchild of Mother's mammy. I
was always very fond of her and always had her at my parties to take off
wraps. She was a perfect picture, with the distinguished Indian features."[36]
Following the funeral, another granddaughter wrote Glasgow,

> From the depths of my heart, I want especially to thank you for the $10.00 you
> sent me by Miss Bennett, the most beautiful spray to cover Birdie's casket, the
> food James brought, the use of your lovely car and chauffeur, the presence
> of Miss Bennett who represented you and last but not least, the gift of your
> wonderful book—"Vein of Iron" which I am reading with great pleasure.[37]

Periodically Glasgow sent a man to the cemetery to mow and shape the turf
of Birdie's grave.

Glasgow tended to mark her life by losses. She also made writing a way
of remembering, of keeping alive people and places. In her middle sixties and
in poor health, Glasgow felt death at hand. She said it did not scare her. By
nature, she had a fatalistic attitude. Pain and loss defined reality, and she often
felt that the sooner she and the world ended the better. Friends complained
about her cynicism. Cabell, for instance, thought that her mind "inclined
toward pessimism" as a flower did toward the sun.[38] Her niece Josephine,

however, thought her attitude something of an intellectual pose. Despite prolonged periods of sickness and occasional protests to the contrary, Glasgow did not want to die. Feeling a renewal of creative fervor, she forged instead a kind of armed truce with life.

Asking nothing of fate except the strength and time to work, Glasgow adopted a schedule that suited her: two hours work in the morning; walking and resting in the afternoon. By nine o'clock at night, she was usually in bed.[39] Above all, she wanted to finish her new novel before she died. "I have to live, more or less, as an invalid," she told Mencken, "and if only my capacity for work will last as long as I do, I shall feel that I am satisfied."[40] The new book would take, she estimated, another two years.

VI

Glasgow purposefully worked slowly on her novel. She dreaded the moment when it would no longer be solely hers, clearly wondering if it would be her last. By dragging the process out, she tricked herself into thinking she could hold death at bay. The year passed tranquilly, as she sat at her typewriter wearing a red kimono and white gloves. Her feet dangled inches from the floor, and the new dog, Bonnie, a woolly, white orphan from the SPCA, bounced in and out.

News from Europe repeatedly disrupted her concentration. "The war haunts in the shape of a nightmare," she wrote Mims in October 1939:

> I feel not only saddened but outraged, and it all seems to me so utterly unnecessary. But never, never, never again shall I surrender to the contagion of war hysteria. I suffered that once and once is enough—or too much. Even the trumpet of the Lord will not awaken me this time; I have lost my faith in salvation through violence, and I do not believe that anything can be saved by murder in masses.[41]

During this time, she thought she could hear her father singing his favorite hymn, "There Is a Fountain Filled with Blood." In the past, she simply turned off her hearing aid. Now she could not ignore the voices of English communists and fascists, who in her mind chanted nothing but "war."

Glasgow barely survived to the end of the year. The first week in December, her heart gave out. The severity of the attack and the accompanying arteriosclerosis made recuperation painful. It took two weeks before she could sit up. The doctors, she told friends, had pronounced her heart entirely inadequate for the work it had to do. They ordered her to stay in bed. Glasgow put on a brave front. Life had taught her that the greatest tragedy consisted not of dying too soon but living too long. She only feared, as she wrote Wilson, that she should be "the last creature on this planet to fight a losing battle" with that ancient hereditary enemy, the cockroach.[42] Cabell told her to keep in mind that she had achieved more than any living American woman, that she had overcome far more handicaps, and that this last illness should be but a "spur to her dear indomitableness."[43] She proved him right. Before a month had passed, she was up and active, reading Carl Sandburg's *Lincoln* and planning to sponsor his membership in the Academy of Arts and Letters.

By summer, Glasgow had completed the second draft of her latest novel, *In This Our Life*. On her way to Castine, she stopped in New York and immediately entered Doctor's Hospital. The cardiologist told her that she might live six weeks or six months. During the next month of convalescence, her heart grew stronger, but she suffered from neuralgia and worried about Carrie Duke who, after a car accident, had been hospitalized with a broken arm and three broken ribs. In Carrie's stead, Bennett arrived to escort her to Castine the last week in July.

On August 9, 1940, Glasgow had her second heart attack. Although seemingly unconscious, she remembered everything that happened. The doctor with his kindly Roman features sat for an hour with a stethoscope on her heart and his finger on her pulse, afraid to do anything lest it push her over "the ragged edge." Glasgow remembered feeling not "the faintest fear or reluctance, or even a wish to hold back a moment." Her philosophy held firm. She knew that there was "nothing to cling to in life and nothing, or less than nothing, to fear in death." As long as she couldn't finish her book, she hoped that she would go quickly. All the while, she could see the face of Rebe and hear the voice of Anne Virginia calling her back. Glasgow experienced a sensation akin to the one in the Swiss Alps after she received Gerald's last letter: "The peace I felt," she wrote in her autobiography,

> was not the peace of possession. It was . . . a sense of infinite reunion with the Unknown Everything or with Nothing . . . or with God. But whether Everything or Nothing, it was surrender of identity. . . . In my death, as in my life, I was still seeking God, known or unknown. . . . When I thought of dying . . . it was of dying not as a cold negation but as a warm and friendly welcome to the universe, to the Being beyond and above consciousness, or any vestige of self. (*WW*, 289–90)

Glasgow spent the summer in bed, staring (like Josiah Oakley in *Barren Ground*) at a tall pointed fir outside her bedroom window. It may be vanity, she wrote a friend, but "I have become much attached to this tree, and I feel that it has a kinship with something deep down in myself." [44]

Forbidden to walk, and permitted only short drives, Glasgow had to promise not to work for more than half an hour or so a day. "What a life and what a world!" she complained good-naturedly. "I shall merely remind you," Cabell scolded her,

> that I, in common with a great many other people, really do love you very much. And I beg you, for all our sake, to do what for you is the hardest possible thing—namely, nothing whatever except to obey your physician, to rest steadfastly, and to put by all thought of writing for the while.—Which of course you cannot do. Still, you might try.[45]

Glasgow had Bennett write (and Rebe witness) final instructions. She worried about the fates of her unfinished book and (as Bennett called it) her "[auto]biography." Bennett felt overwhelmed with Rebe's nervous chatter, news of her own sister's cancer, and visits from Dr. Babcock, who had what Glasgow called a "perfect deathbed manner." [46] She could not leave her patient for more than a few minutes because there was no way of predicting when an attack, like aftershocks of an earthquake, would occur.

Glasgow came home from Castine early in November. From her bedroom, she reached out to old friends—Cabell, Van Vechten, Freeman, Radclyffe Hall, and Bessie Jones—as well as new ones: the critic Van Wyck Brooks, the playwright Clemence Dane, and the novelists Claire Leighton, Margaret Mitchell, and Marjorie Rawlings. Mitchell realized how much she owed to Glasgow's experiments with literary forms, including the historical and the domestic novel. In earlier years, Glasgow had entertained visitors by showing them the sights: the great estates along the James River, the mountainscape of Skyline Drive, the picturesque towns of Williamsburg and Lexington, where Rebe would provide an elegant lunch. Now confined, she entertained them with the more intimate landscape of the heart. "I feel strangely enough," she wrote Brooks, "as if this friendship contained the element, not of time, but of eternity." [47] Glasgow gave and welcomed confidences about children, love affairs, marriages, and miscarriages, and made sure to tell each of her correspondents how much she loved them. She grew closer to her remaining siblings. "Do take care of yourself," she told Rebe. "You are really all I have, and you are bound up with my childhood and with my memories of Mother, who seems nearer to me as I go on." [48] She went so far as to compliment Arthur on his magnificent work for England and the part he had in changing American sentiment. Arthur, who had authored many patents and papers in gas technology, had begun to think about contributing political articles. Dedicating his work to all who want better government, he privately printed a series of diatribes against strikes in restraint of trade, against the Eighteenth Amendment granting universal suffrage, and against the mandatory filing of joint income tax returns for married couples. [49] Glasgow, perhaps remembering her fling with politics, encouraged him to express his own point of view, without commenting on either his beliefs or his style. She saw a person, who, like herself, remained a kind of exile, someone who had taken root and created, if not an inner world she could wholly honor, certainly a world of his own.

VII

With Rebe living in Lexington and Arthur in England, Glasgow increasingly depended on James Branch Cabell for amusement and affection. He came and spent hours by her bedside, reading aloud chapters of her new novel and helping with final revisions. He took a perverse pleasure in knowing that he was almost certainly polishing a Pulitzer Prize winner. The publishers, impressed with Glasgow's "gallantry," refused to let her pay for any author's changes in the corrected plate proofs.

Glasgow acknowledged Cabell's help but never credited him with making substantive changes. She claimed to have rewritten several chapters as well as the whole in proofsheets for style and manner (CM, 263; WW, 292). In his memoir, As I Remember It (1955), Cabell asserted that he had finished the final draft out of love and friendship and honest sympathy. Twice a week, about four o'clock, he would stop by to show her any "slight amendments" he had made in the text. Then he would "kiss her cheek and depart with a fresh batch of typescript," which he returned in the next three or four days. [50] Glasgow would inscribe his copy: "For James Branch Cabell in devoted friendship and admiration from Ellen Glasgow, Richmond, Virginia, March 10, 1941."

Before the book saw print, the American Academy of Arts and Letters honored Ellen Glasgow for the entire body of her work, with special recognition of her recent novel, Vein of Iron. Van Wyck Brooks informed her that despite the usual competition among three nominees she had been the only one considered.[51] Illness prevented her accepting the solid gold medal with a picture of Howells engraved on one side and a quill and inkstand on the other. On November 14, 1940, J. Donald Adams accepted it in her stead. He read a two-sentence speech that Glasgow had asked the secretary of the academy to supply: "A literary award confers a double honor when it is given, in the name of William Dean Howells, by the Academy of Arts and Letters. I accept this distinguished medal with the deepest appreciation."[52]

Glasgow wanted particular care taken with what might be her last book. She hoped it would come into the world warmly received. "Will you please, please, please, promise me that it will be printed in large, clear, open type," she wrote Alfred Harcourt. "I like a long novel, so please do not let the printers try to make the book appear shorter. My eyes have not yet recovered from the small, close, glaring type of the new Virginia Woolf book [*Roger Fry: A Biography*]."[53] As usual, she insisted that her book have an allotted advertising budget and lead Harcourt's list. She also insisted that a sufficient time elapse before allowing book clubs to offer it at a reduced price. When the publicity department promoted her book with "popular piffle" like Jan Struther's *Mrs. Miniver*, she fired off a letter to the president of the company. "If your publicity department is headed this way," she punned to Harcourt, "then please treat me as generously as you treated Sinclair Lewis and *Let Me Go*."[54]

Glasgow concerned herself with every aspect of production from advertising copy to the design of the book jacket, a black cityscape in the setting sun against a gold background. The description of the book troubled her because it contained too much detail. Nowhere did it state the theme of the book, which she saw as "an analysis of the modern mind and temperament in a single community." She wanted it emphasized that the lives of her black characters presented a theme in themselves—"a minor theme, perhaps, but still a theme which is closely woven into the major theme of the book."[55] The final copy read, "The fascinated reader sees unfolding before him an analysis of the modern mind and temper as exhibited in this family and community. . . . And, as always, the story marches to the rhythm of that close-woven, epigrammatic, polished prose, one of the great styles of our time."[56]

As a critically acclaimed and best-selling novelist, Glasgow had an equivocal relationship to popular culture. While she cared to publish in the "better" magazines, she made no demands about the filming of her novels. For the right price, such as the $25,000 she demanded for *They Stooped to Folly*, Hollywood could do what they wanted with her novels. Paradoxically, she did not seem to care that the same people who read the *Cosmopolitan* would see her novel on the big screen. Although she wrote for a general audience, she imagined her own readers as somehow more discriminating than the low-brows who watched movies and read popular magazines of a certain kind. In her complicated and contradictory thinking, a novel and a film, which sacrificed the philosophical in its emphasis on human interest, remained entirely different enterprises. Hollywood gave the public what William Deans Howells claimed it craved: a tragedy with a happy ending. Glasgow forgot that she herself had given the public a happy ending in *The Deliverance*, which became a silent and then a sound film.

Glasgow had liked the film version of *Gone with the Wind*, especially the portrayal of Mammy, which reinforced, or perhaps influenced, her romanticized accounts of Rhoda Kibble and Lizzie Jones in *The Woman Within*. Still, she absolutely refused to see *In This Our Life*, which starred Bette Davis and Olivia de Havilland as Stanley and Roy Timberlake. Hollywood did exactly what she had expected by emphasizing the rivalry between two sisters "fated to hate each other." Under Davis's picture, the advertising copy read, "She didn't give. She only took her husband, his career, his life." Glasgow sold the rights for $40,000, which Joseph Collins told her not to invest. "Spend it," he urged.[57]

Believing that *In This Our Life* would be her last novel, Glasgow wanted it to communicate whatever wisdom she had gained from suffering and joy. The novel follows the fortunes of the Timberlake family: Asa, an aristocrat who works as a laborer in the tobacco company his family once owned; his wife, Lavinia, the hypochondriac niece of the city's leading industrialist; and their two daughters: Stanley, a spoiled beauty, and Roy, a woman searching for meaning, for something greater than herself. As in the movie, Stanley "drives" the plot. After she runs off with her sister's husband, he commits suicide. When she returns home, history repeats itself as Roy's fiancé, Craig Fleming, finds himself drawn to Stanley. Stanley's innocent exterior makes it impossible for people to blame her for anything, even the hit-and-run death of a little girl.

They can, however, believe it of Parry Clay, a black man acting as Stanley's chauffeur. With the creation of Parry, Glasgow realized her goal of freeing black characters from stereotype. Parry, who dreams of studying law but becomes an instrument—as his name suggests—of deflection, has some of the qualities of Faulkner's Joe Christmas (*Light in August* [1932]). To Queenborough residents, Parry seems "nearly white," or, to put it another way, "so little black." He suffers, as Glasgow wrote in *The Battle-Ground* (1902), because white Southerners sacrifice morality for self-preservation. Foreshadowing the thoughts of James Baldwin in "Stranger in the Village" (1953), Asa thinks:

> How little we actually know of the Negro race. Our servants know all about us, while we know nothing of them. They are bound up in our daily lives; they are present in every intimate crisis; they are aware of, or suspect, our secret motives. Yet we are complete strangers to the way they live, to what they really think or feel about us, or about anything else. And the less colored they are, the more inscrutable they become, until, when they have so nearly crossed the borderline, like this boy Parry, they seem almost to speak another language, and to belong to another species than ours. (*ITOL,* 28, 27)

From the beginning of her career to its end, Glasgow had concerned herself with racial characteristics, whether Michael Akershem's illegitimacy, Grandmother Fincastle's vein of iron, or the plight of American Indians, whom she thought denied their constitutional rights.[58] Here she questions not only racial bias in the United States, but also the political, economic, and social separation of whites and blacks whom she sees as part of one human family. Asa has trouble understanding Parry because the "tradition of servitude" that previously determined their roles has broken down. Between him and Parry lies the veil W.E.B. DuBois discussed, "the dark thickness of race, that impenetrable obscurity . . . welling up among the intricate ties of human relationship" (*ITOL,* 30). Neither Asa nor Parry can free himself from a "conspiracy of tradition and of custom, of reason and of economics" (42). Much as he wants to expiate the sins of slavery, Asa's family tries to prevent him from telling the truth that would free Parry: "Colored people don't feel things the way we do . . . not as a young girl would" (415). The converse is precisely Glasgow's point. The young man whom Asa visits in jail bears no resemblance to the Parry he knew. To authenticate the scene, Glasgow had a friend escort her to the city jail — "and, still worse, to the Negro section."[59] What she saw appalled her no less than it does Asa. Beaten into "type," Asa finds Parry speaking the dialect he has always shunned, as though ignorance offers the only remedy (*ITOL,* 402).

Glasgow based the central incident of the novel, the car accident, on a tragedy in her own family. While in Virginia Beach, one of her nephews fatally injured a black pedestrian in a traffic accident. After his arrest, a friend of the family stood bail. The case never came to trial, though the widow filed a suit for damages. The prosecuting attorney at the magistrates' court did not think a charge of manslaughter justified.[60]

When Glasgow's sister heard about the accident, she supposedly burst out, "I hope it wasn't a black man." Rebe knew that Glasgow would see the man's death as another assault on a besieged race.[61] She was right. Glasgow believed that his family deserved both a personal apology and adequate compensation. When Rebe defended her son, Glasgow shifted ground by questioning the morals of his fiancée. Even engaged couples should not stay in the same hotel unchaperoned—the circumstances of the hearing aside. The quarrel resulted in a long rift between the sisters.

Glasgow infused her sympathy for the man who died into her characterization of Parry. She congratulated herself on drawing her black characters from real life. She claimed to have walked with the model for Abel Clay, the family patriarch, in the garden he had grown through "diligence and devotion," and she modeled his wife, Minerva, after Rhoda Kibble's granddaughters, Roberta Richardson and Agnes Reese (*CM*, 257–58). Thanking Glasgow for having a *"beautiful soul,"* Reese told Glasgow that she made her think,

> what a lovely place this world would be today if nations had a little of that kind of [familial] love in their hearts for each other.
>
> Our love for each other teaches me how firm a foundation of love was laid by our first generations for the second and third to build upon.[62]

Like most white readers, Carl Van Vechten found her black characters wholly believable. Thanks "for what you have said in behalf of the Negro race and what you said against their treatment by otherwise gentle people!" he applauded. "If you were dancing in a Spanish Theatre, every man's hat would be flung to the stage; every available dove would be released to circle about your head; and you would stand bowing knee deep in carnations!"[63] But the letter that must have meant the most to her came from Elaine Deane, a high school English teacher from Washington, D.C.:

> My purpose for writing this note is to express profound appreciation for your novel, "In This Our Life." I read with interest every page of the book, and noted with particular zeal your admirable portrayal of colored people. To me, Minerva and Parry were respectable human beings, with dignity, ideas and opinions. As a member of this minority group, I thought as I read, of the many colored people who have ideals, who lead decent lives, who are ambi-

tious, and who, in many instances, do achieve more than an average share of success in life. . . . I want to express my heart-felt and sincere gratitude for the kind heart, the deep understanding of human nature, and the liberal conceptions which assisted you in writing such a novel.[64]

Reviewers echoed Deane's assessment, commenting on the philosophical and moral impact of *In This Our Life*. Many wondered why she had yet to receive the Pulitzer Prize for fiction, if not for a single novel, then for the collective body of her work. She was, as James Southall Wilson wrote, greater than any one of her novels. Together they showed the measure of her genius (*Reviews*, 428).

In June an exhausted Glasgow arrived in Castine. The freshly wallpapered housed pleased her, and she enthusiastically ordered tubs of pink geraniums and a tree of purple heliotrope to brighten the yard. Carrie, who brought four pairs of shoes but none for walking, kept her entertained: "She minces over the country on high spiked French heels," Glasgow wrote Rebe, "just as the women mince along in New York. . . . Feet and legs are played up there at the expense of the rest of female anatomy. They move exactly as Chinese women did in the old sheltered days of China."[65] Berta Wellford joined them later in the summer. Glasgow's health led her to assume it would be her last visit to Maine. She could see no practical reason to buy Appledoor, now on the market. It would only complicate matters for her legatees.

During the summer, Glasgow, again depressed, worked on the prefaces for *A Certain Measure*. "I know that I am over and done with," she wrote Cabell, "and I cannot reconcile myself to being merely a shell with an inadequate heart. . . . May you never know the horror of coming to the end of your work before your life is finished."[66] Since the completion of *In This Our Life*, she had felt as if she were "drifting in an icy vacuum toward something— or nothing." She wondered whether other writers had this sense of "being drained and lost and surrounded by emptiness whenever they have finished a book." Her illness and five years of work intensified her feeling of "being swallowed up in the void."[67]

In September, Glasgow returned to Richmond, where two months later, on December 7, she learned that the Japanese had bombed Pearl Harbor. "War has come," she wrote in her notebook. "Another age of Disenchantment is ending. Another Age of illusion is beginning."[68] Once again, Ellen Glasgow wished herself finished with the world, and once again the world had not finished with her.

CHAPTER 12

A CERTAIN MEASURE

1942–1945

I am not sanguine about our destiny, for I have not, like
Margaret Fuller, made the great acceptance. But I believe in
a gallant endeavor, whether or not we are ever to come into
a finer inheritance.
Ellen Glasgow, letter to Van Wyck Brooks, August 23, 1941

I

ON MAY 4, 1942, Ellen Glasgow won the Pulitzer Prize for fiction. The garbled telegram from the Trustees of Columbia University read: "Take pleasure in advising you award to 'In This Our Life.'" She understood that the award, given on the occasion of her novel, honored the entire body of her work. A reviewer echoed the committee's sentiments when he observed that "Ellen Glasgow occupies a unique position among her contemporaries. Since she first won a national reputation some 25 years ago she has never written a novel unworthy of her great talents" (*Reviews*, 431). Telegrams, including several from Margaret Mitchell, began to flood One West Main. That afternoon, Glasgow wrote Donald Brace, "Please print and sell more copies. Publishers tell me that this prize is excellent for advertising purposes."[1] Not to be outdone, Warner Brothers immediately released its version of *In This Our Life* to packed audiences.

Glasgow was 69 years old. She had endured, even triumphed, but she had been dying for the last decade. And like those Stoics she admired, she intended to die with dignity. In moments of despair, she returned to Plotinus, the spiritual philosopher of light and beauty, for consolation. Pain felt more real to her than any award, and only the response of her friends made her believe that the Pulitzer had not been "too little too late."[2] Their recognition credited what she had seen within: a "truth" that indeed corresponded to others' reality.

In Glasgow's state of health, many writers would have retired. Not her. During the next two years, she did what conceivably kept her alive. She worked on the sequel to *In This Our Life*, published posthumously as *Beyond Defeat* (1966); her book of literary criticism, *A Certain Measure* (1943); and her autobiography, *The Woman Within*. All three projects involved both revisiting the past and assessing her shrinking present. Glasgow's weak heart made writing difficult, but, as one friend warned, "Some fool is going to do a sentimental biography of you one of these days and how your spirit will writhe. Better do it yourself."[3] She lived mostly in her bedroom where she received visitors while lying on a sofa. Bessie Jones felt that Glasgow's bedroom recreated her mother's room, a place steeped in the atmosphere of Victorian ill-health. Most of Glasgow's inner life had been lived in this room and the adjoining study. When she felt well enough, Glasgow would wrap herself in one of the colorful shawls knitted by a woman in Maine and type at a rickety little table. In this study, littered with stacks of newspapers and magazines, with odds and ends of letters and papers, she was most herself. The mask of the "great writer" or the "Southern charmer" dropped. She was every inch the creative artist.[4]

II

The rest of Glasgow's life became a struggle to keep sacrosanct her "private world of beauty and spirituality."[5] Events in the outside world had less and less effect on her daily routine or even consciousness. Surveying her life, she read the diary that Rebe had kept on their trip to Egypt. From so long ago, it seemed to belong to fiction. The two sisters made a pilgrimage to Hollywood

Cemetery, where the graves of their family stood like so many volumes on a library shelf. With friends, Glasgow sought a new candor, and her letters included (almost verbatim) passages that would compose her autobiography. "My one eager desire, as far back as I remember," she wrote Bessie Zaban Jones from Castine,

> has been to start out, quite alone, and go round the world by myself. Yet, though I have travelled a great deal, I have always been shielded and looked after, and advised and warned and retarded. For years, I was so sensitive about my deafness that I would not go into a shop unless someone was with me, and in earlier years I would not even see a caller alone. . . . I suffered from a morbid sensitiveness that was a kind of tepid Hell, and even now, I have not entirely got over it. My whole life has been a struggle not to be helped.[6]

In her friends' eyes, Glasgow's courage gave her life a significance beyond her writing. If she could work with such physical disabilities, then Radclyffe Hall, for example, felt she could surmount her eye and heart troubles. Glasgow talked openly about death, and Hall assured her that she had nothing to fear in being united with "the source of all true and indestructible happiness, with God."[7]

At the end of her life, Glasgow made a special effort to reach out to younger women, including Hall, Rawlings, and Signe Toksvig (the biographer of Hans Christian Anderson), who found in Glasgow a trustworthy confidante and willing mentor. Glasgow told Toksvig how much her "little lonely Hans Christian" reminded her of the time when she "dreamed dreams, and was little and lonely."[8] "It had not occurred to me till last night," Toksvig responded, "that I was sitting at your feet and adopting you for my teacher, but now that it has occurred to me I feel very happy about it!"[9] Glasgow had a knack for giving unfeigned, discerning praise. No book could ever take the place of The Yearling, she wrote Rawlings, but Cross Creek, with its evocation of the Floridian landscape and sustained rhythmic prose, almost did. Glasgow felt that the book had been so tightly constructed, it would bleed if torn apart. (Her one objection concerned the scene in which Rawlings betrayed the confidence of the yellow catch-dog.) After reading that passage, Glasgow had put the book aside for several hours: "You write so vividly that, even then," she confessed, "I could not put the story out of my mind."[10] Ironically Rawlings, the anointed biographer, told Glasgow her own life story. Rawlings, who had a troubled first marriage, sensed that Glasgow had experienced similar emotional entanglements. Her new marriage, she admitted, was "something of a gamble." [11] These friendships gave Glasgow, who craved the company of like minds, a feeling of "intellectual integrity, of a certain rightness of mind and heart . . . [of] breadth, depth, and elevation." [12] They gave her a sense of immanence.

III

From 1942 on, Glasgow spent more and more of her time between bedrooms in Richmond and Castine, a place she would risk her life to reach. She returned to Maine the summer of 1942, accompanied by Bennett and Carrie. The town, which had never failed to delight her, now seemed occupied solely by old women panting with war fever. Still, she told friends, the air smelled like chilled wine and beyond the blue, rippling bay the crystalline hills rose heavenward. She had driven up with rationed gas, stockpiled during the year, to find the new house freezing and everything upholstered in plush: "There are more ways of killing the spirit than smothering it in plush," she wrote Cabell.

Unlike Littleplace or Appledoor, this house seemed inhospitable to writing. In August, Glasgow physically could not write. A window fell on her hand, and though an x-ray revealed no broken bone, she could type with just one finger. Even walking proved beyond her, for the sling made her lose her balance. Yet Glasgow's ennui went deeper. "What is the meaning of it?" she asked Cabell. "For more than forty years I was driven by some inner scourge to commit an act which appears to me, now, as useless, as murder. Shall I feel that way ever again? Or is the impulse dead and buried for good?" [13] Intimates of Ellen Glasgow knew that there could be only one answer to her question. When not writing, she felt as though she ought to be dead. [14]

IV

Glasgow returned to Richmond in October, after a week in New York at the Weylin Hotel and a visit with Nelson Doubleday on Long Island. To think, she wrote Van Wyck Brooks, that she might never again see her old friend or the skyline of New York. [15] Three months later, on the last day of 1942, Glasgow had another heart attack. The doctor made her give up any exertion. The very weather—a sleet storm "slaughtering" the trees outside her window—seemed to reflect the soul of the world.[16] By the end of February, however, she had begun writing—for fifteen minutes a day—the sequel to *In This Our Life*. Why? No matter that "the contemporary scene and the contemporary standards of craftsmanship" had destroyed, for her, "the faith and the work of a lifetime,"[17] she simply had to do it.

Thinking that she would not find any readers in wartime, Glasgow persisted in writing the book that would become *Beyond Defeat*.[18] She finished the first draft in late April or early May 1943, and the third around January of the next year.[19] The news of Stephen Vincent Benét's death in March reinforced her feeling that she was rushing against time. On her seventieth birthday, Irita Van Doren and Frank Morley sent her seventy "Better Times" roses.

Glasgow wanted to finish *Beyond Defeat* because it troubled her "how few reviewers ever see what one regards as the chief, or only, meaning in a work of imagination. Charles Poore thinks *In This Our Life* has 'hope alone' at the end. Lewis Gannett thinks 'the end is without hope.' But," she wrote Van Wyck Brooks, "the meaning was (or is) [that] failure lies not in defeat but in surrender to life."[20] *Beyond Defeat* opens with Roy's return to Queenborough after a three-year interval. In the interim, Stanley has married a Hollywood producer, and Lavinia has inherited an annuity that frees Asa to live in the country with his old friend Kate Oliver. Roy has tuberculosis and must find a temporary home for her illegitimate son, Timothy. Kate agrees to care for him on her farm, a place, like Jerdone Castle, where work, love, and nature coalesce. Glasgow believed in the individual and cultural significance of tradition. She also believed, as *Beyond Defeat* illustrates, in the need for "adjustment," for a living dynamic that "does not repudiate the unknown and the untried."[21] Glasgow doubted whether she would ever publish the novel. She thought it might be better to end her career with her book of prefaces and cap it with the posthumously planned autobiography.

V

In 1943, *A Certain Measure* led Harcourt, Brace's fall list, priced at $3.50—a dollar more than Glasgow, who worried about sales for a book on writing, expected. "Of course," she wrote Cabell,

> the inevitable disappointment has set in. I am not satisfied with the appearance of the book. The print is very good. I selected that, and the best paper

we could find for the first edition, which will take all of this particular kind of paper.

But I dislike the smooth edges, and I think the book [a deep reddish-maroon] looks too much like a text-book. Then, of course, as soon as I open the pages, I see things I should like to do over, and so differently.[22]

Glasgow found the warm response to her book of literary criticism astonishing. *A Certain Measure* seemed to offer readers what it promised, a potpourri of information. The book gave a summary of her career and the impulse behind individual novels. Glasgow educated her readers about Southern cultural history from the 1850s to the present, while presenting an overview of American letters. For readers interested in the process of writing, she provided a handbook on narrative technique. And for those interested in Ellen Glasgow herself, she was as ironical and feisty as ever—"much more than the outstanding woman writer of America," as one friend phrased it, "[she was] one of the great feminine figures in the history of our age—and feminine in all the noblest, most rounded attributes."[23] Glasgow's valuation of memory, manners, and morals appealed to readers in the midst of world chaos: "We find, in a certain measure, what we have to give," she wrote, "if not what we seek, both in the external world about us and in the more solitary life of the mind" (*CM*, 264). Her message carried some consolation.

For her part, Glasgow hoped that the book would generate a long, if limited, demand, and that Harcourt, Brace would keep it in stock. Always the businesswoman, she wondered whether the Book of the Month Club might offer it with another volume. (They declined.) It now happened that she could often be read only in the costly Scribner's edition. Her books had to be available and priced to sell if people were to continue to read them.

VI

A Certain Measure crowned Glasgow's career. Reviewers compared it to Henry James's *Prefaces*. "It is a privilege to be able to salute her in her own time," Hamilton Basso wrote in the *New York Times Book Review* (*Reviews*, 453). To Hunter Stagg, her books were "home."[24] And Marjorie Rawlings cited *A Certain Measure* as one of the three most influential books of the year.

Cabell, whom Glasgow had asked to review the book, did not emulate their chivalry. Glasgow had assumed his support. After all, he had helped with the project, both morally and practically, even down to choosing a title. Original choices had included "The Anatomy of the Novel," "Life and the Novel," and "Life in the Novel" (hers); and "The Facts of Fiction" and "A Certain Measure" (his). With him, she had been, as Bennett was wont to say, "indiscrete." Cabell claimed to have fended off her desire to disclose her "past" (perhaps with Gerald B or Henry Anderson), while trying to lift her spirits. In 1941, he had told her:

> It is dreadful to think of you as a virgin, but your books offer almost irrefut-able testimony to the fact, unless indeed your Virginian ladyhood has stepped in and caused you to become reticent. . . . When people write to me as an authority upon your maidenhood, I become, as befits an aging grandfather, embarrassed. What I really meant, though, is that your last letter was simply silly. Your theme song was The Old Gray Mare She Ain't What She Used to Be, whereas the correct melody is There's Life in the Old Girl yet. What more do you want, you—so to speak—swine? You have had a recognition more wide than Shakespeare ever received during his lifetime, or for that matter, Homer. Should you not ever publish another line, your fame is none the less secure and opulent.[25]

Glasgow responded: "Well, James, I was delighted to hear from you, in spite of the scolding tone of your letter, and in spite, too, of the groundless supposition in your first paragraph. I see nothing in my books, and still less in my conversation, to lead you to assume such a thing."[26] The next day, as a thank you for his help with the prefaces, she sent a handwrought sign for his house in St. Augustine, Florida, named Poynton Lodge.

By 1943, Glasgow felt as if Cabell were part of her family, the brother she might have continued to love if he had survived military school. She de-pended on him without completely trusting him. It worried her, for example, that he saved her letters. The man with whom she had become most inti-mate in her later years also held her—and the world—at a distance. When Bennett, who was later treated for manic-depression, began acting strangely, Glasgow wanted to confide in Cabell: "Now, will you please destroy this let-ter, for, before I finish it, I must add a few warning lines I have wished, for years, to whisper in your inattentive ear," she wrote in September 1943.

> But the opportunity has never come, and probably never will come. Please do not ever, ever, by spoken work or telephone make any allusion to Anne Vir-ginia about my work. I mean never mention it to her, or send me a message through her. And do not mention this request even to Percie. Not to anybody. I may explain, and I may not, but that is all.[27]

He treated this matter, as he did most, lightly—as a sign of Glasgow's re-
pressed sexuality and need for attention. Any service he rendered was, in his
mind, a service to letters.

Glasgow's anxiety about Bennett had a real cause. Bennett later admitted
to opening Glasgow's correspondence to see if she was mentioned. And
Carrie Coleman Duke, Glasgow's friend and surrogate sister, had to have
the First and Merchants National Bank prove to Bennett that she (Bennett)
had done nothing criminal with funds in her trust. Bennett could never be
entirely convinced of her own innocence. This woman, who checked under
her bed and in every cupboard to make sure no one was lurking, always remained something of a cipher. Was she simply paranoid or jealous or overly
protective?[28] She seemed a part of the furnishing of One West Main, but no
one really knew her—perhaps not even Glasgow, whose responsibility she
had become. In the last years of Glasgow's life, she and Bennett had an ongoing contest of wills. Glasgow, sick and impotent, had become something
of a taskmaster and Bennett, worried and overworked, her "guardian" angel
or jailer.

Glasgow had, of course, a very different relationship with Cabell than she
had with Bennett. With Bennett, Glasgow clearly remained the employer.
When she referred to Bennett outside the family, she described her as "my
secretary." With Cabell, she sought a soulmate. To her, their friendship had
not been one-sided. She had done her best to promote his career—from
lobbying for his admittance to the American Academy of Arts and Letters to
promoting advertising for the *Storisende Edition* to writing laudatory reviews
of his books.[29] Her inscription of *A Certain Measure* read: "For James Branch
Cabell, with affection and admiration unbounded, from Ellen Glasgow, Castine, Maine, Sept. 7th, 1943." It can be imagined how his tongue-in-cheek
review of that very book had shocked her.

The title of Cabell's review, "As One Famous Virginia Author Sees Another," assertively stated his own credentials. Published in the *New York Post*
as well as the *Chicago Sun*, it portrays Glasgow as a female incarnation of
Edward Gibbon, the historian whose initials she significantly shares. Cabell
notes that Glasgow's career has followed the same design as Gibbon's, for
after his history of the *Decline and Fall of the Roman Empire*, he turned to memoir. Cabell emphasizes this parallel between history and fiction to suggest
that Glasgow's self-styled social "history" is nothing but "fiction" or, worse,
"histrionics": the actions of young men in love, the resigned sentiments of a
time-tamed husband, the meditations of an illiterate black woman "were no

more comprehensible to Ellen Glasgow, through any vital experience, than was to Gibbon, let us say, the deplorably un-English temperament of the harlot-empress Theodora" (*Reviews*, 467). For obvious reasons, the review infuriated Glasgow. It placed her in the "sentimental" tradition; and it found the woman ("by turns frank, or seductive, or arrogant, or self-contradictory, or rich with wisdom") more interesting than her work (468). Glasgow could not contemplate her life apart from her work, and either Cabell did not, or callously did, understand the connection.

What prompted Cabell, knowing the state of Glasgow's health, to such hurtful malice? Did he resent the stasis of his own career in the wake of her ascendancy? Or the fact that she did not publicly acknowledge his help? If he meant to be funny, or wrote as one coauthor to another, he grossly mistook his audience. He realized his mistake almost immediately: "If you have yet seen the complete article concerning you and Gibbon as it appeared in the N.Y. Post then you have the advantage of me," he wrote Glasgow. "They promised to send me copies here, but none has reached me. The extract printed in the Times-Dispatch appeared carefully to omit the more complimentary parts." [30]

Glasgow did not acknowledge either his letter or the review, though her friend Roberta Wellford took Cabell to task. Six months passed in total silence before she responded from Castine:

In this life-giving air, lifted high above a blue rippling bay and a chain of hills, I find that only a war on the other side of the world, with mankind destroying itself and other more innocent animals, appears really important to bother about. Even the sharpened edge of what Berta Wellford felicitously called your "all-time low" has become harmlessly blunted.

You alone, I suppose, my dear James, know the reason for this abrupt change of front after thirty—or is it nearly forty—years? I am willing to grant you any number of reasons, though I cannot quite understand all the long endeavor to build up a charming appearance of sympathy and comprehension, if this were simply for the need of releasing, in the end, a sudden gust of uninhibited malice. Literary smartness must depend, of course, for its best effects upon caricature and misrepresentation, and, as we both have learned, from the wise or the witty, caricature demands the spicy flavour of malice or flippancy. And yet, even so—the only literary right I deny is the right of misrepresentation. But all this is beginning to sound over-serious. Perhaps, without suspecting it, I am still incurably romantic at heart, and I dislike seeing destroyed a perfection that cannot be restored. I find, as I grow older, that

I cling more firmly to certain ancient beliefs or illusions: to steadfast loyalties, and to truth of the written or spoken word, and to the abiding sincerity of a long friendship.

Glasgow offered an olive branch in closing: "After I reach home, perhaps you will both come down for an old-fashioned. We may still have a laugh together, for I think that ironic amusement will be the last pleasure we give up." [31]
Cabell hated emotional wrangles, and he would rather have lost her friendship than justify his motives. A proud man, he answered with a letter bearing neither greeting nor preamble: "I terminate for this while my un-inhibited malignities with the forwarding of our best love to you and Anne Virginia." He signed it "as always." [32]
Glasgow refused to give up on their friendship. Since those days in Williamsburg when she had seen him—poetical and victimized—he had held a special place in her affections. Returning to her original point three months later, she asked,

Does the pleasure of releasing an inhibited gust of malice make the effort, or the satisfaction, worth more than its costs . . . ? What you might care to say in a newspaper would certainly be no solemn matter, if only it had not denied everything you had said or written, and I had believed, for the past thirty or forty years. [33]

Cabell's response ignored her grievance, and Glasgow did not write again for nearly a year. Then she admitted missing their "old talks on writing and the kind of writing that was worth while." She signed her letter, "With my love to the three of you, and with the old friendship and sympathy, Ellen." Recovering his lost gallantry, Cabell answered: "I must certainly see you in October. There are so many things which may not be written about with profit, because a face to face quarrel, but not a letter, can end with a kiss." [34] Glasgow succeeded by meeting the certain measure of Cabell's hardness with an equal (and unheard of) measure of humility.
The quarrel, which lasted until the last three months of Glasgow's life, could not have helped her health. From 1943 on, she had experienced a good deal of pain. "Yet one can only bear it," she wrote Toksvig, "and pretend not to mind it." [35] Glasgow thought often of that ecstatic, golden afternoon on the Alps when the world had harmony and her life became part of some greater good. That vision, more than love and maybe more than writing, had made the struggle bearable.

For weeks on end, she did not leave her bedroom. In February 1944, her old enemy, influenza, returned, leaving her exhausted and gloomy. She still felt defiant, she told Marion Canby, though no longer young: "I have not yielded an inch in my rebellion against the cruelties of the world."[36] She would die as she had lived: refusing to admit defeat.

VII

Glasgow's last days were marked by displays of pragmatism, courage, and — depending on one's values — pettiness. On April 15, 1944, just a week before her seventieth birthday, Ellen Glasgow signed her will. Her main beneficiaries were Anne Virginia Bennett, who succeeded Glasgow as president of the SPCA, and the SPCA itself. Glasgow cared so strongly about animal rights that since 1932 she had not worn fur. That year she sent her niece Josephine a short coat made of Siberian squirrel. If she could no longer bring herself to wear fur taken from animals not killed in a steel trap, neither did she want to waste a perfectly good coat.[37]

Glasgow left Bennett a life interest in a trust fund of $100,000 administered by the First and Merchants National Bank of Richmond. From that fund, James Anderson, her cook, would receive a monthly bequest of $50. According to his daughter, Sarah Anderson Easter, Glasgow had already helped him to buy their family house as well as a house for his mother in the country. The deed to Anderson's house at 202 West Marshall Street in Richmond, purchased in 1946 (the year after Glasgow's death), indicates that he paid cash, which may have come from the sale of another house on Clay Street or from Glasgow herself. Glasgow's last words to Anderson's daughter were about him. "Take care of Daddy," she said. Sarah thought he died three years after Glasgow from a broken heart: "That was all he knew."

Following Bennett's death, the income from the trust reverted to the Richmond Society for the Prevention of Cruelty to Animals in memory of Glasgow's dog Jeremy. Although Arthur owned One West Main, Bennett could live there as long as she chose. If she did move, she could take, after Rebe, whatever household items she needed. Glasgow made a point of categorizing those items, which included furniture, silver, china, and glass, but not books. They, with all her papers, were to go to her literary executors, Irita Van Doren and Frank Morley.

Glasgow, who left Rebe and Anne Virginia $10,000 outright and Carrie

Duke $5,000, took special care to provide for her other dependents. At the time of her death, Nathaniel Martin, her chauffeur, was to receive $300, and every person in her employ $100. In various codicils written over the next year up to October 31, 1945, Glasgow made specific gifts to friends for keepsakes: she wanted Berta Wellford to have her miniatures of Cary; Rebe the Chinese Chippendale chairs and Thomas Sidney Cooper's "Sheep Reposing." Carrie Duke would inherit her emerald ring, clothes, and ermine cape; Josephine Clark, her bedroom furniture; Anne Virginia, a topaz pin to match her brown hair; Signe Toksvig, the bronze Buddha that had been a gift from Amélie Rives; and Lizzie Patterson, who needed nothing but Glasgow's love, a bowknot pin of onyx and diamonds. The American Academy of Arts and Letters received a portrait of Glasgow in her twenties; the Valentine Museum a collection of about 150 china and pottery dogs in memory of Cary McCormack; not least, her dog Bonnie got a life tenancy of the chaise longue in her bedroom.

Ellen Glasgow accepted the fact that her working days appeared to be finished, though friends—like Alfred Knopf who asked her to edit and introduce a volume of James's short stories and tales—pretended she was immortal. Joseph Collins wrote that a person with such obvious vigor, transcendent energy, and lovely complexion should not be saying her valediction to literature. He insisted that she come to New York for treatment. "I know of no one in the world," he wrote, "to whom it is more hazardous to say 'you must' than to you, but I am going to say it: You must come to New York and let me through the medium of doctors that I shall select restore you to a degree of health that will permit you to live the next few years in comparative comfort free from pain and anguish." If Carrie could not accompany her, he would send his own nurse as an escort. If she could not afford the expense of further hospitalization, he would pay for it in "memory of P[earce]. B[ailey]. who loved you and of J[oseph]. C[ollins]. who admires you and believes that you have in the recesses of your brain something the world wants to hear." [38] Arthur advised her to accept and offered to pay for any treatment. However, recalling the bills of a "previous 'crook' heart doctor in New York," he didn't want to be exploited as a "rich relative." He asked her to tell Collins "to keep the expenses to a minimum." [39] She thanked them all for their concern and decided she would die in Richmond or Castine, where she returned one last time with Josephine. "We shall need your courage," she told her.[40]

Glasgow, who for the sake of her heart religiously drank a glass of scotch each day, could not tell from one moment to the next how she would feel.

Nevertheless, she worked as well or as much as she could, living more and more in books. She read *The World of Washington Irving*, written by her friend Van Wyck Brooks, and followed its characters on Indian trails and through the Louisiana swamps. She felt the "shabby splendor" of Edgar Allan Poe's genius, the intellectual power of Arnold Toynbee, and the subtle humor of Anthony Trollope and Jane Austen. Sympathizing with Henry James, who could not read a contemporary novel without rewriting every sentence, she declared that the novel had ended with the greatest of Victorians, Thomas Hardy.[41] Her favorite books in American literature remained Nathaniel Hawthorne's *The Scarlet Letter*, Mark Twain's *Huckleberry Finn*, and Henry David Thoreau's *Walden*.

When Cabell visited Glasgow in October 1945, her condition horrified him. She seemed a "mere wisp" of herself and confessed that the idea of living like a prisoner in her dark house throughout the winter without literary contacts depressed her. Glasgow both loved and loathed One West Main, which with the windows open seemed engulfed by the noise of traffic and impinging life. Cabell urged Marjorie Rawlings to write her a letter:

> Tell her how wonderful she is in comparison with all other writers, living and dead; that is treatment to which she responds purringly. And urge her to try spending the winter in St. Augustine. I believe this to be a possibility, now that I have discussed the matter with her companion, Miss Bennett, who believes that some such course is imperative. She could then get out and about; she loves to walk; and there would be enough people to make a to-do over her to induce complacence. You and I could acquire merit by discussing literature with her on, say, alternating Thursdays.[42]

Willfully forgetting her tiff with Cabell, Glasgow asserted that none of her friends had once let her down or failed in loyalty and consideration. And for this she felt blessed.

Ellen Glasgow never visited St. Augustine. She did return Cabell's call, stopping by his Richmond house in the afternoon to sip old-fashioned cocktails and talk valiantly about the future. Yet a month before, on October 23, 1945, she had written Bennett instructions that show her anticipating her death: "Do not send Manuscript of Memoirs by post or express. Notify publishers and they will send for it—or Literary Executors."

On November 11, Glasgow felt well enough to keep a hair appointment at the Jefferson Hotel Beauty Parlor. Since 1936, when she bobbed her hair over Anne Virginia's objections, she had worn it short. The idea of having her hair washed, cut, and permed made her feel like one of her own heroines who buys a cocky red hat to face down the world. As the moist heat, the slightly acrid smell of chemicals, and the familiar female voices surrounded her, Ellen Glasgow had another heart attack. Anne Virginia, just about to have her hair washed, called Nathaniel Martin and sent him home to bring the bottle of Scotch sitting on the drawing-room mantel. He returned in minutes, and Glasgow drank half a glass straight. For some reason, Bennett decided that it was not necessary to administer the hypodermic she had been carrying for the last several years for such emergencies. The beautician finished the permanent as quickly as possible, and Bennett took Glasgow home. "What would you have done if I had died there?" Glasgow asked. Bennett, who understood her fear of dying in public, answered, "We would have gotten you right into the car. No one would ever have known."

Ellen Glasgow lived ten more days. The day before she died, she had lunch with her brother Arthur, who happened to be in Richmond. Douglas Southall Freeman wrote, thanking her for successfully lobbying for his admittance to the American Academy of Arts and Letters.[43] That night she donned a red dress with a matching red coat to preside over a meeting of the SPCA, held at One West Main. She went to bed shortly after her last guest left. As usual, she checked to see that a thermos of coffee stood on her nightstand, and then she locked the door.

In the morning, Anne Virginia got up at six-thirty and went downstairs to make sure Nathaniel had built the fires. When Glasgow did not respond to her knock, she unlocked the door. Glasgow lay with her head slightly turned, a wry smile curving her lips. Anne Virginia faithfully remembered the instructions that Glasgow had written to her and Rebe: *Do not forget Jeremy. Remind Dr. Tompkins of his promise.*[44] When Tompkins arrived, he administered what would have been a fatal dosage of strychnine to Glasgow. Glasgow had no intention of being buried—like Madeline Usher—alive. For the remainder of the day, Anne Virginia and Carrie notified friends: "Ellen Glasgow died this morning."[45]

Glasgow requested a simple graveside ceremony, but Anne Virginia and Rebe had their own ideas. Bennett prepared her body for viewing and arranged that a hairdresser from the Jefferson would come every morning to comb her hair. On the day of the funeral, Glasgow's family—her sister Rebe, Anne Virginia, Carrie Duke, James Anderson, and the other members of the household—held hands and prayed in a circle around her bed before the Episcopal service (for seventy-five people) in the drawing room. In this room,

Glasgow had said goodbye to her mother and seen her sisters married. Yellow roses adorned the door, and candles burned at the head and foot of her casket. Glasgow held the last of the daily orchids that had arrived anonymously. Anne Virginia had not invited Henry Anderson, who defied her and all Richmond by standing in the doorway as he had in Glasgow's life—half in and half out. After the funeral, rumor has it that Bennett received a snub that Anderson might have interpreted as poetic justice. A relative, Beulah Branch, whether from cruelty, resentment, or ignorance, made Bennett use the servants' entrance to the Branch house.

Glasgow was buried in Hollywood Cemetery near J.E.B. Stuart, the Confederate general. Douglas Southall Freeman, Virginius Dabney, and Herschel Brickell numbered among her pallbearers. The coffin held both Glasgow's body and that of her dog Jeremy, a gift from, and no doubt a constant reminder of, Henry Anderson.[46] If dogs could not enter heaven, then neither would she. She had chosen her epitaph from John Milton's "Lycidas," his lament for a friend dead before his prime. "Tomorrow," it reads, "to fresh woods and pastures new."

LEGACIES

I could laugh at the end, because I had had my life.
Ellen Glasgow, *The Woman Within*

I

ELLEN GLASGOW HAD ALWAYS thought about life, and about her own life, as a doubtful enterprise. She tended to see herself in a state of war, surrounded by enemies, and fighting for every success.[1] She kept with all save a small number of friends and family an armed truce. At the end, she did her best to make peace with the remaining members of her family, having learned the futility of "denying one's flesh and blood." As she wrote in *The Ancient Law,* "it can't be done" (298).

Although Glasgow had accepted with skepticism the world's estimate of family feeling or unity, she might have expected her will and her requests would be honored, that they would insure some harmony after her death. Rather than drawing the remaining siblings together, her death seemed to have unloosed past rivalries and rancor. Anne Virginia Bennett, for example, was so certain that Glasgow would have wanted periwinkle on her grave that she threatened to rip up the flowers Rebe had planted.[2] Her legatees reminded Marjorie Rawlings of adders she had seen living under a floribunda rose.[3] The discord and rancor that followed Glasgow to Hollywood Cemetery reflected a profound ambivalence about her life, her accomplishments, and the lasting value of her work. Her family had as much difficulty coming to terms with these questions as did later readers and literary historians.

The problems began almost immediately after the funeral, when Henry Anderson offered to buy One West Main and donate it either to the Museum of Fine Arts or the Virginia Historical Society. The idea of a Glasgow memorial delighted Arthur, who wanted to bestow the house himself. He had only two concerns: first, that the designated proprietor maintain the building; and second, that the house appear as it had during his sister's lifetime. He hoped that giving the house to the State of Virginia would guarantee its becoming part of the Museum of Fine Arts.

On the surface, the proposal seemed simple enough. Alas, it hinged on Glasgow's heirs relinquishing their inheritances of household furnishings. It took less than three weeks for the first signs of resistance. After hearing that Henry Anderson might buy West Main, Cabell Tutwiler wrote to Arthur about a counterplan. His wife had very definite ideas about the memorial, which she wanted to reflect Glasgow's work for the SPCA. "I believe," he ended, "that Rebe and Anne Virginia can indicate more accurately than any one else, the kind of memorial Ellen would prefer. Few people realized, I think, how close were the bonds of sympathy, love and understanding between Rebe and Ellen."[4]

Arthur, who of course knew of the long silence between his sisters, judiciously said nothing. He preferred to recognize Ellen's contribution to American literature. For Rebe, the terms of Glasgow's will further complicated her position. If Anne Virginia remained at One West Main, she lost all interest in the contents of the house not specifically bequeathed.[5] "Knowing Ellen as I did," she told Arthur, "it is impossible for me to picture her, the most exclusive of people; her home the most difficult to enter, having any and all classes, privileged to see how she lived her private life; but of course, after all, her life was not lived down stairs, but a very unhappy one in her bedroom and study."[6] Rebe worried that black college-educated women would be able to tour the house.[7]

Unable to comprehend the depth of Rebe's resistance, Arthur thought he could disarm the opposition by promising to reimburse the legatees. Again outlining the advantages of a "Monument d'Etat," he proposed a compro-

mise: a bronze tablet on either side of the entrance door to One West Main
that would read:

(Right)
HERE
ELLEN GLASGOW
Lived and Worked
And Died November 21, 1945

(Left)
President's Office
Richmond Society for
Prevention of Cruelty to Animals
Founded, Presided over, and Endowed
by
ELLEN GLASGOW

In Arthur's plan, Bennett would be able to live in the house and continue her
work for the society.

The Glasgow family negotiations tired Anderson, who began to wish he
had never broached the subject. They exasperated Arthur, who chastised
Rebe for making "nullifying qualifications" and chilling Anderson's zeal. "I
have tried throughout to consider the problem on a practical permanent
basis, rather than on a transitory emotional one," he told her. "A house divided against itself will fall." [8]

With reluctance, Rebe assented to Arthur's plan. It remained for the Virginia Museum of Fine Arts or the Virginia Historical Society to accept the
building. Unfortunately, neither institution believed it had the financial resources to maintain the property. Given the circumstances, Anderson argued that they must abandon the project. "I find some consolation," he told
Arthur, "in the fact that the real memorial to her will exist and continue to
exist in her books which were the products of her mind and spirit." [9]

Arthur finally decided to give the house to the Virginia Historical Society.
They, in turn, sold it to the Association for the Preservation of Virginia
Antiquities. Arthur, who contributed the 1952 purchase price of $20,000, in-
tended the house as a permanent memorial to his "distinguished" sister.
Unlike the houses of Emily Dickinson or Edith Wharton, One West Main is
now a private residence. Readers who want to see where Glasgow lived and
worked must imagine themselves behind its gray stucco facade. Echoing the

protagonist of Glasgow's last novel, Arthur might be forgiven for thinking that "family feeling had stood in the way of everything he had ever wanted to do" (*ITOL*, 16).[10]

II

Glasgow probably suspected that her family would argue about the house and its objects as well as about her life. Even the most carefully defined wills can be broken. While she might not have imagined the particulars of the domestic drama that ensued after her death, she had planned a second line of defense. Practical and ever cynical, she left a larger will and testament, a testament to the shape and meaning of her life. If members of her family had their own ideas about how she should be remembered, so did Ellen Glasgow herself. She relished the idea of speaking from beyond the grave. When, in the months before she died, her literary executors visited her, she would prop herself up with pillows and read the most tantalizing passages from her autobiography.

Published the year of Henry Anderson's death, *The Woman Within* (1954) caused a stir for its revelation of her affair with Gerald B and its sardonic portrayal of Anderson himself. Glasgow had told Cabell that he, too, would not like what she had written about him, and Cabell obliged her. He called the autobiography her best work of fiction.

Glasgow, who considered her story as compelling as most novels, wanted to leave a record of her search for meaning. Throughout her adult life, she had understood the necessity of creating a persona her public could embrace, envy, or admire, a persona that, to some extent, held her suspended in time. The young woman who thought of herself as a rebel had grown old and unsure of any labels, especially those applied to her own identity. *The Woman Within* recounts the major stages of its author's life: her awakening to self, her long apprenticeship to art, and her relentless struggle with "God" (*WW*, 289). Perhaps in no age would Glasgow have felt anything other than a stranger and an exile; nevertheless, she found a home in art where the grace achieved came from work and work alone (279, 296). For all its venom and even exhibitionism, *The Woman Within* shows an almost tangible yearning to be known as she knew (and didn't know) herself.

The bickering between Glasgow's brother and sister, the misunderstanding about the woman and her work, testify to more than family feuds. For in spite of her careful preparation for her posthumous fame or the care she took in both *The Woman Within* and her legal will and testament, it might be said that Ellen Glasgow died intestate. This woman who was her own Memoria, who wrote the memory of Virginia and the South, knew that she might not be read, or, if read, not appreciated by generations to come. Her friendships with critics speak to her growing sense of inconsequence, of a dismissal or a forgetting by posterity.

For fifty years now, Ellen Glasgow has been considered, at most, a weak third to Edith Wharton and Willa Cather. In her presentation of "the first wholly genuine picture of the people who make up and always have made up the body of the South," [11] Glasgow anticipated much that secured the fame of a writer like William Faulkner. Yet she has won little of Faulkner's recognition. Perhaps it does not matter whether a writer is forgotten. Most, after all, are. Who now reads Cabell, for example? Who reads Norris or Howells? Who read Melville for generations after his death? Still, the silence about Glasgow seems a poignant loss.

Near the end of World War II, a young soldier tried to express to Glasgow what she meant to him. "Though you have never been in Pittsburgh," he wrote, "it was there we met, in a bookstore":

> On that day and in that store a copy of Barren Ground came into my hands for the first time; worn, limp, and many times reread, it is a permanent possession. It was something of an adventure in my life, or in that "strangely valid" life that lies beneath the surface consciousness of everyday existence. Undoubtedly I shall never meet you personally, see you, speak to you, but we have met many times in your books in the past few years, and will meet again in times to come. We have a host of mutual friends, Dorinda, General Archbald, Mrs. Dalrymple, and others of the inhabitants of Queenborough and of the Commonwealth. They are durable friends; better than many friends, they have an infinite variety, have a capacity for philosophy, are always dependable, coming unbidden when needed." [12]

He was right. Glasgow has been and will be remembered for the merit of her books. She knew what she wanted to do and did it the best she could. In the process, she found, if not complete happiness, then achievement. "I have known a feeling for beauty that was almost ecstasy," she wrote in summary of her life. "I have had moments of rapture; I have had moments of exaltation; I have had moments of mystic vision" (*CM*, 112). Above all, she has shown us "that life without imagination would be insupportable."[13] How can we fail to admire her?

The witness of a rich and complex past that she could treat as either comedy or tragedy, the voice of America's struggle to rebuild from its Civil War, the novelist who never let personal tragedy or professional failure deter her, Ellen Glasgow deserves better. True, she could be silly, selfish, even autocratic. "In that bland Richmond world," Van Wyck Brooks asked, "how could she have carried on if she had *not* been, if she had not barricaded herself and defended her great interest by nursing an anti-social rebellious ego?"[14] She could also be generous and strong. Over a long career, she refused to interrupt or compromise her work. An almost singular case in American letters, she began early and wrote until the end, getting better all the while. Hailed as the South's "first novelist," rather than "romancer,"[15] she shaped American literature no less than "regionalists" such as Mark Twain, Nathaniel Hawthorne, or Kate Chopin. Living in silence, she understood the larger silence of a world that did not care. Her novels are neither the bagatelles of a Southern lady nor the social chronicles of a Southern city. They are the work of one of America's most dedicated and gifted writers.

ABBREVIATIONS

AA   "Author and Agent: Ellen Glasgow's Letters to Paul Revere Reynolds," ed. and introduced by James B. Colvert, *Studies in Bibliography* 14 (1961): 177–96

AL   Alderman Library, University of Virginia–Charlottesville

BG   Ellen Glasgow, *Barren Ground* (New York: Harcourt Brace Jovanovich, 1985)

Builders   Ellen Glasgow, *The Builders* (Garden City, N.Y.: Doubleday, Page, 1919)

CM   Ellen Glasgow, *A Certain Measure: An Interpretation of Prose Fiction* (New York: Harcourt, Brace, 1943)

CSS   *The Collected Short Stories of Ellen Glasgow*, ed. Richard K. Meeker (Baton Rouge: Louisana State University Press, 1963)

D   Ellen Glasgow, *The Deliverance* (New York: Doubleday, Page, 1904)

EGN   *Ellen Glasgow Newsletter*

FV   "My Fellow Virginians," in *RD*, 60

GL   Glasgow Letters, Harry Ransom Center, University of Texas

ITOL   Ellen Glasgow, *In This Our Life* (New York: Harcourt, Brace, 1941)

Letters   *Letters of Ellen Glasgow*, ed. Blair Rouse (New York: Harcourt, Brace, 1958)

Man   Ellen Glasgow, *One Man in His Time* (Garden City, N.Y.: Doubleday, Page, 1922)

Miller   Ellen Glasgow, *The Miller of Old Church* (New York: Doubleday, Page, 1911)

MP   Macmillan Papers, New York Public Library

Phases   Ellen Glasgow, *Phases of an Inferior Planet* (New York: Harper and Brothers, 1898)

Poems   Ellen Glasgow, *The Freeman and Other Poems* (New York: Doubleday, Page, 1902)

RC   Marjorie Kinnan Rawlings, "Notes for a Biography of Ellen Glasgow," Marjorie Kinnan Rawlings Collection, University of Florida

RC   Ellen Glasgow, *The Romantic Comedians* (New York: Doubleday, Page, 1926; Charlottesville: University Press of Virginia, 1995)

RD   *Ellen Glasgow's Reasonable Doubts: A Collection of Her Writings*, ed. Julius Rowan Raper (Baton Rouge: Louisiana State University Press, 1988)

Reviews   *Ellen Glasgow: The Contemporary Reviews*, ed. Dorothy M. Scura (Cambridge: Cambridge University Press, 1992)

Romance   Ellen Glasgow, *The Romance of a Plain Man* (New York: Macmillan, 1909)

SL   Ellen Glasgow, *The Sheltered Life* (London: Virago, 1981)

ST   Ellen Glasgow, *The Shadowy Third and Other Stories* (Garden City, N.Y.:
        Doubleday, Page, 1923)

TB   Ellen Glasgow, *The Battle-Ground* (New York: Doubleday, Page, 1902)

TD   Ellen Glasgow, *The Descendant* (New York: Arno Press, 1977)

TSF   Ellen Glasgow, *They Stooped to Folly* (New York: Doubleday, Doran, 1929)

Vein   Ellen Glasgow, *Vein of Iron* (New York: Harcourt, Brace, 1935)

Voice   Ellen Glasgow, *The Voice of the People* (New York: Doubleday, Page, 1900)

WL   Ellen Glasgow, *The Wheel of Life* (New York: Doubleday, Page, 1906)

WW   Ellen Glasgow, *The Woman Within* (New York: Harcourt, Brace, 1954)

NOTES

Introduction

1. I am paraphrasing Henry James, *The Golden Bowl*, vol. 1 (New York: Scribner's, 1908), 16.

2. Woodrow Wilson and Thomas Nelson Page became members in 1908. Willa Cather, who was born in Virginia, was inducted with Glasgow in 1938. If we give Cather alphabetical precedence, then Glasgow would become the second Virginian woman admitted to the Academy.

3. For taped interviews with Sarah Anderson Easter, Mary Tyler Freeman McClenahan, and Frances Shield, see "Ellen Glasgow," a video made by the Virginia Writers Club of interviews conducted by Patricia Pearsall and Welford D. Taylor, held at the Richmond Historical Society.

4. See Louis D. Rubin Jr., *No Place on Earth: Ellen Glasgow, James Branch Cabell and Richmond-in-Virginia* (Austin: University of Texas Press, 1959), 43–47. Also see Sara Haardt, "Ellen Glasgow and the South," in *Ellen Glasgow: Critical Essays*, ed. Stuart P. Sherman, Sara Haardt, and Emily Clark (Garden City, N.Y.: Doubleday, Doran, 1929), 15.

5. E. Stanly Godbold Jr., "A Biography and a Biographer," *EGN* 32 (Spring 1994): 4–5. See also Godbold, *Ellen Glasgow and the Woman Within* (Baton Rouge: Louisiana State University Press, 1972).

6. Linda Wagner-Martin, *Ellen Glasgow: Beyond Convention* (Austin: University of Texas Press, 1982); Julius Rowan Raper, *Without Shelter: The Early Career of Ellen Glasgow* (Baton Rouge: Louisiana State University Press, 1971), and *From the Sunken Garden: The Fiction of Ellen Glasgow, 1916–1945* (Baton Rouge: Louisiana State University Press, 1980); Pamela Matthews, *Ellen Glasgow and a Woman's Traditions* (Charlottesville: University Press of Virginia, 1994).

7. Van Wyck Brooks, *An Autobiography* (New York: Dutton, 1965), 477.

8. Virginia Woolf, *Orlando: A Biography* (New York: Harcourt Brace Jovanovich, n.d.), 325.

9. For a discussion of this process, see Bell Gale Chevigny, "Daughters Writing: Toward a Theory of Women's Biography," in *Between Women: Biographers, Novelists, Critics, Teachers, and Artists Write about Their Work on Women*, ed. Carol Ascher, Louis DeSalvo, and Sara Ruddick (Boston: Beacon Press, 1984), 356–79.

10. Leon Edel, *Literary Biography* (Bloomington: Indiana University Press, 1973), 11.

11. See Robert Skidelsky, "Only Connect: Biography and Truth," in *The Troubled Face of Autobiography*, ed. Eric Homberger and John Charmley (New York: Macmillan, 1988), 7.

12. Linda Wagner-Martin, *Telling Women's Lives: The New Biography* (New Brunswick, N.J.: Rutgers University Press, 1994), x.

13. Willa Cather, *On Writing: Critical Studies on Writing as an Art* (New York: Knopf, 1949), 41-42.

14. RC. Glasgow could not believe that Rawlings, never having seen the library at One West Main, could describe its claret-colored curtains.

15. Ibid.

16. Brooks, *An Autobiography*, 477.

17. Mark Twain, letter to William Dean Howells, March 14, 1904, in *Mark Twain Howells Letters: The Correspondence of Samuel L. Clemens and William D. Howells, 1872-1910*, ed. Henry Nash Smith and William M. Gibson (Cambridge, Mass.: Belknap, 1960), 2:782.

18. Godbold, *Ellen Glasgow and the Woman Within*, 219.

Chapter 1. The Deep Past

Epigraph: *The Thoughts of the Emperor Marcus Aurelius Antoninus*, trans. George Long (Philadelphia: Henry Altemus, 1890), 206. Glasgow marked the passage.

1. See RC. These relatives were the Landgrave Christophe De Graffenried, and William Yates, president of William and Mary College.

2. See the will of William Yates Gholson, Accession No. 5060, Box 22, Alderman Library (hereafter 5060/22, AL). Gholson did make provisions for Anne and Samuel Creed in his will. He left three pieces of land and any other subsequently acquired real estate to be divided between his surviving three children, the third being Virginia E. Kittredge, his daughter by Elvira Wright. Samuel and his descendants stood to inherit the bulk of the estate after Elvira's death.

3. Anne Gholson Glasgow, letter to William Yates Gholson, April 29, 1866, ed. Edgar MacDonald, *EGN* 10 (March 1979): 3-4.

4. See "Taylor, Creed," 5060/22, p. 2, AL. Anne Gholson was born on December 9, 1931. Taylor added the codicil to his will on March 7, 1932, leaving Anne and her brother their mother's share of his estate.

5. E.G., letter to Arthur Glasgow, October 3, 1933, Accession No. 5347, AL.

6. "Gholson, William Yates," 5060/22, p. 2, AL.

7. In the 1860 census, Francis Glasgow listed his occupation as "farmer," and the value of his real estate at $10,000 and his personal assets at $6,000.

8. Charles B. Dew, *Ironmaker to the Confederacy: Joseph R. Anderson and the Tredegar Iron Works* (New Haven: Yale University Press, 1966), 19, 26. Also see Marie Tyler-McGraw and Gregg D. Kimball, *In Bondage and Freedom* (Chapel Hill, N.C.: Valentine Museum, 1988), 20-33, 19, 26; and Kathleen Bruce, *Virginia Iron Manufacture in the Slave Era* (New York: Augustus M. Kelley, 1968), esp. 179-230.

9. Tyler-McGraw and Kimball, *In Bondage and Freedom*, 23.

10. Robert S. Starobin, *Industrial Slavery in the Old South* (New York: Oxford University Press, 1970), 8.

11. Dew, *Ironmaker to the Confederacy*, 75.

12. See E.G., letter to Rebe Tutwiler, May 6, 1942, RC. Glasgow's letter to her sister shows her making a good story better: "Do you recall the name of the Colonel or captain who spent the night on Mother's porch, after General Hunter tore up her note asking for a guard? Was it Milroy? I think it began with an 'M', and I remember her telling us several times of that incident."

13. Anne Gholson Glasgow, letter to William Yates Gholson, April 29, 1866, *EGN* 10 (March 1979): 3–4.

14. Virginia Rawlings is not listed on any census report of the Glasgow household from 1860 on, when she was, according to Glasgow's memory, a member of the family.

15. Charles M. Wallace, *The Boy Gangs of Richmond in the Dear Old Days* (Richmond, Va.: Richmond Press, 1938), 8.

16. The Register of Communicants, First Presbyterian Church, lists Kate's baptism as November 13, 1868, and her burial as November 21, 1869.

17. Virginius Dabney, *Richmond: The Story of a City* (Garden City, N.Y.: Doubleday, 1976), 221.

18. E.G., letter to Signe Toksvig, August 14, 1943, Glasgow Letters, Harry Ransom Center, University of Texas (hereafter GL).

19. Jean Purcell, "Developers Will Try to Keep 'Air of Restrained Elegance,'" *Richmond Times Dispatch*, Sunday, Oct. 14, 1973, Section D.

20. Antoinette W. Rhoades, "Fertile Ground," *EGN* 4 (March 1976): 13.

21. For more discussion of this dynamic, see Cheryl Thurber, "The Development of the Mammy Image and Mythology," in *Southern Women: Histories and Identities*, ed. Virginia Bernhard, Betty Brandon, Elizabeth Fox-Genovese, and Theda Perdue (Columbia: University of Missouri Press, 1992), 87. Also see Elizabeth Fox-Genovese, *Within the Plantation Household: Black and White Women of the Old South* (Chapel Hill: University of North Carolina Press, 1988), 292.

22. Family Records and Genealogy, "Judge Thomas S. Gholson," 5060/22, AL.

23. E.G., letter to Signe Toksvig, December 4, 1944, in *Letters*, 364.

24. Rebe Tutwiler, letter to E.G., December 9, 1942, 5060/19, AL.

25. Irita Van Doren, interview with Rawlings, March 13, 1953, RC. Rawlings's interviews with Carrie Duke and Anne Virginia Bennett contain the same information about Francis Glasgow, which over time has been accepted as "truth." See Wagner-Martin, *Ellen Glasgow: Beyond Convention*, 7–8; and Godbold, *Ellen Glasgow and the Woman Within*, 27. The sexual exploitation of female servants seems to have been a common and unacknowledged practice among people of the Glasgows' class and one that her oldest brother supposedly thought his right when visiting One West Main.

26. The number of women who take addictive drugs such as morphine in Glasgow's novels makes one wonder if Anne's nightly pacing might have been a sign of withdrawal. Glasgow also would have firsthand testimony about withdrawal symptoms from her friend Amélie Rives.

27. Francis Glasgow served as chair of the Finance Committee for five years. See Dabney, *Richmond*, 237. Surveying Richmond in 1900, one might have had an optimistic view for the future of race relations. When Josiah Crump, a black postal clerk who served several terms on the Board of Aldermen, died, for example, the entire board showed their respect by attending his funeral and draping his desk and chair in mourning for thirty days. However, that year also marked the end of blacks serving on either the Common Council or the Board of Alderman.

28. See Wyndham Blanton, *The Making of a Downtown Church* (Richmond, Va.: John Knox Press, 1945), 321. The effort, begun in 1885, proved unsuccessful, and the church abandoned it two years later.

29. Arthur Glasgow, interview with Rawlings, RC. Arthur, who became something of a despot himself, liked to think that his father had mellowed with age.

Glasgow made contradictory statements about her father; for example, in a letter to Signe Toksvig, August 15, 1943, she pronounced him "a sterling character and a zealous Calvinist." GL.

30. Glasgow's fictional representation of children seduced by older men, as in *The Sheltered Life* (1932), her possible celibacy, her identification with the voiceless, her illnesses, which more than one doctor felt were largely psychosomatic, might raise the spectre of childhood abuse. Anne Virginia Bennett, who disliked Francis Glasgow and hated men in general, flatly denied any history of incest, though personal and social considerations make any denials suspect. Without any evidence, the question is moot.

31. Edgar MacDonald, "An Essay in Bibliography," in *Ellen Glasgow: Centennial Essays*, ed. M. Thomas Inge (Charlottesville: University Press of Virginia, 1976), 222. MacDonald quotes from a letter of Burton Rascoe to James Branch Cabell.

32. The records of the Second Presbyterian Church are available on microfilm. On April 15, 1910, Francis Glasgow was named as an alternate delegate to represent his church at a meeting of the East Hanover Presbytery three days hence. The last meeting he attended was December 17, 1911.

33. Josephine Glasgow Clark, interview with Rawlings, RC.

34. Lucy Pegram, "Diary of a Richmond Child," RC.

35. Ellen Glasgow, "Only a Daisy," 5060/3, AL, published in Godbold, *Ellen Glasgow and the Woman Within*, 17–18.

36. Pegram, "Diary of a Richmond Child."

37. See Perceval Reniers, *The Springs of Virginia: Life, Love, and Death at the Waters, 1775–1900* (Chapel Hill: University of North Carolina Press, 1941).

38. Ellen Glasgow, "A Modern Joan of Arc," Box 4, 5060/3, 7225-a, AL. Someone has dated this piece about 1900, but its style and handwriting lead me to think it earlier, around 1885. See Pamela R. Matthews, "Glasgow's Joan of Arc in Context," in *Mississippi Quarterly* 49, no. 2 (Spring 1996): 210–26. Matthews, who has edited and published the story in the same issue, 203–9, dates the story similarly.

39. Ellen Glasgow, "The Prairie Flower," 5060/4, 1180-5, AL.

40. Emma Gray Trigg, "Ellen Glasgow," *The Woman's Club Bulletin* (Richmond) 9 (1946): 2. The clipping can be found in 10,137b/2, AL.

41. Georg Lukács, *The Historical Novel* (Boston: Beacon Press, 1963), 30–88.

42. Pocohontas White Edmund, video made by the Virginia Writers Club of interviews conducted by Patricia Pearsall and Welford D. Taylor, the Richmond Historical Society.

43. RC.

44. E.G., letter to Rebe Tutwiler, December 27, 1925, RC.

Chapter 2. Sharp Realities

1. Haardt, "Ellen Glasgow and the South," 15.

2. This clipping is in Notebook no. 3, Ellen Glasgow Collection, 5060/6, AL.

3. Irita Van Doren, interview with Rawlings, March 13, 1953, RC.

4. Wm. Wilmer Page, letter to Mrs. Jane Y. Page, July 26, 1852, Page-Walker Manuscripts, 3098/2, AL.

5. F. T. Glasgow, letter to Gen. F. H. Smith, Jan. 21, 1888, Virginia Military Institute Archives.

6. Julian Meade, *I Live in Virginia* (New York: Longmans, Green, 1935), 157.

7. See Mrs. St. Julien Ravenel, *Charleston, the Place and the People* (New York: Macmillan, 1925), 426–31.

8. John Bennett, Budget, April 21, 1929, John Bennett Manuscripts, South Carolina Historical Society, Charleston, South Carolina. I am indebted to E. Stanly Godbold for the quotation. Glasgow's chaperon was probably Mrs. Washington Jefferson Bennett, an older widow.

9. R. W. B. Lewis, *Edith Wharton: A Biography* (New York: Fromm International Publishing, 1985), 11.

10. Annie Gholson Glasgow (Clark) joined by examination in 1877, and Emily Taylor Glasgow joined in 1893.

11. Anne Jane Gholson had previously joined the First Presbyterian Church by examination on May 25, 1851.

12. Maurice Duke, "The First Novel by a Glasgow: Cary's *A Successful Failure*," *EGN* 1 (October 1974): 7–8.

13. Cary Glasgow, *A Successful Failure: An Outline* (Richmond, Va.: West and Johnson, 1883), 42.

14. "A Renunciation," Ellen Glasgow Collection, Accession No. 7225-b, AL. The story is undated and untitled but appears to be written in Cary's hand. Its style resembles that of *A Successful Failure*, suggesting that she authored, rather than copied, something her sister wrote.

15. Elizabeth Muhlenfeld, "The Civil War and Authorship," in *The History of Southern Literature*, ed. Louis D. Rubin Jr., Blyden Jackson, Rayburn S. Moore, Lewis P. Simpson, and Thomas Daniel Young (Baton Rouge: Louisiana State University Press, 1985), 183–86.

16. Maurice Duke, "Cabell's and Glasgow's Richmond: The Intellectual Background of the City," *Mississippi Quarterly* 27, no. 4 (Fall 1974): 388.

17. Glasgow, *A Successful Failure*, 17.

18. Ellen Glasgow, "The Greatest Good," and Cary Glasgow, "The Virtuoso," Accession No. 7225-c, AL.

19. See Linda Pannill, "Ellen Glasgow's Allegory of Love and Death: 'The Greatest Good,'" *Resources for American Literary Study* 14 (Fall 1984): 161–66.

20. For information on George Walter McCormack, see Julius Rowan Raper, "The Man Ellen Glasgow Could Respect," *EGN* 3 (March 1975): 4–9. Also see Raper, *Without Shelter*, 33–50.

21. See William Graham, *Socialism New and Old* (New York: D. Appleton, 1891). Glasgow wrote the expression on the top of the book's index page.

22. Glasgow's books provide a record of the growth of her imagination. On the title page of Lecky's *History of the Rise and Influence of the Spirit of Rationalism in Europe*, for example, she signed her name in tribute to her mother "Ellen Anderson Gholson Glasgow." Her father's initials, F. T. G., may grace the book's inside cover, but she made it her own. In the margins, she invoked the names of Charles Darwin, Herbert Spencer, John Stuart Mill, Buddha, and Socrates to refute statements about the mystery of free will. The back cover bears a quotation from Montaigne—"The world is but a school of inquisition." Under it she argued that because Montaigne's essays were "the first great work in which

persecution was turned into ridicule," he had prepared "men's minds for a reception of the spirit of toleration."

23. William Irvine, *Apes, Angels, and Victorians: The Story of Darwin, Huxley, and Evolution* (New York: McGraw-Hill, 1955), 181. Aurelius's dictum that "the universe is transformation" (141) reinforced Glasgow's reading of Darwin.

24. Virginius Dabney, *Mr. Jefferson's University: A History of the University of Virginia* (Charlottesville: University Press of Virginia, 1981), 381.

25. "A Beautiful Home Wedding," *Richmond Times Dispatch*, March 25, 1892, 1.

26. Edward L. Ayers, *The Promise of the New South: Life after Reconstruction* (New York: Oxford University Press, 1992), 282.

27. See C. Vann Woodward, *Origins of the New South, 1877-1913* (Baton Rouge: Louisiana State University Press, 1951), 235-36, 252, 261; Ayers, *Promise of the New South*, 214-82, 217, 251, esp. 282; and Beth Barton Schweiger, "Putting Politics Aside: Virginia Democrats and Voter Apathy in the Era of Disfranchisement," in *The Edge of the South: Life in Nineteenth-Century Virginia*, ed. Edward L. Ayers and John C. Willis (Charlottesville: University Press of Virginia, 1991), 194.

28. Edgar MacDonald, "Lellie: Ellen Glasgow and Josephine Clark," *EGN* 4 (March 1976): 11-17.

29. The book is in the Alderman Library, and Josephine dated the poem c. 1897 or 1898.

30. Ellen Glasgow, "What I Believe," *The Nation* 136 (April 12, 1933): 404-6.

31. *Newspapers in Microfilm* lists four newspapers in Perth Amboy, none of which were in existence the years McCormack was alive. The first, *Slovensky Sokoi*, began in 1905. The census contains no S. J. Otey listed at the given address.

32. *New York Herald*, June 19, 1894, 3.

33. Raper, "The Man Ellen Glasgow Could Respect," 7.

34. Rebe Tutwiler, interview with Rawlings, RC.

35. Rebe Tutwiler, 1899-1900 diary, quoted by permission of Carrington Tutwiler (hereafter Tutwiler diary).

36. Ellen Glasgow, "A Point in Morals," *Harper's Magazine* 98 (May 1899): 976-82. For one of the few readings of this story, see William J. Scheick, "The Narrative Ethos of Glasgow's 'A Point in Morals,'" *EGN* 30 (Spring 1993): 1, 3-4. The story reflects Glasgow's reading of Aurelius, Von Hartmann, Schopenhauer, and especially Epictetus, who advised to make no tragedy of dying, but "tell it as it is" (*Epictetus* 96).

37. Alexander Bain, *Mental Science: Compendium of Psychology and the History of Philosophy* (New York: American Book Co., 1868), xxii, xxv, xxvi. The book was used as a text for high school and college students.

38. *Thoughts of the Emperor Marcus Aurelius Antoninus*, trans. Long, 150. When Glasgow read Berkeley, she marked passages on the nature of physical pain. See *The Works of George Berkeley*, vol. 1 (London: George Bell and Son, 1897), 196.

39. Glasgow copied a related saying in her copy of *The Teachings of Epictetus* (New York: John B. Alden, 1889): "Things are as they are and will be brought to their destined issue." The book is inscribed "S. P. C. 1888, given to Ellen Glasgow in 1896. May 1896." AL.

40. *Thoughts of Antoninus*, 135.

41. See ibid., 77, 116, 148, 150, 166-67, 190, 200, 208-9.

42. Ellen Glasgow, "The Freeman," in *Poems*, 13.

43. See Frederick P. W. McDowell, *Ellen Glasgow and the Ironic Art of Fiction* (Madison:

University of Wisconsin Press, 1963), 245. McDowell notes that both McTeague and Aker-shem are driven by hereditary forces.

44. George Frederick Drinka, *The Birth of Neurosis: Myth, Malady, and the Victorians* (New York: Simon and Schuster, 1984), 251–58.

45. For a discussion of this novel, see Raper, *Without Shelter*, 62–83, 73 esp. Also see Matthews, *Ellen Glasgow and a Woman's Traditions*, 26, 32.

46. See Laurence Hutton, "Literary Notes," *Harper's Magazine* 94 (April 1897): 549, reprinted in *Reviews* (Cambridge: Cambridge University Press, 1992), 3. He describes Michael as an Ishmaelite, who "began life by cursing and hating everybody." Glasgow liked Mark Twain's remark when asked about the Jews: "All that I care to know is that a man is a human being—that is enough for me; he can't be any worse." See Notebook no. 3, 5060/6, AL.

47. Susan Haskins, *Mary Magdalen: Myth and Metaphor* (New York: Harcourt Brace, 1994), 14–16, 92–96.

48. Glasgow criticizes this ending, typical of the Victorian novel's domestic ideology. See Nancy Armstrong, *Desire and Domestic Fiction: A Political History of the Novel* (New York: Oxford University Press, 1987), 20–23, 221–24.

Chapter 3. No Place or Time

1. Léonie Villard, letter to E.G., September 6, 1933, 5060/19, AL.

2. Ellen Glasgow, manuscript of *The Woman Within*, 5060/5, AL.

3. Drinka, *Birth of Neurosis*, 249.

4. Leslie Jones, Jim Kyle, and Peter Wood, *Words Apart: Losing Your Hearing as an Adult* (New York: Travistock Publications, 1987), 22.

5. Ibid., 18.

6. Alan J. Thomas, *Acquired Hearing Loss: Psychological and Psychosocial Implications* (London: Academic Press, 1984), 28.

7. See Harriet Martineau, *Autobiography*, 2 vols. (London: Virago, 1983), 2:216. Also see E.G., letter to Mary Johnston, July 2, 1908, 3588/2, AL.

8. Martineau, *Autobiography*, 2:216.

9. See Linda Kornasky, "Ellen Glasgow's Disability," *Mississippi Quarterly* 49, no. 2 (Spring 1996): 281–95.

10. Irita Van Doren, interview with Rawlings, RC.

11. Edgar MacDonald, "The Last Pleasure," *EGN* 14 (March 1981): 12.

12. Maude Williams, interview with Rawlings, RC. The metallic sound of Glasgow's voice may have been largely inherited, for Rebe had a similar voice.

13. Jones, Kyle, and Wood, *Words Apart*, 21–28.

14. Thomas, *Acquired Hearing Loss*, 34.

15. Ellen Glasgow, "Spirit-Loneliness," 5060/4, AL.

16. E.G., letters to Messr. Macmillan & Co., December 28, 1895; letters of George P. Brett and Price Collier, January 29 and 30, 1896; George Brett, letter to E.G., February 2, 1896, Macmillan Authors, New York Public Library. See Godbold, *Ellen Glasgow and the Woman Within*, 38–39.

17. See Susan Goodman, *Edith Wharton's Inner Circle* (Austin: University of Texas Press,

1994); Sharon O'Brien, *Willa Cather: The Emerging Voice* (New York: Oxford University Press, 1987), 126, 132, 136–37, 233–42.

18. Drinka, *Birth of Neurosis*, 189–90.

19. Julius Rowan Raper, "The European Initiation of Ellen Glasgow," *EGN* 5 (October 1976): 2–5.

20. E.G., letters to Cary McCormack, July 31 and August 2, 1896, 5060/14, AL.

21. Ibid., April 28 and September 9, 1896. Glasgow also quoted Aurelius: "For he is a wise man and hath understanding of things divine who hath nobly agreed with necessity."

22. Ibid., July 23, 1896.

23. Ibid., April 28, 1896.

24. Unlike Edith Wharton, who sought the friendship of members of the French Academy, Glasgow knew few intellectuals or writers in Paris. One exception was Louise Chandler Moulton, a friend of Amélie Rives. See Pamela R. Matthews, "Between Ellen and Louise: Female Friendship, Glasgow's Letters to Louise Chandler Moulton, and *The Wheel of Life*," in *Ellen Glasgow: New Perspectives*, ed. Dorothy M. Scura (Knoxville: University of Tennessee Press, 1995), 106–23.

25. E.G., letter to Arthur Glasgow, July 21, 1933, Accession No. 5347, AL.

26. Howard Mumford Jones, "The Earliest Novels," in *Ellen Glasgow: Centennial Essays*, ed. Inge, 75; C. T. Herrick, "The Author of *The Descendant*," *Critic* 27 (May–June 1897): 383.

27. See Ann Ardis, *New Woman, New Novels* (New Brunswick, N.J.: Rutgers University Press, 1990), esp. 11–28.

28. Gaillard Lapsley, "E. W.," Beinecke Library, Yale University, New Haven, 46. Lapsley is repeating a remark that Wharton made to Mary Berenson.

29. See, e.g., Haardt, "Ellen Glasgow and the South," 15.

30. See Bernard Berenson, *The Bernard Berenson Treasury*, ed. Hana Kiel, with an introduction by Nicky Mariano (New York: Simon and Schuster, 1962), 138.

31. James Branch Cabell, *As I Remember It: Some Epilogues in Recollection* (New York: McBride, 1955), 229–30.

32. For male patterns of artistic development, see Maurice Beebe, *Ivory Towers and Sacred Founts: The Artist as Hero in Fiction from Goethe to Joyce* (New York: New York University Press, 1964).

33. See Adrienne Rich, "Education of a Novelist," *The Fact of a Doorframe* (New York: Norton, 1984), 314–17. Also see Pamela R. Matthews, "Education of a Novelist, Education of a Poet: Ellen Glasgow and Adrienne Rich," *EGN* 29 (Fall 1992): 4–5.

34. Hamlin Garland, *Roadside Meetings* (New York: Macmillan, 1930), 349–50.

35. Ibid., 350.

36. See *Commemorative Tributes of the American Academy of Arts and Letters, 1905–1941* (New York: Books for Libraries Presses, 1968), 19–20, 116–18, 399–402.

37. Ellen Glasgow, " 'Evasive Idealism' in Literature: An Interview with Joyce Kilmer," in *RD*, 123. This visit was Glasgow's second to the Author's Club. On January 9, 1896, she had attended their annual meeting. See Raper, *Without Shelter*, 61.

38. See Duffield Osborne, *The Authors Club* (New York: Knickerbocker Press, 1913).

39. See Notebook no. 3, 5060/5, p. 25, AL. Glasgow copied William James's observation that "America does not know the meaning of moral corruption compared with Europe! Corruption is so permanently organized here that it isn't thought of as such." Next to it, she wrote: "Of France—The Dreyfus trial."

40. For Cabell's side of the continuing argument, see Edgar MacDonald, *James Branch Cabell and Richmond-in-Virginia* (Jackson: University Press of Mississippi, 1993), 303-4; and MacDonald, "The Glasgow-Cabell Entente," *American Literature* 41 (March 1969): 76-91.

41. MacDonald, *James Branch Cabell and Richmond-in-Virginia*, 304.

42. See Honoré de Balzac, *Comédie Humaine*, ed. George Saintsbury, vol. 8 (London: J. M. Dent, 1898), 5.

43. E.G., letter to Walter Hines Page [November 22, 1897], in *Letters*, 25.

44. Walter Hines Page, letter to E.G., December 8, 1897, in *The Training of an American: The Early Life and Letters of Walter H. Page: 1855-1913*, ed. Burton J. Hendrick (Boston: Houghton Mifflin, 1928), 336-37.

45. See the Harpers Collection, Columbia University. Glasgow signed the contract on September 23, 1896. Harper's wanted royalties on *The Descendant* to begin after the first thousand copies had been sold.

46. E.G., letter to Paul Revere Reynolds [November, 1897], in AA, 180. Also see E.G., letter to Walter Hines Page, March 26, 1898, in *Letters*, 27. Glasgow asks: "Do you believe that an American writer has as fair a chance of fame as an English one?"

47. E.G., letter to Walter Hines Page, November 22, 1897, in *Letters*, ed. Rouse, 25.

48. Walter Hines Page, *A Publisher's Confession* (New York: Doubleday, Page, 1905), 46.

49. F. N. Doubleday, *The Memoirs of a Publisher*, (New York: Doubleday, 1972), 186-87.

50. Ibid., 187.

51. Ellen Glasgow, "A Woman of To-Morrow," in *RD*, 4. The story was first published in *Short Stories* 19 (1895): 415-27.

52. E.G., letter to Walter Hines Page, March 26, 1898, in *Letters*, ed. Rouse, 26.

53. *Phases*, 28. Also see Ellen Glasgow, "Phases of an Inferior Planet," 5060/3, AL.

54. See Martha Banta, *Imaging American Women: Ideas and Ideals in Cultural History* (New York: Columbia University Press, 1987), 6, 46-47, 254, esp. 258.

55. See Raper, *Without Shelter*, 94-120.

56. Mariana's surname changes from Muzin (musing) in the manuscript to the less obvious Musin in the book. For other changes, see Marion K. Richards, appendix, *Ellen Glasgow's Development as a Novelist* (The Hague: Mouton, 1971), 195-201.

57. The overall changes fall into three interrelated categories: the ordering of material, the addition of ironic commentary, and the search for a larger philosophic significance. For example, the manuscript reads:

> Doffing her conventional dress, she doffed conventionality as well. She was transformed into something weird and seductive and subtle—something in a woman's form as ethereal as sea foam and as vivid as flame. (*Phases*, 15)

By cutting the adjective "weird" and the article "a" before "woman," Glasgow uses the individual woman to represent the category Woman:

> She was transformed into something seductive and subtle—something of woman's flesh as ethereal as sea-foam and as vivid as flame. (*Phases*, 15)

58. Page, *Publisher's Confession*, 47.

59. Ellen Glasgow, "The Biography of Manuel," *Saturday Review of Literature* 6 (June 7, 1930): 1108-9. Also see *RD*, 205-16.

60. See MacDonald, *James Branch Cabell and Richmond-in-Virginia*, 68-75.

61. In *The Woman Within*, Glasgow dates her trip abroad from January to November 1899; however, her letters to Paul Reynolds dated February 3, 1899, and September 7, 1899, state that she is leaving for Egypt on February 4, 1899, and had "just returned to America, reaching New York on the Kaiser Wilhelm last Tuesday." See AA, 189.

62. Ellen Glasgow, "Between Two Shores," *McClure's* 12, no. 4 (Feb. 1899): 345–52.

63. Tutwiler diary, quoted by permission of Carrington Tutwiler. See Rebe Glasgow, "The Eyes of the Sphinx: Selections from Rebe Glasgow's Travel Journal of 1899," ed. Mark Lurie and Shanon Wilson, *EGN* 25 (Fall 1995): 8.

64. Tutwiler diary, 47, 121. Trinity's problem may have been that he had doubts about his calling for the ministry. It is difficult to know anything about him because Rebe erased his given name from her journal and cut sections of pages that would identify him.

65. E.G., letter to Horace Traubel, May 25, 1899, in *Letters*, 27–28.

66. See letters between Ellen Glasgow and Horace Traubel from 1899 to 1914, Ken D. McCormack Collection, Library of Congress.

67. See Edith Wharton, *In Morocco* (New York: Scribner's, 1920).

68. Ellen Glasgow, "Richmonders in Constantinople," *Richmond Dispatch*, April 23, 1899, 7.

69. Tutwiler diary, 99.

70. Frederic Whyte, *William Heinemann: A Memoir* (Garden City, N.Y.: Doubleday, Doran, 1929), 306, 187.

71. Burton J. Hendrick, *The Life and Letters of Walter H. Page*, 2 vols. (Garden City, N.Y.: Doubleday, Page, 1922), 1:64–66.

Chapter 4. Heart Hungry

1. See, e.g., James Branch Cabell, letter to E.G., August 6, 1941, 5060/13, AL, quoted in part in Godbold, *Ellen Glasgow and the Woman Within*, 284. Cabell concluded that Glasgow's novels offered irrefutable proof that she was a virgin.

2. Louise Willcox gave Glasgow a copy of *Thus Spake Zarathustra* (New York: Macmillan, 1902) in 1905. Glasgow marked the paraphrased passage, which can be found on page 34 of the book in the Alderman Library. For some of Glasgow's marginalia, see Carrington Tutwiler, "The Glasgow Library," *EGN* 3 (October 1975): 2–4.

3. Rebe Tutwiler, letter to Marjorie Rawlings, November 14, 1953, RC. Marjorie Rawlings, among others, found Rebe's facts and dates inaccurate at best and possibly changed for her self-interest.

4. Matthews, *Ellen Glasgow and a Woman's Traditions*, 53–55.

5. See Godbold, *Ellen Glasgow and the Woman Within*, 56–58; Raper, *Without Shelter*, 145; Frances W. Saunders, "Glasgow's Secret Love: 'Gerald B' or William T?" *EGN* 31 (Fall 1993): 1, 3, 4.

6. Edgar MacDonald, "An Essay in Bibliography," in *Ellen Glasgow: Centennial Essays*, ed. Inge, 222. MacDonald quotes from a letter of Burton Rascoe to James Branch Cabell. Howland's wife sued him for divorce in 1903 on the grounds that he did not provide.

7. Saunders, "Glasgow's Secret Love," 3.

8. See Matthews, *Ellen Glasgow and a Woman's Traditions*, 53–55.

9. "W. R. Travers Ends Life After Divorce," *New York Times*, September 30, 1905, 1.

10. If the Paris edition of the *Herald* could yield Gerald's identity, other candidates

might be: Robert D. M'Gonnigle of Philadelphia, a writer and philanthropist, of suicide on July 7, 1905; John H. Murray, president of S. S. Beard Co., tea and coffee expert, who died on July 22; James Lowe, artist and magazine writer, on August 2; R. W. Criswell, society author and editor in New York, also a suicide; and Nielson Brown, a Philadelphia banker and horse owner, on August 5. I have found no evidence that any of these men are Gerald.

11. Anne Scott Frior first suggested that this letter may have been written by a woman. See Godbold, *Ellen Glasgow and the Woman Within*, 57–58. Also see E.G., letter to Rebe Tutwiler, December 30, 1906, RC, in which Glasgow mentions Gray's forthcoming marriage.

12. See Matthews, *Ellen Glasgow and a Woman's Traditions*, 53–54.

13. Virginia Woolf, letter to her sister, Vanessa Bell, in *Letters of Virginia Woolf*, ed. Nigel Nicolson and Joanne Trautmann, vol. 6 (New York: Harcourt Brace Jovanovich: 1980), 245.

14. W. J. Cash, *The Mind of the South* (New York: Vintage Books, 1991), 144.

15. Glasgow, "The Freeman," 28. Glasgow dedicated *The Freeman and Other Poems* (August 1902) to her old friend Louise Collier Willcox, whom she had consulted about publishing *The Descendant*. In 1903, Willcox accepted an editing job with Macmillan. In 1910, she began work at E. P. Dutton & Co. From 1906 to 1913, the *North American Review* employed her on its editorial staff. She also served as an editorial writer for *Harper's Weekly* and *Harper's Bazaar*. Her books include *Answer of the Ages* (1900), *The Human Way* (1909), *The Road to Joy* (1911), and *The House in Order* (1917).

The derivative poems in *The Freeman and Other Poems* reflect Glasgow's reading of Browning, Tennyson, Hardy, Arnold, Aurelius, and Nietzsche. For readings of these poems, see Terence Allen Hoagwood, "The Poetry of Ellen Glasgow: *The Freeman and Other Poems*," in *Ellen Glasgow: New Perspectives*, ed. Scura, 59–73; and Hoagwood, "Glasgow's Poetry: A Critique of Ideological Illusion," in *Mississippi Quarterly* 49, no. 2 (Spring 1996): 361–72. Also see Raper, *Without Shelter*, 174–80; and Richards, *Ellen Glasgow's Development as a Novelist*, 68–76.

16. E.G., letter to Howard Mumford Jones, July 8, 1935, in *Letters*, 187.

17. E.G., letter to Walter Hines Page, December 2, 1899, in *Letters*, 28–29.

18. Van Wyck Brooks, *The Confident Years: 1885-1915* (New York: Dutton, 1952), 352.

19. See Raper, *Without Shelter*, 137–44.

20. William Morton Payne, "Recent Fiction," *Dial* 29 (July 1, 1900): 23–24, in *Reviews*, 44–45.

21. Dixon inscribed a copy (now in the Alderman Library) of *The Leopard's Spots* to Miss Ellen Glasgow with "keen appreciation of her genius" for depicting "tragical" characters.

22. Henry James, *The American Scene* (New York: Scribner's, 1946), 350.

23. E.G., letter to Paul Revere Reynolds, February 26, 1900, in AA, 190.

24. Dew, *Ironmaker to the Confederacy*, 288.

25. R. H. W. Dillard, "On Ellen Glasgow's *The Battle-Ground*," in *Classics of Civil War Fiction*, ed. David Madden and Peggy Bach (Jackson: University Press of Mississippi, 1991), 64–81. Also see Raper, *Without Shelter*, 161–62; and McDowell, *Ellen Glasgow and the Ironic Art of Fiction*, 63–65.

26. E.G., letter to Rebe Tutwiler, June 4, 1907, RC. She wrote Rebe that it gave her pleasure to treat the privates the way everybody else treated the colonels and captains. Some of the twenty-three men wept and all sang "God be with you till we meet again!"

27. See EGN 13 (October 1980): 6. Also see the Barrett-Glasgow Collection, Accession No. 6151-5, AL.

28. E.G., letter to Walter Hines Page, January 14, 1902, in *Letters*, 36. Before she com-

pleted *The Voice of the People*, Glasgow had asked Paul Revere Reynolds to see whether he could place her next one as a serial. Since she had decided to devote herself to writing novels, rather than short stories and poetry, Glasgow had less frequent need of an agent's services. She had switched firms without consulting him and preferred to deal directly with publishers herself.

Also see *Time Magazine*, March 31, 1941, 72–73. Glasgow claimed that *The Battle-Ground* sold only 11,000 copies but that she got a $10,000 advance. She wanted another $10,000 spent on advertising.

29. E.G., letter to Elizabeth Patterson, January 2, 1902, in *Letters*, 34.

30. *Richmond Times-Dispatch*, April 29, 1904, 1.

31. E.G., letter to Walter Hines Page, December 26, 1902, in *Letters*, 40. See Godbold, *Ellen Glasgow and the Woman Within*, 71. Godbold notes that the letter is misdated and should read "1904."

32. In the beginning of July 1904, Glasgow and Rebe had sailed on the SS *Bremen* to London. Cary remained in Richmond, where they sent her greetings from Nordhausen and Carlsbad in July, Dresden in August. In September a postcard of Sassure arrived from France, succeeded almost immediately by one from Prague. There is no record that Gerald met the sisters in Europe, though that seems to have been the previous pattern.

33. *Bhagavad Gita* (London: Theosophical Pub. Society, 1896), 29.

34. Ibid., 37.

35. Roberta Wellford, interview with Rawlings, RC.

Chapter 5. The Wheel of Life

1. E.G., letter to Arthur Graham Glasgow, March 27, 1905, in *Letters*, 43–44.

2. For information on Glasgow's relationship with women, see Matthews, *Ellen Glasgow and a Woman's Traditions*, 71–73, 48–55, 155, 177, 104, 155. Also see Raper, *Without Shelter*, 205–8.

3. I am indebted to Welford D. Taylor for information on Amélie Rives. See Welford D. Taylor, *Amélie Rives (Princess Troubetzkoy)* (New York: Twayne, 1973).

4. C. Ronald Cella, *Mary Johnston* (New York: Twayne Publishers, 1981), 18, 21.

5. See L. G. Nelson, "Mary Johnston and the Historic Imagination," in *Southern Writers: Appraisals in Our Time*, ed. R. C. Simonini Jr. (Charlottesville: University Press of Virginia, 1964), 74.

6. E.G., letter to Mary Johnston, March 22, 1904, in *Letters*, 43–44.

7. Ibid.

8. Ibid., February, 3, 1905, in *Letters*, 45–46.

9. Ibid.

10. Tutwiler diary, 1899, by permission of Carrington Tutwiler.

11. Ellen Glasgow, "The Mountain Pine," in *Poems*, 38.

12. E.G., letter to Mary Johnston, August 15, 1906, in *Letters*, 54.

13. E.G., letter to Signe Toksvig, August 14, 1943, GL.

14. Amélie Rives Troubetzkoy, letter to E.G., October 27, 1913, 5060/18, AL.

15. Emily Clark, *Innocence Abroad* (Westport, Conn.: Greenwood Press, 1975), 78–79.

16. E.G., letter to Amélie Rives Troubetzkoy, July 14, 1937, 5060/14, AL.

17. E.G., letter to Mary Johnston, August 15, 1906, in *Letters*, 54.

18. In 1904, Cary had been too sick to travel with her sisters through central Europe. They sailed on the SS *Bremen* on July 6 and returned in the fall.

19. E.G., letter to Arthur Glasgow, March 27, 1905, in *Letters*, 48.

20. Rebe Glasgow, postcard to Josephine Clark, July 18, 1905, Glasgow Family Collection, Accession No. 10127, AL. Also see Edgar MacDonald, "Recent Additions to the Glasgow Collection," and Martha E. Cook, "Miss Ellen and Miss Lucy, The Richmond-Nordhausen Connection," *EGN* 30 (Spring 1993): 12, 13–14.

21. Before returning to the United States, Glasgow visited Paris in the late summer and toured Sienna, Perugia, and Florence in September.

22. E.G., letter to Mary Johnston, August 15, 1906, in *Letters*, 53.

23. E.G., letter to Walter Hines Page, Christmas 1905, in *Letters*, 50.

24. Alice Payne Hackett, *Fifty Years of Best Sellers, 1895–1945* (New York: Bowker, 1945), 22.

25. E.G., letter to Mary Johnston, September 15, 1906, in *Letters*, 55.

26. E.G., letter to Bessie Zaban Jones, April 18, 1938, in *Letters*, 238.

27. See Matthews, "Between Ellen and Louise," 106–23.

28. See Matthews, *Ellen Glasgow and a Woman's Traditions*, for a more sexualized reading of this same idea, 47–48.

29. See Raper, *Without Shelter*, 213. Glasgow was also influenced by her reading of William Graham. See Graham, *Socialism New and Old*, 168.

30. When Glasgow published *The Romance of a Plain Man* (1909), the critic for the *Nation* fell just short of accusing her of plagiarizing Johnston's *Lewis Rand* (1908). Had he remembered *The Voice of the People* (1900), he might have found fault the other way. Like Nicholas Burr, Rand comes from a poor family hostile to education and through the intervention of his "superiors" rises to take his seat in the state legislature.

31. See Raper, *Without Shelter*, 231.

32. Mary P. Edwards, "Tea and Metaphysics: Excerpts from Mary Johnston's Diary," *EGN* (October 1983), 4.

33. E.G., letter to Rebe Tutwiler, December 14, 1906, RC.

34. Ibid., December 7, 1906.

35. E.G., letter to Rebe Tutwiler, December 23, 1906, RC.

36. See ibid., December 26, 1906.

37. Louise Collier Willcox, letter to E.G., August 17, 1924, 5060/20, AL.

38. Frank Paradise, letter to E.G., October 17, 1925, 5060/17, AL. See Raper, *Without Shelter*, 231.

39. E.G., letter to Rebe Glasgow, December 26, 1906, RC.

40. E.G., letter to Rebe Tutwiler, January 18, 1907, RC.

41. E.G., letter to Mary Johnston, August 15, 1906, in *Letters*, 53.

42. E.G., letter to Rebe Tutwiler, January 30, 1907, RC.

43. Edwards, "Tea and Metaphysics," 4.

44. See "Miscellaneous Pungencies," 5060/22, AL.

45. E.G., letter to Rebe Tutwiler, May 24, 1907, RC.

46. Ibid., May 22, 1907.

47. No date. Rawlings transcribed this poem. See 5060/5, AL.

48. See E.G., letter to Arthur Glasgow, August 14, 1907, in *Letters*, 57. Glasgow wrote

Arthur that there must be "some connection between typhoid fever and appendicitis," Frank's previous ailment.

49. E.G., letter to Mary Johnston, July 20, 1907, 3588/2, AL.

50. E.G., letter to Rebe Tutwiler, August 5, 1908, RC.

51. "Life of a Monkey Against the Life of a Man," *World's Work* 16 (July 1908): 104–17.

52. E.G., letter to Walter Hines Page, June 26, 1908, in *Letters,* 58–59.

53. Ibid., 60.

54. E.G., letter to George Brett, December 12, 1908, MP.

55. George Brett, letter to E.G., January 26, 1909, MP.

56. Glasgow made a little over $6,000 on the novel. See George Brett, letters to E.G., January 3 and March 1, 1909, MP.

57. Ibid., September 2, 1909. In all, Macmillan's profit totaled $216.30. Glasgow's royalties were $6,995.10.

58. See AA, 193, 194. Glasgow's agent, Paul Revere Reynolds, had seen her switch to Macmillan as a chance to sell the serial rights of her next novel, *The Miller of Old Church,* to McClure or the American. Because Doubleday, Page paid Glasgow a regular salary, the book rights would inevitably go to them.

59. Francis Hackett, "Amateur Romance," Chicago *Evening Post,* May 14, 1909; and Edwin Francis Edgett, "The Romance of a Plain Man," Boston *Evening Transcript,* May 26, 1909, in *Reviews,* 133, 135.

60. See 5060/18, AL. The first stanza reads:

> In the twilight of the kings
>   When the purple sun of pomp
> Sank on bloody wings
>   Into a sea of spears
>   And Death's mad romp
> Tossed against heaven with a surf of tears,
> When to be royal was to be half cursed,
>   A man stood clean against the waning light,
> By fate, by manhood, and by virtue first
> Of all the hearts he led to Honor's fight.

Chapter 6. Beyond Heartbreak

1. Maude Williams, interview with Rawlings, RC.

2. See Arthur Glasgow, letter to Marjorie Rawlings, February 3, 1953, RC. Arthur first renounced the income from his share to his father and then to Glasgow, who, from about 1915 on, received half of its total current income. By 1953, the trust had a capital value of $250,000 with an annual income of $12,500.

3. Edwards, "Tea and Metaphysics," 6.

4. Ibid., 5.

5. E.G., letter to Cary McCormack, April 28, 1909, 5060/14, AL.

6. Topics for discussion included hypnotism, Tennyson and His School, The Brownings, Modern Musical Composers, The Theory of Evolution, and Goethe's Life. See Sandra Gioia Treadway, *Women of Mark: A History of the Women's Club of Richmond, Vir-*

ginia, 1894-1994 (Richmond: The Library of Virginia, 1995), esp. 42, 61, 112. The club was founded in late April or early May 1894 by Jane Looney Lewis and twenty-five local women interested in literary studies, who met on Saturday afternoons.

7. Sinclair served as a founder-member of London's Medico-Psychological Clinic. See Sidney Janet Kaplan, *Feminine Consciousness in the Modern British Novel* (Urbana: University of Illinois Press, 1975).

8. E.G., letter to Cary McCormack, April 28, 1909, 5060/14, AL.

9. See Theophilus E. M. Boll, *Miss May Sinclair, Novelist* (Rutherford, N.J.: Fairleigh Dickinson Press, 1973), 89.

10. E.G., letter to Elizabeth Patterson, August 17, 1909, 5060/28, AL.

11. Ibid., August 13, 1909.

12. Ibid., September 3, 1909.

13. Ibid., September 2, 1909.

14. Also see Glasgow's interview in the *New York Times*, March 23, 1913, in *RD*, 21. "It is well worth while, even at this somewhat critical juncture of her argument," the interviewer noted, "to stop and look at her as she speaks. "She is both pretty and young [Glasgow was 40 at the time]—an extraordinarily unexpected combination in an author of more than National renown."

15. Carter W. Wormeley, "Woman Suffrage in Virginia: Ellen Glasgow Interviewed," *Jewish Record* 1 (November 28, 1909), 5, 16, in *RD*, 15, 17.

16. See Edgar MacDonald, "Mary Johnston and Henry Sydnor Harrison," *EGN* 20 (April 1984): 2-4.

17. Alexander Weddell, letter to E.G., November 17, 1945, 5060/20, AL.

18. See Godbold, *Ellen Glasgow and the Woman Within*, 91.

19. Sarah Anderson Easter, interview with author, 1994.

20. E.G., letter to James Branch Cabell, May 2, 1940, Accession No. 5947H, AL.

21. Monique Parent locates the apartment on Fifth Avenue and Eighty-Fifth Street. Writing to Elizabeth Patterson on October 12, 1912, Glasgow used black-edged paper with the address One West Eighty-fifth Street.

22. E.G., letter to Grant C. Knight, June 30, 1929, in *Letters*, 94-95.

23. James Lane Allen, letter to E.G., December 8, 1910, 5060/8, AL.

24. James Lane Allen, letter to E.G., January 25, 1910, 5060/8, AL. Glasgow became vice-president of the society in 1911.

25. James Lane Allen, letters to E.G., November 7 and 26, 1911, 5060/8, AL.

26. E.G., letter to Grant C. Knight, June 29, 1929, in *Letters*, 93-94.

27. Glasgow reread Allen's letters after responding to Grant Knight's request for information on Allen, and they prompted her to write immediately, revising what she now considered her overly negative response of the day before. See E.G., letters to Grant C. Knight, June 29 and 30, 1929, in *Letters*, 92-95.

28. James Lane Allen, letters to E.G., August 7, 1923, and January 16, 1922, 5060/8, AL.

29. E.G., letter to Grant C. Knight, June 29, 1929, in *Letters*, 93.

30. See ibid., 94.

31. Edgar MacDonald, "Home Thoughts," *EGN* 10 (October 1983): 10.

32. The poem is published in Godbold, *Ellen Glasgow and the Woman Within*, 92, and *RD*, 18.

33. See Edgar MacDonald, ed., "Ellen Glasgow to Lila Meade Valentine: Three Letters," July 1, 1912, in *EGN* 21 (October 1984): 5.

34. E.G., letter to Elizabeth Patterson, March 29, 1912, 5060/28, AL.

35. See Raper, *Without Shelter,* 241–47; Matthews, *Ellen Glasgow and a Woman's Tradition,* 69–88; and Phillip D. Atteberry, "The Framing of Glasgow's *Virginia,*" in *Ellen Glasgow: New Perspectives,* ed. Scura, 106–23. Also see Wagner-Martin, *Ellen Glasgow: Beyond Convention.* Wagner notes that *Virginia* is the first book that Glasgow narrated from a woman's consciousness.

36. Marjorie Kinnan Rawlings, "Regional Literature of the South," *English Journal* 29, no. 2, pt. 1 (February 1940): 93.

37. Allen Tate, "The New Provincialism," in *Essays of Four Decades,* ed. Tate (Chicago: Swallow Press, 1968), 539, 545.

38. Allen Tate, "The Profession of Letters in the South," in *Essays of Four Decades,* ed. Tate, 532.

39. See Ellen Glasgow, *Virginia* (New York: Penguin, 1989), 338–39. Jenny is "dangerous," intellectual, and spinsterish, all possible hints of her covert sexuality. Even her refusal to marriage whatever its cause would be seen by Virginia's world as subversive.

40. See Francesca Sawaya, " 'The Problem of the South': Economic Determination, Gender Determination, and Genre in Glasgow's *Virginia,*" in *Ellen Glasgow: New Perspectives,* 132–45, esp. 136.

41. Ellen Glasgow, " 'Evasive Idealism' in Literature: An Interview by Joyce Kilmer," in *RD,* 122.

42. See Emily Clark, "Ellen Glasgow," in *Ellen Glasgow: Critical Essays,* ed. Sherman, Haardt, and Clark, 39. Clark writes that no Southerner had ever before written a sentence like this one.

43. *Reviews,* 162, 159, 171, 169.

44. E.G., letter to Rebe Tutwiler, May 31, 1914, RC.

45. Ada Galsworthy, letter to E.G., July 13, 1914, 5060/14, AL.

46. Amélie Rives Troubetzkoy, letter to E.G., October 27, 1913, 5060/18, AL.

Chapter 7. New Beginnings

1. See Alan Price, "Writing Home from the Front: Edith Wharton and Dorothy Canfield Fisher Present Wartime France to the United States, 1917–1919," *Edith Wharton Newsletter* (Fall 1988): 1–5, 8.

2. Vera Palmer, "Mrs. Duke, 77, Faces Life with Charm, Humor," *Richmond Times Dispatch,* March 22, 1953.

3. E.G., letter to Rebe Tutwiler, July 27, 1915, RC.

4. Mayor from 1895–1900, Phelan received a complimentary vote in the California legislature for U.S. senator at the end of his mayoral term.

5. Florence Finch Kelly, "Some Novels of the Month: *Life and Gabriella,*" *Bookman* 43 (March 1916): 80–82, in *Reviews,* 184.

6. Ellen Glasgow, *Life and Gabriella: The Story of a Woman's Courage* (New York: Doubleday, Page, 1916), 125.

7. Joseph Conrad, letter to Frank Doubleday, April 10, 1916, 5060/13, AL.

8. Berta Wellford, interview with Rawlings, RC.

9. Ibid.

10. See James Lane Allen, letters to E.G., October 10 and December 12, 1915, 5060/8, AL.

11. Annie Clark, letter to Glasgow Clark, Glasgow Family Collection, Accession No. 10127-a, AL. See MacDonald, "Lellie," 15.

12. "Miss Glasgow Talks of Literature and War," Newspaper Clippings, 10,137b/2, AL.

13. E.G., letter to Rebe Tutwiler, November 4, 1916, RC. The renovations had been decided upon before Francis Glasgow's death.

14. E.G., letter to Arthur Glasgow, Monday [1916], Accession No. 5347, AL.

15. E.G., letter to Arthur Glasgow, December 14, 1916, Accession No. 5347, AL.

16. For a description of the house during Glasgow's tenancy, see Dorothy M. Scura, "One West Main," *EGN* 1 (October 1974): 3–7.

17. "Miss Glasgow Talks of Literature and War."

18. Edgar MacDonald, "A Gallery of Richmond Portraits," *EGN* 22 (March 1985): 6.

19. See Ann Hobson Freeman, *The Style of a Law Firm: Eight Gentlemen from Virginia* (Chapel Hill, N.C.: Algonquin Books, 1989), 76–103.

20. E.G., letter to Arthur Glasgow, April 5, 1932, RC.

21. See Dorothy M. Scura, "Ellen Glasgow, Henry Anderson, and *The Romantic Comedians*," in *Mississippi Quarterly* 49, no. 2 (Spring 1996): 301–18, esp. 310. Scura suggests that Anderson may have been sexually dysfunctional because of a case of pre-adolescent mumps.

22. Henry Anderson, letter to E.G., June 19, 1916, 5060/8, AL. See Edgar MacDonald, "A Retrospective: Henry Anderson and Marjorie Rawlings," *EGN* 12 (March 1980): 4–16.

23. Maude Williams, interview with Rawlings, RC.

24. RC.

25. Pearce Bailey, letter to E.G., March 8, 1916, 5060/11, AL. The story was published posthumously; see *CSS*, 253–54. Meeker dates the story between 1918 and 1925, though clearly the idea for it predates Glasgow's disillusionment with Anderson.

26. Ellen Glasgow, *Harper's Monthly Magazine* 125 (June 1912): 103; quoted in Godbold, *Ellen Glasgow and the Woman Within*, 110.

27. In Godbold, *Ellen Glasgow and the Woman Within*, 111. The poem is dated August 4, 1916, 5060/8, AL.

28. Henry Anderson, letters to E.G., August 16 and 31, 1916, 5060/8, AL.

29. Ibid., September 6 and 7, 1916.

30. E.G., letters to Paul Revere Reynolds, July 1 and November 26, 1916, in AA, 194–95.

31. James Lane Allen, letter to E.G., July 2, 1916, 5060/8, AL.

32. Ellen Glasgow, "Thinking Makes It So," in *CSS*, 89. See Edgar MacDonald, "From Jordan's End to Frenchman's Bend: Ellen Glasgow's Short Stories," *Mississippi Quarterly* 49, no. 2 (Spring 1996): 319–32.

33. Henry Anderson, letter, September 13, 1916, 5060/8, AL.

34. Glasgow thanked Anderson for his collaboration on *The Builders*, inscribing his copy: "To Henry W. Anderson, with whose help and inspiration this book was written. From Ellen Glasgow, Richmond, Virginia, November the first, 1919."

35. See "France—1916," 5060/4, AL. The poem begins and ends:

> Slain yet immortal she rises; bleeding but strong . . .
> Pure as the sword of the Lord, or the heart of the free,
> France, the beloved Republic, is leading the world!

36. See Henry Anderson, letter to Randolph Williams, April 20, 1919, *EGN* 11 (October 1979): 21. Anderson believed, for example, that civilization advanced from the "love and sympathy" of individuals; that "men and nations must find their lives . . . by losing them for a noble ideal or through an unselfish act."

37. Godbold, *Ellen Glasgow and the Woman Within*, 119.

38. See Hannah Pakula, *The Last Romantic: A Biography of Queen Marie of Roumania* (New York: Simon and Schuster, 1984), 212-17; and Sara Bearss, "Marie of Rumania and Henry Anderson of Virginia," *EGN* 25 (Spring 1988): 7.

39. Pakula, *The Last Romantic*, 227.

40. Queen Marie, letter to Henry Anderson, March 17, 1919, ed. Sara B. Bearss, in *EGN* 30 (Spring 1993): 7.

41. Henry Anderson, letter to E.G., September 8, 1916, 5060/8, AL.

42. Queen Marie, letter to Henry Anderson, February 6, 1919, *EGN* 30 (Spring 1993): 7.

43. Bearss, "Marie of Rumania and Henry Anderson of Virginia," 10.

44. E.G., letter to Arthur Glasgow, October 11, 1919, Accession No. 5347, AL.

45. Freeman, *Style of a Law Firm*, 90.

46. See Edward R. Crews, "A Virginia Hospital Abroad: U.S. Army Base Hospital No. 45 in the Great War," *Virginia Cavalcade* 45, no. 4 (1993): 178-91. The Base Hospital No. 45 was organized in July 1917 at the Medical College of Virginia, and mobilized in March 1918, at Camp Lee, Virginia, where it trained and was equipped. It sailed from Newport News, Virginia, on July 10, 1918, and reached Brest, France, on July 21. The unit was eventually transferred to Toul, Department of Meurthe-et-Moselle, in the advance section, where it became part of the Justice Hospital Center. Their buildings had no lights or plumbing. The hospital functioned as an evacuation hospital. From August 19, 1918, to January 29, 1919, it treated 17,438 sick and wounded.

47. Ibid., 186-87.

48. Marjorie Rawlings noted that Henry Anderson enthused about Queen Marie's beauty and "literary (!!!) ability," in RC.

49. Poem of Henry Anderson, 5060/8, AL.

50. Laura Anderson, letter to E.G., ed. Edgar MacDonald, *EGN* 13 (October 1980): 7.

51. Henry Anderson, letter to Randolph Williams, April 20, 1919, ed. Edgar MacDonald, *EGN* 11 (October 1979): 9.

52. Ibid.

53. Henry Anderson, letter to E.G., Saturday (n.d.), 5060/9, AL.

54. Ibid., September 10, 1929.

55. Henry Anderson, letter to E.G., Friday (n.d.), 5060/11, AL.

56. Godbold, *Ellen Glasgow and the Woman Within*, 124.

57. Tuesday (n.d.) (cited in part in ibid., 125), 5060/11, AL.

58. Godbold, *Ellen Glasgow and the Woman Within*, 125-26.

59. Interview with Maude Williams, *EGN* 12 (March 1980): 14.

60. Henry Anderson, letter to E.G., January 23, 1920, 5060/9, AL.

61. Freeman, *Style of a Law Firm*, 92.

62. Henry Anderson, political speech, 4050/7, AL.

63. See Donald Lisio, *Hoover, Blacks, and Lily-Whites* (Chapel Hill: University of North Carolina Press, 1985), 72-81.

64. Godbold, *Ellen Glasgow and the Woman Within*, 127.

65. Edgar MacDonald published Rawlings's notes of her interviews with Anderson and Maude Williams in *EGN* 12 (March 1980): 7–16.

66. Henry Anderson, letter to Marjorie Rawlings [January 1953], *EGN* 12 (March, 1980): 7.

Chapter 8. What Endures

1. Glasgow decided not to include "The Artless Age" (*Saturday Evening Post*, August 1923), a comedy of manners, foreshadowing *The Romantic Comedians* (1926), in which a flapper vanquishes an old-fashioned girl who then becomes her stepmother.

2. See "The Cabineers," *EGN* 6 (March 1977): 11. The Cabineers met at Reveille, Lizzie Patterson's old house. Ellen Glasgow was a frequent guest. Cabell suggested a reception for Glasgow at the Writers' Club to celebrate the publication of *The Builders*.

3. Dorothy M. Scura, "Mary Dallas Street: Editor, Novelist, and Poet," *EGN* 4 (March 1976): 5.

4. Joseph M. Flora, "Fiction in the 1920s: Some New Voices," in *History of Southern Literature*, ed. Rubin et al., 279.

5. See *Mencken and Sara, A Life in Letters: The Private Correspondence of H. L. Mencken and Sara Haardt*, ed. Marion Elizabeth Rodgers (New York: McGraw-Hill, 1987), 34–35.

6. Clark, *Innocence Abroad*, 55. Also see Maurice Duke, "The Reviewer: A Bibliographical Guide to a Little Magazine," *Resources for American Literary Study* 1 (Spring 1971): 58–103; and Duke, "Ingénue among the Richmonders: Of Emily Clark and Stuffed Peacocks," *EGN* 3 (October 1975): 3–9.

7. Clark, *Innocence Abroad*, 14.

8. For the history of Cabell's relationship to *The Reviewer*, see MacDonald, *James Branch Cabell and Richmond-in-Virginia*, 216–35.

9. Marshall W. Fishwick, *Gentlemen of Virginia* (New York: Dodd, Mead, 1961), 234.

10. H. L. Mencken, *My Life as Author and Editor* (New York: Knopf, 1993), 357.

11. Hunter Stagg, letter to Carl Van Vechten [March 7, 1925], in "Hunter Stagg on Literary Visitors to Richmond," *EGN* 16 (March 1982): 12.

12. Flora, "Fiction in the 1920s," 280.

13. See Hugh Walpole, letter to E.G., April 14, 1920, 5060/19, AL. Walpole writes of Ocean View, Virginia: "This is the *ideal* place and the weather is divine, a warm blue sky and white waves and smiling niggers and not a soul who knows me except the landlord who whispered to me sotto voce this morning."

14. Rupert Hart-Davis, *Hugh Walpole: A Biography* (New York: Macmillan, 1952), 281.

15. See Hugh Walpole, letter to E.G., July 24, 1922, 5060/19, AL. Naively at best and maliciously at worst, Walpole assumed that Glasgow felt *One Man in His Time* a failure: "What happened to you in fact was that your mistrust in your central character was swamped by the sudden life of all the other characters which you scarcely expected. Isn't that so?"

16. Notebook no. 3, 5060/6, AL.

17. The records of the Richmond SPCA are in the James Branch Cabell Library, Virginia Commonwealth University. The agents noted the race of the offenders by the notation "col."

18. Alexander Weddell, letter to E.G., July 18, 1936, 5060/20, AL.

19. E.G., letter to Signe Toksvig, August 14, 1943, GL.

20. RC.

21. See Jane Davenport Reid, "The Ellen Glasgow Collection of Ceramic Dogs," *Commonwealth* 16 (February 1949): 13, 30, 31.

22. RC.

23. Queen Marie, letter to Henry Anderson, December 31, 1919, introduced and edited by Sara B. Bearss, in *EGN* 28 (Spring 1992): 6.

24. Virginius Dabney, "Ellen Glasgow's Pet Sealyham Terrier Had Canine Personality," *Richmond Times-Dispatch*, September 8, 1929, 14, in *EGN* 4 (March 1976): 10.

25. RC.

26. See Ellen Glasgow, "A Plea," in *EGN* 29 (Fall 1992): 6. Also see in the same issue, Terence Allan Hoagwood, "Glasgow's 'A Plea,'" 7–8.

27. For recent reading of *Barren Ground*, see Margaret D. Bauer, "'Put Your Heart in the Land': An Intertextual Reading of *Barren Ground* and *Gone with the Wind*," in *Ellen Glasgow: New Perspectives*, ed. Scura, 162–82. Also see Catherine Rainwater, "Consciousness, Gender, and Animal Signs in *Barren Ground* and *Vein of Iron*," in *Ellen Glasgow: New Perspectives*, ed. Scura, 204–19.

28. See Raper, *From the Sunken Garden*, 1–14. Also see Raper, "*Barren Ground* and the Transition to Southern Modernism," in *Ellen Glasgow: New Perspectives*, ed. Scura, 146–61.

29. See David R. Williams, *Wilderness Lost: The Religious Origins of the American Mind* (London: Associated Presses, 1987). Also see Annette Kolodny, *The Land Before Her: Fantasy and Experience of the American Frontiers, 1630-1860* (Chapel Hill: University of North Carolina Press, 1984).

30. H. L. Mencken, letter to Sara Haardt, May 14, 1925, in *Mencken and Sara*, ed. Rodgers, 210.

31. McDowell, *Ellen Glasgow and the Ironic Art of Fiction*, 257.

32. Clark, *Innocence Abroad*, 132.

33. Edwin Mims, letter to E.G., January 28, 1925, 5060/17, AL.

34. Stuart P. Sherman, letter to E.G., April 23, 1925, 5060/18, AL. Like earlier reviewers of *The Descendant*, Sherman commented on *Barren Ground*'s firm, lucid, and "masculine" style. Times had changed enough, however, for him to offer the description timorously (*Reviews*, 244).

35. Carl Van Vechten, letter to E.G., April 18, 1925, 5060/19, AL.

36. Louise Maunsell Field, "Miss Glasgow at Home," *New York Times Book Review and Magazine*, July 30, 1922, 21.

37. E.G., letter to Signe Toksvig, February 4, 1944, in *Letters*, 342–43.

38. See Dorothy M. Scura, "Afterword," *The Romantic Comedians* (Charlottesville: University Press of Virginia, 1995), 241–65. Also see Caroline King Barnard Hall, "'Telling the Truth about Themselves': Women, Form, and Idea in *The Romantic Comedians*," in *Ellen Glasgow: New Perspectives*, ed. Scura, 183–95.

39. Emily Clark, *Ingénue among the Lions: The Letters of Emily Clark to Joseph Hergesheimer*, ed. Gerald Langford (Austin: University of Texas Press, 1965), 166.

40. Ibid., 172.

41. See E.G., letter to Arthur Glasgow, July 28, 1926, Accession No. 5347, AL. Also see Arthur Glasgow, letter to Marjorie Rawlings, February 3, 1953, in which he says that the

trust was created on March 25, 1926, with $165,000. The trust provided for Bennett in case Glasgow predeceased her.

42. E.G., letter to Rebe Tutwiler, August 7, 1927, 5060/14, AL.

43. Maude Williams, interview with Rawlings, RC. Milk-leg is a painful swelling of the leg soon after childbirth.

44. E.G., letter to Rebe Tutwiler, June 26, 1927, 5060/14, AL.

45. Ibid., June 26, 1927.

46. Ibid., July 23, 1927.

47. Ibid., July 30, 1927.

48. E.G., letter to Anne Virginia Bennett, August 14, 1927, 5060/28, AL.

49. E.G., letter to Rebe Tutwiler, August 24, 1927, 5060/14, AL.

50. The woman had a daughter crippled from tuberculosis, and the two lived together in a tiny room. She promised to name her new salmon-colored rose after Glasgow.

51. E.G., letter to Anne Virginia Bennett, August 25, 1927, in *Letters*, 87–89.

52. E.G., letters to Mr. Ayer, March 14, 1927, and August 23, 1928, in *EGN* 22 (March 1985): 3, 4.

53. E.G., letter to James Branch Cabell, June 27, 1924, Accession No. 5947H, AL.

54. Ibid., December 18, 1929.

55. See Godbold, *Ellen Glasgow and the Woman Within*, 239. Glasgow refused degrees from Rollins College (1935), the University of Wisconsin (1937), Goucher College (1938), the University of Rochester (1939), Middlebury College (1940), and Smith College (1944).

56. Arthur Glasgow, letter to E.G., October 11, 1929, 5060/14, AL.

57. Stark Young, letter to E.G., Thursday [December 1928], 5060/20, AL.

58. Irita Van Doren, interview with Rawlings, RC. Glasgow supposedly worried about the "French boys."

59. Ward A. Holden, letter to E.G., June 5, 1929, 5060/15, AL. Most of the quotation is in Godbold, *Ellen Glasgow and the Woman Within*, 178.

60. Ward A. Holden, letters to E.G., July 2 and July 13, 1929, begun at 6 a.m., 5060/15, AL.

61. Joseph Collins, letter to E.G., September 11, 1929, 5060/13, AL; in Godbold, *Ellen Glasgow and the Woman Within*, 180.

62. Radclyffe Hall, letter to E.G., September 29, 1929, 5060/15, AL.

63. Amélie Rives, letter to E.G., September 28, 1929, 5060/18, AL.

64. Godbold, *Ellen Glasgow and the Woman Within*, 180.

65. Carl Van Vechten, letter to E.G., September 10 [1929], in *Letters of Carl Van Vechten*, sel. and ed. Bruce Kellner (New Haven: Yale University Press, 1987), 108.

66. E.G., letter to Anne Virginia Bennett, October 16, 1929, 5060/28, AL.

67. E.G., letter to Rebe Tutwiler, June 18, 1930, RC.

68. See Eleanor Atkinson, *Greyfriars Bobby* (New York: Harpers and Brothers, 1912).

69. E.G., letter to Anne Virginia Bennett, August 24, 1930, 5060/28, AL.

Chapter 9. *Blood and Irony*

1. E.G., letter to Carl Van Vechten, July 28, 1926, in *Letters*, 80–81.

2. See Dorothy M. Scura, "Glasgow and the Southern Renaissance," in *Ellen Glasgow: Centennial Essays*, ed. Inge, 46–64.

3. Ibid., 50.

4. E.G., letter to Allen Tate, March 25, 1933, in *Letters*, 132.

5. Scura, "Glasgow and the Southern Renaissance," 52. For a description of the conference, see Joseph Blotner, *Faulkner: A Biography* (New York: Random House, 1974), 706–17. Also see Godbold, *Ellen Glasgow and the Woman Within*, 184–89; and Sherwood Anderson, letter to Laura Lou Copenhaver [October 24, 1931], in *Letters of Sherwood Anderson*, ed. Howard Mumford Jones (Boston: Little, Brown, 1953), 250–54.

6. Emily Clark, "A Weekend at Mr. Jefferson's University," *New York Herald Tribune Books*, November 8, 1931, 1–2.

7. Scura, "Glasgow and the Southern Renaissance," 52.

8. Blotner, *Faulkner*, 709.

9. Ibid., 713.

10. See E.G., letter to Signe Toksvig, March 11, 1936, GL. Tate had wanted to include an essay by Glasgow on the "modern woman" for *I'll Take My Stand* (1930).

11. Ellen Glasgow, "Heroes and Monsters," in *RD*, 163.

12. Blotner, *Faulkner*, 711, 715.

13. Allen Tate, letter to Donald Davidson, "The Agrarian Symposium," ed. John Tyree Fain and Thomas Daniel Young, *Southern Review* 8 (October 1972): 872–73.

14. Allen Tate, letter to Stark Young, January 11, 1932, 5060/20, AL.

15. Scura, "Glasgow and the Southern Renaissance," 62.

16. Stark Young, letter to E.G., November 10, 1931, 5060/20, AL.

17. H. L. Mencken, *My Life as Author and Editor*, ed. Charles A. Fecher (New York: Knopf, 1993), 118.

18. Allen Tate, letter to E.G., March 9, 1932, 5060/18, AL.

19. For a reading of the novel that emphasizes the development of Jenny Blair, see Matthews, *Ellen Glasgow and a Woman's Traditions*, 179–88.

20. See Linda Wagner-Martin, "Glasgow's Time in *The Sheltered Life*," in *Ellen Glasgow: New Perspectives*, ed. Scura, 204–19.

21. Barbara Welter, "The Cult of True Womanhood, 1820–1860," *American Quarterly* 18 (Summer 1966): 151–74.

22. Mary Boykin Chesnut, *A Diary from Dixie*, ed. Ben Ames Williams (Cambridge: Harvard University Press, 1980), 122, 21.

23. Also see *BG*, 497.

24. See Raper, *From the Sunken Garden*, 147, 191–202 esp. Raper claims that Archbald bears most responsibility for creating the social ideal that perverts Eva Birdsong's growth (198).

25. "Miss Glasgow Talks of Literature and War," newspaper clippings, 10137b/2, AL.

26. Ibid.

27. Fanny Butcher, "Ellen Glasgow Writes Novels of Old South," *Chicago Daily Tribune*, August 27, 1932, 11, in *Reviews*, 327.

28. E.G., letter to Sara Haardt, October 27, 1932, in *Letters*, 126.

29. H. L. Mencken, letter to E.G., November 29, 1935, 5060/16, AL. See Ritchie D. Watson Jr., "Sara Haardt Mencken and the Glasgow-Mencken Literary Entente," *EGN* 20 (April 1984): 12.

30. Mencken, *The Diary of H. L. Mencken*, 49.

31. E.G., letter to Anice Cooper, August 12, 1932, in *Letters*, 120.

32. E.G., letter to Stark Young, January 12, 1932, in *Letters*, 112.

33. Stark Young, letter to E.G., April 21, 1932, 5060/20, AL.

34. E.G., letter to Allen Tate, September 22, 1932, in *Letters*, 123–26.

35. Stark Young, letter to E.G., January 25, 1932, 5060/20, AL.

36. Ibid., July 14, 1933.

37. E.G., letter to Allen Tate, March 6, 1932, in *Letters*, 114.

38. Brooks, *An Autobiography*, 477.

39. Bessie Zaban Jones, letter to E.G., February 9, 1932, 5060/16, AL.

40. James Branch Cabell, letters to E.G., August 30 and September 13, 1932, 5060/12, AL.

41. Page Cooper, letter to E.G., August 23, 1932, 5060/13, AL.

42. Isa Glenn, letter to E.G., May 7, 1933, in Godbold, *Ellen Glasgow and the Woman Within*, 192.

43. E.G., letter to Allen Tate, July 14, 1933, in *Letters*, 139–40.

Chapter 10. *Vein of Iron*

1. E.G., letter to James Branch Cabell, Saturday [1931], Accession No. 5947H, AL.

2. E.G., letter to Arthur Glasgow, December 16, 1931, RC.

3. Rebe Tutwiler, interview with Rawlings, RC.

4. Arthur Glasgow, letter to E.G., August 7, 1931, RC.

5. See E.G., letter to Arthur Glasgow, June 19, 1931, in *Letters*, 109.

6. Maude Williams and Henry Anderson, interviews with Rawlings, RC.

7. E.G., letter to Arthur Glasgow, April 5, 1932, RC.

8. E.G., letter to Sam Everitt, February 5, 1929, Ken McCormack Papers, Library of Congress.

9. Ken McCormack Papers, Library of Congress.

10. E.G., letter to Signe Toksvig, October 8, 1944, GL.

11. E.G., letter to Daniel Longwell, June 22, 1932, in *Letters*, 117.

12. See Arthur Glasgow, letter to Marjorie Rawlings, February 3, 1953, RC. Glasgow received half of the current income from a trust Arthur established in 1908 and half of the 1926 trust. In 1953 the income from these trusts totaled $18,500 per annum.

13. E.G., letter to Arthur Glasgow, December 30, 1930, in *Letters*, 106.

14. Margaret Dashiell, interview with Rawlings, RC.

15. E.G., letter to Arthur Glasgow, April 5, 1932, RC. Dr. Alexander Brown Jr. thought her illness definitely psychopathic.

16. E.G., letter to Arthur Glasgow, December 16, 1931, RC.

17. James Southall Wilson, "Ellen Glasgow's Novels," *Virginia Quarterly Review* 9 (October 1933): 594–600, in *Reviews*, 363.

18. H. L. Mencken, letter to Sara Haardt, May 14, 1925, in *Mencken and Sara*, ed. Rodgers, 210.

19. See Ellen Glasgow, inscription to *Of Ellen Glasgow: An Inscribed Portrait by Ellen Glasgow and Branch Cabell* (New York: Maverick Press, 1938). In Glasgow's version, they had lived with "equal discretion in the same place and period" and approached their subject from "opposite directions and contrasting angles of vision." In youth, he had exalted the "glamour of chivalry" and she "the shabbiness. But beneath the glamour and the shabbiness, the realities of their surrounding were inseparable."

20. E.G., letter to Sara Haardt, September 14, 1930, in Watson, "Sara Haardt Mencken and The Glasgow-Mencken Literary Entente," 6.

21. E.G., letter to Allen Tate, September 30, 1933, in *Letters*, 145–46.

22. E.G., letter to Arthur Glasgow, October 3, 1933, RC.

23. E.G., letters to Irita Van Doren, August 2 and 12, 1934, in *Letters*, 159–62.

24. Ibid., August 17, 1934, in *Letters*, 163–65.

25. Carl Van Vechten, letter to E.G., February 6, 1935, 5060/19, AL.

26. Frances Williams, interview with Rawlings, RC. Williams helped Freeman research his biography of Washington and wrote children stories and historical books.

27. *RD*, 223.

28. Emma Gray, letter to Marjorie Kinnan Rawlings, April 16, 1953, RC.

29. E.G., letter to Allen Tate, June 4, 1933, in *Letters*, 136–37.

30. Ellen Glasgow, "Random Thoughts on the Artist and the Scholar," 5060/6, AL. Published as "Heroes and Monsters," *Saturday Review of Literature* 12 (May 4, 1935): 3, 4.

31. E.G., letter to John Chamberlain, December 2, 1935, in *Letters*, 200–201.

32. See Lucinda H. MacKethan, "Restoring Order: Matriarchal Design in *The Battle-Ground* and *Vein of Iron*," in *Ellen Glasgow: New Perspectives*, ed. Scura, 89–105. Also see Rainwater, "Consciousness, Gender, and Animal Signs in *Barren Ground* and *Vein of Iron*," 204–19.

33. E.G., letter to Miss Forbes, December 3, 1935, 5060/14, AL.

34. E.G., letter to Alfred Harcourt, June 18, 1935, in *Letters*, 184–85.

35. James Branch Cabell, letters to E.G., July 19, July 25, and August 15, 1935, 5060/12, AL.

36. E.G., letter to Stark Young, n.d., in *Letters*, 190–91.

37. E.G., letter to H. L. Mencken, August 30, 1935, in *Letters*, 195–96.

38. Allen Tate, letter to E.G., September 9, 1932. See Ritchie D. Watson, "The Ellen Glasgow–Allen Tate Correspondence: Bridging the Southern Literary Generation Gap," in *EGN* 23 (October 1985): 3–23.

39. E.G., letter to Stark Young, January 12, 1932, in *Letters*, 112–13.

40. James R. Mellow, *Charmed Circle: Gertrude Stein and Company* (New York: Praeger, 1974), 355. For an account of Stein's trip to Richmond, see also 399–400.

41. Bruce Kellner, "Ellen Glasgow and Gertrude Stein," *EGN* 2 (March 1975): 14. Also see ibid., 399.

42. Gertrude Stein, *Everybody's Autobiography* (New York: Random House, 1937), 245.

43. Kellner, "Ellen Glasgow and Gertrude Stein," 15.

44. Ibid.

45. Godbold, *Ellen Glasgow and the Woman Within*, 204.

46. E.G., letter to James Branch Cabell, July 22, 1935, Accession No. 5947H, AL.

47. Hunter Stagg, interview with Rawlings, RC.

48. Edgar MacDonald, "Glasgow-Stein: Second Meeting," *EGN* 15 (October 1981): 17.

49. Stein, *Everybody's Autobiography*, 245.

50. Godbold, *Ellen Glasgow and the Woman Within*, 204.

51. Kellner, "Ellen Glasgow and Gertrude Stein," 16. Also see Oliver L. Steele Jr., "Gertrude Stein and Ellen Glasgow: Memoir of a Meeting," *American Literature* 33 (March 1961): 76–77.

52. Stein, *Everybody's Autobiography*, 246–47.

53. Rhea Talley, "U. D. C.'s Pity Gertrude Stein for Remarks on General Lee," reprinted in Larry Hall's "A Van Vechten Pose: Mark Lutz and Gertrude Stein in Richmond," *EGN* 18 (March 1983): 8.

54. E.G., letter to Alfred Harcourt, March 21, 1935, in *Letters*, 175–76,

55. Stark Young, letter to E.G., May 1, 1935, 5060/21, AL.

56. Douglas Southall Freeman, letters to E.G., January 2 and May 7, 1935, 5060/14, AL.

57. E.G., letter to Douglas Southall Freeman, n.d., in *Letters*, 195. Freeman tactfully mentioned her deafness in an article he wrote for the *Saturday Review of Literature* (August 31, 1935), entitled "Ellen Glasgow, Idealist."

58. Meade, *I Live in Virginia*, 184–85.

59. E.G., letter to Stark Young, n.d., in *Letters*, 196–97.

60. See Julian R. Meade, letter to Stark Young, March 24, 1937; Stark Young, letter to E.G., April 15, 1937; and copy of letter from Margaret Mitchell to Stark Young, undated, in 5060/21, AL.

61. See Stark Young, letter to E.G., April 19, 1937, 5060/21, AL.

62. Julian Meade, letter to E.G., June 17, 1936, 5060/16, AL.

63. E.G., letter to J. Donald Adams, April 28, 1936, in *Letters*, 211.

64. E.G., letter to Bessie Zaban Jones, September 9, 1936, in *Letters*, 214–15.

Chapter 11. The Ragged Edge

1. E.G., letter to Harry Scherman, January 14, 1937, in *Letters*, 216–17. Anne Virginia Bennett, whose taste in books ran to romances and mysteries, could read none of the selections except J. C. Titzell's *Best in the Greenwood*.

2. *Of Ellen Glasgow*. One evening over dinner, the friends had decided to collaborate on the book.

3. E.G., letter to Bessie Zaban Jones, April 11, 1938, in *Letters*, 240.

4. The house belonged to Mr. and Mrs. John Kerr Branch.

5. Glasgow had imagined *In This Our Life* as early as 1935. See William W. Kelly, *Ellen Glasgow: A Bibliography* (Charlottesville: University Press of Virginia, 1964), 96.

6. Maxwell E. Perkins, *Editor to Author: The Letters of Maxwell E. Perkins*, ed. John Hall Wheelock (New York: Scribner's, 1950), 251.

7. Maxwell Perkins, letters to E.G., August 18, September 9, and May 6, 1937, 5060/21, AL.

8. James Branch Cabell, letter to E.G., January 18, 1939, 5060/12, AL.

9. Ibid., September 16, 1937.

10. E.G., letters to James Cabell, Friday [1937]; Saturday [1937]; Monday [1937]; Tuesday [1937], Accession No. 5947H, AL. Glasgow kept the passage. See *CM*, 52.

11. Maxwell Perkins, letter to E.G., September 17, 1937, 5060/21, AL.

12. Perkins advised her to cut the second paragraph of the original preface.

13. Maxwell Perkins, letters to E.G., September 17, November 17, December 1, and December 8, 1937, 5060/21, AL.

14. Godbold, *Ellen Glasgow and the Woman Within*, 234.

15. Maxwell Perkins, letter to E.G., December 27, 1939, 5060/21, AL.

16. E.G., letter to Bessie Zaban Jones, April 11, 1938, in *Letters*, 236.

17. Ibid., May 9, 1938, in *Letters*, 239.

18. E.G., letter to Howard Mumford Jones, July 22, 1938, in *Letters*, 242.

19. E.G., letter to Douglas Southall Freeman, April 14, 1938, in *Letters*, 237.

20. E.G., letter to Frank C. Brown, June 2, 1938, College of Physicians of Philadelphia, Historical Collections of the Library.

21. E.G., letter to Rebe Tutwiler, June 17, 1939, RC.

22. Once a major port, the community had been a Revolutionary battleground and occupied by enemy British troops in 1814. After the War of 1812, Castine flourished through trade with the West Indies and England, but the Civil War and the era of the railroads heralded the beginning of its decline.

23. Phil Perkins, interview with author, 1995.

24. Francis W. Hatch, "Ellen Glasgow: Pulitzer Prize-Winner at Castine," *Downeast Magazine*, June 1974, 95.

25. E.G., letter to Van Wyck Brooks, September 2, 1939, in *Letters*, 254-55.

26. Hatch, "Ellen Glasgow," 69. Also see Edgar MacDonald, "Remembering Ellen Glasgow—and Elizabeth Branch Bowie," *EGN* 32 (Spring 1994): 1, 3, 6-7.

27. E.G., letter to Van Wyck Brooks, September 2, 1939, in *Letters*, 254-55.

28. Hatch, "Ellen Glasgow," 94.

29. Katharine Butler Hathaway, *The Little Locksmith* (New York: Coward-McCann, 1942), 71.

30. E.G., letter to Van Wyck Brooks, September 2, 1939, in *Letters*, 254-55.

31. E.G., letter to Edwin Mims, October 4, 1939, in *Letters*, 258-59.

32. Irita Van Doren, interview with Rawlings, RC.

33. E.G., letter to Rebe Tutwiler, February 15, 1938, RC.

34. E.G., letter to Amélie Rives, August 23, 1937, in *Letters*, 224-25.

35. Amélie Rives, letter to E.G., September 9, 1937, 5060/18, AL.

36. E.G., letter to Rebe Tutwiler, October 22, 1937, RC.

37. Agnes Reese, letter to E.G., November 1, 1937, 5060/17, AL. See Edgar MacDonald, "Ellen Glasgow's Characterizations of Blacks," *EGN* 10 (March 1979): 8.

38. James Branch Cabell, letter to E.G., July 6, 1931, 5060/12, AL.

39. E.G., letter to Bessie Zaban Jones, February 5, 1939, in *Letters*, 248-49.

40. E.G., letter to H. L. Mencken, January 19, 1939, in *Letters*, 248.

41. E.G., letter to Edwin Mims, October 4, 1939, in *Letters*, 258-60. Also see E.G., letter to Rebe Tutwiler, September 20, 1938, 5060/14, AL. "I take off my hat to Mr. Chamberlain," she wrote:

It seems to me that England would be mad to get entangled with any other Continental quarrel, or to defend any borders except her own. There could be but one end if she were to ally herself with Russia and France, and that would be the end of her government and of English democracy. Of course the Communists, who have a strong following in England, are trying to bring on war, and so of course are the Fascists.

42. E.G., letter to James Southall Wilson, August 2, 1940, in *Letters*, 267–68.

43. James Branch Cabell, letter to E.G., July 15, 1941, 5060/13, AL.

44. E.G., letter to Bessie Zaban Jones, September 25, 1940, in *Letters*, 268–69.

45. James Branch Cabell, letter to E.G., August 9, 1940, 5060/13, AL.

46. Anne Virginia Bennett, letter to James Branch Cabell, August 26, 1940, ed. Edgar MacDonald, *EGN* 27 (Fall 1991): 6.

47. E.G., letter to Van Wyck Brooks, March 28, 1941, in *Letters*, 283.

48. E.G., letter to Rebe Tutwiler, August 21, 1941, RC.

49. Copies of Arthur's pamphlets are in the RC. At the time of his death, Arthur was writing his memoirs, "Collection of Recollections." He left an estate of over $1 million, with contributions to several colleges, including Washington and Lee University, which gave him an honorary degree, the Valentine Museum, and the Virginia Historical Society. He left his collections to Richmond's Museum of Fine Arts.

50. Cabell, *As I Remember It*, 222–23.

51. Van Wyck Brooks, letter to E.G., March 15, 1940, 5060/12, AL.

52. Godbold, *Ellen Glasgow and the Woman Within*, 277.

53. E.G., letter to Alfred Harcourt, November 27, 1940, in *Letters*, 271.

54. Ibid., Thursday, in *Letters*, 272–73.

55. E.G., letter to Helen K. Taylor, December 17, 1940, in *Letters*, 273–74.

56. Book jacket of the first edition of *In This Our Life*.

57. Joseph Collins, letter to E.G., March 9, 1941, 5060/13, AL.

58. See E.G., letter to Colonel Wise, September 26, 1927, "Ellen Glasgow's Letters in the Library of the Virginia Historical Society," ed. Ritchie D. Watson Jr., *EGN* 14 (March 1981): 8. Glasgow writes: "No American can read 'A Plea for the Indian Citizens of the United States' without a feeling of shame and an overwhelming sympathy for the oppressed minority in our midst. . . . However strongly I speak I cannot speak strongly enough on this subject. It is not only pitiable, it is deplorable that this impoverished people should be forced to spend its substance in contending for its constitutional rights."

Also see Helen Fiddyment Levy, "Coming Home: Glasgow's Last Two Novels," in *Ellen Glasgow: New Perspectives*, ed. Scura, 220–34.

59. E.G., letter to Edmund M. Preston, October 1, 1939, Accession No. 10,212, AL.

60. See Glasgow Clark, letter to Cabell Tutwiler, October 31, 1934, 5060/13, AL. The widow asked for $10,000 in damages.

61. I am indebted to Edgar MacDonald for this anecdote, which he heard from Josephine Clark.

62. Agnes Reese, letter to E.G., December 27, 1941, 5060/17, AL.

63. Carl Van Vechten, letter to E.G., May 27, 1941, 5060/19, AL.

64. Elaine J. Deane, letter to E.G., June 26, 1941, 5060/13, AL.

65. E.G., letter to Rebe Tutwiler, June 14, 1941, 5060/12, AL.

66. E.G., letter to James Branch Cabell, August 1, 1941, 5060/13, AL.

67. E.G., letter to Marjorie Kinnan Rawlings, July 24, 1941, in *Letters*, 286–87.

68. Ellen Glasgow, "Miscellaneous Pungencies," 5060/22, AL. Also see *EGN* 15 (October 1981): 1.

Chapter 12. A Certain Measure

1. E.G., letter to Donald C. Brace, May 4, 1942, in *Letters*, 295.
2. E.G., letter to Margaret Mitchell, May 17, 1942, in *Letters*, 297.
3. Bessie Zaban Jones, letter to E.G., February 17, 1945, 5060/16, AL.
4. Marion Canby, letter to Blair Rouse, in *Letters*, 371-72.
5. E.G., letter to Ellen Knowles Harcourt, September 15, 1942, in *Letters*, 307.
6. E.G., letter to Bessie Zaban Jones, July 20, 1942, in *Letters*, 302.
7. Radclyffe Hall, letter to E.G., March 22, 1943, 5060/15, AL.
8. E.G., letter to Signe Toksvig, June 8, 1943, in *Letters*, 321.
9. Signe Toksvig, letter to E.G., November 6, 1944, 5060/18, AL.
10. E.G., letter to Marjorie Kinnan Rawlings, April 20, 1942, in *Letters*, 294.
11. Marjorie Kinnan Rawlings, letter to E.G., January 17, 1942, 5060/17, AL.
12. E.G., letter to Van Wyck Brooks, July 27, 1943, in *Letters*, 327.
13. E.G., letter to James Branch Cabell, June 27, 1942, Accession No. 5947H, AL.
14. E.G., letter to Donald C. Brace, May 4, 1943, in *Letters*, 317.
15. E.G., letter to Van Wyck Brooks, November 5, 1942, in *Letters*, 309.
16. E.G., letter to Frank Morley, February 28, 1942, in *Letters*, 311.
17. E.G., letter to Van Wyck Brooks, March 22, 1943, in *Letters*, 314.
18. Glasgow probably decided against publishing the sequel because her book of prefaces, which included one for *In This Our Life*, addressed the "misreadings" of its conclusion.
19. Luther Y. Gore, "Introduction," *Beyond Defeat* (Charlottesville: University Press of Virginia, 1966), xxiii.
20. E.G., letter to Van Wyck Brooks, March 28, 1941, in *Letters*, 283. He wrote an unsigned reviewed for *Time*. See *Reviews*, 426-27.
21. E.G., letter to Frank Morley, December 7, 1943, in *Letters*, 340.
22. MacDonald, *James Branch Cabell and Richmond-in-Virginia*, 313. For information on the compiling of *A Certain Measure* and the ensuing feud, also see 305-6, 307, 309, 311-14, 317-19, 320-22.
23. James Southall Freeman, letter to E.G., April 24, 1942, 5060/14, AL.
24. Hunter Stagg, letter to E.G., June 8, 1944, 5060/18, AL.
25. James Branch Cabell, letter to E.G., August 6, 1941, 5060/13, AL.
26. E.G., letter to James Branch Cabell, August 30, 1941, Accession No. 5947H, AL.
27. Ibid., September 7, 1943
28. After Glasgow's death, Bennett was prescribed barbiturates, which contributed to or caused a nervous collapse. She received electric shock treatments. See Anne Virginia Bennett, letter to James Branch Cabell, October 8, 1947, "Anne Virginia Bennett to James Branch Cabell: Two Letters," *EGN* 27 (Fall 1991): 8.
29. See Glasgow's "Mr. Cabell as a Moralist," "Van Doren on Cabell," " 'The Biography of Manuel,' " and "Branch Cabell Still Clings to His Unbelief," in *RD*, 198-218.
30. See Godbold, *Ellen Glasgow and the Woman Within*, 90; and MacDonald, *James Branch Cabell and Richmond-in-Virginia*, 318.
31. MacDonald, *James Branch Cabell and Richmond-in-Virginia*, 315.
32. James Branch Cabell, letter to E.G., in *EGN*, 26 (Spring 1991): 9-10.
33. MacDonald, *James Branch Cabell and Richmond-in-Virginia*, 318-19.

34. Godbold, *Ellen Glasgow and the Woman Within*, 295.
35. E.G., letter to Signe Toksvig, September 4, 1943, in *Letters*, 322.
36. E.G., letter to Marion Canby, April 12, 1944, in *Letters*, 346.
37. E.G., letter to Josephine Clark, December 20, 1932, Accession No. 10127-a, AL.
38. Joseph Collins, letters to E.G., February 9 and April 8, 1945, 5060/13, AL.
39. Arthur Glasgow, letter to E.G., April 14, 1941, 5060/14, AL.
40. E.G., letter to Josephine Clark, May 6, 1944, Accession No. 10127-a, AL.
41. E.G., letter to Rebe Tutwiler, Sunday, February 5, 1945, RC.
42. MacDonald, *James Branch Cabell and Richmond-in-Virginia*, 320.
43. Douglas Southall Freeman, letter to E.G., November 20, 1945, 5060/14, AL.
44. E.G., letter to Anne Virginia Bennett and Rebe Tutwiler, October 31, 1944, with last will and testament, RC.
45. Godbold, *Ellen Glasgow and the Woman Within*, 299.
46. Although I have heard an eyewitness account that confirms this story, I have not been able to corroborate it with the Bliley Funeral Home, which handled Glasgow's burial.

Legacies

1. See E.G., letter to Signe Toksvig, May 21, 1943, GL. Glasgow states: "Always I have felt that I was pushing against the stream, against immovable objects."
2. Edgar MacDonald, "The Glasgow Papers," *EGN* 2 (March 1975): 18.
3. Elizabeth Silverthorne, *Marjorie Kinnan Rawlings: Sojourner at Cross Creek* (Woodstock, N.Y.: Overlook Press, 1988), 335.
4. Dorothy M. Scura, "A 'Lost' Memorial to Ellen Glasgow," *EGN* 12 (March 1980): 28.
5. If Bennett changed her residence and died before Rebe, Rebe would be the main benefactor of household goods.
6. Scura, " 'Lost' Memorial," 33.
7. RC.
8. Scura, " 'Lost' Memorial," 37.
9. Ibid., 42.
10. See Arthur Glasgow, letter to Margaret Freeman Cabell, January 1, 1925, James Branch Cabell Library, Virginia Commonwealth University. Arthur told Freeman that "the assurance by James of her feeling for me is profoundly comforting." Arthur was hurt that he had been left out of *The Woman Within*.
11. Cash, *Mind of the South*, 375.
12. Paul W. Donham, letter to E.G., April 10, 1944, 5060/13, AL.
13. Brooks, *An Autobiography*, 476.
14. Ibid.
15. See Cash, *Mind of the South*, 374.

BIBLIOGRAPHY

Ardis, Ann. *New Woman, New Novels*. New Brunswick, N.J.: Rutgers University Press, 1990.

Armstrong, Nancy. *Desire and Domestic Fiction: A Political History of the Novel*. New York: Oxford University Press, 1987.

Atkinson, Eleanor. *Greyfriars Bobby*. New York: Harpers and Brothers, 1912.

Atteberry, Phillip D. "The Framing of Glasgow's *Virginia*." In *Ellen Glasgow: New Perspectives*, ed. Scura, 124–31.

Auchincloss, Louis. "Ellen Glasgow." In *Pioneers and Caretakers: A Study of Nine American Women Novelists*, 56–91. Minneapolis: University of Minnesota Press, 1965.

Ayers, Edward L. *The Promise of the New South: Life after Reconstruction*. New York: Oxford University Press, 1992.

Bagby, George William. "At Last We Were Off: A Trip on the Kanawha Canal (1830)." In *A Richmond Reader, 1733–1983*, ed. Maurice Duke and Daniel P. Jordon, 71–78. Chapel Hill: University of North Carolina Press, 1983.

Banta, Martha. *Imaging American Women: Ideas and Ideals in Cultural History*. New York: Columbia University Press, 1987.

Bauer, Margaret D. " 'Put Your Heart in the Land': An Intertextual Reading of *Barren Ground* and *Gone with the Wind*." In *Ellen Glasgow: New Perspectives*, ed. Scura, 162–82.

Bearss, Sara. "Marie of Rumania and Henry Anderson of Virginia." *EGN* 25 (Spring 1988): 7–11.

Beebe, Maurice. *Ivory Towers and Sacred Founts: The Artist as Hero in Fiction from Goethe to Joyce*. New York: New York University Press, 1964.

Berenson, Bernard. *The Bernard Berenson Treasury*. Edited by Hana Kiel. With an introduction by Nicky Mariano. New York: Simon and Schuster, 1962.

Bernhard, Virginia, Betty Brandon, Elizabeth Fox-Genovese, and Theda Perdue, eds. *Southern Women: Histories and Identities*. Columbia: University of Missouri Press, 1992.

Blanton, Wyndham. *The Making of a Downtown Church*. Richmond, Va.: John Knox Press, 1945.

Bleser, Carol, ed. *In Joy and In Sorrow: Women, Family, and Marriage in the Victorian South, 1830–1900*. New York: Oxford University Press, 1990.

Bloom, Harold. *The Anxiety of Influence: A Theory of Poetry*. New York: Oxford University Press, 1973.

Boll, Theophilus E. M. *Miss May Sinclair, Novelist*. Rutherford, N.J.: Fairleigh Dickinson Press, 1973.

Brantley, Will. *Feminine Sense in Southern Memoir: Smith, Glasgow, Welty, Hellman, Porter, and Hurston*. Jackson: University Press of Mississippi, 1991.

Brooks, Van Wyck. *An Autobiography*. New York: Dutton, 1965.

———. *The Confident Years: 1885–1915*. New York: Dutton, 1952.

Bruce, Kathleen. *Virginia Iron Manufacture in the Slave Era*. New York: Augustus M. Kelley, 1968.

Cabell, James Branch. *As I Remember It: Some Epilogues in Recollection*. New York: McBride, 1955.

———. *Between Friends: Letters of James Branch Cabell and Others*. Edited by Padraic Colum and Margaret Freeman Cabell. New York: Harcourt, Brace and World, 1962.

———. *The Letters of James Branch Cabell*. Edited by Edward Wagenknecht. Norman: University of Oklahoma Press, 1975.

Carroll, Roger Hunt. "Ellen Glasgow and Rockbridge." *EGN* 9 (October 1978): 5–13.

Cash, W. J. *The Mind of the South*. New York: Vintage Books, 1991.

Cather, Willa. *On Writing: Critical Studies on Writing as an Art*. New York: Knopf, 1949.

Cella, C. Ronald. *Mary Johnston*. New York: Twayne Publishers, 1981.

Chandler, Marilyn R. "Healing the Woman Within: Therapeutic Aspects of Ellen Glasgow's Autobiography." In *Located Lives: Place and Idea in Southern Autobiography*, ed. J. Bill Berry, 93–106. Athens: University of Georgia Press, 1990.

Chesnut, Mary Boykin. *A Diary from Dixie*. Edited by Ben Ames Williams. Cambridge: Harvard University Press, 1980.

Chevigny, Bell Gale. "Daughters Writing: Toward a Theory of Women's Biography." In *Between Women: Biographers, Novelists, Critics, Teachers, and Artists Write about Their Work on Women*, ed. Carol Ascher, Louis DeSalvo, and Sara Ruddick, 356–79. Boston: Beacon Press, 1984.

Christian, W. Asbury. *Richmond: Her Past and Present*. Richmond, Va.: L. H. Jenkins, 1912.

Clark, Emily. "Ellen Glasgow." In *Ellen Glasgow: Critical Essays*, ed. Sherman, Haardt, and Clark, 33–48.

———. *Ingénue among the Lions: The Letters of Emily Clark to Joseph Hergesheimer*. Edited by Gerald Langford. Austin: University of Texas Press, 1965.

———. *Innocence Abroad*. Westport, Conn.: Greenwood Press, 1975.

———. *Stuffed Peacocks*. New York: Knopf, 1928.

———. "A Weekend at Mr. Jefferson's University." *New York Herald-Tribune Books*, November 8, 1931, 1–2.

Clark, Suzanne. *Sentimental Modernism: Women Writers and the Revolution of the Word*. Bloomington: Indiana University Press, 1991.

Clinton, Catherine. *The Plantation Mistress: Woman's World in the Old South*. New York: Pantheon Books, 1982.

Clinton, Catherine, and Nina Silber, eds. *Divided Houses: Gender and the Civil War*. New York: Oxford University Press, 1992.

Collins, Joseph. *The Doctor Looks at Literature: Psychological Studies of Life and Letters*. New York: George H. Doran, 1931.

———. *Taking the Literary Pulse: Psychological Studies of Life and Letters*. New York: George H. Doran, 1924.

Commemorative Tributes of the American Academy of Arts and Letters, 1905-1941. New York: Books for Libraries Presses, 1968.

Cook, Martha. "Miss Ellen and Miss Lucy, The Richmond-Nordhausen Connection." *EGN* 30 (Spring 1993): 13-14.

———, ed. "Ellen Glasgow's 'Ideals': A 'New' Story from the 1920s." In *Ellen Glasgow: New Perspectives,* ed. Scura, 22-32.

Crews, Edward R. "A Virginia Hospital Abroad: U.S. Army Base Hospital No. 45 in the Great War." *Virginia Cavalcade* 45, no. 4 (1993): 178-91.

Dabney, Virginius. *Mr. Jefferson's University: A History of the University of Virginia.* Charlottesville: University Press of Virginia, 1981.

———. *Richmond: The Story of a City.* 2nd ed. Charlottesville: University Press of Virginia, 1994.

De Graffenried, Thomas P. *The De Graffenried Family Scrap Book, 1191-1956.* Charlottesville: University Press of Virginia, 1956.

Dew, Charles B. *Ironmaker to the Confederacy: Joseph R. Anderson and the Tredegar Iron Works.* New Haven: Yale University Press, 1966.

Dillard, R. H. W. "Ellen Glasgow's *The Battle-Ground.*" In *Classics of Civil War Fiction,* ed. David Madden and Peggy Bach, 64-81. Jackson: University Press of Mississippi, 1991.

Drinka, George Frederick. *The Birth of Neurosis: Myth, Malady, and the Victorians.* New York: Simon and Schuster, 1984.

Duke, Alastair, Gilliam Lewis, and Andrew Pettegree, eds. and trans. *Calvinism in Europe, 1540-1610: A Collection of Documents.* New York: St. Martin's, 1992.

Duke, Maurice. "Cabell's and Glasgow's Richmond: The Intellectual Background of the City." *Mississippi Quarterly* 27, no. 4 (Fall 1974): 388.

———. "The First Novel by a Glasgow: Cary's *A Successful Failure.*" *EGN* 1 (October 1974): 7-8.

———. "Ingénue among the Richmonders: Of Emily Clark and Stuffed Peacocks." *EGN* 3 (October 1975): 3-9.

———. "The Reviewer: A Bibliographical Guide to a Little Magazine." *Resources for American Literary Study* 1 (Spring 1971): 58-103.

DuPlessis, Rachel Blau. *Writing beyond the Ending: Narrative Strategies of Twentieth-Century Women Writers.* Bloomington: Indiana University Press, 1985.

Edel, Leon. *Literary Biography.* Bloomington: Indiana University Press, 1973.

———. *Writing Lives: Principia Biographica.* New York: Norton, 1984.

Edkins, Carol. "Quest for Community: Spiritual Autobiographies of Eighteenth-Century Quaker and Puritan Women in America." In *Women's Autobiography: Essays in Criticism,* ed. Estelle C. Jelinek, 39-52. Bloomington: Indiana University Press, 1980.

Edmund, Pocohontas W. "Ellen Glasgow, Social Historian." In *Virginians Out Front,* 245-90. Richmond: Whittet and Shepperson, 1972.

Edwards, Mary P. "Tea and Metaphysics: Excerpts from Mary Johnston's Diary." *EGN* 19 (October 1983): 2-9.

Fain, John Tyree, and Thomas Daniel Young, eds. "The Agrarian Symposium." *Southern Review* 8 (October 1972): 847-82.

Field, Louise Maunsell. "Miss Glasgow at Home." *New York Times Book Review and Magazine*, July 30, 1922, 21.

Fishwick, Marshall W. *Gentlemen of Virginia*. New York: Dodd, Mead, 1961.

————. *Virginia: A New Look at the Old Dominion*. New York: Harper and Brothers, 1959.

Flora, Joseph M. "Fiction in the 1920s: Some New Voices." In *The History of Southern Literature*, ed. Louis D. Rubin Jr., Blyden Jackson, Rayburn S. Moore, Lewis P. Simpson, and Thomas Daniel Young, 279–90. Baton Rouge: Louisiana State University Press, 1985.

Fox-Genovese, Elizabeth. *Within the Plantation Household: Black and White Women of the Old South*. Chapel Hill: University of North Carolina Press, 1988.

Freeman, Ann Hobson. *The Style of a Law Firm: Eight Gentlemen from Virginia*. Chapel Hill, N.C.: Algonquin Books, 1989.

Garland, Hamlin. *Roadside Meetings*. New York: Macmillan, 1930.

Glasgow, Cary. *A Successful Failure: An Outline*. Richmond, Va.: West and Johnson, 1883.

Glasgow, Ellen. *The Ancient Law*. New York: Doubleday, Page, 1908.

————. "Author and Agent: Ellen Glasgow's Letters to Paul Revere Reynolds." Edited and introduced by James B. Colvert. *Studies in Bibliography* 14 (1961): 177–96.

————. *Barren Ground*. New York: Harcourt Brace Jovanovich, 1985.

————. *The Battle-Ground*. New York: Doubleday, Page, 1902.

————. "Between Two Shores," *McClure's* 12, no. 4 (Feb. 1899): 345–52.

————. *Beyond Defeat: An Epilogue to an Era*. Edited by Richard K. Meeker. Baton Rouge: Louisiana State University Press, 1966.

————. "The Biography of Manuel." *Saturday Review of Literature* 6 (June 7, 1930): 1108–9.

————. *The Builders*. Garden City, N.Y.: Doubleday, Page, 1919.

————. *A Certain Measure: An Interpretation of Prose Fiction*. New York: Harcourt, Brace, 1943.

————. *The Collected Short Stories of Ellen Glasgow*. Edited by Richard K. Meeker. Baton Rouge: Louisana State University Press, 1963.

————. *The Deliverance*. New York: Doubleday, Page, 1904.

————. *The Descendant*. New York: Arno Press, 1977.

————. *The Freeman and Other Poems*. New York: Doubleday, Page, 1902.

————. *In This Our Life*. New York: Harcourt, Brace, 1941.

————. *Letters of Ellen Glasgow*. Edited by Blair Rouse. New York: Harcourt, Brace, 1958.

————. *Life and Gabriella*. Garden City, N.Y.: Doubleday, Page, 1916.

————. *The Miller of Old Church*. New York: Doubleday, Page, 1911.

————. *One Man in His Time*. Garden City, N.Y.: Doubleday, Page, 1922.

————. *Phases of an Inferior Planet*. New York: Harper and Brothers, 1898.

————. "A Point in Morals." *Harper's Magazine* 98 (May 1899): 976–82.

————. "Richmonders in Constantinople." *Richmond Dispatch*, April 23, 1899, 7.

————. *The Romance of a Plain Man*. New York: Macmillan, 1909.

————. *The Romantic Comedians*. New York: Doubleday, Page, 1926; Charlottesville: University Press of Virginia, 1995.

————. *The Shadowy Third and Other Stories*. Garden City, N.Y.: Doubleday, Page, 1923.

————. *The Sheltered Life*. London: Virago, 1981.

————. *They Stooped to Folly*. New York: Doubleday, Doran, 1929.

————. *Vein of Iron*. New York: Harcourt, Brace, 1935.

————. *Virginia*. New York: Doubleday, Page, 1913; New York: Penguin, 1989.

————. *The Voice of the People*. New York: Doubleday, Page, 1900.

————. "What I Believe." *The Nation* 136 (April 12, 1933): 404–6.

————. *The Wheel of Life*. New York: Doubleday, Page, 1906.

————. *The Woman Within*. New York: Harcourt, Brace, 1954.

Glasgow, Ellen, and Branch Cabell. *Of Ellen Glasgow: An Inscribed Portrait by Ellen Glasgow and Branch Cabell*. New York: Maverick Press, 1938.

Glasgow, Rebe. "The Eyes of the Sphinx: Selections from Rebe Glasgow's Travel Journal of 1899." Edited by Mark Lurie and Shanon Wilson. *EGN* 25 (Fall 1995): 1–10.

Godbold, E. Stanly. "A Biography and a Biographer." *EGN* 32 (Spring 1994): 4–5.

————. *Ellen Glasgow and the Woman Within*. Baton Rouge: Louisiana State University Press, 1972.

Goodman, Susan. "Composed Selves: Ellen Glasgow's *The Woman Within* and Edith Wharton's *A Backward Glance*." In *Ellen Glasgow: New Perspectives*, ed. Dorothy M. Scura, 42–58. University of Tennessee Press, 1995.

————. *Edith Wharton's Inner Circle*. Austin: University of Texas Press, 1994.

Gordon, Marshall. *Presbyteries and Profits: Calvinism and the Development of Capitalism in Scotland, 1560–1707*. New York: Oxford University Press, 1980.

Gusdorf, Georges. "Conditions and Limits of Autobiography." In *Autobiography: Essays Theoretical and Critical*, ed. James Olney, 28–48. Princeton: Princeton University Press, 1980.

Haardt, Sarah. "Ellen Glasgow and the South." In *Ellen Glasgow: Critical Essays*, ed. Sherman, Haardt, and Clark, 11–31.

Hackett, Alice Payne. *Fifty Years of Best Sellers, 1895–1945*. New York: Bowker, 1945.

Hackett, Alice Payne, and James Henry Burke. *Eighty Years of Best Sellers, 1895–1975*. New York: Bowker, 1977.

Hall, Caroline King Barnard. " 'Telling the Truth about Themselves': Women, Form, and Idea in *The Romantic Comedians*." In *Ellen Glasgow: New Perspectives*, ed. Scura, 183–95.

Hall, Larry. "A Van Vechten Pose: Mark Lutz and Gertrude Stein in Richmond." *EGN* 18 (March 1983): 5–16.

Harrison, Elizabeth Jane. *Female Pastoral: Women Writers Re-Visioning the American South*. Knoxville: University of Tennessee Press, 1991.

Hart-Davis, Rupert. *Hugh Walpole: A Biography*. New York: Macmillan: 1952.

Haskins, Susan. *Mary Magdalen: Myth and Metaphor*. New York: Harcourt, Brace, 1994.

Hatch, Francis W. "Ellen Glasgow: Pulitzer Prize-Winner at Castine." *Downeast Magazine*, June 1974, 66–69, 94–96.

Hendrick, Burton J. *The Life and Letters of Walter H. Page*. 2 vols. New York: Doubleday, Page, 1922.

——, ed. *The Training of an American: The Early Life and Letters of Walter H. Page, 1855–1913*. Boston: Houghton Mifflin, 1928.

Herrick, C. T. "The Author of *The Descendant*." *Critic* 27 (May–June 1897): 383.

Hoagwood, Terence Allen. "Glasgow's 'A Plea.'" *EGN* 29 (Fall 1992): 7–8.

——. "Glasgow's Poetry: A Critique of Ideological Illusion." *Mississippi Quarterly* 49, no. 2 (Spring 1996): 361–72.

——. "The Poetry of Ellen Glasgow: *The Freeman and Other Poems*." In *Ellen Glasgow: New Perspectives*, ed. Scura, 59–73.

Hoge, Preston H. *Moses Drury Hoge, Life and Letters*. Richmond: Presbyterian Committee of Publication, 1899.

Howard, Victor B. *Conscience and Slavery: The Evangelist Calvinist Domestic Missions, 1837–1861*. Kent, Ohio: Kent State University Press, 1990.

Humphries, Jefferson, ed. *Southern Literature and Literary Theory*. Athens: University of Georgia Press, 1990.

Hutchinson, William R. *The Modernist Impulse in American Protestantism*. Cambridge: Harvard University Press, 1976.

Inge, M. Thomas, ed. *Ellen Glasgow: Centennial Essays*. Charlottesville: University Press of Virginia, 1976.

Irvine, William. *Apes, Angels, and Victorians: The Story of Darwin, Huxley, and Evolution*. New York: McGraw-Hill, 1955.

James, Henry. *The American Scene*. New York: Scribner's, 1946.

Jones, Howard Mumford. "The Earliest Novels." In *Ellen Glasgow: Centennial Essays*, ed. Inge, 67–81.

Jones, Jacqueline. *Labor of Love, Labor of Sorrow: Black Women, Work, and the Family from Slavery to Present*. New York: Basic Books, 1985.

Jones, Leslie, Jim Kyle, and Peter Wood. *Words Apart: Losing Your Hearing as an Adult*. New York: Travistock Publications, 1987.

Kaplan, Sidney Janet. *Feminine Consciousness in the Modern British Novel*. Urbana: University of Illinois Press, 1975.

Kellner, Bruce. "Ellen Glasgow and Gertrude Stein." *EGN* 2 (March 1975): 13–16.

Kelly, William W. *Ellen Glasgow: A Bibliography*. Charlottesville: University Press of Virginia, 1964.

Kolodny, Annette. *The Land Before Her: Fantasy and Experience of the American Frontiers, 1630–1860*. Chapel Hill: University of North Carolina Press, 1984.

Kornasky, Linda. "Ellen Glasgow's Disability." *Mississippi Quarterly* 49, no. 2 (Spring 1996): 281–95.

Lacan, Jacques. *Feminine Sexuality*. Edited by Juliet Mitchell and Jacqueline Rose. Translated by Jacqueline Rose. New York: Norton, 1982.

Lears, T. J. Jackson. *No Place of Grace: Antimodernism and the Transformation of American Culture, 1880–1920*. New York: Pantheon, 1981.

Letters of Carl Van Vechten. Selected and edited by Bruce Kellner. New Haven: Yale University Press, 1987.

Letters of Sherwood Anderson. Edited by Howard Mumford Jones. Boston: Little, Brown, 1953.

Levy, Helen Fiddyment. "Building on Barren Ground: Ellen Glasgow." In *Fictions of the Home Place: Jewett, Cather, Glasgow, Porter, Welty, and Naylor,* 97–130. Jackson: University Press of Mississippi, 1992.

———. "Coming Home: Glasgow's Last Two Novels." In *Ellen Glasgow: New Perspectives,* ed. Scura, 220–34.

Lewis, R. W. B. *The American Adam: Innocence, Tragedy, and Tradition in the Nineteenth Century.* Chicago: University of Chicago Press, 1955.

———. *Edith Wharton: A Biography.* New York: Fromm International Publishing, 1985.

"Life of a Monkey Against the Life of a Man." *World's Work* 16 (July 1908): 104–17.

Lisio, Donald. *Hoover, Blacks, and Lily-Whites.* Chapel Hill: University of North Carolina Press, 1985.

Lukács, Georg. *The Historical Novel.* Boston: Beacon Press, 1963.

MacDonald, Edgar, ed. "Ellen Glasgow to Lila Meade Valentine: Three Letters." *EGN* 21 (October 1984): 5.

———. "Ellen Glasgow's Characterizations of Blacks." *EGN* 10 (March 1979): 8.

———. "An Essay in Bibliography." In *Ellen Glasgow: Centennial Essays,* ed. Inge, 191–226.

———. "From Jordan's End to Frenchman's Bend: Ellen Glasgow's Short Stories." *Mississippi Quarterly* 49, no. 2 (Spring 1996): 319–32.

———. "A Gallery of Richmond Portraits." *EGN* 22 (March 1985): 6–7.

———. "The Glasgow-Cabell Entente." *American Literature* 41 (March 1969): 76–91.

———. "The Glasgow Papers." *EGN* 2 (March 1975): 18.

———. "Glasgow-Stein: Second Meeting." *EGN* 15 (October 1981): 17.

———. "Home Thoughts." *EGN* 10 (October 1983): 10.

———. *James Branch Cabell and Richmond-in-Virginia.* Jackson: University Press of Mississippi, 1993.

———. "The Last Pleasure." *EGN* 14 (March 1981): 12.

———. "Lellie: Ellen Glasgow and Josephine Clark." *EGN* 4 (March 1976): 11–17.

———. "Mary Johnston and Henry Sydnor Harrison." *EGN* 20 (April 1984): 2–4.

———. "Recent Additions to the Glasgow Collection." *EGN* 30 (Spring 1993): 12.

———. "Remembering Ellen Glasgow—and Elizabeth Branch Bowie." *EGN* 32 (Spring 1994): 1, 3, 6–7.

———. "A Retrospective: Henry Anderson and Marjorie Rawlings." *EGN* 12 (March 1980): 4–16.

McDowell, Frederick P. W. *Ellen Glasgow and the Ironic Art of Fiction.* Madison: University of Wisconsin Press, 1963.

McGrath, Alister E. *A Life of John Calvin: A Study in the Shaping of Western Culture.* Oxford: Basil Blackwell, 1990.

MacKethan, Lucinda H. "Restoring Order: Matriarchal Design in *The Battle-Ground* and *Vein of Iron.*" In *Ellen Glasgow: New Perspectives,* ed. Scura, 89–105.

Marcosson, Isaac F. *Before I Forget: A Pilgrimage to the Past.* New York: Dodd, Mead, 1959.

Marie, Queen of Roumania. *The Story of My Life.* New York: Scribner's, 1934.

Martineau, Harriet. *Autobiography.* 2 vols. London: Virago, 1983.

Mason, Mary Grimley. "Introduction." *Journeys: Autobiographical Writings by Women,* ed. Mary Grimley Mason and Carol Hurd Green, xiii–xvii. Boston: G. K. Hall, 1979.

Matthews, Pamela R. "Between Ellen and Louise: Female Friendship, Glasgow's Letters to Louise Chandler Moulton, and *The Wheel of Life.*" In *Ellen Glasgow: New Perspectives,* ed. Scura, 106–23.

———. "Education of a Novelist, Education of a Poet: Ellen Glasgow and Adrienne Rich." *EGN* 29 (Fall 1992): 4–5.

———. *Ellen Glasgow and a Woman's Traditions.* Charlottesville: University Press of Virginia, 1994.

———. "Glasgow's Joan of Arc in Context." In *Mississippi Quarterly* 49, no. 2 (Spring 1996): 210–26.

Meade, Julian. *I Live in Virginia.* New York: Longmans, Green, 1935.

Mencken, H. L. *The Diary of H. L. Mencken.* Edited by Charles A. Fecher. New York: Knopf, 1989.

———. *My Life as Author and Editor.* New York: Knopf, 1993.

Mencken and Sara, A Life in Letters: The Private Correspondence of H. L. Mencken and Sara Haardt. Edited by Marion Elizabeth Rodgers. New York: McGraw-Hill, 1987.

Miller, Nancy K. *The Heroine's Text: Readings in the French and English Novel, 1722–1782.* New York: Columbia University Press, 1980.

Moss, Elizabeth. *Domestic Novelists in the Old South.* Baton Rouge: Louisiana State University Press, 1992.

Muhlenfeld, Elizabeth. "The Civil War and Authorship." In *The History of Southern Literature,* ed. Louis D. Rubin Jr., Blyden Jackson, Rayburn S. Moore, Lewis P. Simpson, and Thomas Daniel Young, 178–87. Baton Rouge: Louisiana State University Press, 1985.

Nelson, L. G. "Mary Johnston and the Historic Imagination." In *Southern Writers: Appraisals in Our Time,* ed. R. C. Simonini Jr. Charlottesville: University Press of Virginia, 1964.

Newman, Frances. *The Hard-Boiled Virgin.* New York: Arno Press, 1977.

O'Brien, John Thomas. *From Bondage to Citizenship: The Richmond Black Community, 1865–1867.* New York: Garland Publishing, 1990.

O'Brien, Michael. *Rethinking the South: Essays in Intellectual History.* Baltimore: Johns Hopkins University Press, 1988.

O'Brien, Sharon. *Willa Cather: The Emerging Voice.* New York: Oxford University Press, 1987.

Osborne, Duffield. *The Authors Club.* New York: Knickerbocker Press, 1913.

Page, Walter Hines. *A Publisher's Confession.* New York: Doubleday, Page, 1905.

———. *The Southerner: A Novel Being the Autobiography of Nicholas Worth.* London: Heinemann, 1910.

Pahl, Jon. *Paradox Lost: Free Will and Political Liberty in American Culture, 1630–1970*. Baltimore: Johns Hopkins University Press, 1992.

Pakula, Hannah. *The Last Romantic: A Biography of Queen Marie of Roumania*. New York: Simon and Schuster, 1984.

Palmer, Vera. "Mrs. Duke, 77, Faces Life with Charm, Humor." *Richmond Times Dispatch*, March 22, 1953.

Pannill, Linda. "Ellen Glasgow's Allegory of Love and Death: 'The Greatest Good.' " *Resources for American Literary Study* 14 (Fall 1984): 161–66.

Perkins, Maxwell E. *Editor to Author: The Letters of Maxwell E. Perkins*. Edited by John Hall Wheelock. New York: Scribner's, 1950.

Price, Alan. "Writing Home from the Front: Edith Wharton and Dorothy Canfield Fisher Present Wartime France to the United States: 1917–1919." *Edith Wharton Newsletter* (Fall 1988): 1–5, 8.

Pulley, Raymond H. *Old Virginia Restored: An Interpretation of the Progressive Impulse, 1870–1930*. Charlottesville: University Press of Virginia, 1968.

Purcell, Jean. "Developers Will Try to Keep 'Air of Restrained Elegance.' " *Richmond Times Dispatch*, Sunday, October 14, 1973, Section D.

Putnam, Sarah A. Brock. *Richmond during the War: Four Years of Personal Observation by a Richmond Lady*. New York: G. W. Carleton, 1867.

Rachleff, Peter J. *Black Labor in the South*. Philadelphia: Temple University Press, 1984.

Rainwater, Catherine. "Consciousness, Gender, and Animal Signs in *Barren Ground* and *Vein of Iron*." In *Ellen Glasgow: New Perspectives*, ed. Scura, 204–19.

———. " 'That Abused Word, Modern,' and Ellen Glasgow's 'Literature of Revolt.' " In *Mississippi Quarterly* 49, no. 2 (Spring 1996): 345–60.

Raper, Julius Rowan. "*Barren Ground* and the Transition to Southern Modernism." In *Ellen Glasgow: New Perspectives*, ed. Scura, 146–61.

———. "The European Initiation of Ellen Glasgow." *EGN* 5 (October 1976): 2–5.

———. *From the Sunken Garden: The Fiction of Ellen Glasgow, 1916–1945*. Baton Rouge: Louisiana State University Press, 1980.

———. "The Man Ellen Glasgow Could Respect." *EGN* 3 (March 1975): 4–9.

———. *Without Shelter: The Early Career of Ellen Glasgow*. Baton Rouge: Louisiana State University Press, 1971.

———, ed. *Ellen Glasgow's Reasonable Doubts: A Collection of Her Writings*. Baton Rouge: Louisiana State University Press, 1988.

Rawlings, Marjorie Kinnan. "Regional Literature of the South." *English Journal* 29, no. 2, pt. 1 (February 1940): 89–97.

———. *Selected Letters of Marjorie Kinnan Rawlings*. Edited by Gordon E. Bigelow and Laura V. Monti. Gainesville: University Presses of Florida, 1983.

Reid, Jane Davenport. "The Ellen Glasgow Collection of Ceramic Dogs." *Commonwealth* 16 (February 1949): 13, 30, 31.

Reniers, Perceval. *The Springs of Virginia: Life, Love, and Death at the Waters, 1775–1900*. Chapel Hill: University of North Carolina Press, 1941.

Rhoades, Antoinette W. "Fertile Ground." *EGN* 4 (March 1976): 13–15.

Rich, Adrienne. "Education of a Novelist." In *The Fact of a Doorframe*, 314–17. New York: Norton, 1984.

Richards, Marion K. *Ellen Glasgow's Development as a Novelist.* The Hague: Mouton, 1971.

Rubin, Louis D., Jr. *No Place on Earth: Ellen Glasgow, James Branch Cabell, and Richmond-in-Virginia.* Austin: University of Texas Press, 1959.

Samuels, Shirley. *The Culture of Sentiment: Race, Gender, and Sentimentality in Nineteenth-Century America.* New York: Oxford University Press, 1992.

Saunders, Frances W. "Glasgow's Secret Love: 'Gerald B' or William T?" *EGN* 31 (Fall 1993): 1, 3, 4.

Sawaya, Francesca. " 'The Problem of the South': Economic Determination, Gender Determination, and Genre in Glasgow's *Virginia*." In *Ellen Glasgow: New Perspectives*, ed. Scura, 132–45.

Scheick, William J. "The Narrative Ethos of Glasgow's 'A Point in Morals.' " *EGN* 30 (Spring 1993): 1, 3–4.

Schweiger, Beth Barton. "Putting Politics Aside: Virginia Democrats and Voter Apathy in the Era of Disfranchisement." In *The Edge of the South: Life in Nineteenth-Century Virginia*, ed. Edward L. Ayers and John C. Willis, 194–218. Charlottesville: University Press of Virginia, 1991.

Scott, Anne Firor. *The Southern Lady from Pedestal to Politics, 1830–1930.* Chicago: University of Chicago Press, 1970.

Scura, Dorothy M. "Afterword." In Glasgow, *The Romantic Comedians*, 241–65. Charlottesville: University Press of Virginia, 1995.

———. "Ellen Glasgow, Henry Anderson, and *The Romantic Comedians*." *Mississippi Quarterly* 49, no. 2 (Spring 1996): 301–18.

———. "Glasgow and the Southern Renaissance." In *Ellen Glasgow: Centennial Essays*, ed. Inge, 46–64.

———. "A 'Lost' Memorial to Ellen Glasgow." *EGN* 12 (March 1980): 23–43.

———. "Mary Dallas Street: Editor, Novelist, and Poet." *EGN* 4 (March 1976): 3–9.

———. "One West Main." *EGN* 1 (October 1974): 3–7.

Scura, Dorothy M., ed. *Ellen Glasgow: The Contemporary Reviews.* Cambridge: Cambridge University Press, 1992.

———. *Ellen Glasgow: New Perspectives.* Knoxville: University of Tennessee Press, 1995.

Sherman, Stuart P., Sara Haardt, and Emily Clark, eds. *Ellen Glasgow: Critical Essays.* Garden City, N.Y.: Doubleday, Doran, 1929.

Silverthorne, Elizabeth. *Marjorie Kinnan Rawlings: Sojourner at Cross Creek.* Woodstock, N.Y.: Overland Press, 1988.

Skidelsky, Robert. "Only Connect: Biography and Truth." In *The Troubled Face of Autobiography*, ed. Eric Homberger and John Charmley, 1–16. New York: Macmillan, 1988.

Smith-Rosenberg, Carroll. "The Female World of Love and Ritual: Relations between Women in Nineteenth-Century America." *Signs: Journal of Women in Culture and Society* 1 (1975): 1–29.

St. Julien Ravenel, Mrs. *Charleston, the Place and the People.* New York: Macmillan, 1925.

Starobin, Robert S. *Industrial Slavery in the Old South.* New York: Oxford University Press, 1970.

Steele, Oliver L., Jr. "Gertrude Stein and Ellen Glasgow: Memoir of a Meeting." *American Literature* 33 (March 1961): 76–77.

Storr, Anthony. *Solitude: A Return to the Self.* New York: Free Press, 1988.

Tarrant, Desmond. *James Branch Cabel: The Dream and the Reality.* Norman: University of Oklahoma Press, 1967.

Taylor, Welford D. *Amélie Rives (Princess Troubetzkoy).* New York: Twayne, 1973.

Thomas, Alan J. *Acquired Hearing Loss: Psychological and Psychosocial Implications.* London: Academic Press, 1984.

Thomas, Emory M. *The Confederate State of Richmond: A Biography of the Capital.* Austin: University of Texas Press, 1971.

Thurber, Cheryl. "The Development of the Mammy Image and Mythology." In Bernhard et al., eds., *Southern Women,* 87–108.

Treadway, Sandra Gioia. *Women of Mark: A History of the Women's Club of Richmond, Virginia, 1894–1994.* Richmond: The Library of Virginia, 1995.

Trigg, Emma Gray. "Ellen Glasgow." *The Woman's Club Bulletin* (Richmond) 9, no. 2 (1946): 2.

Tutwiler, C. C. *Ellen Glasgow's Library.* Charlottesville: Bibliographical Society of the University of Virginia, 1967.

———. "The Glasgow Library." *EGN* 3 (October 1975): 2–4.

Twelve Southerners. *I'll Take My Stand: The South and the Agrarian Tradition.* 2nd ed. New York: Peter Smith, 1951.

Tyler-McGraw, Marie, and Gregg D. Kimball. *In Bondage and Freedom.* Chapel Hill, N.C.: Valentine Museum, 1988.

Wagner-Martin, Linda. *Ellen Glasgow: Beyond Convention.* Austin: University of Texas Press, 1982.

———. "Glasgow's Time in *The Sheltered Life.*" In *Ellen Glasgow: New Perspectives,* ed. Scura, 196–203.

———. *Telling Women's Lives: The New Biography.* New Brunswick, N.J.: Rutgers University Press, 1994.

Walker, Nancy A. "The Romance of Self-Representation: Glasgow and *The Woman Within.*" In *Ellen Glasgow: New Perspectives,* ed. Scura, 33–41.

Wallace, Charles M. *The Boy Gangs of Richmond in the Dear Old Days.* Richmond, Va.: Richmond Press, 1938.

Washington, Joseph R. *Anti-Blackness in English Religion.* Lewiston, N.Y.: Edwin Mellon, 1984.

Watson, Ritchie D., Jr. "The Ellen Glasgow-Allen Tate Correspondence: Bridging the Southern Literary Generation Gap." *EGN* 23 (October 1985): 3–23.

———. "Sara Haardt Mencken and the Glasgow-Mencken Literary Entente." *EGN* 20 (April 1984): 5–16.

Watson, Ritchie D., Jr., ed. "Ellen Glasgow's Letters in the Library of the Virginia Historical Society." *EGN* 14 (March 1981): 5–8.

Welter, Barbara. "The Cult of True Womanhood, 1820–1860." *American Quarterly* 18 (Summer 1966): 151–74.

Wharton, Edith. *The Fruit of the Tree*. New York: Scribner's, 1907.

———. *The House of Mirth*. New York: Scribner's, 1905.

———. *In Morocco*. New York: Scribner's, 1920.

Whyte, Frederic. *William Heinemann: A Memoir*. New York: Doubleday, Doran, 1929.

Williams, David R. *Wilderness Lost: The Religious Origins of the American Mind*. London: Associated Presses, 1987.

Williamson, Joel. *New People: Miscegenation and Mulattoes in the United States*. New York:
Free Press, 1980.

———. *William Faulkner and Southern History*. New York: Cambridge University Press,
1993.

Woodward, C. Vann. *The Burden of Southern History*. 2nd ed. Baton Rouge: Louisiana State
University Press, 1968.

———. *Origins of the New South, 1877–1913*. Baton Rouge: Louisiana State University Press,
1951.

Woolf, Virginia. *Orlando: A Biography*. New York: Harcourt Brace Jovanovich, n.d.

Young, Stark. *Stark Young: A Life in the Arts, Letters, 1900–1962*. Edited by John Pilkington.
2 vols. Baton Rouge: Louisiana State University Press, 1975.